FINDING IT
ON THE
INTERNET

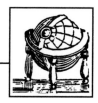

FINDING IT
ON THE
INTERNET

The Essential Guide to archie, Veronica, Gopher, WAIS,
WWW (Including Mosaic), and Other Search and Browsing Tools

Paul Gilster

John Wiley & Sons, Inc.

NEW YORK • CHICHESTER • BRISBANE • TORONTO • SINGAPORE

Publisher: Katherine Schowalter
Editor: Paul Farrell
Assistant Editor: Allison Roarty
Managing Editor: Maureen B. Drexel
Editorial Production & Design: Editorial Services of New England, Inc.

This text is printed on acid-free paper.

This publication is designed to provide accurate and authoritative information in regard to the subject matter covered. It is sold with the understanding that the publisher is not engaged in rendering legal, accounting, or other professional service. If legal advice or other expert assistance is required, the services of a competent professional person should be sought.

Library of Congress Cataloging-in-Publication Data
Gilster, Paul
    Finding it on the internet : the essential guide to archie, Veronica, Gopher, WAIS,
WWW (including Mosaic), and other search and browsing tools / by Paul Gilster.
        p. cm.
    Includes index.
    ISBN 0-471-03857-1 (paper)
    1. Internet (Computer network) I. Title.
TK5105.875.I57G53 1994
025.04—-d20   94-17024
                                                                                CIP

Printed in the United States of America

10 9 8 7 6 5 4 3 2 1

I know of nothing more pleasant, or more instructive, than to compare experience with expectation, or to register from time to time the difference between idea and reality. It is by this kind of observation that we grow daily less liable to be disappointed.

Samuel Johnson

Contents in Brief

1. Internet Navigation Tools   1

2. archie: Finding Files   9

3. Gopher: Finding Resources by Menu   37

4. Veronica: Gopher as Search Engine   77

5. WAIS: Searching for Text   99

6. World Wide Web: Hypertext As Browsing Tool   133

7. HYTELNET: The Database on Your Computer   183

8. WHOIS, netfind, X.500: Finding People   207

9. E-Mail: Non-Interactive Searching   243

10. CNIDR: The Future of Internet Searching   275

Glossary   285

Index   294

Contents

FOREWORD *by George H. Brett II*   xv
PREFACE   xvii

1. Internet Navigation Tools   1

A WORD ON METHODOLOGY   2
THE TOOLS AND THEIR POTENTIAL   3
   WAIS   4
   Gopher   4
   Veronica   4
   World Wide Web   5
   HYTELNET   6
   archie   6
   WHOIS, x.500 and More   6
A SEARCH METHODOLOGY   7
THE REALISTIC SEARCH   8

2. archie: Finding Files   9

THE NATURE OF FILE TRANSFER PROTOCOL   10
ARCHIE SCOUTS THE INTERNET TERRAIN   11
USING ARCHIE   13
USING TELNET TO SEARCH WITH ARCHIE   14
   A Sample Search Using archie with Telnet   17
   archie's Command Options Using Telnet   20
     Setting archie Up   20
     Changing Your Search Parameters   21
   Where and What archie Searches   22
   Controlling archie's Output   23
   Choosing an Output Format   24
     Mailing Your Results   25
   Miscellaneous archie Commands   25
THE (SOMETIMES) HELPFUL WHATIS COMMAND   26
   A Brief Aside on *regex*   28

ARCHIE THROUGH A CLIENT PROGRAM   30
    Using archie's Command Switches   30
    An archie Search Methodology   33

3.   Gopher: Finding Resources by Menu   37

THE NATURE OF GOPHERSPACE   38
ACCESSING GOPHER   42
    Using a Gopher Client   42
    Using Telnet to Access Gopher   43
WHAT'S AVAILABLE VIA GOPHER?   44
LEARNING TO USE GOPHER   46
MASTERING THE GOPHER COMMANDS   51
    Gopher's File Viewing Commands   51
    Gopher's File Management Commands   52
    Using Gopher with Bookmarks   53
    Gopher's Search Commands   59
    Other Gopher Commands   61
EXAMINING GOPHER'S RESOURCES   62
    Using Gopher's Telnet Connection   62
    Using Gopher with FTP   66
    Using Gopher with WAIS   70
    Using CSO Name Servers with Gopher   70
    Gopher's Sights and Sounds   72
KEEPING UP WITH GOPHER   75

4.   Veronica: Gopher as Search Engine   77

HOW VERONICA WORKS   78
ACCESSING VERONICA   79
    Using a Gopher Client to Reach Veronica   79
    Using Telnet to Reach Veronica   80
A SIMPLE VERONICA SEARCH   80
    Refining the Search   83
    Using Gopher's Data Types with Veronica   84
A SAMPLE SEARCH FOR INFORMATION ABOUT CD-ROMs   85
A VERONICA STRATEGY EMERGES   88
COMBINING KEYWORDS TO SEARCH   88
SUMMARIZING VERONICA'S SEARCH OPTIONS   91

SAMPLE VERONICA SEARCH TERMS   93

    Occasional Frustrations of Using Veronica   94

USING JUGHEAD   96

    Locating a Jughead Server   97

5.   WAIS: Searching for Text   99

HOW WAIS WORKS   100

WHAT YOU CAN FIND WITH WAIS   101

ACCESSING WAIS   102

A SAMPLE WAIS SEARCH USING TELNET   103

THE NATURE OF CONTENT NAVIGATION   108

THE BASIC WAIS COMMANDS   109

    swais Movement Commands   109
    swais Search Commands   110
    Miscellaneous swais Commands   110

WAIS KEYWORD LIMITATIONS   110

A WAIS SEARCH USING RELEVANCE FEEDBACK   111

    Step One: Selecting Our Sources   111
    Step Two: Telling swais to Search a Particular Server   112
    Step Three: Running the Initial Search   112
    Step Four: Marking Items for our Next Sweep   113
    Step Five: Putting Relevance Feedback to Work   114

A ROUTINE WAIS STRATEGY   115

USING GOPHER TO ACCESS WAIS   118

USING waissearch FOR SPECIFIC SERVERS   121

INTERESTING WAIS SITES   123

KEEPING UP WITH WAIS   130

6.   World Wide Web: Hypertext As Browsing Tool   133

THE NATURE OF HYPERTEXT   134

THE WEB'S RESOURCES   134

ACCESSING THE WORLD WIDE WEB   137

EXPLORING THE WEB   138

    Reading a Document On-Line With the Web   138
    Using a Local Client With the World Wide Web   140
    World Wide Web Terminology   143
    A Sampling of the Web's Reach   144

A TYPICAL SEARCH ON THE WEB   147

A PANOPLY OF DIVERSE INFORMATION   150

The *I Ching*   150
Black Beans and Other Recipes   151
The Dead Sea Scrolls at the Library of Congress   151
Exploring a University   152
Software for Astronomy   153
Reading USENET with the Web   153
By Gopher to the National Institute of Health   155

COMMANDS FOR THE WWW BROWSER   155

SEARCHING AN INDEX WITH THE WWW BROWSER   158

USING TELNET TO SEARCH THE WORLD WIDE WEB   161

Using The Lynx Browser   161
Using the NJIT Browser   165

WORLD WIDE WEB TIPS   165

MOSAIC: THE WEB GOES TECHNICOLOR   168

WHAT IS MOSAIC?   169

Mosaic and SLIP   171
How to Get Mosaic   173
Mosaic and Internet Tools   173
Speeding Up Mosaic   177
Using the Hot List   178

MOSAIC AT WORK: GLOBAL NETWORK NAVIGATOR   178

MOSAIC'S FUTURE   179

7.   HYTELNET: The Database on Your Computer   183

USING HYTELNET   184

HYTELNET Servers   184
Downloading HYTELNET   185

PUTTING HYTELNET TO WORK   186

THE HYTELNET COMMANDS   190

HYTELNET AS SEARCH TOOL   190

Searching for the WELL   191

HYTELNET AND LIBRARY RESOURCES   194

USING HYTELNET THROUGH GOPHER   195

KEEPING UP WITH HYTELNET   196

LIBTEL—AN ON-LINE LIBRARY RESOURCE   197

USING LIBS TO SEARCH REMOTE LIBRARIES   200

GOPHER AS A LIBRARY TOOL 202
USING CATALIST AS AN ON-DISK LIBRARY SOURCE 204

8. WHOIS, netfind, X.500: Finding People 207

X.500 AND THE SEARCH FOR ADDRESSING STANDARDS 208
X.400: WHAT IT IS AND HOW IT WORKS 209

How X.400 Differs from TCP/IP Electronic Mail 209

X.500 AS A DIRECTORY SERVICE 210
THE PARADISE PROJECT: A DIFFERENT INTERFACE 212
USING GOPHER TO RUN AN X.500 SEARCH 214
WHOIS AS A SEARCH TOOL 216

Accessing WHOIS 216
Using WHOIS Through Telnet 216
Tips on Using WHOIS by Telnet 220
Using WHOIS with a Client Program 223

NETFIND: FINGERING THE RIGHT PERSON 225

Accessing netfind 225
Accessing netfind with Telnet 226
How netfind Works 227
netfind Search Strategies 229

WHAT IS FINGER INFORMATION? 231
KNOWBOTS AND INTELLIGENT SEARCHING 233

Using the Knowbot by Telnet 233
Using the Knowbot by Electronic Mail 235

CSO DIRECTORIES 236
SEARCHING THE USENET ARCHIVES 238
CAMPUS WIDE INFORMATION SYSTEMS 240
MAIL TO THE SOURCE 240

9. E-Mail: Noninteractive Searching 243

ARCHIE THROUGH ELECTRONIC MAIL 244

archie by E-Mail Commands 244
A Sample archie Search Using Electronic Mail 245
archie Courtesy 246

WAIS BY ELECTRONIC MAIL 246

Constructing a WAISmail Search 247
A Sample WAISmail Search 247

The WAISmail Commands   250
Binary Files through WAISmail   252

GOPHER BY ELECTRONIC MAIL   253

A GopherMail Query   254
Limiting GopherMail's Output   255
A GopherMail Search Using Veronica   256

FINGER BY ELECTRONIC MAIL   258

WHOIS BY ELECTRONIC MAIL   259

CHECKING INTERNET IP ADDRESSES   260

SEARCHING A LISTSERV ARCHIVE SITE   262

A BITNET Search Paradigm   262
Targeting the Right Mailing List   263
Sending for an Index   264
Constructing the Search   266
Requesting Messages from the LISTSERV   267
The Typical BITNET Search   268
The View from Middle Earth   268
Reading More on BITNET Searching   270

FINDING AND USING OTHER MAIL SERVERS   270

A Sample Mail Server Search   271
Interesting Mail Server Sites   272

10.   CNIDR: The Future of Internet Searching   275

THE EMERGENCE OF CNIDR   276
BUILDING SEARCH ENGINES   278
TAMING THE KUDZU PATCH   279
THE NATURE OF THE INTERNET SEARCH   280
WHAT THE INTERNET NEEDS   282
GROWING INTO A WORLDWIDE CYBERSPACE   283

Glossary   285

Index   294

Foreword

There was a time that the floppy disk of my desktop microcomputer would store only about 126,000 bytes of information. Now I can easily store more than 1,400,000 bytes on a smaller, cheaper diskette. Ten times the storage for less cost. We see a similar scenario in the hard disk arena. My earliest hard disk stored 5 megabytes of data and cost nearly $8,000. Recently I purchased a 500 megabyte disk for less than $900: a hundred times the storage at one-tenth the cost. All of this power for my desktop. As I increase my storage space, I save more data, and collect more programs. For me, a hopeless pack rat, I also forget more easily what it is that I have on my diskettes and hard drives. Publishers have been making a lot of money selling disk library software and directory searching tools like Lotus Magellan, gofer, sonar, and others to folks like me (and perhaps, you) who have been "losing" files.

And now we're faced with a global network of networks with millions of directories, subdirectories, files, programs, news files, and other stuff. How are we going to make this transition from our desktops, cluttered as they are, to this even more cluttered universe?

In 1989, I wrote about spelunking for online resources—exploring a deep dark cave of information resources on the network. At that time, we did not have any of the Internet applications that are currently available. All we had were rudimentary applications like e-mail, news, and a few menu-oriented information systems. The community was relatively small and well-known, and newcomers had to rely on the experienced old timers to find their way. Since that time, I and others have been working with various people, groups, and professional organizations to develop software that will permit people to locate online resources, access them, and, if possible, manipulate them. We are no longer groping in the dark, but we still are trying to make sense of the numerous maps and signs. And we are working in ever larger, more diverse groups.

Similarly, due to technical, economic, and cultural factors, there has been an explosion of interest in doing work remotely with computer networks, in particular with the Internet. This interest has been intensified by national and regional efforts to promote the construction and use of an "Information Highway." During May 1994, there were no fewer than 35 books about the Internet. Some even included software to help you connect to the Internet. Other books were as large and thick as a metropolitan city telephone directory. Most, if not all, of these books do not explain the Internet navigation software in depth, nor do they describe how these tools can be used most efficiently.

Finding It on the Internet is a very necessary next step for anyone who wants to effectively use the many resources of the global Internet. Paul Gilster presents a clear explanation of where the Internet tools came from, how they fit into the complex matrix that is the Internet, and how you can use them to light the way of your travels on the Internet—whether you experience the net as a briar patch, another Mammoth Cave, an ocean, or an Information Highway after dark.

In North Carolina we have a vine by the name of kudzu. This plant was introduced in the late 1800s from Japan to provide ground cover and help renovate property ravaged during the Civil War. The vine did the job all too well. It grows at a prodigious rate of 12 1/2 inches per day and lives for years. Now one can see the plant everywhere growing up and over roadsides, trees, telephone poles, and even on the telephone wire. A recent agricultural journal estimated that there are more than 9 million acres of kudzu in the southeast. Needless to say, most folks consider this plant a weed.

This same weed, however, is a useful crop in Japan. So much so that recently a Japanese agribusiness bought several thousand acres of land in Alabama for the purpose of raising kudzu commercially. It is the root of the plant that is of most value. It can grow to a size that exceeds 6 feet long and 400 pounds in weight. A lot of root and a lot of work produces a powder for cooking.

The Internet is an electronic form of kudzu. The hallmarks of the network are very much similar to the vine: It is growing at a rapid, almost unbelievable pace in the numbers of attached networks, people, and information resources. It appears to be a large confused mass of services, resources, connections, people, and computers. All diagrams and maps appear as three-dimensional tangles of lines here and there with no apparent beginning or end. It is almost impossible to find anything in that fertile collection. Some folks say that there is little information of value on the Internet. So, we have a digital weed patch that is huge, tangled, hard to use, and very confusing. But, that is only apparently the case. If we think of ourselve as gardeners or stewards of this digital landscape, we can make it into a productive environment where we will work, play, make new aquaintances, and learn all our lives long.

— George H. Brett II
Clearinghouse for Networked Information
Discovery and Retrieval
Research Triangle Park, North Carolina
george.brett@cnidr.org

Preface

The Internet poses unusual challenges to explorers. Tales from network veterans imply that treasures can be found there in abundance, everything from free software to graphic images, unique text files, and numerous databases. But how do we find what we need? Given the Internet's unyielding interface, which provides few clues to the uninitiated, most newcomers are left frustrated in their attempts to discover information. This book aims to relieve that frustration through a step-by-step explanation of the Internet's tools. Using these programs can cut our search time and help us go straight to what we need.

Two types of tools assist our navigation. A *search* tool is one that allows computers on the network to find what we need; using a search tool, we can harness computer power to do our work after providing initial keywords and other parameters. **WAIS** is a search tool, as is **Veronica**. **Gopher**, on the other hand, like **World Wide Web**, is a *browsing* tool. A browser requires a person to do the searching. Think of **Gopher** or **World Wide Web** sessions as the equivalent of rummaging around in a flea market or a badly organized library. You may find what you need, but chances are you'll also discover much that you hadn't realized was out there. Browsing is serendipitous and great fun, but it offers frustrations of its own when we need to target a particular resource and go straight to it.

This book examines both browsers and search engines primarily from the standpoint of the dial-up user to the Internet. Such a user has access to the ubiquitous VT-100 terminal emulation that allows a desktop computer to pretend to be a terminal of a remote machine. With the Internet's numbers swelling through legions of new service providers, we can expect huge growth in the population of dial-up customers, most of whom are encountering the Internet for the first time. Thus, I focus on character-based client programs like **www** (for **World Wide Web**), **swais** (**WAIS**) and **Gopher**, which are used to interact with the underlying application. A thorough grounding in the basics of these tools makes moving to a graphical environment relatively simple. (Users who already work with graphical environments through SLIP accounts or full network access will still find the basics of browsing and searching explained, and can apply them to whatever client programs they choose to run.)

Each search tool receives a chapter, beginning with **archie**. We progress through **Gopher**, **Veronica**, **World Wide Web**, **WAIS**, and into the lesser-known tools, such as **HYTELNET**, **LIBTEL**, and **LIBS**. Dial-up users will also receive information on how to use Internet search and browsing tools through electronic mail, an important consideration given the number of people who only have e-mail access to the net. I include a chapter on finding people through a variety of tools, one that demonstrates that Internet directories are in their infancy. The final chapter discusses the work being done at CNIDR—The Clearinghouse for Networked Information Discovery and Retrieval, in Research Triangle Park, North Carolina—where search and browsing tools occupy the attention of some of the finest minds in networking.

And what about **Mosaic**, the network's premier browsing tool? The beneficiary of much attention in the last six months, **Mosaic** brings a graphical interface with pull-down menus, point-and-click commands, and stunning visual and audio capabilities to the Internet. As a browser for **World Wide Web**, **Mosaic** is simply unequaled; hence my chapter on the **Web** contains numerous screen shots and an explanation of how **Mosaic** works. But regular dial-up users should keep in mind that the VT-100 terminal emulation they work with does *not* allow **Mosaic** to run. It takes a SLIP account or a full network connection to use **Mosaic**, which may be the primary motivation for moving to the SLIP environment. I discuss SLIP and related matters in Chapter 6. The Macintosh screen shots of **Mosaic** were provided by my friend and neighbor, David Warlick.

It is inevitable that finding things would be a major Internet challenge. After all, the network comprises thousands of separate networks linked together, with FTP sites and databases in profusion. The right hand often doesn't know what the left is doing, and information discovery is frequently a matter of chance. Search and browsing tools bring some order to the process and point to a future in which the Internet can grow into a true information center. But as we'll see, all the available tools have their quirks. This book's sample searches will walk you through the process, glitches and all. Internet searching is rarely as efficient as it ought to be, but the thrill of encountering the unexpected often makes the trip worthwhile.

1

Internet Navigation Tools

- Somewhere on the Internet, a text file exists that details recent archaeological discoveries in Egypt, including findings in the royal tombs of Luxor. You're writing a research paper for a class in ancient history and would like to have a look at this file. How do you find it? And even if you can track it down, how do you know whether it's an authoritative study, or merely a random set of sketches by a dilettante?

- Somewhere at one of thousands of FTP sites around the globe, an executable file exists that can help you organize your crowded schedule and extract more productivity out of your day. It comes highly recommended, and you know that it's available at numerous locations. But how do you learn the FTP address to make the retrieval? Just as important, how do you know you've received the latest version, rather than a beta copy of shareware that was posted years ago?

- Somewhere in a major university an old friend from college now works as a faculty member. You'd like to send electronic mail to renew the acquaintance, but you've no idea what her address is. Is there a way to track down an electronic mail address without calling up the person in question and simply asking? You know that numerous directories are found on the Internet. Which do you use, and how? Perhaps most important, how do you know the address you finally get is accurate?

1

Some of these questions are relatively straightforward; this book is about finding the answers to them. We can certainly go out and find information on the Internet. In fact, the range of tools at our disposal is relatively large. We can look at **Gopher**, search with **Veronica**, check for names with **WHOIS**, move between linked data with **World Wide Web**, and run text searches in large databases with **WAIS** (Wide Area Information Servers). I will show you the techniques that make this possible, along with sample searches that will allow you to test your new skills.

A second series of questions, however, is harder to answer. Yes, we can find information, but what is its quality? How do we establish its authoritativeness, or determine its age, or keep ourselves from finding the same information under different names at different sites? Just how good is information on the Internet anyway, and how far should we trust it? If the notion of a digital library intrigues you, I would like to raise a warning flag. The Internet is far from being a satisfactory library. As we'll see in Chapter 2, "networked" information is in its infancy, and a generation of frustrated librarians know that it's true.

We must, then, separate the hype from the reality. You can do more with the Internet than you probably thought possible by way of finding information, but you probably can't do as much as you would like to, at least not until the tools to expand our present holdings and validate our archives become more precise. So as we take this journey, examining Internet search methods and the tools that make them fly, we must remember to keep our eyes on the future. This is a book about a subject that has never been in so great a state of flux. The evolution of the tools we will work with is a critical story in the future of knowledge dissemination. How it turns out depends upon us.

A WORD ON METHODOLOGY

While this book does not exclude graphical software (and we consider **Mosaic** in particular in Chapter 6), the emphasis is upon character-based clients in the UNIX environment. The reason for this is simple: These programs are the way most users first learn about navigation tools, whether they be full-blown search engines like **WAIS** or browsers like **Gopher** and **World Wide Web**. To run graphical programs like **Mosaic** and the various Macintosh, XWindows (for UNIX systems), and PC-based client programs of this ilk requires at minimum a SLIP connection to the Internet. The average dial-up user can't use them, despite their appeal.

Standard dial-up accounts use a modem to connect to a service provider's computer; it is the service provider's machine that is on the Internet, using the Internet's protocols and working with various client programs. The dial-up user takes advantage of whatever client programs the service provider has made available on its machine. The interface is character-based and works through terminal emulation, making the remote computer think that it is talking to a terminal rather than a separate computer.

A SLIP (**S**erial **L**ine **I**nternet **P**rotocol) connection, on the other hand, makes it possible for the user's desktop machine to go directly on the Internet. Rather than working with someone else's clients, the user decides which clients he or she would like to run on the computer. And because the machine is now running TCP/IP (the set of protocols that makes the Internet function) itself, it is possible to use a wide variety of client programs. In short, such a user is no longer limited to terminal emulation and character-based programs. Instead, his or her own computer is a full-fledged part of the Internet and can act like it.

We will discuss SLIP as it pertains to **Mosaic** in Chapter 6. This book is concerned more with search methods than with client programs, and it is written in the firm belief that making the Internet's tools available to the widest number is the wisest course of action. Hence the character-based UNIX bias—this is what millions of new users are encountering as they dial into the Internet for the first time, and it does them little good to learn that graphical browsers simplify the navigation process when they don't know what the process is in the first place. Using the almost universally available tools discussed here, users can explore the network no matter what kind of connection they have available. Dial-up users can upgrade to SLIP or higher-speed connections if and when the need should arise.

THE TOOLS AND THEIR POTENTIAL

Just a few years ago, the Internet search problem was rarely considered. Resources were appearing at sites worldwide, from text files to programs of various kinds, from images to sound, and people went about their work within relatively small communities that shared knowledge. You knew about the local database on meteorology because you saw someone tap it from his or her terminal; perhaps you passed the information along at a later date to a colleague. The directory of campus information was useful because you could check out concert schedules; but perhaps it didn't occur to you that other campuses were building directories. In any case, you found out about such projects by word of mouth.

The great story of the Internet in the past three years is the movement away from this anecdotal approach to data gathering and toward a rational system of organization. Not that we have arrived at this goal—the horizon is distant. But the concept that we could use networked computer power to organize an inherently chaotic sea of information has taken hold. Or perhaps an aeronautical metaphor is more apt. For we are in an era much like the early days of aviation, when it seemed that every week brought some new record set, some new design tested, and people were out building experimental aircraft in their garages. It was a time when almost anything could happen, and often did.

Thus, **Gopher**. This superb approach to organizing information came about not through some central plan handed down by committee but through the efforts of a team of computer programmers and system administrators who were simply thinking on their feet. The University of Minnesota was computerizing, its networks jammed with faculty and students, many of whom had questions. How to answer them, without spending all day every day as teachers, was the motivation for Mark McCahill and the team that built **Gopher**. How were they to know that it would catch, that by early 1994 there would be over 1,300 **Gophers** around the globe, linking together, growing, pointing to data?

Call it serendipity. In any case, we have seen the development of search tools that grew out of user frustrations. Word of the tool spreads as users find it helpful; soon it is adopted at another site, and the two begin to exchange information. Before long, the tool is worldwide; system administrators realize they need to tap its power, and its momentum becomes unstoppable. At this point, perhaps the tool's designers realize they are dealing with a commercial proposition. **Gopher** is now a commercial product, as is **archie**, as is **WAIS**. In Chapter 10, we will examine how such commercialization may affect the continuing development of these tools in the light of the necessity for standards. Our tools, after all, must operate together.

The same is true of all of the search tools that have brought such excitement—and, let's face it—such frustration to the Internet. Their number is presently stable, and we will examine each in turn. In addition to **Gopher**, this book is about these tools, and how to use them:

WAIS

Wide Area Information Servers is a different take on making information accessible. Developed through research efforts at Thinking Machines Corp. in Cambridge, MA, with the help of corporate sponsorship from Apple Computer, KPMG Peat Marwick, and Dow Jones and Co., **WAIS** has become a major search engine for examining large collections of information.

We will learn how to run such searches even as we cope with inherent **WAIS** limitations which you, the end user, will experience. Dial-up users will find the interface primitive and hard to manipulate. Those with better client programs will nonetheless experience the frustrations of any searcher—a lack of databases in the needed field, an inability with some clients, to combine terms using standard Boolean procedures, a puzzling tendency to produce seemingly unrelated search results.

These are problems we will address because it will do you no favors to paint an over-optimistic view of Internet searching. Each search tool has powerful advantages and, as we'll see, limitations. We can find ways around some of them; for others, we will have to supplement our searching with one tool by reference to another. In many cases, we will find what we need; in some, we won't. The good news is that things are getting better. All of these tools remain under active development; in the case of **WAIS**, WAIS Inc. pursues new commercial applications under the guidance of Brewster Kahle, the creator of **WAIS**. And the Clearinghouse for Networked Information Discovery and Retrieval in Research Triangle Park, North Carolina, supports an active program of research and development, centered around the **freeWAIS** program and related issues.

Gopher

Gopher is all about menus. Show people that they can reach your resource, not by issuing a complex command at the system prompt, but simply by moving an arrow around on the screen with their cursor keys, then pressing a **RETURN** to examine the document. As we'll see, **Gopher** also opens doors. You can move to what appears to be an item of local information on a **Gopher** submenu, only to discover that it actually exists on a distant computer. Press a **RETURN**, and you activate a Telnet session to visit the site. **Gopher**, we will learn, is dynamic, referring to resources throughout a worldwide Gopherspace.

Veronica

Fred Barrie and Steven Foster at the University of Nevada at Reno realized that along with **Gopher**'s powerful interface came several inherent problems. **Gopher** was propagating as a client/server tool throughout the Internet, but there was no way to know what was on the menus at another **Gopher** site without actually logging on there to look. As more and more system administrators began putting useful resources on-line, the dimensions of this problem grew. There had to be some way to identify **Gopher** files.

Veronica grew out of this need. Essentially an indexing system, **Veronica** servers regularly check **Gopher** sites around the globe to examine their menu titles. When you run a **Veronica** search, you are consulting this database and checking it against your own keywords. A **Veronica** search never leaves the **Gopher** environment, producing results that appear as **Gopher** menus, and which, like any **Gopher** items, can be accessed by pointing to them and pressing the **RETURN** key.

We examine **Veronica** as an essential adjunct to **Gopher**; indeed, it's hard to imagine how you could draw maximum benefit from the **Gopher** system other than with the help of **Veronica**. Unfortunately, **Veronica** also illustrates a growing problem throughout the Internet: Demand is intense, the load on the limited number of **Veronica** servers is high, and delays and inability to connect are a common occurrence. **Veronica**, as we will see, demands patience, and an understanding that the tools we use and the sprawling network that supports them are still very much under construction.

World Wide Web

Hypertext provides an entirely different take on displaying information. By adding hypertext links to a document, you are enabling your reader to jump from one item to another within the document; reading takes on a non-sequential flavor driven not by the original author's sense of organization but by the information needs of the reader. For some kinds of text, this approach is a valuable way to cut to the chase, drawing maximum benefit from a document with the least amount of time. Add in hypertext links *between* documents and you begin to create an information space with no formal pathways. You begin at one end and explore. No two paths through the labyrinth are precisely the same.

The **Web** comes from CERN, the huge physics research laboratory in Switzerland; it owes its origins to the talented Tim Berners-Lee and his colleagues. In the company of **Mosaic**, perhaps the most effective interface for general-purpose Internet use yet released, **World Wide Web** becomes a comprehensive approach to information retrieval. Like **Gopher**, it links to numerous resources, from FTP to Telnet to **WAIS** indices. Material from USENET newsgroups is accessible through the **Web**, as are graphics images and sound files. As a browsing environment, the **Web** offers unparalleled access to network resources with little overhead; you can become proficient on this tool within minutes, and spend hours moving through the data sea.

But for all its seductions, the **Web** and its hypertext links cannot offer everything. The price of browsing is time. Your ramblings through the **Web** will reveal sites and files you never dreamed existed, but the ability to cut directly to the material you need is lacking. When your search demands a swift response and your needs are precise, the **Web** is not always the tool of choice. At times, a **Veronica** search will serve you better, or a quick run with **archie** through a bank of FTP sites. Experience with each tool will suggest which is best for a given situation.

HYTELNET

Another take on hypertext is provided by **HYTELNET**, a program developed by Peter Scott at the University of Saskatchewan. Available as a stand-alone program as well as a networked tool, and accessible as well through Telnet, **HYTELNET** points to resources and can be a quick way for you to determine everything from the location of a database on agriculture to the address needed to search an on-line library in New Zealand. The program is maintained at an FTP site and is frequently updated to reflect network changes.

The library community has been fertile ground for the development of Internet tools. And no wonder. The diverse needs of those who access voluminous information through computers have prompted the widespread appearance of library catalogs on the network. We also examine the library question through such tools as **LIBTEL** and **LIBS**. We are a long way from the "digital library" spoken of so enthusiastically in the press, but the appearance of such tools points to a future where networks take on the task of providing high-quality reference material on-line.

archie

Think of information for a moment in the way Peter Deutsch and Alan Emtage once saw it. McGill University's School of Computer Science needed useful software. Examining FTP sites around the Internet was a necessity, but the process was labor-intensive, calling for the user to tap into a site and check, directory by directory, to see what was available. Information as fortress, with each fiefdom containing its own archives, and no link between castles but a single FTP connection. Something had to be done.

The **archie** tool that resulted from this dilemma automated what Deutsch and Emtage did manually; it conducted sweeps of selected FTP sites and stored the results in an indexed database. When you consult an **archie** server, you are checking your search term against such a database, which then produces hits showing you where to find the file you need. The public domain organizer program you would have spent hours locating by happenstance is now provided to you in a series of sites with appropriate directories and filenames. You have but to FTP to the site and retrieve a copy.

Now in commercial development through Bunyip Information Systems, **archie** is expanding in significant new directions. The critical need: bring more information to bear on the results of the typical **archie** search. As things now stand, your search will produce sites and filenames, but you have no way of knowing whether the program you're retrieving is the most recent version or an older implementation. Bunyip is responding to this dilemma by encouraging the implementation of *templates*, which will contain file information about the holdings at various FTP sites. The widespread use of such templates would make **archie** searching considerably more effective.

WHOIS, x.500, and More

Sooner or later, the problem of how to find people on the Internet will surface. If you're used to thinking of computers as marvelous data managers, you'll presume that somewhere an Internet directory exists, allowing you to query it by name or location to determine an electronic mail address. To your astonishment, you will quickly learn that instead of a single, comprehensive directory, there exist hundreds of tiny directories. Often they cover the people at a particular organization. What's worse, you can't query them until you know the separate address for each directory.

Millions of people use the global Internet, but only a tiny fraction of them are accessible through electronic searching. The tools we use, from **WHOIS** to the automated Knowbot program to the White Pages directories using the X.500 standard, compel us to master diverse techniques, search widely through distributed databases, and as often as not, come up short in our search. We will examine the frustrations and occasional breakthroughs of people-oriented searching by working through sample searches for each tool.

A SEARCH METHODOLOGY

The truth about Internet searching is this: Both the network and its navigational instruments are in their infancy. Searching can uncover unexpected terrain, sometimes rich with promise. It can just as likely turn up parched earth, with little or no potential. You must learn how to search effectively, know where and how to look, and perhaps just as important, know when to stop. A measure of frustration simply comes with the turf.

That said, the Internet search tools we will use provide us with numerous ways to examine the Internet's resources. We will use each in a variety of ways, running sample searches to display their features, and to give you an example of what can be done. In each case, the searches are not prepackaged. I have not gone out on the network to verify resources and then reverse-engineered a search to make any search tool look better than it is. When our searches come up with less than we'd like, you will see the result. When they hit paydirt, that will also be obvious.

The effective Internet searcher will think in terms of building a methodology. The only way to construct one is to learn the ins and outs of the various tools and then bring this knowledge to bear upon the problem at hand. What I recommend most strongly is that you do not make the mistake of focusing upon a single tool because it seems easier to use than the rest. The quickest way to limit yourself is to become trapped inside one set of commands and a single interface. Do this and the limitations of your tool will catch up with you.

No, the correct method is to run sample searches like those shown to you in this book until you have an understanding of how the various tools work. Then, when confronted with a real-world search problem, ponder which of the tools gives you the best angle on your information. Do you need to cut to the chase, entering a search term to pin down resources? If so, **World Wide Web** lacks the ability to search from the top; its browser structure takes you down numerous datapaths which may distract you from your purpose. Perhaps **Veronica** is the way to go in this case, launching a search for menu items on **Gopher** servers around the net.

But don't stop there. For after running your **Veronica** search and examining the **Gopher** resources, you can move back to the **Web** for a different kind of searching. Using hypertext links, you can look for the less obvious data, the items that didn't appear on **Gopher** menus, the Telnet links and FTP sites which may have escaped the attention of **Gopher** compilers. Don't hesitate to mine **WAIS** if full text is in the picture; perhaps a **WAIS** database exists with information germane to your task. A swift run through the Directory of Servers database at Thinking Machines Corp. may flag unexpected treasures.

Rarely, you see, does a search reach completion through a single resource. Serious Internet work requires combining search tools, looking into issues from a variety of perspectives. None of them is complete, but each can contribute to your knowledge of the available information. One tool leads to another, if you will let it. A frustrating search in **WAIS** may prompt you to a solid hit with **World Wide Web**, but you won't know to make the effort unless you master the rudiments of each tool now.

The Realistic Search

Research and development into Internet search tools continues through the efforts of the teams behind our current tools, other independent researchers and developers, and through the Clearinghouse for Networked Information Discovery and Retrieval in Research Triangle Park, NC. Funded largely by the NSF, the Clearinghouse, known as CNIDR (pronounced "snyder"), is performing yeoman work on the issue of standards and the interoperability of our tools by making sure that developers from the various software communities stay in communication and address common needs.

In Chapter 10, we examine the work of CNIDR, and through the comments of its leading figures, learn about the problems of today's search tools, and how these problems can be addressed in future versions. No one would have imagined five years ago that the number of tools available for our use would grow so large in so short a time. At this point, the influx of new users to the Internet calls up the question of the quality of our data and what we can do to enhance it. Most of what is currently available on the network is freely available material, and for good reason. We have lacked until recently the necessary tools for security and intellectual property protection that would allow us to place genuinely original information on-line. This is our next challenge.

Boswell reports what Samuel Johnson said when he observed a man who had had an unhappy marriage decide to marry again after the death of his first wife. The marriage, said Johnson, was the triumph of hope over experience. No seasoned Internet searcher would deny that an element of that same phenomenon is present in working with the network today. It is easy to glorify our ready access to resources, but experience teaches that all too often what we can obtain is limited in scope and often falls short of expectations. Fortunately, the work of CNIDR and the ongoing development of network standards leads us to hope that one day the so-called "digital library," an electronic Alexandria, will become a reality.

2

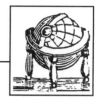

archie: Finding Files

The Internet is by its nature a system in which information is "distributed." This means that there is no central site, no archival storage place for all of its riches. We can see why this must be. After all, the data packets that carry the traffic moving across and through the Internet have no single source, move along no fixed pathway, and arrive at sites determined entirely by the header information they carry. To ask that such a system be centralized is to misunderstand the nature of networking.

A constant tension is maintained, then, between the virtual anarchy of thousands of data "conversations" between the computers that route the Internet's data, and the needs of individuals to find particular computer files. The big three Internet applications—electronic mail, FTP, and Telnet—function to help us communicate and exchange information. We can use both electronic mail and Telnet if we have an address, and the same is true of FTP. The question for Internet explorers is, how do I get the critical address?

In this chapter, we examine the first of our Internet tools, and the one with the longest history. **archie** is in many ways representative of the networks it serves. The idea of using the Internet as a vast repository of software, from executable programs to graphics to textual documents, could not exist without **archie**. Yet the program, command-driven and intimidating to the newcomer, places its own demands upon the user. What you will need here and with other Internet tools is a willingness to learn a set of commands and their options. No, the average **archie** command isn't intuitive. But neither is it difficult to understand once you comprehend how **archie** goes about its job. Using **archie**, you begin to make the Internet a genuine resource.

THE NATURE OF FILE TRANSFER PROTOCOL

File Transfer Protocol, or FTP, is a way of moving computer files from one site to another. We are concerned here with a particular variant of FTP called *anonymous FTP*. The reason: Anonymous FTP is open to anyone. The administrators at computer sites around the world have made directories full of information available to anyone who logs in as **anonymous** (the convention is to use your Internet address as your password). Because you need no special permission to get into these sites, they constitute a kind of Internet "swap box," where everything is freely available. The range of programs available at these sites is staggering and growing every day.

Consider the number of networks alone, close to 30,000 as of June 1994 (compared to the 16,000-plus found in October of 1993 in SRI's International Internet Domain Survey). Then realize that each site will differ according to the wishes of its administrators. One may specialize in Macintosh software, as does **mac.archive.umich.edu**. Another may focus on a broad range of computers, as does the huge **wuarchive.wustl.edu** site at Washington University in St. Louis. A third may collect textual information, such as the valuable **pit-manager.mit.edu**, which houses background documents called Frequently Asked Questions (FAQs); these supply information about USENET newsgroups.

Obviously, software is also duplicated at many sites; you can imagine a popular public domain or shareware program appearing on anonymous FTP directories around the globe: thousands of sites, some large, some small, with new ones appearing daily. No wonder estimates of the number of files available over the Internet go as high as 6 terabytes, or 6,000 gigabytes, of stored programs, text files, and data. Directory follows directory, subdirectories branch into still more subdirectories, and soon the file you need is buried six layers deep at a site whose name you've never heard of in a country half a world away.

How to Find FTP Site Lists

Macintosh FTP sites are compiled in a list maintained by Bruce Grubb. You can retrieve it by FTP.

Address: **sumex-aim.stanford.edu**
Directory: *info-mac/info-mac/comm/info*
File name: **info**

PC FTP sites are compiled in a list that is copyrighted by Rhys Weatherley and Timo Salmi.

Address: **oak.oakland.edu**
Directory: */pub/msdos/info*
File name: **moder*.zip**

You can also find the same file maintained at:

Address: **garbo.uwasa.fi**
Directory: *pc/pd2*

Where to begin? Even before you begin using Internet tools, one place to check is a directory of FTP sites. Fortunately, there are several such documents for Macintosh as well as PC users. Realize that these lists are by nature limited; they're bound to be behind the times, as is any compilation that tries to track such a rapidly shifting landscape. Second, they're not open to the kind of interactive searching that **archie** will allow you to run; a printed list is a static thing. But you may find them helpful in establishing particular sites for further exploration.

The challenge faced by the people who developed **archie** was to find a way to sort through the Internet's embarrassment of riches in order to track down particular computer files. Ideally, the system would allow the user to specify a search term, and the system would then hunt it down. This posed considerable problems of logistics, given the Internet's constantly changing landscape. The solution, as I think you'll agree, is an ingenious one.

ARCHIE SCOUTS THE INTERNET TERRAIN

archie was developed at McGill University's School of Computer Science by Alan Emtage, Bill Heelan, and Peter Deutsch. Like many good computer tools, the program developed out of a university's need to save money. Looking for public domain software, the McGill team began searching anonymous FTP archive sites, and eventually began to automate the process of scanning their findings. From this evolved an information tool that is among the most widely used on the Internet. Deutsch and Emtage, as we'll see shortly, went on to found Bunyip Information Systems of Montreal, which licenses the **archie** server system and provides upgrades and support. **archie** version 3.0, a commercially supported version of the search tool, was released by Bunyip in the fall of 1992; future versions will include a variety of new information gathering tools.

There are various ways you can keep up with **archie** developments. Here are the alternatives:

- Join an **archie** mailing list. Send electronic mail to: **archie-people-request@bunyip.com**. This is an Internet mailing list that tracks the development of **archie** and provides many insights into its function. In the body of your message, write: **subscribe *your address* archie-people**.

- Read the USENET newsgroup **comp.archives.admin**, which often contains discussions about **archie**.

- Use FTP to examine the holdings of the various **archie** servers. There you will find documents about the **archie** system in the directory **pub/archie/docs**. Your command would be in the form **ftp archie.ans.net**. A list of **archie** servers is provided later in this chapter.

An aside on money: The fact that **archie** is now being offered as a commercial system, with support and enhancements, does not mean that you, the end user, will suddenly have to pony up hard cash to use it. Bunyip Information Systems has added functionality to the original tool and marketed it to the sites that want to carry it. A public domain implementation remains available. The people who deal with the commercial aspects of **archie**, then, are the system administrators who are putting **archie** on-line at their site. The end user's job is simply to figure out the best ways to use this powerful tool.

Consider **archie** a set of related functions. The software maintains a list of Internet FTP sites known as the Internet Archives database (the term **archie**, as you're doubtless beginning to realize, is a play on "archive" (the subsequent appearance of the tool called **Veronica** reminds us that it's also the name of a memorable cartoon character). The database is searchable by a variety of servers across the Internet. Note, then, that **archie** does not make data sweeps across the entire Internet; rather, it targets specific sites, with the permission of their administrators, and searches them.

Going through the directories at these sites manually would, obviously, take 24 hours per day for the individual user, who would, in any case, constantly be falling behind as new files and directories were added to one or another site. By automating the process, **archie** can make its own sweep of FTP directories, compiling them and storing the results in its database. Each site's holdings therefore stay relatively up-to-date at any given moment, although there may be a slight overlap; an **archie** search could, for example, point to a file that had been removed shortly after the last **archie** database update. And, of course, a new file that a given **archie** server doesn't yet know about could be added to the holdings at a specific site.

Although the system began at McGill University, the need to spread the wealth soon became apparent. By late 1992, there were over 20 public-access **archie** servers available in the Internet community, with locations scattered around the globe; by mid 1993, that number had increased to 27. Four copies were being operated by the InterNIC, along with U.S. sites at Advanced Network & Services, SURAnet, Rutgers University, the University of Nebraska at Lincoln, and the Clearinghouse for Networked Information Discovery and Retrieval (the last is not publicly accessible).

These server computers query database listings from over 1,500 sites, which are scattered through corporations, government agencies and a variety of other organizations. Within the **archie** system alone, some 230 gigabytes of files are available for searching; and remember, **archie** covers only a subset of the files available throughout the entire network. **archie** servers are averaging 30,000 queries every day.

If you like doing things the hard way, you could always retrieve and examine the listings that **archie** creates for its database; they're available at the individual server sites. In doing so, and in finding a way to search these materials, you would be re-creating the original process that led to **archie**. But fortunately, there is no reason to reinvent the wheel. And as useful as it is in terms of searching FTP directories, **archie** is no longer limited to making directory searches alone. Indeed, the technology behind **archie** is adaptable to any kind of database, which is how the **whatis** database, cataloguing descriptions of software, came to be made available in 1991.

To go to the source for **archie** information, contact its developers. The address is:

Bunyip Information Systems
310 St-Catherine St West, Suite 202
Montreal, Quebec H2X 2A1
Voice: 514-875-8611
Fax: 514-875-8134
E-mail: **info@bunyip.com**

You can expect more such databases using the **archie** system in the near future. Be aware, too, that **archie**'s popularity has led to its being incorporated into a variety of other Internet tools, including **WAIS**, **Gopher**, and **World Wide Web**. The convergence of search technology makes it possible to work with many tools in a range of formats, allowing you to choose the user interface best suited to your needs. We will examine **archie**'s connections to the other major search tools later in this book.

USING ARCHIE

There are three ways to access **archie** directly (which is to say, without going through the medium of one of the other search tools). Here are your options:

- Use Telnet to contact an **archie** server. To do so, the command is **telnet *server-name***. For example, if I choose to contact the **archie** server at SURAnet, I would send the command **telnet archie.sura.net**. At the login prompt, I would enter **archie**.

- Use a client program to access **archie**. To do this, type **archie** followed by a **RETURN** at your system's command prompt. If an **archie** client is available, you should get a list of system commands. If no client is available, you'll be forced to use either Telnet or the third option.

- Contact **archie** by electronic mail. This involves sending a message with your search commands to an **archie** server. To do this, you add the term **archie@** to the server address. Thus, to send electronic mail to the **archie** server at SURAnet, I would send my message to **archie@archie.sura.net**.

As we'll see, there are reasons why you may want to take the electronic mail route even if you have Telnet capabilities, or even the services of a local client program. But when choosing between Telnet and a local client, the local program is best because you are less likely to run into difficulties. The traffic load on the server can be intense, particularly at peak periods during business hours. Using your own system's client program to forward your query can save you time, and is also the best way to conserve network resources. We'll encounter this principle again with other Internet search tools.

USING TELNET TO SEARCH WITH ARCHIE

A list of **archie** servers is presented in Table 2.1. If you examine this list, you'll see that there are servers throughout the world. Bear in mind this fundamental principle: It is less demanding on network resources to use Telnet to a location near to you. Resist the temptation to contact an **archie** server in Australia if you happen to live in the southern United States, where the server at SURAnet would do just as well. International traffic can be heavy and there is no need to cause further congestion on already crowded circuits.

Table 2.1 archie Servers Worldwide

Server Address	Location	Country
ds.internic.net	AT&T InterNIC Directory and Database Services, South Plainfield, NJ	USA
archie.sura.net	SURAnet, Baltimore, MD	USA
archie.unl.edu	University of Nebraska, Lincoln	USA
archie.rutgers.edu	Rutgers University, NJ	USA
archie.ans.net	Advanced Network & Services, Inc., Elmsford, NY	USA
archie.au	University of Melbourne	Australia
archie.univie.ac.at	University of Vienna	Austria
archie.edvz.uni-linz.ac.at	Johannes Kepler University, Linz	Austria
archie.uqam.ca	University of Quebec	Quebec
archie.doc.ic.ac.uk	Imperial College, London	United Kingdom
archie.funet.fi	Finnish University and Research Network	Finland
archie.th-darmstadt.de	Technische Hochschule, Darmstadt	Germany
archie.ac.il	Hebrew University of Jerusalem	Israel
archie.unipi.it		Italy
archie.wide.ad.jp	WIDE Project, Tokyo	Japan
archie.sogang.ac.kr	Sogang University	Korea
archie.kr	Telecom Research Center, Seoul	Korea
archie.nz	Victoria University, Wellington	New Zealand
archie.rediris.es	RedIRIS, Madrid	Spain
archie.luth.se	University of Lulea	Sweden
archie.switch.ch	SWITCH, Zurich	Switzerland
archie.ncu.edu.tw	National Central University, Chung-li	Taiwan

Remember that the ranks of **archie** servers are likely to be supplemented by the time you read this. Many of the **archie** sites update you when you log on, with a list of alternative server sites presented on-screen. More servers will take some of the load off the existing sites, but you should continue to target only those sites nearest you. And, as we'll see, doing so isn't always an intuitive process.

If you are a dial-up user, for example, consider the nature of your connection before you log onto **archie** using Telnet. CompuServe routes its traffic through a central site in Columbus, OH. This is true no matter where its customers happen to live. So if you are based in, say, Portland, OR, but are using CompuServe to send an electronic mail query to an **archie** server, it should be the server nearest to Columbus rather than the one nearest to Portland. The same is true of DELPHI and BIX (Massachusetts), America Online (Virginia), and any other commercial on-line service. Keeping your provider's location in mind will keep you within the bounds of proper network etiquette.

Once you've chosen your server, the command **telnet** *server-name* takes you there; log in as **archie**. Be advised that, as the traffic load on these systems increases, users more frequently encounter busy signals. These occur in the form of a message when you attempt to log on, telling you that due to the number of Telnet connections already in place, you are unable to use the system at this time. An example of this kind of message is shown in Figure 2.1.

As you can see, this server, the one at **archie.sura.net**, provides you with alternative server sites even as it informs you that there are too many users currently logged on for you to use the system. You are also given the opportunity to use a login of **qarchie**, which activates a much simplified **archie** capability that is limited to queries only. We'll concentrate, though, on the full-bore **archie** search as mediated through Telnet to a different site.

The **archie** search screen you'll receive when you do make the connection is a spare one; it's illustrated in Figure 2.2.

Certain relevant information is presented immediately. Terminal type we can assume; it's set to VT100, which is the standard for character-based terminal emulation. Pay particular attention to the cryptic comment *'search' (type string) has the value 'sub'*. At this juncture, it doesn't make much sense, but as we'll see, the values set in this field can be changed and have great bearing on how we conduct an **archie** search.

The basic search command for **archie** is **find** *searchterm*. When you enter this information followed by a **RETURN**, **archie** will search the directories and files in its database for items that match. For example, **find astronomy** is a

Figure 2.1
Trying to log on to an **archie** site when there are too many connections.

```
SunOS UNIX (yog-sothoth.sura.net)

login: archie
Last login: Thu Nov  4 10:00:35 from oak.grove.iup.ed
SunOS Release 4.1.3 (NYARLATHOTEP) #3: Thu Apr 22 15:26:21 EDT 1993
Sorry, there are too many people already logged on.
You can log in as qarchie which uses the prospero server to do searches.
Telnet to archie.sura.net and log in as user qarchie.

The following is a list of other archie servers:
    archie.ans.net              147.225.1.10     (ANS server, NY (USA))
    archie.au                   139.130.4.6      (Austrailian Server)
    archie.doc.ic.ac.uk         146.169.11.3     (United Kingdom Server)
    archie.edvz.uni-linz.ac.at  140.78.3.8       (Austrian Server)
    archie.funet.fi             128.214.6.102    (Finnish Server)
    archie.internic.net         198.49.45.10     (AT&T server, NY (USA))
    archie.kr                   128.134.1.1      (Korean Server)
    archie.kuis.kyoto-u.ac.jp   130.54.20.1      (Japanese Server)
    archie.luth.se              130.240.18.4     (Swedish Server)
    archie.ncu.edu.tw           140.115.19.24    (Taiwanese server)
    archie.nz                   130.195.9.4      (New Zeland server)
    archie.rediris.es           130.206.1.2      (Spanish Server)
    archie.rutgers.edu          128.6.18.15      (Rutgers University (USA))
    archie.sogang.ac.kr         163.239.1.11     (Korean Server)
```

Figure 2.2
Logging on to **archie**
at the InterNIC.

```
*******************************************************************************
                Welcome to the InterNIC Directory and Database Server.

*******************************************************************************


# Message of the day from the localhost Prospero server:


         Welcome to Archie  server for the
         InterNIC Directory and Database Services.




# Bunyip Information Systems, 1993

# Terminal type set to `vt100 24 80'.
# `erase' character is `~?'.
# `search' (type string) has the value `sub'.
archie> _
```

search statement that will likely retrieve a number of directories named *astron-omy*. When I entered this search at the InterNIC's Directory and Database Services **archie** site, two things happened. First, I received information about the status of the search, and my own position in the queue of those waiting to use **archie**.

```
archie> find astronomy
# Search type: sub.
# Your queue position: 1
# Estimated time for completion: 00:05
working... \
```

Soon after, **archie** delivered the information I needed. A portion of this material is shown in Figure 2.3.

Examine this result with care. We're looking at one of several screens of results. One of the "hits," the first one, is actually a file, found at a site that has already scrolled off the screen in this figure. The rest are directories, each of them at the site shown immediately above its name. Thus, the directory *pub/mac/mirror-umich/misc/misc/astronomy* is to be found at the FTP address **ftp.sunet.se**, while *pub/msdos/astronomy* is located at **rigel.acs.oakland.edu**, and so forth. Keep in mind your ability to search for directories; doing so can help you locate archives you'll want to return to for particular types of software in the future.

Having located the file or directory we're interested in, we can then use FTP to move directly to that site, where we can explore and retrieve files as we please. All of which makes **archie** seem like a simple search tool that homes in on exactly what we need. But in fact, the kind of files we're looking for, and the methods we use to search for them, are highly variable. **archie** contains numerous options

Figure 2.3
Partial results from an
archie search using
the term "astronomy."

```
        Location: /pub/music/lyrics/b/blue.oyster.cult
          FILE    -rw-rw-r--   1332 bytes  00:00 15 Nov 1991  astronomy


  Host ftp.sunet.se   (130.238.127.3)
  Last updated 07:53  3 Nov 1993

        Location: /pub/mac/mirror-umich/misc
          DIRECTORY  drwxrwxr-x   1024 bytes  06:20  1 Nov 1993  astronomy


  Host rigel.acs.oakland.edu   (141.210.10.117)
  Last updated 08:20 23 Oct 1993

        Location: /pub/msdos
          DIRECTORY  drwxr-xr-x   1024 bytes  04:30 21 Oct 1993  astronomy


  Host ftp.uwasa.fi   (128.214.87.1)
  Last updated 05:55  7 Oct 1993

        Location: /mirror/umich.macarchive/misc
          DIRECTORY  drwxr-xr-x   1024 bytes  13:47 25 Jun 1993  astronomy
```

that can modify the search you run and make it more precise. These commands can also help reduce congestion on the networks, so using **archie** effectively involves learning what they are.

An aside on names: the Internet changes faster than most things in this transitory world, so it's no surprise that the standard **archie** search command, which was once **prog**, has been renamed **find**. **prog** had a certain elegance, in that it named the type of resource—programs—it was looking for. But **find** is easier to remember and more accurate, since many of the items turned up by a standard **archie** search are not, in fact, programs, but directories, documents, and other kinds of information. If you've become accustomed to the **prog** command, however, you can still use it.

A Sample Search Using archie with Telnet

Let's illustrate how you can adapt **archie** to meet more precise needs by setting up a search for a software program. I've been told by a friend about a shareware package called **2Do**, developed by William P. Anderson and made available on bulletin board systems and at FTP archive sites around the world. **2Do** is a handy program that sets up lists of necessary tasks—to-do lists, in other words. Not only does it sort them using a variety of different, user-defined methods, but it also tags items with different colors depending on their priority. Clearly, this is a handy program to evaluate and, if it proves its mettle, to register for use.

The basic **archie** search, then, would be **find 2do**. But this time, let's think about limiting the results of the search. After all, the astronomy hunt we just concluded actually retrieved numerous screensful of information. We could use many "hits" if we were looking for directories of general information, as we would assuredly find in directories called *astronomy*. But when searching for a particular program, we don't need to pull in screenful after screenful; we just need a few good sites.

archie allows us to do this with a modified command. Before entering **find 2do**, we'll enter a command that changes the way **archie** does business. **set maxhits 10** tells **archie** that we only want a maximum of ten hits; the search should stop after reaching that point. This command should be given before the **find 2do** command because it sets **archie** to search under these constraints. There are a variety of other commands that we can use the same way; for now, let's see what happens when we run the search.

```
archie> set maxhits 10
archie> find 2do
# Search type: sub.
# Your queue position: 1
# Estimated time for completion: 00:06
working... |
```

And soon we have our information, as shown partially in Figure 2.4.

We've also got a problem, because if you examine the results, looking in each case at both the directory and the name of the file we've generated, you can see that none of these is likely to be the **2Do** program we're hoping to find. In fact, we seem to have wandered into a number of selections having to do with images. And while **archie** has indeed found the search term we gave it, which was **2do**, that search term is embedded in a longer word, **pln2dot**.

Two lessons emerge from this result. First, when you limit **archie**'s maximum number of hits, you always have to bear in mind that you may set the number too low, and thus retrieve only material that doesn't meet your needs.

Figure 2.4
Searching for the **2Do** program.

```
Host roxette.mty.itesm.mx    (131.178.17.100)
Last updated 08:33   4 Nov 1993

     Location: /pub/X11R5/mit/extensions/test/InsPEX/refimages
       FILE    -r--r--r--    2464 bytes  01:00 13 Feb 1991  pln2dot


Host emx.cc.utexas.edu    (128.83.186.11)
Last updated 08:23   4 Nov 1993

     Location: /pub/mnt/source/X11R5/mit/extensions/test/InsPEX/refimages
       FILE    -rw-r--r--    2464 bytes  01:00 13 Feb 1991  pln2dot


Host ftp.sunet.se    (130.238.127.3)
Last updated 07:53   3 Nov 1993

     Location: /pub/X11/R5untarred/mit/extensions/test/InsPEX/refimages
       FILE    -r--r--r--    2464 bytes  23:00 12 Feb 1991  pln2dot


Host cs.tut.fi    (130.230.4.2)
Last updated 06:49   3 Nov 1993
```

You would then have to go back and reset this number. The second lesson is that **archie** is clearly searching not just for the standalone term we gave it—**2do**—but also for that sequence of three characters as found inside any other words. We get **pln2dot** as a result because the search term is nestled inside the larger expression. Surely there must be some way to avoid retrieving such unnecessary material.

And, of course, there is. Recall the introductory **archie** screen we retrieved when we first opened the Telnet connection into this site. It contained the statement *'search' (type string) has the value 'sub'*. The time has come to disentangle this arcane expression and put it to work. Search values within **archie** can be set by another set of commands. The new **archie** software, version 3.0, defaults to the search type *sub*, for "substring." Upper- and lowercase are ignored. This means that the program will hunt just as it did in the example above, looking for any name that contains the searchstring we specify.

And, of course, that value can be changed. If we want to find only the exact program name as we look for the **2Do** program, we can do so by setting the search type to *exact*. The syntax is **set search exact**. This would seem to solve our problem, but in fact, it actually opens up another can of worms, because programs aren't listed this way in file archives. We would be unlikely to find **2Do** under that precise name; more likely it would be **2do.exe**, or **2do.zip**, and any number of other variations.

Can we also search using wildcard characters, so we might be able to locate any file that *begins* with the term **2do**, no matter what its ending? The answer is yes. The way to do this is through a UNIX *regular expression*, which is the way **archie** client software handles the search by default (the Telnet client, by contrast, uses the *substring* searchtype, as already mentioned). When you're using a Telnet client, you have to specify that you want to **set search regex**, for regular expression. A regular expression in UNIX terminology is a way of fine-tuning your search. Here I've already set the searchtype to *regex*, and am now entering a command that specifies how I want **archie** to search for the file.

```
archie> find ^2do.*
# Search type: regex.
# Your queue position: 1
# Estimated time for completion: 00:07
working...
```

The command is cryptic, as **regex** statements tend to be. We'll untangle it in a moment. If you look at the results, as they appear in Figure 2.5, you'll see that I've isolated only those files *beginning* with the term **2do**.

Now we're in business. We've located something called **2dov10.zip**, a file which, as we would find out upon unpacking it, contains **2Do** version 1. This is the file we need, and our only remaining task is to go to the site using FTP and retrieve the file. The actual set of hits I received for this search was limited to eight, whereas if I had left the search type at *sub*, I would have generated a large number of hits, most of them irrelevant. By focusing our search using the search type *regex*, then, we've saved ourselves time and we've reduced the network's workload.

The principle is this: Although you can achieve many successful searches simply by using the **find** *searchterm* command at the **archie** prompt, you will

Figure 2.5
Refining the **2do** search;
now we receive only
those files that begin with
the term **2do**.

```
Host wuarchive.wustl.edu     (128.252.135.4)
Last updated 07:37   4 Nov 1993

     Location: /systems/ibmpc/win3/util
        FILE    -r--r--r--   847427 bytes   00:00 28 Apr 1993   2dov10.zip


Host ftp.sunet.se     (130.238.127.3)
Last updated 07:53   3 Nov 1993

     Location: /pub/pc/windows/mirror-cica/util
        FILE    -r--r--r--   847427 bytes   22:00 28 Apr 1993   2dov10.zip


Host halcyon.com     (198.137.231.1)
Last updated 07:02 18 Aug 1993

     Location: /dec/.2/micro/msdos/win3/util
        FILE    -r--r--r--   847427 bytes   17:07 28 Apr 1993   2dov10.zip


Host kum.kaist.ac.kr     (128.134.1.1)
Last updated 09:33 17 Jun 1993
```

search more effectively and certainly more efficiently if you learn to use **archie**'s search options. In a moment, we'll examine the structure of a UNIX regular expression, so that the oddball cryptography of my search statement above will make more sense. But first, let's examine the range of **archie** options, and try to formulate an effective search strategy.

archie's Command Options Using Telnet

archie version 3.0 is loaded with command-line options that allow you to tune up your search. **archie** actually functions by means of a set of variables, the values of which can be changed to reflect the kind of search you want to run. Some variables are *Boolean,* meaning you simply choose to turn them on or off. Others are *numeric*—you enter a number with them. The third kind of variable is a *string* variable; this just means you enter a "string," or sequence of characters to set the variable as needed.

Don't be put off by all this talk of variables. **archie** doesn't require that you do high-level programming to make it work. I will present the major variables below. Each is typed at the command prompt before you begin your search. We use the **set** command to change the settings for each variable.

Setting Up archie

To learn what the current settings are, type the command **show**. Here is the result of entering such a command when using Telnet to the InterNIC's **archie** server at **ds.internic.net**.

```
archie> show
# 'autologout' (type numeric) has the value '60'.
# 'collections' (type string) is not set.
# 'compress' (type string) has the value 'none'.
# 'encode' (type string) has the value 'none'.
# 'language' (type string) has the value 'english'.
# 'mailto' (type string) is not set.
# 'match_domain' (type string) is not set.
# 'match_path' (type string) is not set.
# 'max_split_size' (type numeric) has the value '51200'.
# 'maxhits' (type numeric) has the value '100'.
# 'maxhitspm' (type numeric) has the value '100'.
# 'maxmatch' (type numeric) has the value '100'.
# 'output_format' (type string) has the value 'verbose'.
# 'pager' (type boolean) is not set.
# 'search' (type string) has the value 'sub'.
# 'server' (type string) has the value 'localhost'.
# 'sortby' (type string) has the value 'none'.
# 'status' (type boolean) is set.
# 'term' (type string) has the value 'vt100 24 80'.
archie>
```

This is, in fact, a pocket list of the **archie** variables, many of which we'll be dealing with below. We'll now examine some of these parameters to explain how they function. In each case, we'll change the variable by using the **set** command, followed by the name of the variable and the value we have chosen for it. When I refer to giving the command **set pager**, I could just as easily have stated "set the pager variable." We are changing the values by which **archie** operates to make our search work.

Changing Your Search Parameters

set search sub

This is the default for Telnet searches with **archie** version 3.0. The search will retrieve any file or directory name containing your search term within it, regardless of case. This is why a search under **2do** retrieved the **pln2dot** hits. **2do** is a "substring" of **pln2dot**. Searching for **tin** would retrieve **bulle*tin*** and ***sting***, among other hits.

set search subcase

This is a case-sensitive *substring* search. It works like the regular *substring* search, except that it differentiates between upper- and lowercase letters. A search for **2DO** with searchtype set to *subcase* would ignore any files named **2do** because of the difference of case.

set search exact

Here **archie** looks for an exact match. This works well if you are looking for directories, as we saw when we asked **archie** for information about astronomy. But it can be a problem when you search for individual files, since they may often have extensions that would cause the *exact* search to miss them. A search for **astronomy** would not flag the text file **astronomy.txt** or the compressed file **astronomy.Z**. But an *exact* search is a quick one, and if you know the exact listing of the file you need, this is how to get it.

set search regex

This uses UNIX regular expressions to conduct the search. Used without further specification, a *regex* search becomes a *substring* search, because regular expressions assume a wild-card character at the beginning and end of the search term. You can, however, specify that the search term should only appear at the beginning of the retrieved file or directory name by using the caret (^) character. A dollar sign ($) specifies that the search term is to appear at the end of the retrieved file or directory name.

Confused? Don't worry. I'll have more on *regex* searches at the end of this section.

You should also be aware of three other options that combine the search strategies above.

set search exact_sub

Here you are searching for an exact hit, but if **archie** finds no matches, it will then try the substring search strategy.

set search exact_subcase

The search begins using the *exact* strategy, but if it fails, it switches to a subcase or case-sensitive *substring* search.

set search exact_regex

This begins with the exact search method, but switches to *regex* if no matches are found.

As you can see, the range of options under search terms is broad. Shortly, we'll put the search strategies to work to find files, changing our searchtypes as we go. For now, though, concentrate on another set of options that determines the particular place **archie** should run its search.

Where and What archie Searches

You can tell **archie** to search particular places for a specified search term, again using the **set** command.

set match_domains *string*

This means that you can determine a particular domain that you want to search. Perhaps you want to limit your search to universities. If so, you could use the command **set match_domains edu** to limit **archie** to **edu** sites. Or you could take a geographical slant on things. Perhaps you need a file from Switzerland. Your command **set match_domains ch** would limit the search to that domain.

set match_path

Here you are able to restrict your search by examining the directories **archie** will look in for your search term. This would make sense if you had a fair idea that your files fit into a general category. If you were looking for a file that compiled statistics on the planets, and you knew its name was **planet.zip**, you could restrict your search to directories called *astronomy* by entering the command **set match_path astronomy**. If you needed a particular graphics tool, you might use **set match_path graphics**.

The search pays no attention to case. If you want to use multiple terms, you can separate them with colons. Thus, **set match_path beer:brewing** will retrieve files with one or both of these components—beer or brewing—in the names of the directories that lead to them.

Controlling archie's Output

Fortunately, **archie** allows you a great deal of control over what it sends you. You should consider the output commands among the most important in your **archie** repertoire. Using them properly will save you time.

set maxhits *number*

Depending on what you're searching for, an **archie** hunt can rack up quite a few hits. This is particularly true if you are looking for a fairly common shareware program or a text document that has been receiving wide circulation. Your need is to find a good, preferably nearby site from which to download this file. What you don't need is a huge list of file sites, all of them offering the same file. In fact, the **archie** system will function that much better if you reduce its workload. Why not call up just a few hits, assuming your search terms are tightly chosen?

set maxhits 25 is a command that reduces the number of matches to 25 (and, of course, you can set the number where you choose, providing it is between 0 and 1,000). Once **archie** hits the upper limit, the search stops. You will see quite a difference between this search limitation and the default, which is 1,000 matches (individual servers, of course, may set the default at whatever value they choose).

set maxhitspm *number*

Two other output variables are associated with the **maxhits** command. The statement **set maxhitspm 10** will return ten files for each filename that **archie** matches. The reason that there is a separate **maxhitspm** command has to do with the way the **archie** database works. A filename can have several files associated with it, each of them sharing the same name; the name of the file in the database points to the location of each of the other files throughout the FTP sites on the Internet that share the same name.

set maxmatch *number*

The associated command **set maxmatch *number*** sets a maximum number of matching files that **archie** will find.

Think of the output commands this way. The number you use with **set maxhits** determines the total number of hits returned by **archie**. **set maxmatch** determines the total number of filenames that match the search term. **set maxhitspm** determines the number of files returned for each filename that **archie** is able to match. These distinctions can be useful in cases where we are trying to search for a common filename, one that the **archie** database shows occurring at numerous sites. In most cases, however, simply restricting your search with **maxhits** is a sufficient to limit your search output.

Sorting Commands

Perhaps you prefer to see **archie**'s output sorted alphabetically or by file size. A number of sorting commands are available.

set sortby *filename*

   This command sorts **archie**'s output alphabetically by the name of the files it retrieves.

set sortby *hostname*

   Sorts alphabetically by the name of the host computer.

set sortby *none*

   Does not sort the output.

set sortby *size*

   Sorts **archie**'s output by largest to smallest files.

set sortby *time*

   Sorts by time, with the most recent files listed first.

   Important note: All the sorting commands can be run in reverse order by prefixing the **sortby** statement with the letter **r**. To sort in reverse order by size, for example you would enter **set sortby rsize**. To sort by reverse alphabetical order of filenames, enter **set sortby rfilename**, and so on.

Choosing an Output Format

The normal results of an **archie** search are in **verbose** mode, as illustrated in Figure 2.5; they provide host name and IP number, the date of the file's last updating, its directory location, and associated file information. You may, on the other hand, prefer to look at the output in terse mode, which reduces the information for each file into a single line. Here, for example, is what the output looks like when restricted to terse mode. I've entered a search for the shareware communications program **Qmodem**, from Mustang Software, Inc. I've restricted the number of hits to 10 (**set maxhits 10**) and have requested terse mode:

```
ftp.std.com  00:00  6 Oct 1990 512 bytes /src/pc/comm/qmodem
wuarchive.wustl.edu  14:53  1 Nov 1993 8192 bytes /systems/ibmpc/msdos/qmodem
wuarchive.wustl.edu  22:02  1 Nov 1993 8192 bytes /systems/ibmpc/umich.edu/commm
rigel.acs.oakland.edu  04:31 21 Oct 1993 512 bytes /pub/msdos/qmodem
uhunix2.uhcc.hawaii.edu  01:00 18 Jan 1992 512 bytes /pub/ibmpc/comm/qmodem
ftp.uu.net  00:08 16 Aug 1993 1024 bytes /systems/ibmpc/msdos/simtel20/qmodem
cair.kaist.ac.kr  00:00 16 May 1992 1776 bytes /pub/msdos/bbs/pcb/qmodem.dir
cair.kaist.ac.kr  00:00 19 May 1992 1674 bytes /pub/msdos/bbs/rbbs/qmodem.dir
```

As you can see, the output is now reduced to a single line for each hit. The commands needed to achieve this result follow.

set output_format terse

For terse output as shown above.

set output_format verbose

For standard, full-length **archie** output.

set output_format machine

Useful when you want to manipulate the **archie** results through another program.

Activating the Status Line

archie's status line shows the progress of your search as it's running. You can activate it with the command **set status**.

Mailing Your Results

Rather than examining your results during the Telnet session, you may prefer to have them sent to you via electronic mail. To do so, you can use the **mailto** variable. Once you have set this variable, you can then use the **mail** command to have the output of your last command sent to you.

set mailto *username*

Entering **set mailto vprice@eapoe.com**, for example, sends the output of your search to the specified address. You can also specify more than one address in case you want to forward your results to someone else. You can use the **mail** command to mail your results without setting the **mailto** variable, but if you do, you will need to enter an address each time you invoke the **mail** function.

Paging Through archie

One problem with an **archie** search is that your results can scroll past before you have the chance to examine them. Using the **mail** command to send the output to your mailbox is one option. Another is to change the way **archie** displays material on the screen. The **pager** variable allows you to slow **archie** down. With it, you can cause the system to display your results in single screens of information; you move between screens by pressing the **SPACEBAR**. To do this, give the command **set pager**. After you have read the material in question on-screen, you exit the pager program (it's called **less**, by the way) by entering a **q**, followed by a **RETURN**.

Miscellaneous archie Commands

Although you'll use the **set** command more than any other, because it functions to change the key variables that determine how **archie** works, there are a number of other commands that can make your work with **archie** easier.

list

This command can be used by itself to indicate all the sites in the database at the server site, or in conjunction with a UNIX regular expression to limit the search to particular domains. I could, for example, use **list** to search for all sites in the United Kingdom, using a *regex* term:

```
list .*uk$
```

This command returns any site with the **uk** domain name, and excludes all others. The **$** sign at the end of the statement specifies that no text should follow the search term; the **.*** allows any text to exist in front of the search term.

The (abbreviated) output of a **list** command looks like this:

```
ftp.uu.net                    192.48.96.9      06:23 20 Sep 1993
ftp.x.org                  198.112.44.100      06:20 20 Sep 1993
interviews.stanford.edu       36.22.0.175      06:26 21 Sep 1993
jaguar.cs.utah.edu         155.99.212.101      06:28 24 Sep 1993
julian.uwo.ca               129.100.2.12      06:21 24 Sep 1993
june.cs.washington.edu        128.95.1.4      06:38 24 Sep 1993
kauri.vuw.ac.nz             130.195.11.3      06:16  9 Nov 1993
labrea.stanford.edu           36.8.0.112      06:15 24 Sep 1993
mammoth.cs.berkeley.edu    128.32.149.78      06:16 24 Sep 1993
munnari.oz.au              128.250.1.21      06:27 27 Sep 1993
```

help

Don't overlook **archie**'s extensive help system. While it's impenetrably written and as terse as any UNIX manual page, it nonetheless can bail you out of a jam while you're still on-line. Having given the **help** command, you can use a **?** at the help prompt to list the available subtopics. To exit help, type **done** at the help prompt.

quit

Use this command to exit from **archie**. You can also use **exit** or **bye**.

servers

Enter the **servers** command to generate a list of publicly available **archie** servers known to the site you are currently using. This is a good way to keep up to date as new **archie** servers come on-line.

THE (SOMETIMES) HELPFUL WHATIS COMMAND

Any method of specifying a search presupposes certain constraints. **archie**, for example, allows you to search for files with particular names, or to specify parts of those names and retrieve any files that match your specifications. The method works when you have one of two things: 1) a reasonable expectation of what the filename is or 2) a more general term that can be used to search for directories at the various sites that may contain the software or documents you need. Where the method fails is in those instances when you have a rough idea of what you need but not the faintest idea of what its name might be.

To work around such problems, **archie** maintains a second set of data called the *Software Description Database,* in which are found short descriptions and the names of numerous files stored around the Internet. As with **archie**'s *Internet Archives Database,* you should realize that not all these files are executable programs; many are documents, and some are simply stored data. Whatever the case, using the *Software Description Database* through the **whatis** command can help you find what you need.

To search the database, use **whatis** followed by the term you are looking for. I might, for example, want to find programs or text files relating to satellites.

```
archie> whatis satellite
RFC                     346             Postel, J.B. Satellite consider.
RFC                     357             Davidson, J. Echoing strategy f.
RFC                     829             Cerf, V.G. Packet satellite tech
n3emo-orbitf            Track earth satellites
```

A useful list; we have three Requests for Comments documents involving satellites and one file, apparently a program, that tracks earth satellites. Since we are returned to the **archie** prompt after this search, we can now simply enter the **find** command to track down one of these files. Alas, entering **find n3emo-orbitf** produces no hits, and reveals a major limitation of the **whatis** database. Because the database is not updated regularly, it's often possible to find a file within it that has been removed from the holdings of the various FTP sites.

Be advised, too, that you are at the mercy of the indexers when you use **whatis**. Suppose you were looking for a program that would catalog your collection of rare wines. You could try the **whatis wine** command. But note the result:

```
archie> whatis wine
RFC                     109             Winett, J.M. Level III Server P.
RFC                     110             Winett, J.M. Conventions for us)
RFC                     147             Winett, J.M. Definition of a so)
RFC                     167             Bhushan, A.K.; Metcalfe, R.M.; .
RFC                     183             Winett, J.M. EBCDIC codes and t.
RFC                     393             Winett, J.M. Comments on Telnet.
RFC                     466             Winett, J.M. Telnet logger/serv.
```

The database has looked for the term **wine** and has found it—within the name of the author of the RFCs listed here, J. M. Winett. As you can see, **whatis** searches for the substring exactly as you enter it (ignoring case).

On the other hand, there are times when **whatis** can home in directly on what you're after. Suppose we were looking for a program that would help us catalog audio tapes. The **whatis** command now produces quite a few hits, many of them clearly oriented toward computer storage.

```
archie> whatis tape
ansitape            ANSI tape program
arch                Let users archive and unarchive files to tape in a bat
buffer              Helps write remote tapes *fast*
cassette            Generate a label for a cassete tape or compact disc c)
cktar               Compare tar tape against file system
cmstape             Read and write IBM VM/SP CMS dump tapes
copytape            Magtape copy program
cpio                Various public domain program to read "cpio" format ts
exebyte_toc         Table of Contents for Exebyte 8mm tapes
magtape             Read and write ANSI labeled tapes, copy tapes even wis
```

```
magtapetools            Magtape handling package
makeddtape              Reads a tape and produces a shell script to read the s
mdump                   Multiple dump per tape utility
multivol                Multi-volume tape utility. Splits its input across ms
pdtar                   A PD tar(1) replacement. Writes P1003 (POSIX) standa.
read-vms-backs          Read VMS backup tapes
read20                  Read TOPS-20 "DUMPER" tapes on UNIX
remote                  Remote mag tape routines
remote-magtape          Library routines to handle reading tapes from remote s
remtape                 Remote magtape library for 4.3BSD
rename                  Rename files from their inode numbers after using ress
rmtlib                  Remote magtape library for BSD
rtar                    Diffs to tar to use a remote system's tape drive
tape                    An audio tape database program
tapetest                Test magnetic tapes by writing a test pattern and thek
tar                     PD versions of the tar(1) (Tape ARchive) program
tar_aids                Tools to read damaged tar tapes
tarfix                  Fix and convert tape archives
vms-backup              Read VMS BACKUP tapes
whichtape               Simple database tools to help find files on backup tas
```

We might be interested in the one listed as

```
tape                    An audio tape database program
```

To track it down, we simply type the command **find tape** at the **archie>** prompt. But wait; since **find tape** will generate many hits with the default search variable **sub**, let's change the setting to *regex*. Entering **set search regex**, I then give the command **find ^tape.***, which should narrow the list considerably. Soon we have a number of possibilities, including this one:

```
Host qiclab.scn.rain.com    (147.28.0.97)
Last updated 11:33  8 Nov 1993

    Location: /pub/database
       FILE    -rw-rw-r—  15930 bytes  00:00  8 Nov 1992  tape-database.shar.Z
```

Is this the file we need? Unfortunately, we won't know without going to the site to check it out. Neither the *Internet Archives Database* nor the *Software Description Database* can verify which of the possibilities is ours.

Keep the limitations of the **whatis** command in mind as you use it. The most important is the fact that any **whatis** search you run does not search the entire set of FTP sites available through the standard **archie** database. Instead, it searches the separate *Software Description Database*. This sharply limits its ability to run a comprehensive search. Second, remember that the *Software Description Database* itself is limited by the fact that the people who created the file you need may not have penned a description of it, and therefore could not have sent their description to the database administrators at Bunyip Information Systems. All in all, this remains an extremely limited database.

A Brief Aside on *regex*

UNIX regular expressions can be complicated, but you don't have to master every nuance of their usage to put them to work. The idea is that regular expressions allow you to search for specific patterns. If you're familiar with wildcards as used in MS-DOS, you'll find some of what follows familiar, although regular expressions go far beyond what DOS wildcards allow. Here are some basic principles:

- Using a search term without further *regex* expressions causes the search to be treated as a hunt for substrings; the effect is as if you entered **set search sub**. Thus, **find geotype** is the same as entering the *regex* expression **find .*geotype.***, Why? Read on.

- In a regular expression, the period (**.**) stands for *any single character*. In the *regex* expression **.*geotype.***, the period at the beginning means the search term can be preceded by *any one* letter. The same principle holds at the end, only in reverse. *Any one* letter can follow the search term **geotype**.

- In regular expressions, an asterisk (*****) stands for *zero or more occurrences of the preceding regular expression*. Thus, in the statement **.*geotype.***, the period lets the search term be preceded by any *one* letter, while the asterisk means that *any number* of letters can occur before the **geotype** string occurs. (In other words, the asterisk looks to the preceding expression, which is a period, and determines that it can occur any number of times). At the end of the statement, the asterisk has the same meaning. Any number of letters can follow the basic search string **geotype**.

- A caret (**^**) in the first position sets the search term at the beginning of the word. The statement **find ^geotype**, then, would return only hits that *began* with the term **geotype**. Always use the caret if you know the search string begins the filename.

- A dollar sign (**$**) means that the search term may occur *only at the end of a word*. Thus, **find geotype$** would retrieve **123geotype**, but not **geotype.exe**. Always use the dollar sign if you know that the search string ends the filename.

- Use brackets to show a set of characters you want to match. Thus, **find [djrt]une** will retrieve **dune**, **june**, **rune**, and **tune**, matching any of the four bracketed characters to the string that follows. It will also find **june-92-meeting.tar.Z**, **thesis.june29.ps**, and **system-7-tune-up**. This is because regular expressions have **.*** at the beginning and at the end, unless the caret (**^**) or dollar sign (**$**) appears. This is why I said earlier that a search under **find geotype** is the same as a search using the term **find .*geotype.***.

- If you want to exclude particular characters, you can do so by using brackets and the caret character combined. Thus, **find [^tj]une** will retrieve **dune** and **rune**, but not **tune** and **june**.

- You can use a special character (i.e., one that would normally be treated as part of a *regex* expression) in your search term if you use a backslash (****) in front of it. For example, if I were searching for a file about faxing with a particular extension, such as **.001**, I could search this way: **find .*fax\.001**. The **.*** at the beginning would allow the term **fax** to occur with any number of letters in front of it. The backslash would indicate that the period (**.**) following it is to be treated as part of the search term, and not in its normal *regex* manner (matching any single letter).

As you can see, regular expressions are complicated, and these notes barely scratch the surface. Bear in mind, however, that basic *substring* searches, or a combination of *exact* and *substring,* as in the setting **set search exact_sub**, will handle most of the work you need to accomplish. Use *regex* searching when your needs are extremely specific, and you wish to exclude as many options as possible from your results. Used properly, a *regex* search is your most precisely tuned tool for using **archie**. I doubt, though, that you'll need to use it often.

If you want to learn more about regular expressions, I recommend *A Student's Guide to UNIX,* by Harley Hahn (McGraw-Hill, 1993).

ARCHIE THROUGH A CLIENT PROGRAM

Using **archie** through Telnet to an **archie** server works well, but you do run into the fact that some servers are getting a lot of work these days, and the load on their systems often means they must limit the number of simultaneous users. Therefore, you may run into a screen advising you to try again later, along with a list of alternative sites. This complication needn't trouble you if you have access to an **archie** client on your system. The client programs are not limited by the same restrictions that hold Telnet sites to only a few users, and they're fast, too.

To find out whether there is an **archie** client on your system, type **archie** at your command prompt. If the client is available, you should receive a list of commands. If not, the response will be *Command not found,* which will mean you have no alternative but to use Telnet or electronic mail (as discussed next) to run your search. If, on the other hand, **archie** is available, then running the search is simplicity itself. The basic command is simply **archie** *searchterm*. Thus, **archie chess** searches for files with the string **chess** contained within them. It will also, of course, pull up any directories using the name *chess*. The results of this search are shown in Figure 2.6. This figure shows one screen from several that scrolled past when I ran this search.

But wait. Just as we used variables, changing their values as necessary, to alter the way we worked with Telnet, **archie** client programs also provide ways of modifying your search. Rather than doing so through **set** commands, however, the **archie** client uses *command switches*. A switch is simply an optional letter you enter after the **archie** command; adding it causes the client program to search in the specified way. Let's now examine the primary **archie** options.

Using archie's Command Switches

By typing **archie** at my system's command prompt, I receive the set of command switches available, preceded by a line that reads more like nuclear physics than computing:

```
Usage: archie [-acelorstvLV] [-m hits] [-N level] string
```

But don't be put off by the imposing brackets and dashes. The statement means that the **archie** command is to be followed by any of the switches shown, in the order shown, followed by the search term or "string" that you choose. A command, for example, might read as follows:

```
archie -c -m15 laserjet
```

This would tell **archie** to search for the term **laserjet**, matching only files listed in lowercase, and retrieving no more than 15 matches. Build your query with care, using the correct command switches, and you'll save yourself time. Here are the switches:

-a   Lists all matches as **Alex** filenames. **Alex** is a tool that allows you to read files at remote sites.

-c   Sets up a case-sensitive *substring* search. You could, for example, differentiate between files labeled **dsck3.exe** and **DSCK3.EXE** or, for that matter, **DSck3.exe** and **dscK3.exe**. This is the same as entering **set search subcase** with a Telnet connection.

-e   Matches the search term exactly. This is the default setting for the line-oriented **archie** UNIX client. The equivalent command with an **archie** server is **set search exact**.

-r   Sets up a UNIX regular expression search. The command to do this with an archie server through Telnet would be **set search regex**.

-s   Creates a case-insensitive *substring* search. The equivalent command is **set search sub**, which is the default setting for **archie** version 3.0 when accessed by Telnet.

Figure 2.6
Using an **archie** client
to search for chess
files.

```
Host krynn.efd.lth.se

        Location: /pub/hp-calc/educalc/horn_disk_6/games
                FILE -rwxrwxr-x        9165  Jun  3 1992  chess

Host ftp.luth.se

        Location: /pub/386BSD/386bsd-0.1/filesystem/usr/othersrc/games
            DIRECTORY drwxr-xr-x       512  Apr 12 00:00  chess
        Location: /pub/misc/lyrics/c
            DIRECTORY drwxr-xr-x       512  Apr 15 00:00  chess
        Location: /pub/unix/4.3bsd/net2/games
            DIRECTORY drwxrwxr-x       512  Mar 13 1993  chess

Host nctuccca.edu.tw

        Location: /Operating-Systems/Coherent/mwcbbs
            DIRECTORY drwxr-xr-x       512  Jul 23 00:00  chess
        Location: /Operating-Systems/bsd-sources/games
            DIRECTORY drwxr-xr-x       512  Jul 23 00:00  chess
        Location: /UNIX/bsd-sources/games
            DIRECTORY drwxr-xr-x       512  Jul 23 00:00  chess
        Location: /USENET/FAQ/news/answers/games
            DIRECTORY drwxr-xr-x       512  Oct 18 00:00  chess
```

-l   Lists one match per line. This is the same command as **set output_format machine** with a Telnet connection to **archie**. It produces output that you can then use for further processing with a variety of UNIX tools.

-t   Sorts the results by time and date, with the most recent date first. It is the equivalent of **set sortby time**.

-m *number-of-hits*   Sets the number of items the **archie** search will return. Thus, **-m15** returns 15 hits. It is the equivalent of the server command **set maxhits**. If you fail to specify a maximum number of hits, **archie** will default to an *exact* search and provide a maximum of 95 matches.

-o *filename*   Stores the results of your search in the file whose name you specify; thus, **archie graphics -o graphics.txt**. This can be handy when you're retrieving a large number of hits and don't want to scroll through all the material on-screen.

-h *hostname*   Allows you to specify a server host for your search. Thus, **archie -h archie.sura.net** tells the client to use the server at SURAnet to run its search.

-L   Lists the servers known to the archie client, as well as the server the client defaults to when it searches. When **archie** is set up at your site, the system administrator decides to which **archie** server the client will connect. As shown above, you can always use the **-h** switch to search a different server site. Here is the output from this command at my site:

```
% archie -L
Known archie servers:
        archie.ans.net (USA [NY])
        archie.rutgers.edu (USA [NJ])
        archie.sura.net (USA [MD])
        archie.unl.edu (USA [NE])
        archie.mcgill.ca (Canada)
        archie.funet.fi (Finland/Mainland Europe)
        archie.au (Australia)
        archie.doc.ic.ac.uk (Great Britain/Ireland)
        archie.wide.ad.jp (Japan)
        archie.ncu.edu.tw (Taiwan)
 * archie.sura.net is the default Archie server.
 * For the most up-to-date list, write to an Archie server
     and give it
     the command 'servers'.
```

-N   Allows you to adjust how fast your search proceeds. The **archie** system refers to this as the *query niceness level*, which is in itself a nice touch. It means that if your search isn't urgent, you can choose to inform the system of this fact in order to give more urgent requests priority. You can choose a niceness level between 0 and 35,765, with the default at 0. The higher the number, the nicer you are.

Ponder the **-N** option with care. If you insert no value, your job simply joins the queue and moves on through. But choose a value of **-N 1000**, and you are allowing the system to handle your request with a little less urgency. You may want to avoid the highest settings, however. Setting **-N 32765** tells **archie** to run your job only after the queue is empty. Nobody is that nice.

-V

A long archie search can be baffling; your screen seems to be frozen, and you don't know for sure whether the system is still responding. You can fix this with the **-V** command, which causes **archie** to insert a statement on occasion. What you'll see is this:

```
Searching...
```

Note several things about these command options. First, if you compare this list with the extensive set of server commands available through a Telnet connection, you'll see that your choices are relatively limited, although the major features certainly are available. And be aware that we didn't even explore many of the lesser-traveled byways of server site commands; the list of possibilities through an **archie** client can seem rather limiting when compared to the Telnet option.

Another thing to remember is that the **whatis** command is not available through a client program like the line-oriented **archie** client for UNIX. **whatis** is of very limited utility, of course, so that may not strike you as a major limitation.

On the other hand, the client approach is easy to use, with the command switches available at your system prompt merely by typing **archie**. For most searches, using a client when one is available is the preferred method of access.

An archie Search Methodology

The wealth of variables and switches that **archie** makes available through server sites and local clients allows you to tailor your search to virtually any specification. As you begin to use **archie** to gather information and find the files you need, however, there are certain key precepts that will enable you to search more effectively. They involve setting up a basic set of defaults that can save you time and trouble.

The **archie** UNIX client, for example, defaults to a maximum of 95 hits and an *exact* search, unless you specify otherwise. Using **archie** through Telnet results in a default search type of *sub*, rather than an *exact* search. A server default of a maximum of 100 hits is common, but the number may go as high as 1,000. Server sites allow you to send the results of your search to yourself in the form of a mail message, while **archie** clients let you save the output of your search in a file. Both allow you to sort the output in a variety of ways (although the Telnet option clearly gives you a wider range). In other words, paying attention to how each system is set will allow you to search either with the same set of parameters.

To search effectively, ask yourself these questions:

1. *What are the current options at the system I'm using?*

You can check them at a server site by using the **show** command. If you're using the **archie** UNIX client, simply type **archie** at the system prompt. The resulting list will remind you that the default search type is *exact*, and that the maximum number of hits is 95. You can check the current server with the **archie -L** command.

2. *How do I want to view the results?*

You'll waste time if you construct a careful search and then lose the results as most of them scroll off your screen. If using Telnet, consider setting the pager variable (**set pager**), which allows you to read one screen at a time. Alternatively, send the results to your mailbox, using the **mailto** variable and the **mail** command.

If you're using an **archie** client, consider directing the output of your search to a file using the **-o** *filename* switch.

3. *How do I establish my search type?*

This can be the hardest decision you'll have to make with **archie**. How you search depends upon what you're after. Consider the following possibilities:

- Use an *exact* search when you know the name of the file as it is stored. If you are sure there is a **sam.johnson.txt** file out there, then the *exact* setting should take you right to it, provided it's available at one of **archie**'s FTP sites.

- Use an *exact* search when you're looking for directories of information about general topics. If, for example, I want to know where I can find directories labeled **chemistry**, I could search under that term, knowing that I would retrieve numerous directories but few filenames that matched.

- Use a *sub* search when you know the name of the program you're after but don't necessarily know how it's packaged. I might want to find a program called **switch.exe**, but I know it could be available as **switch.zip**, or **switch20.exe**, or any number of possible variations. A *sub* search can help you ferret out such materials.

- Consider an **exact_sub** search. Available only through a server site, the command **set search exact_sub** lets the system look for the precise search term you enter; if it fails to find it, it looks using *substring* methods. The advantage is that you may get lucky and land your file right off the bat; if you don't, you don't need to run a separate *substring* search for it.

- Use a *regex* search if you feel confident of only part of the name of the file you're searching for. Although a *substring* search would also reveal your search term buried inside a larger string, it may be that you're sure the search term appears at the beginning or the end of the file name. Searching for a program called **pqx**, for example, I might suspect that it's labeled with its version number, as in

pqx13.exe, or some such. I can use a *regex* search to look for the **pqx** search term and to specify that it appear only at the beginning of any matches.

4. *How many hits am I willing to work with?*

One hundred may be more than you need, so why not speed up the search with a **set maxhits 15** command, or its client equivalent, **archie -m15**?

5. *Should I sort my output to show the most recent files first?*

Doing so, you are ensuring that you're getting the latest version of the program or text file in question. The server command is **set sortby time**; the **archie** client command is **archie -t**.

6. *Should I used the "niceness level settings"?*

By all means, if you're not in a hurry to get your results, use these settings. Set your niceness level high and, even if your request takes longer, you'll have helped reduce the workload at the server site. This is particularly applicable if you're submitting a long search. Another possibility is to submit your **archie** query by mail. We'll talk about how to do that in Chapter 9.

3

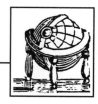

Gopher: Finding Resources by Menu

The search process, on the Internet or anywhere else, is generally collaborative. We look for things through clues or pointers brought to our attention by other people. Those who have made it their job to create locator tools do the entire on-line community a service. They also impose a particular vision of order upon a mass of unstructured information. The key to good searching, then, is to understand the nature of their vision. Each search tool operates from within the boundaries its creators have set.

To understand **Gopher**, you need to realize the benefits, and drawbacks, of menued information. A menu is infinitely better than an unadorned prompt, such as the **&** or **%** symbols that confound so many new users of UNIX systems. The prompt encourages action, but which one? Clueless, the novice can only type commands, learning the process through tedious trial and error. Presenting newcomers with a menu of choices simplifies their task, but it also imposes a new kind of limitation. The user is now dependent upon the developer's sense of what is important and what is not. The menu reflects the priorities of the person who made it.

Gopher was created at the University of Minnesota in 1991, where Mark P. McCahill and an inspired team of programmers (Robert Alberti, Daniel Torrey, Paul Lindler, and Farhad Anklesaria) set about streamlining the help facilities on their campus. The problem faced by the university's Microcomputer, Workstation, and Networks Center was this: The computer systems available on campuses demanded a high degree of user sophistication. Answering the same questions over and over again took time; surely there was a way to make the basic tasks of network information gathering intuitive, so that even the first-timer could work productively and with minimal assistance.

Aware of the issues that troubled neophytes, McCahill's team designed **Gopher** to make campus on-line navigation simple. **Gopher** has spread beyond its home campus to become one of the Internet's major browsing tools.

Hint:

Although the names of many Internet tools are actually acronyms, don't look for one lurking behind the name **Gopher**. It's actually a reference to the Golden Gophers of the University of Minnesota. It also refers to the software's ability to "go for" information and, in the eyes of the imaginative, to burrow through uncharted Internet terrain.

THE NATURE OF GOPHERSPACE

Ponder the implications of menu-driven information. Resources must be identified and organized into sensible units—campus news items under one head, library information under another, perhaps; the developer assigns discrete items to categories as a way of creating a shape for his or her data. Menus proceed relentlessly inward. You choose item 3, from which another menu opens, from which you choose item 6, from which another menu opens, until you reach the terminus: the resource you are looking for.

Think of menus, then, as a linear presentation of information, one in which your options are limited by the shape of the search tool. Probe deeply into a menued structure and then change your mind; now your only recourse is to retrace your steps, backing out of the menu in reverse order until you once again reach the top. Movements *across* the fields of nested data are trickier. **Gopher** allows us to jump to its main menu from anywhere in the environment, but we can't readily cross from a third-level menu under item 3 to a second level menu under item 4 on the main menu. Our data hunt is a series of descents and resurfacings, dependent on an imposed structure which we assume is logical. At first blush, this seems restrictive.

Fortunately, the creators of **Gopher** had something up their sleeves. They included a bookmark feature, which we'll discuss in a moment; it is your key to using **Gopher** wisely. Every time you see a **Gopher** item of interest, you can add it to your bookmark list, which becomes a kind of personal menu. At the end of your browsings, you can move to that menu and choose from the items on it. Your search has moved from the broad survey of information to a tightly focused search. Don't even think of using **Gopher** without bookmarks.

Gopher also involves a way of nesting information that brings a remarkable new dimension to traditional menus. **Gopher's** menus are dynamic; they change as the resources available to the system change, for as **Gopher** moves out over the

Internet, it provides links to a wide variety of resources. **Gopher** can open the door to a Telnet session to a site; the user merely presses the **RETURN** key with the highlight bar over the item in question. **Gopher** can connect you to FTP archives with the help of **archie**, and can let you read USENET news, consult **WAIS** databases, probe X.500 and other white pages directories, and talk to other **Gophers**. These resources, of course, constantly change, and thus, so do **Gopher's** menus.

Figure 3.1 illustrates a typical **Gopher** top menu. This is what you see when you use the **Gopher** at the University of Minnesota, known whimsically as the "mother **Gopher**,' just as the resources connected by **Gopher** systems worldwide have become known as "Gopherspace." In this figure, you see a mixture of resources, some of them of local interest at the University, others pointing in the direction of Internet destinations elsewhere. **Gopher** is anchored to its local site, providing useful tools for users in the neighborhood, but it also opens out to the worldwide flow of networked information.

Gopher isn't a search tool as much as it is a browser. True searching involves a computer performing search work at your behest; browsing is when a human is the search engine. As we'll soon see, **Gopher** can be come a search environment with the help of **Veronica**, but by itself, this tool's menu structure is perhaps best likened to a library's bookshelves. Rather than searching a card catalog electronically, you wander into the stacks to browse. What you find may surprise and delight you, but it's not, strictly speaking, the result of a targeted search.

A **Gopher** is an excellent browsing tool for a university, whose blend of academics in various fields and students without computer backgrounds makes a menu structure a natural. Students at the University of Minnesota would have no difficulty, for example, in finding out more about their school's administrative policies with this **Gopher**. By choosing item 12 from the main menu,

Figure 3.1
The top menu at a
typical **Gopher** site.

```
        Internet Gopher Information Client v1.11

                University of Minnesota

  -->  1.  Information About Gopher/
       2.  Computer Information/
       3.  Discussion Groups/
       4.  Fun & Games/
       5.  Internet file server (ftp) sites/
       6.  Libraries/
       7.  News/
       8.  Other Gopher and Information Servers/
       9.  Phone Books/
      10.  Search Gopher Titles at the University of Minnesota <?>
      11.  Search lots of places at the University of Minnesota  <?>
      12.  University of Minnesota Campus Information/
```

Press ▓ for Help, ▓ to Quit, ▓ to go up a menu   Page: 1

University of Minnesota Campus Information/, they would quickly be presented with the screen shown in Figure 3.2. Choice 3, *Administrative and Financial Policies/* holds the most promise. Notice how broad a range of campus information is presented in this submenu. Note, too, that each of these items is followed by a backslash (*/*). The symbol indicates the presence of further menu choices beyond this item.

But item 8 on the top menu, *Other Gopher and Information Servers/*, shows us how broad **Gopher**'s reach is. By choosing it, we find ourselves at the submenu shown in Figure 3.3, where there are options like *All the Gopher Servers in the World/*, along with more specific menu items that reduce the choice to single continents like Asia or Africa. These menus open to further choices, until we select a particular **Gopher** we would like to contact. **Gopher** will then make the necessary connection, and soon we have a **Gopher** at a distant site on our screen. Figure 3.4 displays the **Gopher** at the University of Edinburgh in Scotland.

The point of this quick tour is that the resources **Gopher** points to are not static items on a menu. Because of its dynamic linkages with other resources on the Internet, **Gopher** becomes a powerful user interface that shields many network transactions from the user, who would otherwise have to set up Telnet sessions, **WAIS** searches, and the like by entering a series of commands. As the resources contacted by **Gopher** themselves change, so do the menus. What we seem to lose by resorting to a framework of nested menus we regain by virtue of **Gopher**'s ability to talk to other machines and to engage in a continuous process of updating. Coupling **Gopher** with the new tool called **Veronica** (discussed in the next chapter) gives us one of the Internet's better search engines.

Figure 3.2
Exploring the **Gopher** at the University of Minnesota.

```
             Internet Gopher Information Client v1.11

             University of Minnesota Campus Information

       -->_ 1.  University Planning/
            2.  Academic Staff Advisory Comittee/
            3.  Administrative and Financial Policies/
            4.  Admissions Services/
            5.  Bursar's Office/
            6.  CLA Student Board/
            7.  Campus Events/
            8.  Campus Services/
            9.  Children, Youth, and Family Consortium Clearinghouse/
           10.  College Bulletins/
           11.  Council on Liberal Education/
           12.  Department and College Information/
           13.  Education Student Affairs Office--Job Vacancy Information/
           14.  Employee Benefits/
           15.  FacultyWrites/
           16.  General Information/
           17.  Human Resources-Personnel/
           18.  Institute of Technology Placement Office/

       Press ? for Help. ? to Quit. ? to go up a menu          Page: 1
```

Figure 3.3
Gopher's submenus
open to other
Gophers around the
world.

```
                    Internet Gopher Information Client v1.11

                       Other Gopher and Information Servers

           -->_  1.  All the Gopher Servers in the World/
                  2.  Search titles in Gopherspace using veronica/
                  3.  Africa/
                  4.  Asia/
                  5.  Europe/
                  6.  International Organizations/
                  7.  Middle East/
                  8.  North America/
                  9.  Pacific/
                 10.  South America/
                 11.  Terminal Based Information/
                 12.  WAIS Based Information/




           Press ▒ for Help, ▒ to Quit, ▒ to go up a menu          Page: 1
```

Figure 3.4
Connecting to a
Gopher in Scotland.

```
                    Internet Gopher Information Client v1.11

                         University of Edinburgh, (UK)

           -->  1.  Information about this Gopher Service.
                2.  Message of the Day (Thu 09 Dec '93).
                3.  METEOSAT weather images/
                4.  The University of Edinburgh Campus Wide Information/
                5.  Anonymous FTP Services/
                6.  Current Local Time.
                7.  Index to public domain X sources/
                8.  Other Gopher Servers/
                9.  Other WAIS Information Servers/
               10.  Other World-Wide Web Information Servers/
               11.  Testing Area (Abandon Hope All Ye Who Enter Here)/
               12.  Whois Servers/




           Press ▒ for Help, ▒ to Quit, ▒ to go up a menu          Page: 1
```

Hint:

Which **Gopher** do you encounter when you enter the **gopher** command at your site? If your computer system offers a **Gopher** server of its own, that's the one you'll see. If not, the **Gopher** client you're using can reference any **Gopher** server on the Internet. Don't be surprised if what seems to be a local **Gopher** turns out to be running on a server a state or two away. And given the interconnected nature of Gopherspace, the physical location of the server you use turns out in some ways to be an unimportant issue.

ACCESSING GOPHER

There are two ways to reach a **Gopher**. The first is by using a Telnet connection to a public access **Gopher** site. The second is to use a local client program to make the connection. Between the two, as is the case with all Internet search tools, a client program is best. It is more responsive, less demanding of system resources, and gives you the greatest flexibility in your search. Using **Gopher** by Telnet, for example, while allowing you to perform most basic **Gopher** functions, does restrict your ability to save files, and you may find that other **Gopher** features are unavailable as well.

Always check, then, to see if you have a client program before relying on Telnet. To do so, type **gopher** at your service provider's system prompt. If there is no **Gopher** program on your system, you will see something like this:

```
gopher: Command not found.
```

In the absence of a client, use one of the Telnet addresses provided in the section on Telnet below.

If a **Gopher** client is installed, you will quickly see its main menu. You may then want to check to see what other **Gopher** clients may be available, depending on the type of system you use.

Using a Gopher Client

As with other Internet tools, the kind of client you use depends on the kind of connection you're using. The **Gopher** client we illustrate here is the one that runs on basic UNIX systems using vt100 terminal emulation; because it operates with any text-based terminal, it is the client most widely available, and certainly the one that dial-up users will need to invoke.

But perhaps you're lucky enough to be computing with a full TCP/IP connection to some sophisticated hardware, or a SLIP or PPP connection through a modem. **xGopher** is a client program for the X Window system, allowing full use of graphical screen elements, mouse-driven commands, pull-down menus and scroll bars, and a variety of other tools to make using **Gopher** an intuitive process. Or perhaps you're a Macintosh user. If so, **TurboGopher** should be just the ticket. Developed at the home **Gopher** burrow at the University of Minnesota, **TurboGopher** supports the new **Gopher+** extensions that add features to **Gopher** information, and as with **xGopher**, provides a point-and-click interface.

Gopher programs for DOS, Microsoft Windows, the NeXT computer, VMS, OS/2, and more are available. The software may be found by using FTP to reach the following address:

Site: **boombox.micro.umn.edu**

Directory: *pub/Gopher*

Again, this is for people with full TCP/IP connections only; dial-up users will need to use the client programs available on their service providers' computers, or, in the absence of such programs, a Telnet connection.

Using Telnet to Access Gopher

A number of public access **Gopher** sites have become available for those without local client programs. Their addresses and login information follows in Table 3.1. As always, choose Telnet sites as close to you as possible.

Table 3.1 Public Access Gopher Sites

Address	Location	Login
ux1.cso.uiuc.edu	University of Illinois at Urbana-Champaign	**gopher**
panda.uiowa.edu	University of Iowa	———
gopher.msu.edu	Michigan State University	**gopher**
consultant.micro.umn.edu	University of Minnesota	**gopher**
gopher.unc.edu	University of North Carolina at Chapel Hill	**gopher**
gopher.ohiolink.edu	Ohio Library and Information Network	**gopher**
ecosys.drdr.virginia.edu	University of Virginia	**gopher**
pubinfo.ais.umn.edu	University of Minnesota (note: Access this system with tn3270 rather than Telnet.)	———
gopher.virginia.edu	University of Virginia	**gwis**
wsuaix.csc.wsu.edu	Washington State University	**wsuinfo**
info.anu.edu.au	Australian National University	**info**
gopher.puc.cl	Pontificia Universidad Catolica de Chile	**gopher**
gopher.denet.dk	DENet (Danish research and academic network)	**gopher**
ecnet.ec	EcuaNet; Corporacion Equatoriana de Informacion (Ecuador)	**gopher**
gopher.brad.ac.uk	University of Bradford (United Kingdom)	**info**
gopher.th-darmstadt.de	Technische Hochschule Darmstadt (Germany)	**gopher**
gopher.ncc.go.jp	National Cancer Center, Tokyo	**gopher**
gopher.uv.es	Universidad de Valencia (Spain)	**gopher**
gopher.chalmers.se	Chalmers University of Technology, Gothenburg, Sweden	**gopher**
info.sunet.se	Sweden	**gopher**

Hint:

The number of Telnet sites for **Gopher** and other Internet tools is constantly changing. Moreover, many of the sites themselves may change, as greater system load is exerted on their resources by the vast number of new users coming onto the net. If you try a Telnet site and find that you are asked for a password as well as a login, it may be that the system administrator has decided to close the site to public access. In that case, try another site.

You should also make it a habit to get the latest Special Internet Connections list by Scott Yanoff, which updates **Gopher** sites and many more resources as well. The simplest way to do this is to join the USENET newsgroup **news.answers**, where the list is posted each time it is updated. But you can also retrieve it by anonymous FTP:

Site: **csd4.csd.uwm.edu**

Directory: *pub*

Filename: **inet.services.txt**

WHAT'S AVAILABLE VIA GOPHER?

When you enter the **Gopher** command, you are launching a client program that connects to a **Gopher** server. And these servers come in all descriptions. Through your **Gopher** entry point, you can easily move to other **Gophers**. You can also, as we'll see, invoke a remote **Gopher** directly (assuming you have a client program available). Expect the breadth of information available in this medium to increase exponentially. **Gopher** is, above all, a superb means of publishing, which can allow any organization to make documents available in a logical and user-accessible way. As of March of 1994, over 1,300 **Gopher** servers were registered at the University of Minnesota.

Hint:

An unregistered **Gopher** is simply one that you won't find on the master list at the University of Minnesota **Gopher**; in other words, the **Gopher** team doesn't know about it yet, or else the site is restricted. Be aware, then, that any list of **Gopher** servers you see is only a subset of the entire **Gopher** population. Though harder to find than registered **Gophers**, their unregistered brethren are growing in number.

The range of subjects covered by these servers is impressive. Consider the eclectic nature of just a few:

Armadillo, the Texas Studies **Gopher (chico.rice.edu port 1170)**: This is a **Gopher** specializing in the natural and cultural history of Texas.

Base de Dados Tropical (**bdt.ftpt.br**): A Brazilian **Gopher** dedicated to biodiversity and biotechnology data.

The Electronic Frontier Foundation (**gopher.eff.org**): Mailing lists and archives related to the work of the EFF, which focuses on studying and clarifying issues of law and privacy on the network.

The Electronic Newsstand (**gopher.internet.com**): Magazines, reviews, and other publishing ventures on-line.

Hungarian *Gopher (***andrea.stanford.edu**): Specializing in all things Hungarian, from archives of Hungarian mailing lists and news services to a directory of Hungarian people on the net.

The Internet Wiretap (**wiretap.spies.com**): Classical literature from Greece and Rome in digital form, plus archival information on electronic texts of all kinds.

The InterNIC *Gopher* (**internic.net**): This **Gopher** links all three InterNIC **Gophers** into a single interface; information on service providers, networking, Internet organizations, directories, and much more.

NASA Goddard Space Flight Center *Gopher* (**gopher.gsfc.nasa.gov**): NASA flight information and imagery.

Panix (**gopher.panix.com**): Maintained by Panix, a New York-based Internet provider. Contains the Del Rey Internet newsletter, the Tor Books online newsletter and archives of the Society for Electronic Access.

RIPE Network Coordination Centre *Gopher* (**gopher.ripe.net**): RIPE provides support for Internet activities in Europe. A wide range of documents on European networking.

Technet, Singapore (**gopher.technet.sg**): Information about Singapore, news bulletins, and the National Technology Plan of the island nation.

University of Minnesota *Gopher* (**gopher.tc.umn.edu**): This is the mother **Gopher**; it contains campus news, a listing of all **Gopher** servers around the world, movie reviews, recipes, and more.

Venezuela *Gopher* (**figment.mit.edu 9999**): Venezuelan news, forums, and tourist information, along with pointers to other Venezuelan **Gopher** servers.

This sampler is provided only to whet your appetite. To keep up with the rapidly changing list of **Gophers** on the net, your only effective recourse is to learn to extract the information from **Gopher** itself.

Hint:

A new mailing list called Gopher Jewels is a good way to follow interesting **Gopher** sites. Gopher Jewels is simply a mailing list that posts the **Gophers** found by its members. Quite a few intriguing servers can be located this way.

   To subscribe to Gopher Jewels, send e-mail to **listproc@einet.net**. In the body of your message, place the statement **subscribe gopherjewels** *firstname lastname*; for example, **subscribe gopherjewels paul gilster**.

LEARNING TO USE GOPHER

The **Gopher** interface is easy to master. The basic process is to move around the menus by using the arrow, or cursor, keys. This action moves an arrow from one menu item to another. Pressing the **RETURN** key then selects a menu item and takes you to it. We'll discuss the complete set of **Gopher** commands below. Figure 3.5, for example, shows what the top menu looks like at the **Gopher** maintained by *WiReD Magazine,* a monthly journal about the on-line scene.

   At the bottom of the screen is a set of elementary commands. It's useful, for example, to know that at any point while using **Gopher**, you can enter a **?** to create a help screen, with the basic commands listed on it. All Internet search tools need this capability, and all dial-up users need to use it, because the keystroke commands necessary to use **Gopher**, **WAIS**, and the rest are often counter-intuitive.

Hint:

Before using any search tool, master its help system. This is the equivalent of travelling to a new city, where your first task should be to learn about the city's public transportation system. In the case of **Gopher**, work through the help menus by pressing the **?** key and reading the information on-screen. Then, remember that the help screens themselves are part of a document. **Gopher** can save this document in your home directory or mail it to you. Continue reading to learn how to perform these tasks.

   We can also see that a **q** is the command to exit **Gopher**, while a **u** will move us up one menu level. Since I am accessing the *WiReD Magazine* **Gopher** from a **Gopher** at MCNC in North Carolina, pressing a **u** would take me back up to the **Gopher** menu at my home site. If we were already at the top menu level, pressing a **u** would only cause that menu to be redisplayed. The **u**, then, moves us back up one level at a time until we again reach the top. And there is one further bit of information, found at the bottom right of the screen:

Figure 3.5
WiReD Magazine's
Gopher. Note
commands at bottom
of screen.

```
     Internet Gopher Information Client v1.11

        Root gopher server: gopher.wired.com

   -->_ 1.  Volume 1 Number 1/
        2.  Volume 1 Number 2/
        3.  Volume 1 Number 3/
        4.  Volume 1 Number 4/
        5.  WiReD's Wonders of the World.
        6.  New Voices, New Visions.
        7.  Guidelines for writers.
        8.  Advertising Rates.
        9.  WiReD's Infobot.
```

```
 Press ? for Help, q to Quit, u to go up a menu              Page: 1
```

This means that this menu page is the only one available at this level. As we'll see shortly, this information is handy when we generate multiple page menus; it tells us how many screens of information we'll be given to choose from.

The first four options on the WiReD **Gopher** allow us to examine *WiReD Magazine* on-line, issue by issue, with the full text of major features. We know there is more information behind these menu items because of the slash following them: *Volume 1 Number 1/,* and so on. Number 5 on the menu, though, lacks the slash. It appears as:

```
-->  5. WiReD's Wonders of the World.
```

Because there is no slash, we can assume that pressing a **RETURN** at this item will generate a text file, as indeed it does. A page from the file is displayed in Figure 3.6.

A period after an entry, then, tells us we are dealing with a text file. Having called up this material, we are able to read through the document by using the basic **Gopher** movement commands. Important ones are shown at the bottom of the screen. Note the material presented there:

```
--More--(11%)[Press space to continue, "q" to quit.]
```

We're told, first of all, that there is more to this document than we've seen so far. The "More" statement is followed by a percentage; this indicates how far we have read into the document at the moment—useful information if it turns out we're examining a large file and would like to get a sense of where we are in the document.

Figure 3.6
Examining a text file
for *WiReD Magazine*.

```
on the broad frontier of high technology. Each of these persons --
scientists, artists, theorists, and social gadflies -- was invited to send
in nominations for a new list: The Seven Wired Wonders of the
World.

The results were dizzying. There was some overlap, of course (for
example, the telecommunications net and various vestiges of our
once-great space program) but not much. Some people named
projects, some people named people. Some of the lists were corny
and cerebral, while others sailed in from some ontological outfield.

On the following pages, then, just in time for the fin de millennium,
appear the Seven Techno-Wonders of the World. The final list was
compiled by our editors, based (for the most part) on the
nominations we received. As you read, it might be interesting to bear
this in mind: of the original Seven Wonders, only one -- the Great
Pyramid -- remains. We can only imagine the glorious Lighthouse at
Alexandria, the Temple of Artemis at Ephesus, or the vast
Mausoleum at Halicarnassus. One has to wonder what future Wired
readers -- 3,000 years hence -- will recall of our own generation's
noblest works.

Only time (lots of it) will tell. In the meantime, have fun -- and let us
--More--(11%)[Press space to continue, 'q' to quit.]
```

The **SPACEBAR** is the critical key here; we use it to move to the next screen of information, pressing it every time we want to see a new page. On the other hand, we can always type a **q** (no **RETURN** necessary) at any point. This will allow us to leave the document and will generate a new command line at the bottom of the screen:

```
Press <RETURN> to continue, <m> to mail, <s> to save, or <p> to print:
```

What we have here is a set of options for handling the document we are reading, one of which is a bit confusing: Pressing the **RETURN** key will not, in fact, take us back into the document for further reading. Instead, it will return us to the next higher **Gopher** menu level, in this case, the top level. We'll see the same screen we did when we first logged in. The **RETURN** key is your route *out* of the document. To leave **Gopher** entirely, press the **RETURN** and then enter a **q**. You will receive the following prompt:

```
Really quit (y/n) ? y
```

The default is a **y**. You can press a **RETURN** to accept it, a **y** to achieve the same result, or an **n** if you've changed your mind and wish to return to **Gopher**.

Perhaps, on the other hand, you'd like to read the document off-line; computer screens are hard on the eyes where large amounts of text are involved. There are two ways to accomplish this. The first is with the **m** command. Pressing the **m**, for "mail," key, creates the screen shown in Figure 3.7.

As you can see, we have been given a blank form to fill out. Enter your Internet address in the space provided (or, if you choose, forward the document

Figure 3.7
Gopher allows you to
mail files to any
Internet address.

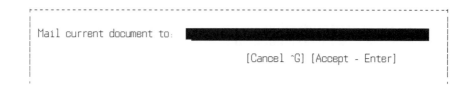

```
+-------------------------------------------------------------------+
|                                                                   |
| Mail current document to:  ██████████████████████████████████     |
|                                                                   |
|                            [Cancel ^G] [Accept - Enter]           |
|                                                                   |
'                                                                   '
```

to some other address), press a **RETURN**, and the document will be mailed to you. A **Ctrl-G** cancels the operation.

Another possibility is to save the document in your home directory. To do so, use the **s** command. Pressing an **s** followed by a **RETURN** creates the screen shown in Figure 3.8.

Gopher has created another form for us to fill in. In this case, however, it has inserted the name of the document in question, assuming this is what we would enter anyway. We can always change the name if we choose.

Pressing the **RETURN** key at this point causes the file to be saved in your home directory. You can use it there or, if you're a dial-up person, download the file for use on your own computer, printing it out as you choose or saving it on disk. But note: When you are accessing **Gopher** by Telnet, you can't print documents or save them on a remote computer (after all, you don't have an account on that system). The best option available to you under such circumstances is to mail the file to your address.

Hint:

When you're asking **Gopher** to save a file, it makes sense to shorten the filename if it's as long as the one in Figure 3.8. If you're a dial-up user, you'll need to download the file once it's safely on your service provider's computer. Change the name to something that's easy to type and to remember. In this above, I would probably change **WiReD's Wonders-of-the-World** to something like **wonder.doc**.

Figure 3.8
Saving a document
with **Gopher.**

```
+-------------------------------------------------------------------+
|                                                                   |
| Save in file:  WiReD-s-Wonders-of-the-World                       |
|                                                                   |
|                            [Cancel ^G] [Accept - Enter]           |
|                                                                   |
+-------------------------------------------------------------------+
```

                                                            Saving File...

One other possibility is to download the file directly, bypassing the need to save it at your service provider's site and then download it in a separate transaction. To do so, you can use the **D** command (note the uppercase). The **D** command is somewhat different from the save and mail commands already discussed. The latter are invoked when you've entered a **q** to quit the document you're reading (or, if you've already come to the end of the document, the save and mail options are presented to you automatically at the bottom of the screen). The **D** command, however, is used from the menu.

Assume we want to download the file we've just looked at, for example. Rather than opening **WiReD's Wonders of the World** by pressing a **RETURN** once we had moved the arrow to that document, we would instead enter a **D** at that spot on the menu. This would generate the menu shown in Figure 3.9.

As you can see, we are given a set of download options, protocols from Zmodem to Kermit to a straight ASCII transfer. We select the item we want by pressing the appropriate number, and **Gopher** will begin the transfer.

But wait. There's a fourth option: We can choose a **p** to print the file. At least, we can do so if we are using a direct TCP/IP connection to the Internet. For modem users, this option is unavailable. They must use either an **m** for mail, **s** for save, or **D** for download command to move the file to their service provider's computers and thence to their own. And, obviously, the print option will not be available if you are reaching **Gopher** through a Telnet session.

Figure 3.9
Downloading a file
with the **D** command.

```
           Internet Gopher Information Client v1.11

                 Root gopher server: gopher.wired.com

          1.  Volume 1 Number 1/
          2.  Volume 1 Number 2/
          3.  Volume 1 Nu+---WiReD's Wonders of the World-----+
          4.  Volume 1 Nu|                                     |
   -->    5.  WiReD's Won|  1. Zmodem                          |
          6.  New Voices,|  2. Ymodem                          |
          7.  Guidelines |  3. Xmodem-1K                       |
          8.  Advertising|  4. Xmodem-CRC                      |
          9.  WiReD's Inf|  5. Kermit                          |
                         |  6. Text                            |
                         |                                     |
                         |  Choose a download method: _        |
                         |                                     |
                         |  [Cancel ^G]  [Choose 1-6]          |
                         |                                     |
                         +-------------------------------------+


        Press ? for Help, q to Quit, u to go up a menu      Page: 1
```

Hint:

With **Gophers** proliferating, you may learn the name of an interesting one and decide you'd prefer not to wade through all the usual **Gopher** menus to reach it. To avoid this, access a **Gopher** client program by entering the name of the **Gopher** server in question after your initial **gopher** command.

Suppose, for example, that I'd like to reach the wonderful **Gopher** at The WELL, The Whole Earth 'Lectronic Link in Sausalito, CA. I know the address:

gopher.well.sf.ca.us

To move directly to this **Gopher**, I enter the command **gopher go-pher.well.sf.ca.us.** The opening screen then appears.

Some **Gophers** have nonstandard port numbers (**Gopher** usually defaults to port 70). If you see such an address, always add the port number to your command. For example, to reach the Venezuelan **Gopher** discussed earlier, whose address is **figment.mit.edu 9999**, we would need to enter the complete address with port number. Thus, the command would be:

```
gopher figment.mit.edu 9999
```

The basic **Gopher** commands are not hard to master. Browse through a **Gopher** menu on your own to get a feel for the medium. In the next section, we look at the complete command set and show what you can do with the more advanced capabilities of this fine tool.

MASTERING THE GOPHER COMMANDS

Although it's an exceptionally powerful tool, **Gopher**'s command set is not conceptually difficult. Here, we examine the basic **Gopher** commands and explain how to use them. In the following sections, we'll use **Gopher** to generate information, and consider the kinds of things it can do best. As with any search tool, **Gopher**'s strengths are best utilized for particular kinds of research needs.

Gopher's File Viewing Commands

Here are the basic **Gopher** commands for file viewing and moving about in a document:

<RETURN>	Allows you to view a document. Place the arrow on the document in question; then press **RETURN**.
<SPACEBAR>	Moves to the next page of the document. Note: You can also use several other keys to achieve the same result. In addition to the **SPACEBAR**, you can use the plus key (**+**), the **PageDown** key, or the right bracket key (**>**).

b   Allows you to view the previous page. You can also use the
                             left bracket key (**<**), the minus key (**-**), or the **PageUp** key
                             to do the same thing.

<number>   Enter the number of the menu item to which you wish to
                             go, followed by a **RETURN**. Or you can move the arrow
                             using the keys described in the next section to do the same
                             thing.

Hint:

You'll save time when working with long menus if you enter the number
of the item to which you wish to go, and follow it with a **RETURN**. This
takes you directly to that item and bypasses the rest of the menus, saving you the need to move menu by menu until you reach the page you
want.

    Another tip: When dealing with several pages of data, go through the
entire list all at once, jotting down the numbers of items you'd like to
examine. It's much faster to do this and then enter, from the last page, the
number of each item you want to see, than it is to pause each time and
examine the documents individually. Remember, **Gopher** can hang up due
to network problems when you ask to see a given document. If this happens, and you've already compiled your entire list before you try to see a
document, it's easy to go back, run the search again, and use the same
numbers to find what you need.

Up arrow   Moves the arrow to the previous line. You can also use
                             Ctrl-P or **k** to do the same thing.

Down arrow   Moves to the next line. You can also use **Ctrl-N** or **j** to do
                             the same thing.

Left arrow   Exits the current item and moves up one level. You can
                             also use the **u** command.

Right arrow   Selects the current item.

m   Returns to main menu.

Gopher's File Management Commands

Here are the basic commands for saving and mailing files. These commands are
critical, because they allow you to bring **Gopher** information to your own
computer for searching, printing, and other uses. Make sure you understand
these commands before using **Gopher** for research.

s   Saves the current item to a file. Remember: You can use this command
                             only if you are running a **Gopher** client on your own system. You can't
                             use it if you're using a Telnet session to reach a **Gopher**.

m Mails the file to the address you specify. This is the route to take when you use **Gopher** through Telnet. The command becomes available only at the document level; i.e., as you are reading a document, and have reached its end or have given a **q** command to exit it.

p Prints the file selected. This command becomes operative at the end of a document, or when you have typed a **q** to exit it. You can use it only if you have a direct TCP/IP connection to the Internet.

D Downloads the item selected to your computer.

Using Gopher with Bookmarks

One handy, though often misunderstood, feature of **Gopher** is that it allows you to use bookmarks to keep your place. Bookmarks can help to surmount the menu limitation we discussed earlier—the fact that menu-driven searches so often have you moving deeper and deeper into layered information, then backing out one menu at a time. With bookmarks, you can jump immediately to the data you have marked, thus streamlining a complicated search.

When you mark an item with an **a**, you add it to your bookmark list. Let's examine how this works. Suppose we are browsing through a **Gopher** looking for various kinds of information about the so-called "information highway," the massive and thus far unorganized attempt to bring high-speed networking to average citizens.

In Figure 3.10, I am using the **Gopher** at Software Tool and Die in Brookline, MA; this company runs one of the major dial-up service provider operations on the

Figure 3.10
Using The World's
Gopher to track
development along the
information highway.

```
              Internet Gopher Information Client v1.1

                       Government Information

    -->_  1.  Americans Communicating Electronically/
           2.  Clinton Speeches and Position Papers/
           3.  Clinton's Economic Plan/
           4.  Internet Sources of US Government Information.
           5.  Library of Congress - Marvel/
           6.  NSF's list of U.S. Government Gopher Servers/
           7.  North Atlantic Treaty Organization.
           8.  Resources for White House Information.
           9.  U.S. House Gopher/
          10.  U.S. Senate Gopher/
          11.  United States Bureau of the Census/
          12.  United States GOVERNMENT Gophers/
          13.  White House Press Release Service/




    Press ? for Help, q to Quit, u to go up a menu          Page: 1
```

East Coast, called The World. I have moved to a menu on its **Gopher** that offers government information, where I've found several items of interest. Item 1, *Americans Communicating Electronically/* certainly looks promising, and the slash after the entry indicates another menu with further choices beneath it. Also intriguing are the entries marked *NSF's List of U.S. Government Gopher Servers/* (after all, the National Science Foundation is a major player in the development of the Internet, and in the high-speed testbeds so crucial to the growth of gigabit-speed networking). And then there's *Internet Sources of U.S. Government Information* (item 4). This one is obviously a document; no slash follows its entry.

Let's begin by marking the first item as a bookmark, because I plan to come back to it later. To do so, I use the command key **a**. Figure 3.11 shows what happens when I press the **a** key with the arrow pointing at item 1.

As you can see, a dialog box has popped up asking what I want to name this bookmark. I press the **RETURN** key to indicate that I will accept the choice shown. I'll also mark item 4, *Internet Sources of U.S. Government Information*, by moving the arrow to it and pressing the **a** key. Again, I'll press a **RETURN** to accept the bookmark name suggested.

Now I move to item 6, *NSF's List of U.S. Government Gopher Servers/*. By pressing a **RETURN** here, I move into a menu of **Gophers**. Here I find two items that may be interesting. The first, *National Coordination Office for HPCC (NCO/HPCC) Gopher/*, is clearly related to the subject in question; HPCC stands for High Performance Computing and Communications, an integral part of the

Figure 3.11
Setting up a **Gopher** bookmark.

```
                      Internet Gopher Information Client v1.1

                              Government Information

      -->  1.  Americans Communicating Electronically/
           2.  Clinton Speeches and Position Papers/
           3.  Clinton's Economic Plan/
           4.  FTP access to Senate.Gov/
      +-------------------------------------------------------------------
      |
      | Name for this bookmark?   Americans Communicating Electronically
      |
      |                                 [Cancel ^G] [Accept - Enter]
      |
      +-------------------------------------------------------------------




      Press ? for Help.  q to Quit.  u to go up a menu              Page: 1
```

emerging National Information Infrastructure. Figure 3.12 shows what I see when I press a **RETURN** at this item to access the **Gopher**.

Moving to item 10, *White House Statements/Policy Papers/*, I press a **RETURN** to access three White House papers, including one called *Clinton Technology Initiative Announcement*. Because this seems useful, I'll mark it with an **a**.

Backing out of the HPCC **Gopher**, I also decide I want to make a stop at the NSF **Gopher**, which is listed on the same menu where I found the HPCC materials. Pressing the **RETURN** here takes me to a **Gopher** that contains a compilation of documents and data from the National Science Foundation. Deep in its menu structure, I encounter the following:

```
-->  31. pr9362     - NSF 93-62 NSFNET TO BOOST NETWORK ACCESS AS IT ENTER...
```

This is a text file, and it sounds interesting; major improvements to the network obviously have ramifications for the emerging information infrastructure. I'll mark this with an **a** as well.

Having marked all these items, I can use the **v** key to examine my bookmark list. Figure 3.13 shows that the list is itself a **Gopher** menu. But in this case, it's a customized menu that I've created for my own research.

I can move to any of the items on the list by pressing the **RETURN** key after positioning the arrow where I want it. As you can see, using bookmarks has enabled me to move beyond many of the limitations of the menu structure which **Gopher** superimposes upon its information.

Figure 3.12
The HPCC **Gopher**, a resource for those interested in government communications and computing policy.

```
                        Internet Gopher Information Client v1.1

                   National Coordination Office for HPCC (NCO/HPCC) Gopher

            -->_ 1.  About this Gopher Server.
                 2.  About the National Coordination Office (NCO)/
                 3.  HPCC-NCO Fact Sheets/
                 4.  HPCC-Toward a National Information Infrastructure (1994 Blue Book)/
                 5.  HPCC-Related Reports/
                 6.  HPCC-Related Legislation/
                 7.  HPCC-Related Testimony at Congressional Hearings/
                 8.  HPCC-Grants and Research Contracts/
                 9.  Links to Other HPCC Related Gophers/
                10.  White House Statements/Policy Papers/
                11.  What's New at NCO/HPCC [November 29, 1993]/



            Press ? for Help, q to Quit, u to go up a menu          Page: 1
```

Figure 3.13
A menu of bookmark
items, accessible
through the v
command.

```
                        ┌──────────────────────────────────────────┐
                        │ Internet Gopher Information Client v1.1    │
                        └──────────────────────────────────────────┘

                                      Bookmarks

         -->_ 1.  Americans Communicating Electronically/
              2.  Internet Sources of US Government Information.
              3.  Clinton Technology Initiative Announcement.
              4.  pr9362      - NSF 93-62 NSFNET TO BOOST NETWORK ACCESS AS IT ENTER.




         Press ? for Help, ? to Quit, ? to go up a menu                 Page: 1
```

Hint:

When you use your **Gopher** bookmark page, the best part of the story is
that it doesn't disappear when you log off your service provider's computer.
Gopher uses a local file called, on UNIX systems, **.gopherrc**; this file
maintains the configuration of **Gopher** as you use it. Whenever you add a
bookmark item to your list, the new entry is added to the bookmarks section of the **.gopherrc** file. Thus, when you log in again, the list you have
created is still available to you. In the next chapter, we'll see how this fact
can be a particular help in constructing an easy-to-use menu of **Veronica**
sites for searching.

Our new menu is as elastic as any other menu **Gopher** can offer. We're
actually pointing to different **Gophers** in it—the one at the National Coordination Office for High Performance Computing and Communications, and the
National Science Foundation **Gopher**, along with the **Gopher** at The World that
we've started our session with. To see our bookmark list at any time, I simply
enter the **v** command. What I will get is a redisplay of the menu shown in Figure
3.13. Our own **Gopher** remembers where we are and makes the list of bookmarks available at any time during our search.

Bookmarks can refer to more than single menu items. It might be helpful,
for instance, to keep an entire menu at the National Coordination Office for High
Performance Computing and Communications available for later reference.
Let's move back to this **Gopher** and mark its entire top menu. Instead of

using the **a** command, which only marks a single menu item at a time, we'll use the **A** command, which marks the whole menu. Again, we receive a dialog box asking what to name this new item on our bookmark list, and offering a default choice. We accept it with a **RETURN**. The new list can be seen in Figure 3.14.

So there we have it: five menu items; a customized **Gopher** hit list. I've marked what I think is germane for the present. Now, as I proceed to browse through the **Gopher** at The World looking for further insights, I can always return to my interest list without backing out through a sequence of menus. I can choose **Gopher** menus and menu items from **Gophers** all over the world, building them all into a custom menu structure. Then I can examine the entire list at once and move easily between its items. Nothing shows off the dynamic nature of **Gopher**'s menus as well as the ability to use its bookmarks.

Hint:

The problem with tools like **Gopher** and the **World Wide Web** is that the resources they point to are so varied that keeping track of what you've found as you continue through cyberspace is extremely difficult. The best kind of **Gopher** session is a foraging expedition, proceeding through the menus, going ever deeper in search of data, always noting interesting destinations along the way by marking them with bookmarks. At the end of this time, you return to the bookmark screen to evaluate what you've found and to decide which of these items are now worth your closer attention.

Figure 3.14
The updated
bookmark list.

```
                  Internet Gopher Information Client v1.1

                                  Bookmarks

            -->_ 1.  Americans Communicating Electronically/
                 2.  Internet Sources of US Government Information.
                 3.  Clinton Technology Initiative Announcement.
                 4.  pr9362      - NSF 93-62 NSFNET TO BOOST NETWORK ACCESS AS IT ENTER...
                 5.  National Coordination Office for HPCC (NCO/HPCC) Gopher/
```

Let's summarize the bookmark commands:

a   Adds the current item to your bookmark list.

A   Adds the current menu to your bookmark list.

v   Allows you to view the current bookmark list.

d   Deletes a bookmark entry.

What is really compelling about **Gopher** bookmarks is their ability to save an entire search. For example, I often use a searchable database on The World that offers both the UPI and Reuters news services. The menu items look like this:

```
        The World's ClariNews UPI/Reuters newswire index

        1.   Information About The ClariNews UPI and Reuters newswire indexes.
-->     2.   Search ClariNews UPI newswire index <?>
        3.   Search Reuters newswire index <?>
```

As you see, I've chosen item 2, the UPI newswire index. The question mark inside the brackets following the entry (**<?>**) tells us that we are dealing with a searchable index. Pressing the **RETURN** key here calls up a search box, in which I can enter what I'm looking for. For example, I follow economic and political news in Latin America with some interest, so I set up a search under the terms **latin american business briefs**. I happen to know that UPI makes reports under this title available daily. Figure 3.15 shows the results of a typical search.

Figure 3.15
Searching UPI for information about Latin America.

```
             Internet Gopher Information Client v1.1

        Search ClariNews UPI newswire index: Latin American Business Briefs

   --> 1.   Latin American Business Briefs    /UPI-data/1993/Dec/Dec 14/biz/.
       2.   Latin American Business Briefs    /UPI-data/1993/Dec/Dec 14/news/.
       3.   Latin American Business Briefs    /UPI-data/1993/Dec/Dec 13/biz/.
       4.   Latin American Business Briefs    /UPI-data/1993/Dec/Dec 13/news/.
       5.   Latin American Business Briefs    /UPI-data/1993/Dec/Dec 15/biz/.
       6.   Latin American Business Briefs    /UPI-data/1993/Dec/Dec 15/news/.
       7.   Canada Business Briefs    /UPI-data/1993/Dec/Dec 16/news/.
       8.   Canada Business Briefs    /UPI-data/1993/Dec/Dec 15/news/.
       9.   Japan Business Briefs    /UPI-data/1993/Dec/Dec 16/news/.
      10.   Canada Business Briefs    /UPI-data/1993/Dec/Dec 14/news/.
      11.   Texas Business News Briefs    /UPI-data/1993/Dec/Dec 16/local/.
      12.   Illinois Supreme Court rules against American frequent flyer    ..iz
      13.   Illinois Supreme Court rules against American frequent flyer    ..ws
      14.   Texas Business News Briefs    /UPI-data/1993/Dec/Dec 15/local/.
      15.   Texas Business News Briefs    /UPI-data/1993/Dec/Dec 14/local/.
      16.   Texas Business News Briefs    /UPI-data/1993/Dec/Dec 13/local/.
      17.   Ohio Business News In Brief    /UPI-data/1993/Dec/Dec 17/local/.
      18.   Briefs Washington (Dec 13 12 am PST)    ..data/1993/Dec/Dec 13/local

   Press ? for Help, q to Quit, u to go up a menu          Page: 1/
```

There is a lot of Latin American news here, along with much else that is business related but not specifically about Latin America. The reason for this is that this is a **WAIS** database, which searches by ranking items in order of what it perceives to be their relevance to your search. (More about **WAIS** and its eccentricities in Chapter 5.)

Further, I would like some way to check on Latin American news every day. To do so, I can enter an **A** *after* I have retrieved this search screen (that is, after the search itself has been run). This enters the search onto my list of bookmarks. When I call up the bookmark list by entering a **v**, I find the following entry:

```
-->  1.  Search ClariNews UPI newswire index: Latin American Business Brief../
```

Perhaps the big picture is emerging. By using bookmarks, I can go into The World's **Gopher** every day and, rather than wade through the menu structure, simply call up the bookmark list with a **v** command from the main menu. There I find my search; all I have to do to run it is press the **RETURN** key. Voilà—updated Latin American news on a daily basis, with a minimum of fuss.

Hint:

The more you use your list of bookmarks, the more valuable it will become. If you want to start **Gopher** with your bookmark list as the top menu, you can do so by entering the **gopher -b** command at your service provider's prompt. Your bookmark menu will be the first thing you see. You will also see an additional menu item like the following:

```
6. Root Gopher server: Gopher.interpath.net/
```

This gives you a menu choice that leads you back to the top menu of the **Gopher** server you normally contact when you start the program.

Gopher's Search Commands

Gopher's search commands are limited, but you should be aware of your ability to move quickly through extended menus of information. Some key commands follow.

/   Searches for a particular item on a **Gopher** menu.

Suppose, for example, that I happened to be dealing with a particularly long, multipage **Gopher** menu. A list of library catalog sites is an example; libraries from all over the U.S. might be listed there. If all I needed were the library connections in North Carolina, I could set up a search using the **/** command. In Figure 3.16, you see the result of pressing the **/** key. A box has popped up offering me the chance to insert my search term, which I have done.

The result appears quickly on my screen:

```
-->  36. North Carolina State University Happenings <TEL>
```

Pressing the **RETURN** key at this point takes me to the catalog in question.

Figure 3.16
Using the / key to
search a **Gopher**
menu.

```
          Internet Gopher Information Client v1.11

                      North American Libraries

    -->  1.  Air Force Institute of Technology <TEL>
         2.  Appalachian State University <TEL>
         3.  Arizona State University <TEL>
         4.  Bates College <TEL>
   +---------------------------------------------------------------
   |
   | Search directory titles for  north carolina
   |
   |                                 [Cancel ^G] [Accept - Enter]
   |
   +---------------------------------------------------------------
        12.  Case Western Reserve University <TEL>
        13.  Cleveland Public Library System <TEL>
        14.  Colorado Alliance of Research Libraries -- CARL <TEL>
        15.  Columbia University Library -- CLIO <TEL>
        16.  Dartmouth College <TEL>
        17.  Harvard's OnLine Library Information System -- HOLLIS <TEL>
        18.  Indiana University <TEL>

   Press ? for Help, q to Quit, u to go up a menu          Page: 1
```

n   Allows you to search for the *next* occurrence of your search term.

In the previous example, I retrieved my first hit at North Carolina State University. But I happen to know there are other North Carolina libraries available. To find out where, I enter the **n** command and retrieve this:

```
-->  78. University of North Carolina at Greensboro MINERVA <TEL>
```

Another application of the **n** command produces this:

```
-->  79. University of North Carolina at Wilmington SEABOARD <TEL>
```

and so on. Clearly, the search commands can be a major help when long menus are involved. Be aware, however, that you are searching **Gopher**'s menu items, not text in the documents themselves.

Hint:

Don't be alarmed if a **Gopher** search doesn't come off as planned. Network usage may be heavy or a node on the net may fail; if that occurs, **Gopher** may simply leave you hanging. The best advice in such circumstances is to wait a while and try again, when usage may be less heavy.

Other Gopher Commands

Here are the balance of the **Gopher** commands you'll need to know.

=　　Use the equal sign to produce technical information about the item in question.

In the preceding example, we found a connection to North Carolina State University's library. With the arrow on that menu item, we could press the **=** key and would quickly see the following information:

```
Name=North Carolina State University Happenings
Type=8
Port=23
Path=INFO
Host=ccvax1.cc.ncsu.edu


Press <RETURN> to continue, <m> to mail, <s> to save, or <p> to print:
```

Now, it may not be particularly useful to have port or path information, and we already know the name of the service, which is the NCSU Happenings Campus-Wide Information System. But it can be handy in some instances to know the address of the service; in this case, it's **ccvax1.cc.ncsu.edu**.

Here, for example, is a **Gopher** menu item:

```
-->  4.  Search Electronic Books <?>
```

The question mark (**<?>**) tells us this is an index that is searchable. Where is it located? We'll use the **=** key to find out. Entering it, we learn the following:

```
Name=Search Electronic Books
Type=7
Port=70
Path=7/indexes/etext-index/index
Host=joeboy.micro.umn.edu
```

Our server is located at **joeboy.micro.umn.edu**; it's on the campus of the University of Minnesota, using port 70.

Back to the rest of the **Gopher** commands:

O　　The capital letter **O** is used to display the options of the **Gopher** system you are using.

You can change these options if you choose, but in most cases, it won't be necessary. Figure 3.17 shows an example of what you might see using the **O** command.

We learn, for instance, that the pager function, which allows us to read through the documents provided by **Gopher**, is set to work with the UNIX **more** program. This can be interesting for those with an eye for detail, but there is little reason to make any changes to the default settings.

q　　Quits **Gopher**, leaving you with a prompt in case you change your mind. Type a **y** to exit.

Q　　Quits **Gopher** immediately; no prompt.

Figure 3.17
Gopher options are
shown by using the
O key.

Press **?** for Help, **q** to Quit, **u** to go up a menu   Page: 1

EXAMINING GOPHER'S RESOURCES

As we've seen, **Gopher** is a flexible tool; it can show us not only where information is located and let us read it, but it can also make the necessary network
connections behind the scenes. This is precisely what we'd like a good browser to
do. One of the major barriers to retrieving Internet information is that it is necessary
to approach data from different directions. One site offers files via FTP, another
requires the interactivity of a Telnet session, while a third allows you to read key
documents on-line through its own **Gopher** server. The ideal world is one in
which we don't need to keep the various procedures and addresses straight.

Gopher displays its offerings by adding tags to menu items that explain either
what the resource is or how it can be reached. An example is shown in Figure 3.18.

In this figure, we can see that each entry is followed by the **<TEL>** designation for Telnet; in other words, each of these sites—the Food and Drug Administration BBS, ISAAC—Advanced Academic Computing Info, and HPCwire—High
Performance Computing Info and so on—is accessible by choosing it with the arrow
keys and then pressing the **RETURN** key.

Using Gopher's Telnet Connection

Let's see what happens when we choose a **Gopher** item with Telnet links. I will
choose an item from Figure 3.18, ISAAC—Advanced Academic Computing
Information, to see what it is. By pressing the **RETURN** key, I generate the
information shown in Figure 3.19.

Figure 3.18
Gopher marks its
Telnet items with the
<TEL> suffix.

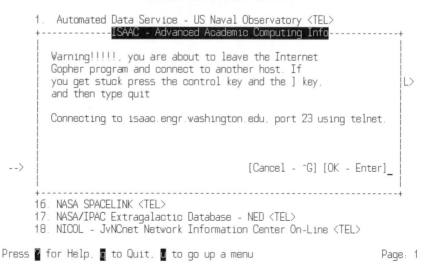

```
         ▌Internet Gopher Information Client v1.11▐

                    General Information Servers

    --> 1.  Automated Data Service - US Naval Observatory <TEL>
         2.  Cleveland Free-Net <TEL>
         3.  Contel DUATS - Pilot info <TEL>
         4.  E-Math - American Mathematical Society <TEL>
         5.  Electronic mail address query program <TEL>
         6.  Federal Information Exchange - Minority On-line Info Service <TEL>
         7.  Food and Drug Administration BBS <TEL>
         8.  Geographic Server - University of Michigan <TEL>
         9.  Guelph's Cosy <TEL>
        10.  HPCwire - High Performance Computing Info <TEL>
        11.  Ham Radio Callbook Server - SUNY at Buffalo <TEL>
        12.  Heartland Free-Net <TEL>
        13.  ISAAC - Advanced Academic Computing Info <TEL>
        14.  Knowbot Information Server <TEL>
        15.  Lunar & Planetary Institute - NASA <TEL>
        16.  NASA SPACELINK <TEL>
        17.  NASA/IPAC Extragalactic Database - NED <TEL>
        18.  NICOL - JvNCnet Network Information Center On-Line <TEL>

    Press ▌ for Help, ▌ to Quit, ▌ to go up a menu            Page: 1
```

Figure 3.19
Preparing to begin a
Telnet session through
Gopher.

```
         ▌Internet Gopher Information Client v1.11▐

                    General Information Servers

      1.  Automated Data Service - US Naval Observatory <TEL>
      +-------------▌ISAAC - Advanced Academic Computing Info▐-------------+
      |                                                                    |
      |  Warning!!!!!, you are about to leave the Internet                 |
      |  Gopher program and connect to another host. If                   |
      |  you get stuck press the control key and the ] key,               |L>
      |  and then type quit                                                |
      |                                                                    |
      |  Connecting to isaac.engr.washington.edu, port 23 using telnet.    |
      |                                                                    |
      |                                                                    |
      |                                                                    |
    --> |                                      [Cancel - ^G] [OK - Enter]_ |
      |                                                                    |
      +--------------------------------------------------------------------+
        16.  NASA SPACELINK <TEL>
        17.  NASA/IPAC Extragalactic Database - NED <TEL>
        18.  NICOL - JvNCnet Network Information Center On-Line <TEL>

    Press ▌ for Help, ▌ to Quit, ▌ to go up a menu            Page: 1
```

Hint:

When you press the equal sign key (**=**) to get information about a particular menu item, the information listed under Type is interesting. The type field is used to describe the kind of object this item represents. Remember that **Gopher** can access many different kinds of resources. A 7 stands for an index search, while an 8 is a Telnet session. You may not think you'll ever have to use these, but in the next chapter, when we get into **Veronica** searches, you'll see how important they will become.

0	A file.
1	A directory or menu. These are marked on **Gopher** menus with the slash symbol (*/*).
2	A **CSO** phone book. This is a directory service to help you find people on the Internet, about which more in a moment. Marked as **<CSO>** on **Gopher** menus.
3	Error.
4	A Macintosh file in the BinHex format. These items are marked on **Gopher** menus as **<HQX>**.
5	A DOS binary file in archived form. This means the files are probably in .ZIP or .ARC format, although other types of archiving are in use. These items are found on the menus with the **<PC Bin>** suffix.
6	A file in **uuencoded** form. Requires the **uudecode** program to extract.
7	An index search. Marked with the **<?>** suffix on the menus.
8	A Telnet connection (**<TEL>**).
9	A binary file (**<Bin>**).

There are also a number of still experimental types. Among them:

g	A GIF file.
h	An HTML file (used by **World Wide Web**).
I	An image file.
i	An inline text file used by **panda** (an Internet front-end based on **Gopher**).
M	A MIME file (an evolving standard for multimedia mail communications).
s	A sound file.
T	A Telnet 3270 session.

Note the warning screen **Gopher** has interposed between its own interface and the session we are about to enter. Once **Gopher** fires up the Telnet connection to a remote computer, we are in the hands of the system we have accessed. In this case, the system is **isaac.engr.washington.edu, port 23**. By pressing the **RETURN** key now, we initiate the Telnet session. By pressing **Ctrl-G**, we abort our request and **RETURN** to the **Gopher** menus.

Figure 3.20 shows what happens when we press the **RETURN** key and make the Telnet jump. We've reached IKE, the IBM Kiosk for Education. By reading the material provided, we learn that IKE is a set of user forums for educators, with particular emphasis upon IBM systems in instruction and research. We also see that this IKE system requires an access code. What to enter here is provided at the prompt. By entering register, we receive a new screen, as shown in Figure 3.21.

Now we've been given the limitations for system access. Educators can apply, as can students and staff at institutions of higher education. In other words, the system is closed to a broad category of users, but if we qualify, we can proceed.

The point of this exercise is to demonstrate that each Telnet session you initiate will have its own set of parameters and procedures. Once you have left the **Gopher** menu, the system you have accessed is the one that is calling the shots. You can explore it as you choose or leave, but you should look carefully, no matter what the system, to discover what its commands for exiting are. There are two ways to leave a Telnet session:

1. You can determine the exit commands at the remote site and use them to leave when your session is over.

2. You can use the Telnet escape command, **Ctrl-]**, to exit. If you take this route, you'll wind up with a prompt like the following:

```
telnet>
```

Figure 3.20
The actual Telnet session begins. We jump to the IBM Kiosk for Education.

```
 _   _          _       _
| | | | /|  |  __|      IBM Kiosk for Education
| | | |< |  |  __|         Office: (206) 543-5604
|_| |_|\_| |____|          E-mail: ike@ike.engr.washington.edu
```

```
================================================================================

Welcome to the IBM Kiosk for Education (IKE) User Discussion Forums.  These
Forums are for the exchange of information among educators about how they
are using IBM systems for instruction and research.  This system is available
for use by faculty, staff, and students in higher education for this purpose.

You must register to use this service.  Please enter your access code and
password (in lower case) in the spaces provided below.  New users should
enter 'register' as their access code and follow the on-screen instructions.

ISAAC USERS: ISAAC has been enhanced with the addition of the gopher server.
Please log in with your current ISAAC access code and password.  Follow
instructions for non-gopher users to access full ISAAC services.

Access code:
```

Figure 3.21
Registering at IKE.

```
                        I K E   R e g i s t r a t i o n


    IKE OBJECTIVE
         IKE, the IBM Kiosk for Education, provides information for
         IBM users about software and hardware for instruction and
         research in higher education.

    ELIGIBILITY
         IKE is free to faculty, staff, and students in higher education
         for the purpose described above.

    ACCESS
         IKE can be accessed by either an IBM PS/2 or PC and modem,
         or via the Internet computer network.

  * * *  If you are eligible for IKE access, press <Enter> to complete
         online registration or type 'q' and press <Enter> to quit.
```

At this point, typing **quit** will take you back to the **Gopher** menu from which you gave the Telnet command.

Hint:

You may run into menu items which, rather than showing **<TEL>** as a suffix, use **<3270>**. **tn3270** is a version of Telnet designed to handle the various screen-drawing techniques of IBM mainframe computers. A Telnet session to one of these sites is accomplished the same way as a regular Telnet session—by pressing the **RETURN** key with the item selected.

But note: Getting out of such a session can be problematical. As opposed to a regular Telnet session, where **Ctrl-]** invariably takes you back to the **telnet>** prompt if you get stuck, many **tn3270** sessions have their own escape mechanisms. If you can't remember the system's command for exiting, and a **Ctrl-]** doesn't work, try a **Ctrl-C**. You should wind up at a **tn3270>** prompt. From there, you can enter **quit** to exit.

Using Gopher with FTP

Gopher works just as well at initiating an FTP session; indeed, you can use **Gopher** with **archie** to find the files you need, and then move directly to the necessary site to retrieve them. The advantage of searching for and retrieving files this way is that the interface shields you from the complexities of the search. Instead of running a tricky **archie** session, you let **Gopher** do the work.

How to find an FTP site with **Gopher**? A typical **Gopher** menu, like the one shown here, displays a tag at the end of each item, which is a question mark inside brackets. The **<?>** tells us that rather than dealing with a text file (in which case there would have been no bracketed information following the menu item) or a Telnet session (**<TEL>**), we are going to retrieve a searchable index if we take this option.

```
            Anonymous FTP Site Search - ARCHIE
-->   1.  Exact search of archive sites on the internet <?>
      2.  Substring search of archive sites on the internet <?>
```

Notice the nature of these menu items. When we used **archie**, we discovered that the best way to search was with the *substring* option, which means that your search term can be embedded within a larger word and **archie** will still find it. Using an *exact* search proved to be a problem because it would miss many files that might be of interest. Suppose we were looking for a program that helped us chart commodity prices. An exact search for a program called **future.exe** would pull up only that file; it would not locate **futures.exe**, or **future2.exe**, or other variants. A *substring* search would find them all.

So, it's best to use the substring option by choosing item 2 on the menu, and use exact searches when we know the exact filename in advance. Choosing item 2, then, we retrieve a screen box prompting us to enter a search term. As you'll recall from the previous chapter, **archie** searches from the command prompt can be set up with a number of options. Be aware that **Gopher**'s interface doesn't yet give us the bells and whistles available in a straight **archie** search. If your search is truly complex, you'll be able to fine-tune it using the methods of Chapter 2 and a regular **archie** client. But for most searching, **Gopher**'s interface will suffice.

Let's go retrieve a file. Anyone who has used PKware Inc.'s powerful compression utilities knows how useful they are. PKZIP and PKUNZIP give you the ability to reduce a file to a fraction of its former size, or to expand it when needed. Both **PKZIP** and **PKUNZIP** run from the DOS command line, but I've heard about a Windows shareware program called WINZIP that gives the whole process a Windows interface. Can we find it using **Gopher**? Let's enter **winzip** as the search term after selecting the substring search option. The results of that search are partially shown in Figure 3.22.

As you can see, many of these items are followed by the **<Bin>** suffix, which indicates we are dealing with a binary file. And indeed, the very first item looks compelling:

```
server.uga.edu:/pub/msdos/mirror/windows3/winzip50.zip <Bin>
```

This, a binary file, seems to be the program we're looking for. Pressing the **RETURN** key with the arrow on this file calls up the following box:

```
+ - - - - - - - - - - - - - - - - - - - - - - - - - - - - - - - - - +

|                                                                   |

| Save in file:    server.uga.edu:-pub-msdos-mirror-windows3-winzip50.zip    |

|                                                                   |

|                               [Cancel ^G] [Accept - Enter]        |

|                                                                   |

+ - - - - - - - - - - - - - - - - - - - - - - - - - - - - - - - - - +
```

Figure 3.22
Results of an **archie**
search as run through
Gopher.

```
┌─────────────────────────────────────────────────────────────┐
│Internet Gopher Information Client v1.11                       │
└─────────────────────────────────────────────────────────────┘

        Substring search of archive sites on the internet: winzip

  --> 1.  server.uga.edu:/pub/msdos/mirror/windows3/winzip50.zip <Bin>
      2.  van-bc.wimsey.bc.ca:/upload/winzip50.zip <Bin>
      3.  knot.queensu.ca:/course/chee115/peppard-picks/winzipx.exe <Bin>
      4.  ousrvr.oulu.fi:/pub/msdos/tools/winzip.exe <Bin>
      5.  ousrvr.oulu.fi:/pub/msdos/tools/winzip.hlp.
      6.  ousrvr.oulu.fi:/pub/msdos/tools/winzip32.dll.
      7.  ousrvr.oulu.fi:/pub/msdos/tools/winzip.doc.
      8.  nic.switch.ch:/mirror/novell/netwire/novuser/11/winzip.zip <Bin>
      9.  swdsrv.edvz.univie.ac.at:..novell/netwire/novuser/11/winzip.zip <Bi
     10.  novell.com:/pub/netwire/novuser/11/winzip.zip <Bin>
     11.  sun0.urz.uni-heidelberg.de:/pub/msdos/novell/11/winzip.zip <Bin>
     12.  nic.switch.ch:/mirror/msdos/windows3/winzip50.zip <Bin>
     13.  athene.uni-paderborn.de:/pcsoft/msdos/windows3/winzip50.zip <Bin>
     14.  oak.oakland.edu:/pub/msdos/windows3/winzip50.zip <Bin>
     15.  plaza.aarnet.edu.au:/micros/pc/oak/windows3/winzip5.zip <Bin>
     16.  plaza.aarnet.edu.au:/micros/pc/oak/windows3/winzip50.zip <Bin>
     17.  sun0.urz.uni-heidelberg.de:/pub/simtel/windows3/winzip50.zip <Bin>
     18.  terra.stack.urc.tue.nl:/pub/simtel/windows3/winzip50.zip <Bin>

    Press ? for Help, ? to Quit, ? to go up a menu              Page: 1
```

Gopher is suggesting a name for the file we are about to retrieve. The name is gigantic; it's the name of the entry as found on the **Gopher** menu. We can edit this lengthy title, however, to whatever we want. Let's use the name of the program itself: **winzip50.zip**. Having changed the name, we can download the file by pressing the **RETURN** key.

Not bad. Now the file **winzip50.zip** is on our service provider's computer; if we're dial-up users, we can proceed to download it directly onto our own hard disks. **Gopher** has allowed us to combine two operations within a single interface. First we searched for a file we needed, then we downloaded that file, all without leaving **Gopher**. The best Internet tools are expert at this kind of behind-the-scenes manipulation; they do the hard work, while the user specifies the needed information and chooses which of the resultant files to retrieve.

Of course, you don't use **archie** just to find specific files; it can also be used to look for broad categories of information. Assume we're looking for information on genetics. One way to go about a search like this is to enter a term in hopes of finding directories. This clues you in to which sites to search for the kind of material you need; a subsequent FTP session to the site can track down materials you may not have known existed. Figure 3.23 shows the results of entering **genetics** in the search box and pressing the **RETURN** key.

This is an interesting screen; it illustrates a number of different types of information. There are directories here, just the thing we were looking for. Doubtless they'll include numerous files on various aspects of genetics. There are also text files. Entry 6, for example, is:

Figure 3.23
Using **archie** through
Gopher to search for
material on genetics.

```
            ┌─────────────────────────────────────────────┐
            │ Internet Gopher Information Client v1.11      │
            └─────────────────────────────────────────────┘

            Substring search of archive sites on the internet: genetics

    -->_  1.  net.bio.net:/pub/BIOSCI/BIO-JOURNALS/HUMAN_GENETICS//
          2.  net.bio.net:/pub/BIOSCI/BIO-JOURNALS/CURRENT_GENETICS//
          3.  net.bio.net:/pub/BIOSCI/BIO-JOURNALS/MOL_GENL_GENETICS//
          4.  net.bio.net:/pub/BIOSCI/BIO-JOURNALS/IMMUNOGENETICS//
          5.  ucselx.sdsu.edu:/pub/stepinfo/Matlab-Ex/genetics.m.
          6.  nic.sura.net:..rchie/sites/local/evolution.genetics.washington.edu.
          7.  plaza.aarnet.edu.au:..e/listings/evolution.genetics.washington.edu.
          8.  ucselx.sdsu.edu:/pub/equestrian/color_genetics.
          9.  ftp.uu.net:/government/umich-poli/P_News/genetics.and.racism.gz.
         10.  nic.cic.net:..er/e-serials/alphabetic/p/p-news/genetics.and.racism.
         11.  nic.cic.net:..r/e-serials/alphabetic/p/p-news/genetics.and.racism.g
         12.  dorm.rutgers.edu:..rchie.ans.net/evolution.genetics.washington.edu.
         13.  walton.maths.tcd.ie:/src/misc/genetics//
         14.  plaza.aarnet.edu.au:../medical/hypercard/mendelgenetics.cpt.hqx <HQ
         15.  sunsite.unc.edu:../mac-medical/hypercard/mendelgenetics.cpt.hqx <HQ
         16.  fly.bio.indiana.edu:/biology/mac/mendelgenetics.hqx <HQX>


    Press ? for Help, q to Quit, u to go up a menu              Page: 1
```

```
nic.sura.net:..rchie/sites/local/evolution.genetics.washington.edu.Z.
```

At the far left, of course, is the address: **nic.sura.net**. It's followed by the directory and subdirectory chain that leads to the file in question, **evolution.genetics.washington.edu.Z**. The **Z** reminds us that this is a compressed file; if we retrieve it, we'll need to run it through the UNIX **uncompress** program. (Although a text file, this material turns out to be of little value to us; it's actually an **archie** directory listing itself.)

We also find Macintosh files in compressed form, as denoted by the HQX suffix at the end of entries like:

```
fly.bio.indiana.edu:/biology/mac/mendelgenetics.hqx <HQX>
```

Perhaps we're interested in learning more about current work in genetics. In that case, the second item on this menu is of interest. It looks to be a directory with back issues of a journal specializing in genetics:

```
net.bio.net:/pub/BIOSCI/BIO-JOURNALS/CURRENT_GENETICS//
```

Whatever the resource, **Gopher** can move us to it quickly. Incorporating **archie** within **Gopher** goes a long way toward expanding **Gopher**'s search capabilities. Add in **Veronica**, as we'll see in the next chapter, and you have access to an effective search engine.

Hint:

Gopher occasionally seems to lock up. You'll know this has happened when you have been waiting interminably for a response as the bottom right-hand corner of the screen shows a seemingly frozen statement:

```
Retrieving Directory..
```

To exit this loop, enter a **Ctrl-C**. The result will be the **Gopher** quit prompt:

```
Really quit (y/n) ?
```

At this point, enter an **n** for no instead of the usual **y**. You'll then receive a box telling you what happened to your connection, as shown in Figure 3.24.

At this point, you can press the **RETURN** key to return to the **Gopher** menu you were just using. Such hangups are not uncommon with **Gopher**. When they happen, you may want to wait and try to run your search at a later time.

Using Gopher with WAIS

Just as **Gopher** can be used to track down files with **archie** and retrieve them through FTP, it can also cope with the Wide Area Information Servers (**WAIS**) system. We'll examine **WAIS** carefully in Chapter 5, but for now, we'll consider **WAIS** in its simpler form as an index searchable through **Gopher**. While **Gopher** does not offer you the full power you can muster through a direct **WAIS** search (that is, not all **WAIS** options are available), it does make it possible to run a search through its relatively simple interface.

To use **WAIS**, look for a menu entry like the following:

```
WAIS Based Information/
```

Pressing a **RETURN** at this prompt calls up a **Gopher** screen listing the **WAIS** databases, as shown in Figure 3.25. From this point on, you simply select the database you would like to search and press a **RETURN** to activate **Gopher**'s search screen.

Using CSO Name Servers with Gopher

Although we'll discuss how to find people on the Internet in a Chapter 8, you should be aware at this stage of another kind of **Gopher** resource that does that. A **CSO** name server is named after the Computing Services Office at the University of Illinois at Urbana-Champaign, which first developed the software. **CSO**s are used to find people on the Internet, and they're found in an ever-widening number of institutions.

Figure 3.24
The failure of a
Gopher connection
attempt.

```
                    Internet Gopher Information Client v1.1

                     Other Gopher and Information Servers

    -->  1.  All the Gopher Servers in the World/
         2.  Search titles in Gopherspace using veronica/
         3.  Africa/
         4. +---------------------Network Error----------------------+
         5. |                                                        |
         6. |   Cannot connect to host gopher-gw.micro.umn.edu, port 70. |
         7. |                                                        |
         8. |   Connection refused by host.                          |
         9. |                                                        |
        10. |                          [Cancel - ^G] [OK - Enter]    |
        11. |                                                        |
        12. +--------------------------------------------------------+




       Press ? for Help, q to Quit, u to go up a menu           Page: 1
```

Figure 3.25
WAIS databases as
listed by **Gopher**.

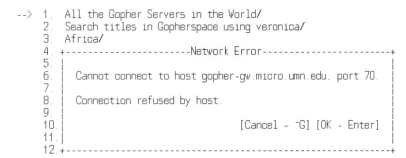

```
                Internet Gopher Information Client v1.11

                        List of all WAIS Sources

    -->  1.  AAS_jobs.src <?>
         2.  AAS_meeting.src <?>
         3.  AAtDB.src <?>
         4.  ANU-Aboriginal-EconPolicies.src <?>
         5.  ANU-Aboriginal-Studies.src <?>
         6.  ANU-Ancient-DNA-L.src <?>
         7.  ANU-Ancient-DNA-Studies.src <?>
         8.  ANU-Asian-Computing.src <?>
         9.  ANU-Asian-Religions.src <?>
        10.  ANU-AustPhilosophyForum-L.src <?>
        11.  ANU-Australia-NZ-History-L.src <?>
        12.  ANU-Australian-Economics.src <?>
        13.  ANU-Buddhist-Electrn-Rsrces.src <?>
        14.  ANU-CAUT-Academics.src <?>
        15.  ANU-CAUT-Projects.src <?>
        16.  ANU-CanbAnthropology-Index.src <?>
        17.  ANU-Cheng-Tao-Ko-Verses.src <?>
        18.  ANU-Coombseminars-Listserv.src <?>

       Press ? for Help, q to Quit, u to go up a menu           Page: 1/
```

In Figure 3.26, for example, we are looking at a screen of **CSO** name servers, any of which is accessible through **Gopher** by pressing the **RETURN** key. Note that this is but one screen out of thirteen and you'll realize how far the **CSO** servers have spread in academe. (Note: Not all of the servers illustrated are **CSO** name servers; others, indicated by **<?>**, are directories based on other technology.)

Pressing the **RETURN** key on any of the **CSO** entries will take you to a screen in which you can set up a search. You will be asked to fill in fields of information: name, e-mail address, department, and so on. You enter whatever information you know and press the **RETURN** key again. The fields are set up in a simple form; you move between them by pressing the **TAB** key. This form is shown in Figure 3.27.

As you can see, pressing a **Ctrl-G** at any point will cancel the search and take you back to the previous menu. **CSO**s are not difficult to use, and their growth addresses a key Internet problem—the need for more comprehensive directories of people and institutions. We'll examine this problem, and run a sample **CSO** search, in Chapter 8.

Gopher's Sights and Sounds

Text has always been the backbone of the Internet's communications structure; in fact, RFC 822, which specifies how mail messages are to be handled over the network, limits such messages to 7-bit ASCII characters. But increased bandwidth and the efforts of network pioneers to create software tools have recently placed a new emphasis upon sight and sound. And **Gopher** is not exempt; it is now possible to retrieve photographs and other pictures through its menus, as well as to fetch binary files that contain sounds. We will be seeing more and more of these resources as audio and video become more established on the Internet.

Figure 3.26
CSO name servers presented by **Gopher**. Note that each menu item has a suffix.

```
┌────────────────────────────────────────────────┐
│Internet Gopher Information Client v1.11          │
└────────────────────────────────────────────────┘

                   North America

    -->_ 1.  Albert Einstein College of Medicine <CSO>
         2.  American Mathematical Society Combined Membership List <?>
         3.  Arizona State University <?>
         4.  Auburn University <?>
         5.  Bates College <CSO>
         6.  Baylor College of Medicine <CSO>
         7.  Board of Governors Universities (Illinois) <CSO>
         8.  Boston University <CSO>
         9.  Bradley University <CSO>
        10.  Brigham Young University <CSO>
        11.  Brown University <CSO>
        12.  Bucknell University <CSO>
        13.  Bull HN Information Systems <?>
        14.  California Institute of Technology <?>
        15.  California Polytechnic Institute <CSO>
        16.  California State University - Fresno <?>
        17.  California State University - Hayward <?>
        18.  California State University - Sacramento <?>

    Press ? for Help, q to Quit, u to go up a menu          Page: 1/7
```

Figure 3.27
The **CSO** search form.

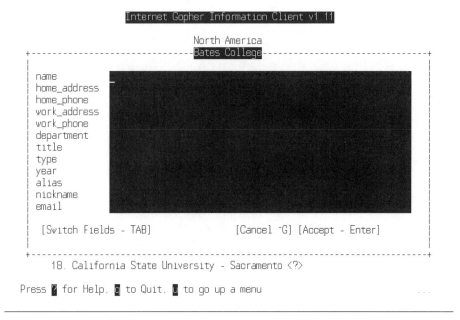

Regular binary files are flagged with the **<Bin>** suffix. Pictures, on the other hand, are given the special designation **<Picture>**. Purdue University, for example, places pictures of its faculty and staff on-line on the university's **Gopher**. The entries look like the following:

```
         Internet Gopher Information Client v1.11

       Pictures of Purdue CS Department Faculty and Staff

-->  1.  Abhyankar, S. (ram@cs.purdue.edu) <Picture>
     2.  Apostolico, Alberto (axa@cs.purdue.edu) <Picture>
     3.  Atallah, Mike (mja@cs.purdue.edu) <Picture>
     4.  Bajaj, Chandrajit (bajaj@cs.purdue.edu) <Picture>
     5.  Bhargava, Bharat (bb@cs.purdue.edu) <Picture>
```

Using the **D** command, we can download the file to our own computer for viewing.

Let me give you another example. In January 1993, the Library of Congress created an electronic version of an exhibit called *Rome Reborn: The Vatican Library And Renaissance Culture*. The University of Virginia Library made the exhibit accessible by **Gopher**. You can see some of the results in Figure 3.28.

Each item is marked with the **<Picture>** suffix. I have placed the arrow next to the image I'd like to retrieve, Antonio Tempesta's *View of Rome*. To get it, I now enter a **D** command. A box pops up asking which download protocol I plan to use. I chooze Zmodem, and soon the file is being shipped to my computer.

Figure 3.28
Retrieving an image
with the help of
Gopher.

```
┌─────────────────────────────────────────────────┐
│     Internet Gopher Information Client v1.11      │
└─────────────────────────────────────────────────┘

            VATICAN LIBRARY  (Exhibit, Part A)

     1.  THE CITY REBORN:  How the City Came Back to Life.
     2.  THE VATICAN LIBRARY:  Books for Popes and Scholars.
     3.  THE CITY RECOVERS:  From Wasteland to Metropolis.
     4.  Image of Rome.
     5.  Image of Rome <Picture>
     6.  Ugo Pinard, Plan of Rome.
     7.  Ugo Pinard, Plan of Rome <Picture>
     8.  Antonio Tempesta, View of Rome.
-->_ 9.  Antonio Tempesta, View of Rome, pt. a <Picture>
    10.  Antonio Tempesta, View of Rome, pt. b <Picture>
    11.  Antonio Tempesta, View of Rome, pt. c <Picture>
    12.  Antonio Tempesta, View of Rome, pt. d <Picture>
    13.  Antonio Tempesta, View of Rome, pt. e <Picture>
    14.  Antonio Tempesta, View of Rome, pt. f <Picture>
    15.  Antonio Tempesta, View of Rome, pt. g <Picture>
    16.  Antonio Tempesta, View of Rome, pt. h <Picture>
    17.  Antonio Tempesta, View of Rome, pt. i <Picture>
    18.  Antonio Tempesta, View of Rome, pt. j <Picture>


Press ? for Help, q to Quit, u to go up a menu        Page: 1
```

Hint:

Plan to take advantage of the images available over the Internet. They're sure to grow dramatically in number as the data pipeline is widened and more powerful processors come to our desktops. To do so, you'll need a program to view the graphics files you download. Standalone PC users can track down shareware file viewers by using **archie** over the Internet. Among the best are **vpic** and **cshow**; each is available at numerous FTP sites.

   To find them, enter the name of either in an **archie** substring search. My search with **Gopher**, for example, quickly turned up **cshow**:

```
-->  1.  m.ehd.hwc.ca:/pub/upload/cshow860.zip <Bin>
```

A similar search for **vpic** found this:

```
-->  22. apocalypse.engr.ucf.edu:/usr/ssd/msdos/vpic60e.zip <Bin>
```

   Sound is also becoming more widely available on the Internet. Again, you need the right hardware to be able to play such a file back, but if you own a multimedia PC, you can always download a file the same way we did with the image above, playing it back on your own equipment (be careful about file types, though; some sound files are designed to be played back, for example, on a Sun Microsystems computer; you may not be able to play these).

The G. Robert Vincent Voice Library at Michigan State University is an example of how rich a resource sound may eventually become on the Internet. The library contains speeches, performances, lectures, and other audio files from over 40,000 people recorded over the past 100 years. Thus far, only a fraction of these are presently available over the Internet. Following is a sample of the information you can pull in today, drawn directly from a **Gopher** menu:

```
6.   Amelia Earhart Talks of Science's Aids to Women in 1935 (1:08) <)
7.   Anwar Sadat Calls for Everlasting Peace in 1970 (0:58) <)
8.   Babe Ruth, Dying of Cancer, Talks About Baseball in 1947 (1:04) <)
9.   Betty Ford on Being Married to an Insecure Man in 1975 (0:15) <)
10.  Big Ben Rings in the Twentieth Century as Bob Vincent Explains (.. <)
11.  Charles F. Kettering Talks About Painting Cars at GM in 1955 (2:.. <)
12.  Edwin Booth Reads from Othello in 1890 Onto an Edison Cylinder (.. <)
13.  Florence Nightingale (Bob Vincent Interpolates) in 1890 (0:50) <)
14.  Franklin D. Roosevelt in Accepting the Nomination in 1936 (0:34) <)
15.  George Washington Carver Talks About Peanut Research in 1930's (.. <)
16.  Isaac Asimov at MSU in 1974 (2:39) <)
```

As you can see, each sound file has its own suffix. The **<)** (think of a stereo speaker) tells you that this is a file that can be played back. Note that the descriptions contain information about the length of each sound.

KEEPING UP WITH GOPHER

Gopher news is fast breaking, as indeed are Internet communications developments in general. You'll want to keep up with **Gopher** happenings if you find the tool useful. To do so, consider signing up for a **Gopher** newsgroup on USENET. The group is **comp.infosystems.gopher**. Another possibility (particularly if you're limited to e-mail access to the Internet alone) is to sign up for the **Gopher-News** mailing list. Send your request for a subscription to **gopher-news-request@boombox.micro.umn.edu**.

4

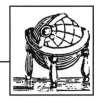

Veronica: Gopher as Search Engine

As a browsing tool, **Gopher**'s great talent is that it simplifies the process of information retrieval by allowing us to concentrate on what we need rather than upon the complexities of accessing it. On the other hand, using menued information, even with so bulletproof an interface, contains built-in obstacles. Although we have learned to put **Gopher**'s bookmarks to work to tag items, our session remains a lengthy process of exploration, more hit and miss than targeted strategy.

We can, of course, uncover quite a bit this way, including precisely the data we need. But what we would like is a way to cut through all the unnecessary menu stops. How much simpler it would be if we could build an engine that could search Gopherspace. Such a program would take the guesswork out of our searching by returning a list of menus containing the terms we specified. We could enter **information highway** as our search term and a list of **Gophers** with that term somewhere in their menu structure would appear. Hours of search time and menu scanning could be condensed into seconds.

Such an idea came to Steven Foster and Fred Barrie at the University of Nevada at Reno's System Computing Department. **archie** provided a precedent; it allowed users to locate text, data, and executable files at sites throughout the Internet community. Why not create something similar for **Gopher**? Using **Gopher**'s ability to create menus out of diverse information sources, this new tool would produce a customized menu based on the results of its search. And, as with any **Gopher** menus, each item would thereby be accessible through the usual **Gopher** commands.

Make no mistake about it, Barrie and Foster's work has created one of the Internet's premium search tools. Called **Veronica**, the new engine was developed in November 1992, and has quickly sprung to prominence as users have experienced its many advantages. For most of my own information gathering, **Veronica** is the first stop. Using it, I can quickly find out what's available on any **Gophe**r server known to the University of Minnesota's **Gopher**, some 1,300 servers plus as of this writing. Given the range of information being fed into the expanding base of **Gophers**, the use of **Veronica** as a search tool is indispensable.

Hint:

Where do they dream up these names? Intriguingly, most Internet tools seem to have multiple referents. Thus, **Gopher**'s origins as a school mascot as well as a retriever that "goes for" data. **Veronica**, likewise, owes a debt to several sources. Readers of the Archie comic strip or listeners to the old Archie Andrews radio show may remember **Veronica** as Archie's girl friend. And we already know about **archie** itself, a search tool known for its software's ability to search archives (take out the "v"). So if **Veronica** is a kind of **archie** for **Gophers**, then it makes sense that it have a name associated with **archie** (**archie**, by the way, was *not* originally named after Archie Andrews).

On the other hand, maybe we should give credence to the Frequently Asked Questions document about **Veronica**. With a straight face, it claims the name means this: **v**ery **e**asy **r**odent-**o**riented **n**et-wide **i**ndex to **c**omputerized **a**rchives. And brace yourself for a new search tool, working closely with **Gopher** and **Veronica**, called **Jughead**. More about the meaning of its reverse-engineered acronym later in this chapter.

How Veronica Works

Menu items presented by **Gopher** are references to the files—whatever their type—found beneath them in the menu structure. **Veronica** is able to search these titles by consulting an index it maintains. By entering a keyword, you are able to run your search past this index. You should, therefore, think of **Veronica** in somewhat the same terms you think of **archie**. **Veronica** must collect data from the **Gopher** servers it consults and then make searches of that database available to the **Gopher** clients that access it. The database is updated on a biweekly (sometimes weekly) schedule by a **Veronica** server, which queries the **Gopher** servers it knows about and asks for their menus.

The results of the search are presented on your screen as a **Gopher** menu, which you can then use in the same way you use any **Gopher** item, pressing the cursor keys to move to the item you wish to inspect, followed by a **RETURN** to examine that document. As you can see, **Veronica** is not a standalone program; there are no **Veronica** client programs in the same sense that **Gopher** clients have proliferated on the network. Rather, **Veronica** remains a cohesive link to

Gopher, working with the **Gopher** client of your choice to present the results of its searches and make their connections available to you.

ACCESSING VERONICA

Veronica's tight links with **Gopher** mean that you can connect to it through a **Gopher** client, which will allow you to reach a **Gopher** server that provides its own link to **Veronica**. The new search tool is expanding so rapidly in usage that, chances are, your usual **Gopher** site will offer a **Veronica** link. But if it does not, many other **Gopher** sites are available that do. If, on the other hand, you lack access to a **Gopher** client, you can still use **Veronica** through a Telnet connection to a public **Gopher** client.

Using a Gopher Client to Reach Veronica

You can look for **Veronica** at your service provider's site by calling up **Gopher**, as discussed in Chapter 3. The best place to look is under any menu item that refers to other Internet information servers. For example, here is what I see when I dial into the **Gopher** at MCNC in Research Triangle Park, NC, and look for **Gopher**-related materials:

```
7.   Search of GopherSpace - Veronica/
```

This is obviously the menu choice I want. On the other hand, perhaps it's not a choice found on your **Gopher** server. In that case, look for a menu item referring to other **Gopher** servers. **Veronica** will likely be found on such a list.

If it still doesn't turn up, you can take a quick shortcut by going to the mother **Gopher** at the University of Minnesota. The address is **gopher.micro.umn.edu**. You can reach it either by calling it up on the command line, in the form **gopher gopher.micro.umn.edu** (this assumes your service provider is offering a **Gopher** client program), or by moving through **Gopher**'s menus of other **Gophers** until you isolate the Minnesota site. In either case, you'll wind up with ready access to **Veronica** by following the menu choices. Look for the menu item labelled *Other Gopher and Information Servers/* and press a **RETURN** there. **Veronica** should appear as a menu choice like this one:

```
2.   Search titles in Gopherspace using veronica/
```

Pressing a **RETURN** at this point will call up the **Veronica** servers available to you, along with related information:

```
2.   FAQ:  Frequently-Asked Questions about veronica  (1993/08/23).
        3.   How to compose  veronica queries (NEW June 24) READ ME!!.
        4.   Search Gopher Directory Titles at NYSERNet <?>
        5.   Search Gopher Directory Titles at PSINet <?>
        6.   Search Gopher Directory Titles at SUNET <?>
        7.   Search Gopher Directory Titles at U. of Manitoba <?>
        8.   Search gopherspace at NYSERNet <?>
        9.   Search gopherspace at PSINet <?>
       10.  Search gopherspace at SUNET <?>
       11.  Search gopherspace at U. of Manitoba <?>
```

Examine this menu with interest. Obviously, the Frequently Asked Questions document is of value. The date will change with updates, so keep an eye on it and whenever a new version comes out, save and print it out for reference. Item 3 is also one to watch for updates; it contains information about the proper form to use in composing your search statements for **Veronica**. The tool continues to change as improvements are added, and the first word you may get about these changes is in this document.

Notice, too, that you have received a list of several **Veronica** servers. It's possible that your own site may contain fewer server references, or even different ones. The **Gopher** at MCNC, for example, includes reference to two **Veronica** servers available there, one of which is not listed on the Minnesota list. It's helpful to know about other servers, because you may connect to one and receive a message that there are too many connections ongoing for you to carry out your search on that server. In that case, using a different server may be your only route.

Using Telnet to Reach Veronica

Because **Gopher** and **Veronica** are so tightly interwoven, you know that in the absence of a **Gopher** client on your system, you will need to use Telnet to access a **Gopher** site from which you can tap into **Veronica**. The list of sites is the same given in Chapter 3. As always, use the site nearest to you to minimize network congestion. And as mentioned before, use a client program if at all possible. A client will provide a faster search and will take the best advantage of the equipment you have available.

A SIMPLE VERONICA SEARCH

To illustrate the workings of **Veronica**, let's run the simplest kind of search. As with **Gopher**, the search you'll see here represents the kind of activity the average user brings to **Veronica**. And just as you learned that using **Gopher** without bookmarks was ignoring the true potential of the medium, so using **Veronica** without proper attention to its various search options sharply reduces the effectiveness of your search. Consider what follows, then, as a paradigm that is under construction.

We'll start with the basics and gradually build a much more comprehensive search routine. First, an easy-to-answer information request. I'd like to learn about QWK mail readers, which allow various kinds of bulletin board systems to work with mail to and from the Internet. A friend is interested in establishing a bulletin board with Internet links, but doesn't know what is available that would help him download and distribute messages to his callers. He'd also like to learn more about QWK in general, not only in terms of the software programs out there, but the theory behind the data transfer.

I call this a simple request because of its narrow focus. I'm looking for information about a named subject—QWK. I can specify this in full knowledge that everything I generate will have something to do with my topic. It's not as if I were searching under broad terms like **reader** or **mail**. The ability to focus is a key tenet in any Internet search strategy. Always ask yourself how narrowly you can specify your data needs and still retrieve what you need. Too narrow a focus pulls up no "hits." Too broad a strategy results in long search times and huge numbers of hits to wade through (although, as we'll see, there are times when a broad search is essential; more on this in a moment). Each search calls upon you to juggle these possibilities. A practiced eye soon develops.

To search using **Veronica**, I simply press a **RETURN** at the **Veronica** menu. In this case, I will use the **Veronica** at PSInet, the Internet service provider in Reston, VA. The search screen is shown in Figure 4.1. As you can see, this screen is familiar: It contains the same dialog box that **Gopher** pops up when you want to search an indexed database.

I've already entered my search term—**QWK**—in the space provided. I could just as easily have used **qwk**, for **Veronica** is not sensitive to case.

Hint:

Memorize what I just said: ***Veronica*** *is not sensitive to case.*

When I press a **RETURN** after entering my search term, the **Veronica** search begins. This is shown in **Gopher** fashion by a statement in the right-hand corner of the screen:

```
Searching..-
```

Figure 4.1
Preparing to run a
Veronica search at
PSInet.

```
                    Internet Gopher Information Client v1.11

                                  Bookmarks

          1.  Search gopherspace using veronica (Server 1)  <?>
          2.  Search gopherspace at NYSERNet <?>
     -->  3.  Search gopherspace at PSINet <?>
          4.  Search gopherspace at U. of Manitoba <?>
     +-------------------------Search gopherspace at PSINet--------------------
     |
     | Words to search for   QWK
     |
     |                              [Cancel ^G] [Accept - Enter]
     |
     |
     +-------------------------------------------------------------------------



       Press ? for Help, q to Quit, u to go up a menu              Page: 1
```

Hint:

Don't be alarmed if **Veronica** occasionally hangs up at this point, leaving you with the searching prompt on and a seemingly frozen connection. When this occurs, it may be because a necessary network connection is congested or down. The solution is to do the same thing you would do with **Gopher**; remember, **Veronica** works *through* **Gopher**. Press a **Ctrl-C**, then answer **n** when you're prompted whether you want to quit **Gopher**. This should pop you out of cyberspace limbo and let you try again.

This method works most of the time. When it doesn't, repeating **Ctrl-C** several times may take you back to your provider's prompt. And don't be surprised if there are times when you have no choice but to hang up to break out of the frozen system.

When the search is complete, you'll get a screen full of information or, more likely, several screens. Figure 4.2 shows one of three screens that this search generated.

Let's examine this screen with some care. As you can see, it's a regular **Gopher** menu, and it's clear that if we were to move the arrow to any of these items and press a **RETURN**, we could call up the information. But every item on this menu refers in some manner to QWK. It's important, too, to note the kinds of information we've been presented.

Item 29, *Blurb of QWK_1.12_blurb*, for example, is clearly a text file; we assume this because of its title, and because **Gopher** uses a period after it;

Figure 4.2
Partial results of the PSInet search.

```
Internet Gopher Information Client v1.11

         Search gopherspace at PSINet: QWK

     19. Re: HP100LX cc: Mail and QWK.
     20. QWK-Door-for-Waffle.
     21. cstone    WafMail or other QWK mail for Waffle 1.65
     22. seb3      Re: Looking for QWK processor
     23. QWK mail READER.
     24. Re: QWK mail READER.
     25. QWK mail READER.
     26. QWK Door.
     27. QWK mail READER.
     28. QWK mail READER.
 --> 29. Blurb of QWK_1.12.blurb.
     30. 92.11 123K  QWK'n'Dirty 1.1 Terminal program and QWK reader/
     31. 92.09  60K  QWK 1.12/
     32. Contents of QWK_1.12.hqx.
     33. Contact Address for QWK Program Authors.
     34. Current QWK Related Products.
     35. QWK Mail Packet File Layout.
     36. QWK file stuff/

Press ? for Help. ? to Quit. ? to go up a menu            Page: 2
```

therefore, it's not a directory. Item 36, on the other hand, is a directory, shown by its distinctive slash after the menu entry, *QWK file stuff/*. And if we were to page through the rest of the material, we'd find other kinds of information and files. Examine the entries I found on page 3 of our **Veronica** results:

```
39.    qwk-reader.hqx <HQX>
40.    qwk-reader.hqx <HQX>
41.    qwk-130.hqx <HQX>
42.    qwk-130.hqx <HQX>
43.    qwk-reader.hqx <HQX>
44.    qwk-reader.hqx <HQX>
45.    qwk-130.hqx <HQX>
46.    qwk-reader.hqx <HQX>
47.    qwk-130.hqx <HQX>
48.    qwk-reader.hqx <HQX>
49.    Silly Little Mail Reader (Offline QWK mail reader) <PC Bin>
50.    mtn_qwk.lzh <PC Bin>
51.    qwk_idx.zip <PC Bin>
```

Interesting stuff! First, the **<HQX>** suffix tells us we're looking at Macintosh material in the Binhex archival format. This is followed by three items with the suffix **<PC Bin>**, which, as we saw in Chapter 3, refers to material that has been compressed in a format like PKZIP or another of the popular archival methods for the PC. These are likely to be QWK programs themselves, interesting for future reference, but not what we're looking for at the moment.

Just what are we looking for? Again, we need to define our mission. It's useful to know that we can retrieve various executable files here, but we are really concentrating on text files, because we're looking for background information. This reduces the population of files to consider by quite a bit. We might, for example, look in the directory I mentioned above—*QWK file stuff/*. By pressing the **RETURN** key on this item, I retrieve this:

```
QWK file stuff
-->    1.    Contact Address for QWK Program Authors.
       2.    Current QWK Related Products.
       3.    QWK Mail Packet File Layout.
```

Here are three text files, and they look to be just what we need: a list of current products, a file containing information on QWK's mail packet structure, and the addresses of people who write QWK programs. We can use the usual **Gopher** methods to mail or save these files.

Refining the Search

If you are happy with the preceding search because it tracked down the QWK information we needed, you should reexamine your search methodology. Yes, we did find what we wanted, but the search we ran was inexcusably slack. It produced three screens full of information, but much of the material was not what we wanted. It consisted of executable files, and we weren't yet ready to do anything with those. The fact that **Veronica** called up so much also meant that we had to spend time sifting through all the results. This may not seem like a big challenge when you're dealing with three screens, but when the screen count goes to 12, it is.

How could we home in more precisely on our search materials? By tuning up **Veronica** through a series of search options. In the case above, we want to find text files and directories (which may contain text files, as we just saw). To do so, we will restrict **Veronica** to finding certain **Gopher** data types. (Recall that we looked at these data types in Chapter 3.) **Gopher** marks its retrieved material through a series of official data type suffixes; there are also a number of experimental types being developed for pictures and sound. **Veronica** can be restricted to search for just the types you specify—the automated equivalent of going through menu after menu looking for particular kinds of files and directories.

The key is to add **-t** to our search request. Directories, for example, correspond to data type 1. It would make sense to search for directories in our search for QWK material; an entire directory devoted to QWK is likely to contain background materials. To search for directories alone, we frame our query this way: **qwk -t1**. **Veronica** doesn't care where we drop in the **-t** modifier, so we could also enter **-t1 qwk** for the same result (note that there is no space between the **-t** and the number following it). This is the result of the modified search:

```
Search gopherspace at PSINet: -t1 qwk

-->   1.  92.11 123K  QWK'n'Dirty 1.1 Terminal program and QWK reader/
      2.  92.09  60K  QWK 1.12/
      3.  QWK file stuff/
```

Notice that three pages of material have been reduced to three items, each of which has the search term **QWK** in its entry. And we know from our earlier search that the third of these entries contains the material we need.

Using Gopher's Data Types with Veronica

The list of data types shows us that we can specify to a fair degree of precision what it is we'd like to find. Let's explore the options now within the framework of a highly targeted search. Suppose we'd like to determine what Internet databases exist with information about geology. One way to do this would be to look for Telnet connections that are available on **Gopher** menus. **Veronica** is made for this kind of searching.

Remember the Telnet data type: Telnet connections are given the suffix **<TEL>** and correspond to data type 8. This means we can search for them using the search term **geology -t8**. We have narrowed our search to only Telnet items. The result:

```
              Search gopherspace at PSINet: geology -t8

-->   1.  Resources on Geology, Geophys, Astron., Astrophys. (Login: lp.. <TEL>
      2.  Resources on Geology, Geophys, Astron., Astrophys. (Login: lp.. <TEL>
      3.  USGS Pacific Marine Geology (PMG) data catalog <TEL>
```

Does the big picture begin to emerge? We have more control over a **Veronica** session than we realized. The issue is not how to narrow these choices—as we're finding, **Veronica** is not that difficult to master—but rather how to exercise good judgment in setting up an initial search strategy and then following through to the best possible result. With this in mind, let's create several searches and consider how they can best be managed.

Hint:

It's time to refresh your memory about **Gopher**'s data types and the numbers associated with them. Briefly:

0	A file
1	A directory
2	A CSO server
3	ERROR
4	A Macintosh file in BinHex format
5	A DOS binary archive
6	A uuencoded file
7	A searchable index
8	A Telnet connection
9	A binary file

And here are the experimental types:

s	A sound file
g	A GIF image file
M	A file containing MIME data, which is an evolving method of multimedia mail communications
h	An HTML file (See Chapter 6 on **World Wide Web** for more information on HTML.)
I	An image file
i	An inline text file used by **panda** (an Internet front end based on **Gopher**)
T	A Telnet 3270 session

A SAMPLE SEARCH FOR INFORMATION ABOUT CD-ROMS

The goal: we'd like to learn more about Internet resources that are available on CD-ROM disks. The number of such disks seems to be growing, with providers supplying everything from TCP/IP software to disks mirroring huge shareware collections like SIMTEL20 and others. UNIX public domain software is also out there, along with such implementations as LINUX, a UNIX system configured for the PC. We want to find out more comprehensively what's out there and how to get it.

We can try a **Veronica** search at its widest setting simply by entering the search term **cdrom** and pressing a **RETURN**. But by doing so, we run into an immediate difficulty. The results of such a search are illustrated in Figure 4.3. True, there's much that proves useful. Right off the bat, we find a Frequently Asked Questions document for CD-ROM, along with what seem to be numerous text files about the medium. The problem shows up when we examine the bottom right-hand corner of the screen, where we find this:

```
Page: 1/12
```

Twelve pages of material is a lot to wade through. On the other hand, it's certainly worth doing if we find what we need here. But a second problem arises if we go to that twelfth page. There, we find the final item:

```
200.   NEC CDROM Driver?.
```

Is it just chance that in our search, we've generated precisely 200 hits? Not by a long shot. The number of hits can be regulated at the site of each **Veronica** server. What you see, in other words, isn't always a full set of what's available. When a search generates a large number of hits, a cut-off must be found to avoid bombarding you with thousands of entries (and, for that matter, to avoid overloading network connections). This can be seen graphically if we run the same search at a different **Veronica** server.

The previous search took place on the PSInet server. When I ran the search at NYSERNET's server, I generated not 200 but 201 hits. The 201st was a dandy:

```
201.   ** There are 1487 more items matching the query "cdrom" available ...
```

Figure 4.3
A **Veronica** search for
CD-ROM materials.

```
 Internet Gopher Information Client v1.11 

        Search gopherspace at PSINet: cdrom

  --> 1.  cdrom-faq.
      2.  SUMMARY: converting bootable cdrom to bootable tape format...
      3.  Booting Via CDROM Over Net.
      4.  Help with mount CDrom .
      5.  SUMMARY: Toshiba CDROM on Solaris 2.2.
      6.  Info needed on Exabyte Stackers and Pioneer CDROM Changers.
      7.  SUMMARY: Help with mount CDrom.
      8.  4.1.2 cdrom permission problems.
      9.  SUMMARY: hsfs (4.1.2 cdrom) permission problem.
     10.  SUMMARY: Info needed on Exabyte Stackers and Pioneer CDROM Changer.
     11.  add_services can't use cdrom on the server.
     12.  Sun CDROM.
     13.  Danish texts on CDROM.
     14.  CDROM's writable.
     15.  Problem with SunOS 4.1.3 and Toshiba CDROM.
     16.  CDROM's again.
     17.  SUMMARY: Problem with SunOS 4.1.3 and Toshiba CDROM.
     18.  Mac CDROM on SS10 undef 413?.

   Press ? for Help, q to Quit, u to go up a menu            Page: 1/
```

If twelve pages of hits totals 200 items, then 1,487 more items should mount up to roughly *89 pages* of additional **Gopher** items. Of course, we can use **Gopher**'s **/** command to search these pages, but given that we don't yet have specific search terms to work with, this is impractical; so, too, is the idea of paging through a grand total of 101 screens of **Gopher** items hoping to find what we need.

Let's try to narrow the search. You might think we could use data type 0 to do this; type 0 is listed as referring to "files." But as used in this context, the word "file" doesn't mean text file, even though it would be phenomenally useful if we could isolate our search to text files to the exclusion of all else. If we enter **cdrom -t0** as our search term, we retrieve precisely the same list as when we enter **cdrom** by itself. Type 0, in other words, tells **Veronica** to bring in any **Gopher** items it finds; for our purposes, it is useless.

So let's get creative. First, we'll examine the list of data types and make a decision about what might be useful. In the preceding example, we used the directory data type to narrow our search for QWK readers to directories only; we found three. We might want to try that with CD-ROM materials, discovering possible archival sites that might be interesting to examine (note that we could run the equivalent search using **archie**). And let's take a look at data type 7, which consists of indexed databases, as well. Perhaps something exists for CD-ROM in this format.

Let's run the search with the term **cdrom -t17**. Note that it isn't necessary to separate the numbers for the various data types; **cdrom -t17** searches for the term **cdrom** in any directory (data type 1), as well as in any indexed database (directory type 7). And when we run the search, we retrieve eight pages of information, most of which consists of directories like those shown:

```
-->    1.  cdrom/
       2.  cdrom/
       3.  cdrom on bramble (Jim Robb)/
       4.  cdrom(a) on manitou (Carol Brown)/
       5.  cdrom(b) on manitou (Carol Brown)/
       6.  cdrom on quissett (Eric Schmuck) /
       7.  (Soon) GLORIA mosaics and data on CDROM (with DOS graphics) /
       8.  Local Woods Hole USGS WORKSTATIONS: login, anon ftp, or cdrom/
       9.  cdrom    Drivers for various CD ROM devices/
```

The last two items on page 8 turn out to be searchable databases, as shown by their **<?>** suffix:

```
     140.  Life Sciences Collection CDROM List of Journals <?>
     141.  CDROM Applied Science and Technology <?>
```

Eight pages, with 141 entries, is workable if we are conducting a broad sweep for background information. And indeed, we can find a substantial amount of background material by running the search in this form. We learn about the existence of several USENET newsgroups and their archives:

```
      53.  comp.publish.cdrom.hard Hardware used in publishing with CD-ROM./
      54.  comp.publish.cdrom.mult Software for multimedia authoring & publis../
      55.  comp.publish.cdrom.soft Software used in publishing with CD-ROM./
```

We learn about CD-ROM journals:

```
92.  Online & CDROM Review—E2EO01/
```

We also find directories under various aspects of CD-ROM installation and usage:

```
131.  CDROM Installation Program/
132.  CDROM Products/
133.  CDROM Product Appearance Images/
```

And finally, we find one of the major suppliers of CD-ROM disks of Internet information:

```
137.  Walnut Creek CDROM ............................ 6 entries/
```

By combining the information we find inside key directories with the Frequently Asked Questions document we retrieved from our first search, we have built up a battery of knowledge about our subject.

A VERONICA STRATEGY EMERGES

Earlier, I said that there were times when it made sense to run a broad search first before narrowing your focus. Our search for CD-ROM materials is such a time. Remember, our search under the broad term **cdrom** did find the Frequently Asked Questions file. It's okay to generate the big list as the first step in such a search, but treat the first few pages as the critical ones. This is where you are likely to find any documents **Veronica** has found that correspond to your search materials. If you search through pages 1 through 3 of your hit list looking for text files and retrieving what you need, you can use these as your core documents. After examining them, you can then begin the process of progressively narrowing your search.

Consequently, you can see that any **Veronica** search, save for the most simple, depends on at least two passes through the material. The first is a sweep for text files germane to your subject. The second is based on the first, attempting to fill in the gaps left by that initial search, and to save you the effort of wading through page after page of **Veronica** hits. To summarize, then: Step 1: the broad search, examining only the first three pages of hits for the most relevant. Step 2: the narrowed search, examining the resources you think most effective in following up your search. A third sweep may, of course, be suggested by what you find in the first two.

COMBINING KEYWORDS TO SEARCH

Now we can start to get crafty. Rather than using a single keyword, we'll branch out into multiple keywords with Boolean-style connections. We'll also learn to specify the number of hits we'd like to examine. Adding this level of search capability to **Veronica** makes it capable of finding files quickly, which otherwise might take hours of searching, if you ever found them at all.

But before you begin a new search, you should make a necessary adjustment to your **Gopher** menus. If you are going to use **Veronica** frequently, and anyone who searches the Internet with any degree of consistency should do so, then you need to make it easier to reach your search tool. To do this, use the **Gopher** bookmark page.

> **Hint:**
>
> The **Gopher** client most dial-up users will work with makes narrowing a search a simple matter. When you enter your search term into the search field, that term stays there after the search has been run. Type, for example, **cdrom** as your search term and run the search. Then, when you want to refine the search, go back to the search screen. The term **cdrom** is still there, with the cursor waiting at the end of the word. Now you can add another term to it. Perhaps add **-t1**, so that your entire search term is now **cdrom -t1**. Press the **RETURN** key and the revised search is run. Adding yet another search term or modifier is done the same way.
>
> For the same reason, moving your search to another **Veronica** server is easy. Leave the search screen and go back to the list of **Veronica** servers. Change the server you want to search and press **RETURN**. Voilà! The same search strategy is fed to the new server.

As shown in Chapter 3, putting the marker arrow next to an item and entering an **a** will add that item to your bookmark page. This is how I built up the following bookmark page, which is what I see when I type a **v** from within **Gopher**:

```
-->    1.  Search gopherspace using veronica (Server 1)  <?>
       2.  Search gopherspace at NYSERNet <?>
       3.  Search gopherspace at PSINet <?>
       4.  Search gopherspace at U. of Manitoba <?>
       5.  Search gopherspace at UNR <?>
       6.  University of Minnesota/
```

As you can see, I've compiled a list of **Veronica** servers, and have included the **Gopher** at the University of Minnesota, where I picked up the links to these **Gophers** in the first place. Now, when I sign on to **Gopher**, all I have to do is to enter a **v** and the list is ready to be used.

Remember, the changes you make to your bookmark list are reflected in changes in the **.gopherrc** file, which determines **Gopher**'s configuration. They'll stay there until you change them.

Now, let's begin a new search. In this session, let's say we are trying to learn about current research into cancer; specifically, we want to know what treatments or research investigations are underway on the subject of breast cancer. We can begin by running a basic **Veronica** search under the term **cancer**, which will generate numerous hits. When I used the **Veronica** server at the University of Manitoba, in fact, I wound up with 28 pages of **Gopher** items on the subject. This result is what we would expect on a topic as important as cancer; and indeed, the last item on the 28th page notes that there are more than 2,000 additional entries.

Don't be put off by this. Remember the key principle: When your subject is broad, begin with a broad sweep, looking for text files. Carefully search the first few screens of entries for anything germane. In this context, several good materials suggest themselves on the initial page of our sweep, as shown in this segment of our results:

```
-->    1.  Faulty-math-heightens-fears-of-breast-cancer..
       2.  Fatalismo-toward-cancer;.
       3.  Fear-of-breast-cancer..
       4.  Tenneco-s-chief-has-brain-cancer..
       5.  U.S.-ties-secondhand-smoke-to-cancer..
       6.  Study-ties-DDT-to-cancer-cases..
       7.  Cancer-causing-gene-found,-with-a-clue-to-how-it-works..
       8.  Coincidence-or-link-between-cancer-and-hereditary-diseases?.
       9.  Colon-cancer-screening;-contradictory-results-puzzle-researchers..
      10.  Little-benebit-seen-in-prostate-surgery;-study-finds-sixfold-incre...
      11.  Power-lines-didn-t-cause-girl-s-rare-cancer,-jury-finds;.
      12.  Report-call-simple-test-effective-in-reducing-colon-cancer-deaths..
      13.  Advances-in-detection-create-dilemma-on-prostate-cancer..
      14.  New-study-links-liquor,-cancer..
      15.  Stories-on-cancer's-causes-are-said-to-be-misfocused;-media-overpl...
      16.  Study-find-less-family-breast-cancer-risk..
      17.  Cancer-victims-may-sue-over-effects-of-radiation-theraphy..
      18.  Study-says-some-cancer-may-be-linked-to-'junk'-DNA..
```

Later in the listing, we find interspersed entries of interest, like this one:

```
22.  Breast-cancer:-success-is-imminent-in-search-for-key-gene..
```

or this one:

```
25.  Rivalry-holds-up-discovery-of-breast-cancer-gene;-Scientists-bicke...
```

But clearly, going through the entire list is going to be a major headache because it's so big. To get around it, let's combine terms.

We're interested in breast cancer, and we can enter that as our search term. When we put two words together this way an AND connector is implied, so we would retrieve any menu items using the term breast cancer, but also such entries as "cancer of the breast," where the two words are not adjacent. So let's search under **breast cancer**. Doing so reduces our hit list to 16 pages, quite an improvement. You can see this result in Figure 4.4.

We find numerous files of interest in these screens, but again, we're wondering if there is some way to reduce our search time still further. Progressively, we are homing in on our target, and now that we know we can combine terms, let's search under the following:

`cancer (breast and treatment)`

By nesting the "breast and treatment" terms in parentheses, we are asking **Veronica** to search for any entry that includes the term **cancer** as well as the terms **breast** and **treatment**. This turns out to be a productive search; we narrow our hit list to just over one page. Here are a few of our hits:

```
-->    1.  P1: PA-93-083 STUDIES ON THE PREVENTION, ETIOLOGY, CONTROL, BIOLOG...
```

Figure 4.4
Results of a search for
breast cancer materials.

```
           Internet Gopher Information Client v1.11

       Search gopherspace at U. of Manitoba: cancer and breast

  -->_ 1.  Faulty-math-heightens-fears-of-breast-cancer..
       2.  Fear-of-breast-cancer..
       3.  Study-find-less-family-breast-cancer-risk..
       4.  Breast-cancer:-success-is-imminent-in-search-for-key-gene..
       5.  Cancer-study-error-found;-Key-finding-unchanged-on-breast-disease-.
       6.  Rivalry-holds-up-discovery-of-breast-cancer-gene;-Scientists-bicke.
       7.  Breast-cancer-abortion-link-under-attack;-authors-outraged-by-reli.
       8.  MN-Free Breast & Cervical Cancer Testing.
       9.  Faulty-math-heightens-fears-of-breast-cancer..
      10.  Fear-of-breast-cancer..
      11.  Study-find-less-family-breast-cancer-risk..
      12.  Breast-cancer:-success-is-imminent-in-search-for-key-gene..
      13.  Cancer-study-error-found;-Key-finding-unchanged-on-breast-disease-.
      14.  Rivalry-holds-up-discovery-of-breast-cancer-gene;-Scientists-bicke.
      15.  Breast-cancer-abortion-link-under-attack;-authors-outraged-by-reli.
      16.  101993 Breast Cancer Coverage Under The Health Security Plan (Oct .
      17.  102093 President to the National Breast Cancer Coalition (Oct 20).
      18.  SPECIALIZED PROGRAMS OF RESEARCH EXCELLENCE IN BREAST CANCER.

  Press ? for Help, q to Quit, u to go up a menu              Page: 1/
```

```
       2.  PA-93-083 STUDIES ON THE PREVENTION, ETIOLOGY, CONTROL, BIOLOGY, D...
       3.  Autologous Bone Marrow Transplantation in the Treatment of Breast ...
       4.  Patients Needed for Clinical Trials for New Treatment for Breast C...
       5.  SUPERSEDED-15.  THE TREATMENT OF PRIMARY BREAST CANCER:.
       6.  81.  TREATMENT OF EARLY-STAGE BREAST CANCER.
```

If we choose, we could get fancier still. Perhaps we're interested in any kind of treatment *except* bone marrow transplantation. To ask for **Gopher** items concerning the treatment for breast cancer *not* including bone marrow methods, we could use this search statement:

`cancer (breast and treatment) not (bone marrow)`

Figure 4.5 shows the result. We have isolated precisely what we were after, using **Veronica**'s ability to nest and combine search terms. As you can see, this is a very powerful tool, which has taken us from thousands of items of **Gopher** information down to a one-page menu with 15 items closely related to our topic.

SUMMARIZING VERONICA'S SEARCH OPTIONS

The **Veronica** search options we have discussed so far, along with several new ones, are listed here. Let's take a moment to review these before we proceed.

Figure 4.5
Narrowing the search
by tightening the
search statement.

```
                     Internet Gopher Information Client v1.11


     -->  1.  NCI Treatment Referral Center Trial for Breast Cancer.
          2.  Patients Needed for Breast Cancer Treatment Clinical Trials.
          3.  Patients Needed for Clinical Trials for New Treatment for Breast C.
          4.  PA-93-083 STUDIES ON THE PREVENTION, ETIOLOGY, CONTROL, BIOLOGY, D.
          5.  Patients Needed for Clinical Trials for New Treatment for Breast C.
          6.  Patients Needed for Clinical Trials for New Treatment for Breast C.
          7.  P1: PA-93-083 STUDIES ON THE PREVENTION, ETIOLOGY, CONTROL, BIOLOG.
          8.  NCI Treatment Referral Center Trial for Breast Cancer.
          9.  Patients Needed for Clinical Trials for New Treatment for Breast C.
         10.  Autologous BM Transplantation in the Treatment of Breast Cancer  c.
         11.  81. TREATMENT OF EARLY-STAGE BREAST CANCER.
         12.  NCI Treatment Referral Center Protocol for breast cancer. . . .[40.
         13.  Patients Needed for Clinical Trials for New Treatment for Breast C.
         14.  Patients Needed for Breast Cancer Treatment Clinical Trials.
         15.  SUPERSEDED-15. THE TREATMENT OF PRIMARY BREAST CANCER:.




     Press ? for Help, q to Quit, u to go up a menu             Page: 1
```

-t(*datatype*)   The **-t** type specifier tells **Veronica** what type of **Gopher** item to
                      search for. The ones you're likely to use are these:
                      -t1 for directories
                      -t2 for CSO phonebooks
                      -t7 for indexed databases
                      -t8 for Telnet sessions

   The **-t** specifier can appear anywhere in your search term; it makes no
difference, for example, whether you enter **mongolia -t1** or **-t1 mongolia**; you'll
get the same result. Note that no spaces are allowed between the **-t** and the
number following it. Note, too, that to specify more than one data type, you put
the numbers together behind the **-t**. Thus, **-t18** searches for directories and
Telnet sessions.

-l   Asks for link files containing the results of your search.

   A link file? This means that **Veronica** will generate a file showing where all
the resources it uncovers are to be found, along with the usual information
generated by the **=** command. When I ran the search for information on breast
cancer, and include the **-l** statement, I received, as the first item on the list, a
Gopher item containing the link file:

```
     -->   1.   *** Link info for cancer (breast and treatment) not (bone marrow) ...
```

   By pressing a **RETURN** at this point, I was able to view a file of all the links.
A snippet of this is shown:

```
Type=0
Name=NCI Treatment Referral Center Trial for Breast Cancer
Path=0/NUS-NCI CancerNet/allfiles/4060/400008
Host=nuscc.nus.sg
Port=70
#
Type=0
Name=Patients Needed for Breast Cancer Treatment Clinical Trials
Path=0/NUS-NCI CancerNet/allfiles/4060/600713
Host=nuscc.nus.sg
Port=70
```

Obviously, asking for a link file may be important if you need information about the location of the resources before proceeding.

-m   Limits the number of items **Veronica** will retrieve.

By itself, **-m** requests **Gopher** not to limit itself to 200 items (or whatever limit has been set at the site); instead, you will retrieve the entire file list. Used with a number, **-m** specifies how many items you want to see. If I were looking for information about the space shuttle, for example, I could specify 500 items through the search term **space shuttle -m500**.

and   Allows you to combine search terms. Thus, **japan and history** retrieves **Gopher** items containing both terms.

not   Allows you to exclude a term. Thus, **germany not kohl** retrieves any **Gopher** item containing the word **germany**, but not those with the term **kohl** in them.

Let's drive these basics home through a series of search terms.

Sample Veronica Search Terms

To begin **Veronica** searches, always use a single term. Thus:

```
books
```

will retrieve any **Gopher** menu item with that term in it. This search pulls a huge amount of entries, as shown:

```
-->    1.  C-New Books Women and Feminism.
       2.  Books and Literary Events/
       3.  Electronic Books/
       4.  Phone Books/
       5.  Intro Ph (phone books).
       6.  UNIX BOOKS.
       7.  Books, journals, ref's/
       8.  New books on European forest history during the eighties. .
       9.  About Phone Books.
```

At this point in the discussion, you know how to narrow a search in the following ways:

1. The **AND** operator: **books and history** is a valid search strategy. It searches for any **Gopher** items containing both terms, but will not retrieve items with only one or the other term. Remember, you could also write this search term as **books history**. **Veronica** assumes the **AND** connection whenever you use more than one word as your search term. You could, therefore, retrieve menu items where the two words were not adjacent. An item called *Electronic books and journals in History/* is just as likely to appear as one called *crypto-history-books.txt/* (both of these are actual menu items).

2. The **OR** operator: **books or e-text** tells **Veronica** to look for menu items containing *either* term, but not necessarily both.

3. The **NOT** operator: **books not electronic** tells **Veronica** to find all menu items including the word **books** but not the term **electronic**. This rules out, for example, electronic text archives like Project Gutenberg's, or any others that fall under the rubric "electronic books."

4. Parentheses: Use parentheses when you want to nest search terms for maximum effectiveness. **electronic books and (gutenberg or wiretap)**, for example, searches for any menu items composed of both the term **electronic books** along with either the term **gutenberg** or **wiretap** (the latter being another collection of electronic text archives).

5. Wild card searching: Use an asterisk (*****) in place of characters at the end of a word. For example, suppose you need books about art. You could search under the combined term **books and art**. But then you might miss anything using the term **artistic**, **artisans**, or similar terms (**Veronica** will not search for embedded words). To get around this, you can search for **books and art***. The asterisk tells **Veronica** to retrieve any **Gopher** menu item *beginning* with the letters **art-**.

Hint:

Don't make the common Internet mistake of misunderstanding **Veronica**'s search capabilities. **Veronica** is a searchable index of the titles of menu items on the various **Gophers** scattered throughout the network. **Veronica** does not run full-text searches of the files it finds; it can only tell you when there is a *menu item* that corresponds to your search term. The document or file *behind* the menu item is yours to explore; **Veronica** doesn't see it.

Occasional Frustrations of Using Veronica

Veronica is a useful search engine, but it has limitations. In my mind, there is no question that its biggest drawback is its inability to limit searches to text files. It would be so useful to be able to specify, say, a search for **germany and econ*** and limit the search to text files alone. At present, unfortunately, there is no way to do this; we have to content ourselves with directories, assuming that an entire directory labelled with our search terms probably contains germane materials. But the solution is hardly ideal.

Other **Veronica** problems are obvious. First of all, **Gopher** menus correspond to no universal standard. Each system administrator makes his or her own call about how to build a **Gopher** menu. This makes your searches of necessity reliant on your own ingenuity. You are forced to think not only of obvious search terms but also of less likely ones, under the theory that someone, somewhere, might have used those terms to list your data on a **Gopher**. We've seen this problem before, in a hundred ways, on the Internet at large. Because there is no central organization, what the network offers can surprise you. This is a major weakness of the network as a data source, yet it also makes exploring the Internet a challenging and sometimes exciting activity.

Another **Veronica** drawback is the fact that your hit lists contain numerous duplications as **Veronica** tracks down the same material made available at different **Gopher** sites on the network. There is no way to sift through and eliminate every instance of duplicates, because often the same file will appear under a different name. Then, too, you'll occasionally run a search that you know should generate hits, only to receive a message that there is nothing available:

```
+- - - - - - - - - - + - - - - Gopher Error - - - - -+- - - - - - - - - - +
|                    |                               |                      |
| Words to search for |  Nothing available.          |                      |
|                    |                               |                      |
|                    |  [Cancel - ^G] [OK - Enter]   | [Accept - Enter]     |
|                    |                               |                      |
+- - - - - - - - - - + - - - - - - - - - - - - - - -+- - - - - - - - - - --+
```

There is little to do in this case but to try again.

Or perhaps you'll see this message:

```
-->   1.   *** Too many connections - Try again soon. ***.
```

This, however, isn't a **Veronica** problem; it's a result of demand exceeding supply in terms of the resources available; there just aren't that many **Veronica** servers out there. Trying at a different time of day may be the best approach if you run into this message frequently.

Another puzzling result can occur when you retrieve a menu of items and then try to access one in particular. Rather than calling up the file you were expecting you see, **Veronica** delivers something like this:

```
-->   1.   Server error: - Cannot access that directory.
```

Here, the likely culprit is a change at the **Gopher** site in question. A menu item has changed since the last time **Veronica** checked its records for that site. The item still appears on the menu generated by **Veronica**, but it's no longer where it's supposed to be.

Finally, you may see something like this:

```
Bookmarks
      1.   Search gopherspace using veronica (Server 1)  <?>
      2.   Search gopherspace at NYSERNet <?>
      3.   Search gopherspace at PSINet <?>
```

```
    4.  S+- - - - - - - - - -Network Error- - - - - - - - - - +
+- - - - -|                                                            |- - - - -+
|         |   Cannot connect to host comics.scs.unr.edu, port 800.  |         |
| Words to|                                                            |         |
|         |   Connection refused by host.                              |         |
|         |                                                            |         |
|         |                            [Cancel - ^G] [OK - Enter]  |         |
+- - - - -|                                                            |- - - - -+
          +- - - - - - - - - - - - - - - - - - - - - - - - - +
```

Note what has happened here: From the bookmark page, I've tried to run a search at the **Veronica** server at the University of Nevada in Reno. The connection has been refused, for a variety of possible reasons. Wait a while and try your search again if you receive such a message; or attempt the search at another **Veronica** server. This is one more reason that setting up your bookmark page with multiple **Veronica** servers as menu items can save you time.

Using Jughead

Despite its occasional frustrations, it is difficult to name a more comprehensive search tool than the **Gopher/Veronica** combination. It should be your first choice for complicated searching when you know the basic terms about which you need information but don't know where to begin. It is less useful as a browsing tool, though, where it cedes pride of place to **World Wide Web** or the other hypertext browser, **HYTELNET**. But its ability to limit itself to certain data types gives it unquestionable power in searches for Telnet sites of a certain description or binary files under your search term. You should get to know **Veronica** now and learn it well.

Also of interest is a new search engine that takes up where **Veronica** leaves off. And like the whimsically named **Veronica**, **Jughead** is another clever acronym: **J**onzy's **U**niversal **G**opher **H**ierarchy **E**xcavation **a**nd **D**isplay. "Jonzy" is Rhett Jones, who works at the University of Utah Computer Center where **Jughead** made its first appearance in 1993. And like **Veronica**, **Jughead** takes an existing concept and refines it to make the tool in question more effective.

Veronica expands **Gopher** by allowing you to consolidate your information gathering in gopherspace; **Jughead** moves in the opposite direction. Its concept is to allow you to search Gopherspace, but in a user-delimited fashion. For example, suppose you know about a great **Gopher** but you don't want to work through every one of its menus to find what you need. With **Jughead**, you can search that **Gopher** alone. A **Jughead** server maintains a database of the menu items at that site and allows users to search them.

Jughead is easier to demonstrate than to explain because, like **Veronica**, it is so closely linked with **Gopher**. This, for example, is what a **Jughead** item looks like at the University of Minnesota **Gopher**:

```
-->  10.  Search Gopher Titles at the University of Minnesota <?>
```

Pressing a **RETURN** with the arrow on this item generates the search screen we've come to expect from **Gopher**, and allows us to enter a search term. As with **Veronica**, search terms can include **AND**, **OR**, and **NOT**; the **AND** is assumed unless you use one of the other terms. Case is irrelevant.

Jughead, however, does sport a few commands of its own, as follows:

?all *searchterm*   Retrieves all hits **Jughead** finds on a particular term. Example: **?all philos*** returns all hits at the site containing the root term **philos-**.

Note the question mark, which must be included for this strategy to work. The default number of hits is a maximum of 1,024 items; you would use **?all** *searchterm* if you anticipated a greater number and wanted to see them all. In most cases, this command will be unnecessary. If you're searching at a particular site, it is unlikely that there will be this many items corresponding to your search term unless the site is running quite a large **Gopher**!

?help [*searchterm***]**   Produces the **jughead** help file, along with any hits on your search term. Entering **?help** by itself produces only the help file.

?limit=n *searchterm*   Limits the results of your search to the number of items (**n**) you designate. Thus, **?limit=10 faculty** produces the first ten hits and no more for this term.

?version [*searchterm***]**   Returns the version number of **jughead**, plus the hits on your search term. Entering **?version** by itself produces only the version number.

Locating a Jughead Server

The only way to track down a **Jughead** server, other than by trial and error, is to use **Veronica**, which can tell you where many of them are operating. Remember, it would be pointless to search under the broad term **Jughead**, because you would wind up with such things as text files about **Jughead**. So limit your search to indices by using the **-t7** command. Thus, your search term would be **jughead -t7**. This will retrieve any **Jughead** menu item that points to a searchable index; it will not, unfortunately, find a **Jughead** server that has been labelled, like the one at the University of Minnesota, *Search Gopher Titles at the University*, or other such variants. **Veronica**, remember, is very precise; it's looking for the term **jughead** in the menu item itself.

Here are a few of the hits this search generated:

```
Search gopherspace at NYSERNet: jughead -t7
-->     1.   Search this gopher (jughead) <?>
        2.   Search directories in GopherSpace: jughead (U.Birmingham,UK) <?>
        3.   Searching with jughead from Utah <?>
        4.   Search CSIE gopher by jughead (regexp, AND, OR, NOT)  <?>
        5.   jughead Test <?>
        6.   Test jughead Search <?>
        7.   Search Gopher Items at Technet using jughead <?>
        8.   Use jughead to search menus of UW-Superior <?>
        9.   jughead test <?>
        10.  Search all local menu items for "string" (uses jughead) <?>
```

```
11.   Search all Monash CWIS menus using jughead <?>
12.   Search High-Level Gopher Menus by JUGHEAD at W&L <?>
```

Note the additional problem here. Most of these **Jughead** servers aren't labelled as to location. But if you have read carefully, you already know the answer to this. Use the **-l** command to create a link file showing all the addresses. Thus, a better search strategy would be **Jughead -t7 -l**. Now you can access the link file and see where the **Jughead** servers are (at least, the ones labelled as such on their **Gopher** menus).

5

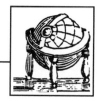

WAIS:

Searching for Text

A close look at the intricacies of **Gopher** and **Veronica** shows how versatile they are at finding files on the Internet. In fact, given the riches we can uncover through their combined efforts, it seems churlish to raise any doubts about their effectiveness. But technology is always redefining itself, and each new advance leads invariably to the next question. There are things that **Gopher** and **Veronica** simply cannot do; we must consider what they are and how a hot new networking concept addresses them.

When you run a **Veronica** search, you are retrieving information from **Gopher** menus scattered throughout the worldwide Internet. But this information is, in a sense, surface-level; it produces the titles of individual programs, graphics images, text files, and directories, but it does not tell us what is inside them. A file labelled "A New Approach to Networking," for example, might be about the merger of Bell Atlantic and TCI, or it might be an examination of ATM switching technology. The point is, we can't tell from the title alone what it is, and thus must rely on the people who choose these titles to do their jobs well.

What's missing is the ability to search the contents of a database for specific text. Perhaps I want to know something about Alfred the Great. I can search in a variety of ways for articles and even directories about the great king of Wessex, but I would miss a directory called */medieval*, which could, for all I know, contain a lot about him. But if I could find a database stuffed with textual information with an appropriate search engine, I could then descend to the document level, searching for words within the text. And if the database were properly designed, I could retrieve a list of "hits" which would be ranked in order of importance.

The system I am describing is called **WAIS**—**W**ide **A**rea **I**nformation **S**ervers. The brain child of Brewster Kahle, the concept was refined by him while working at Thinking Machines Corp., a producer of massive parallel computers and information retrieval engines. Apple Computer also played a role, as did KPMG Peat Marwick and Dow Jones and Co. The result is a public domain implementation as well as a series of more sophisticated versions which bring these powerful capabilities to computers of all descriptions. Kahle himself, meanwhile, has founded his own firm, WAIS Inc., to focus on **WAIS** and the future of data retrieval.

How WAIS Works

To understand **WAIS** and its improvement on prior search methodologies, you need to know something about its history. Driving the enterprise was the need to make text-based information systems more accessible to corporate executives (this accounts for the heavy corporate sponsorhip of the project). A key to the concept is that a good search interface must be usable by nontechnical people. (We might wish, given the success of **WAIS**, that all search tools were designed for executives and others not proficient with computer technology. The interface industry would doubtless improve!)

Another key: A good retrieval engine must be able to address a wide variety of data through a *single* interface. We can see why this would be so in business, where numerous sources are important, yet frequently accessed by different types of software. The **WAIS** project (pronounced "ways") sought to circumvent that obstacle by bringing a new search method to database access, one that not only provided an easy-to-use interface, but that produced its results in a way strikingly different from conventional database methods.

Graft these needs into the network environment and you get a system that can draw information from widely dispersed databases through a common front end. The client/server relationship of the network is the key. When you decide to search a **WAIS** database, you set up a search by choosing key terms, which are then sent to the appropriate server computer. The **WAIS** system will return a list of documents that contain the keywords you've specified. The **WAIS** servers are linked to databases that can reside anywhere on the Internet. **WAIS** clients exist for a wide variety of computers, from DOS to UNIX and the Macintosh.

The answers to your initial query are only the beginning of the process. Once the remote server has sent the results of its search, the client program displays these "hits" in a sequence that is ranked by the number of occurrences of the search terms in the files in question. Thus, a document that contains numerous examples of your search term ranks high on the list, while one containing a single reference ranks at the bottom. You then can refine your query by noting which of the search results is closest to what you need, and run a new search. This process is called *relevance feedback*.

WHAT YOU CAN FIND WITH WAIS

Unlike **Gopher**, which offers collections of local information as well as links to remote files and services of a diverse nature, **WAIS** servers are specialized. The nature of the Internet means they may be located anywhere in the network; each will focus on particular topics. We find, for example, servers dealing with specialties like mathematics, or physics, or astronomy. Because **WAIS** allows textual searching (and finely tuned textual searching at that), bringing USENET newsgroups, as well as archived BITNET and Internet mailing lists, into the system is a natural. We also find binary data. Although **WAIS** searches for text, the element downloaded can be a program, or an image.

Given the history of the Internet as a research and communications tool within the academic and research communities, it is no surprise to learn that a research slant permeates the current crop of servers. The network itself is a prime area for **WAIS** to catalog. The popular **com-priv** mailing list, for example, which discusses issues involving the privatization and commercialization of the Internet, is available in a **WAIS** server called **com-priv.src** (**src** is the **WAIS** server suffix; it stands for "source"). Documents from the Electronic Frontier Foundation are catalogued at another server (**eff-documents.src**), while articles from the monthly Matrix News newsletter are available as **matrix_news.src**. Whimsy, too, has its place. The USENET cookbook, drawn from recipes posted by cooking aficionados all over the world, is here as **usenet-cookbook.src**. So, too, are Internet standards-documents (**internet-rfcs.src**) and network information documents (**internet_info.src**).

Chris Christoff has compiled a listing of **WAIS** sources that demonstrates the system's range. We find servers holding documents on everything from aeronautics and astronomy to music, food, and robotics. Although sources in the humanities are comparatively rare, their number will grow as **WAIS** expands. From specialized items like the *Bryn Mawr Classical Review* (**bryn-mawr-classical-review.src**) to the *Journalism Periodicals Index* (**journalism.periodicals.src**), servers in arts and letters today merely suggest the possibilities. The on-line poetry server (**poetry.src**) is perhaps a better gauge of what is to come; it contains the complete works of Shakespeare and Yeats. The notion of a distributed literature available for keyword search throughout the network is an exciting one. So, too, is the concept of a comprehensive on-line encyclopedia, a tool the Internet currently lacks but which **WAIS** seems designed for.

Brewster Kahle likes to speak of **WAIS** as a publishing tool; its beauty is that it can provide the necessary vehicle enabling anyone with information to contribute that knowledge to the network. "Everybody has something to say," Kahle notes. "Everybody has a newsletter, a piece of expertise,a favorite recipe. Maybe they're an expert on car types or IBM PC clones. If we can make a system that helps people share that expertise, we as a societal organism become richer." And because **WAIS** is interactive, you don't compile information only to have it molder away in an attic. You get the data you need when you need it. Kahle considers **WAIS** a new medium for publishing. (True to his interests, the founder of the technology keeps a printing press in his basement.)

> **Hint:**
>
> If you're interested in seeing a current list of **WAIS** sources, you can find it by anonymous FTP to **wais.com**. The directory is:
>
> `/pub/wais-inc-doc/txt/`
>
> There are two files to consider. The first lists servers alphabetically, and is called **Source-List-Alpha.txt**. The second lists servers by category, and is called **Source-List-Cat.txt**. This list does not purport to contain every **WAIS** server, but currently includes over 400 servers that are registered with WAIS, Inc. By contrast, the number of **WAIS** servers found by a recent **Gopher** search at **sunsite.unc.edu** revealed 652 servers. Clearly, the medium is growing quickly, and these numbers will change, perhaps dramatically, by the time you read this.
>
> European users should try FTP to **funet.fi** to reduce network workload when they retrieve these documents. The directory there is *pub/networking/services/wais*. Users in the Pacific can retrieve the documents at **kirk.bu.oz.au**; there, the directory is *pub/Bond_Uni/doc/wais*.

ACCESSING WAIS

To tap **WAIS** resources, three methods are available:

- You can access the system through a local host's client program. Clients exist for most operating systems. Both **swais** and **waissearch** are used with UNIX, while **xwais** is the preferred interface for X Window systems. Others include **mxqwais** (OSF-Motif), **olwais** (for OpenWindows), **sunsearch** (for SunView), **waisserver** (VMS), **WAIStation** (for the Macintosh), and **HyperWais** (also for the Macintosh, using a Hypercard client interface). **wwais** works with Microsoft Windows, as does **WinWAIS**, while **os2wais** works with OS/2.

- You can access **WAIS** by Telnet to a remote site, which maintains a public access **WAIS** client. Such sites operate with the **swais** client. For the balance of this chapter, save for a brief digression about **waissearch**, we will be dealing with **swais**, the most common client for **WAIS**. The public access **WAIS** clients are listed in Table 5.1.

Table 5.1 Public access **WAIS** clients.

Address	Site	Login
swais.cwis.uci.edu	University of California at Irvine	swais
nnsc.nsf.net	NSF Network Service Center, Massachusetts	wais
quake.think.com	Thinking Machines Corp., Massachusetts	wais
sunsite.unc.edu	University of North Carolina at Chapel Hill	swais
kudzu.cnidr.org	Clearinghouse for Networking Information Discovery and Retrieval, North Carolina	wais

- You can run a **WAIS** search through **Gopher**. We discuss how this is done in Chapter 3. This method has considerable advantages for those using **WAIS** through a dial-up connection, in that it frees them from the limitations of the public access **swais** client. The **Gopher** interface is considerably easier to work with.

A SAMPLE WAIS SEARCH USING TELNET

Let's begin a **WAIS** session now by setting up a Telnet connection to one of the publicly available **WAIS** clients as shown in Table 5.1. To do so, we enter the Telnet command followed by the address. Thus:

```
telnet quake.think.com
```

takes us to the server at Thinking Machines Corp. in Cambridge, MA, where so much of the original **WAIS** development took place. The initial logon is unexceptional, but the message following it is important. The logon and message are shown in Figure 5.1. Press a **RETURN** when you see the message **TERM = (vt100)**; this will set the default terminal emulation.

Figure 5.1
Logging into **WAIS** at Thinking Machines Corp.

```
& telnet quake.think.com
Trying 192.31.181.1 ...
Connected to quake.think.com.
Escape character is '^]'.

SunOS UNIX (quake.think.com)

login: wais
SunOS Release 4.1.3 (SUN4C-STANDARD) #9: Wed Oct 27 18:18:30 EDT 1993
Welcome to swais.
Please type user identifier (optional, i.e user@host): gilster@rock.concert.net
TERM = (vt100)
Starting swais
This is the new experimental "wais" login on Quake.Think.COM

As the total number of sources has passed the 500 mark, we've found it's
become virtually impossible to find a source from the 25 screens of
sources.

I have decided that instead of presenting you with all the sources, I'll
just give you the Directory of Servers as a starting point. To find
additional sources, just select the directory-of-server.src source, and ask
it a question. If you know the name of the source you want, use it for the
keywords, and you should get that source as one of the results.  If you
don't know what source you want, then just ask a question that has
something to do with what you're looking for, and see what you get.

Once you have a list of results, you should "u"se the result you desire.
You can "v"iew a result before you "u"se it, paying close attention to the
"description".

Please let us know how you like this approach by sending feedback to
"wais@quake.think.com".

- WAIS at Think.COM

(press "q" to continue)
(END)
```

If you have used the server at **quake.think.com** in the past, you will quickly see a difference in how the system is managed. Before, the initial screen was one of many containing the list of **WAIS** servers. But with the number of servers expanding as quickly as it has, this site has taken a new approach. It will take you initially to a directory of servers, from which you can run searches to determine which servers you actually want to use. Having made this determination, you then run the search.

Figure 5.2 shows the opening screen at **quake.think.com**, once you get past the logon material. As you can see, the screen is spare and simple. Along the top is the server you will search initially, which is the directory of servers at Thinking Machines Corp. Along the bottom are a few of the basic commands needed to run your search. Unfortunately, the most important of these are not included. Let's run through a sample search to demonstrate how to use this system, and then we'll proceed to more complicated **WAIS** retrievals using this and other servers.

Hint:

Don't be put off by the interface you see here. **swais** is not user-friendly, but neither is it downright hostile. The commands I will provide will show you how to use the system. Later, running **WAIS** searches through **Gopher** will also be an option, though one without some of the features **swais** can provide. And, of course, as you become more accomplished in **WAIS** searching and begin to realize how powerful it can be, you may want to consider a SLIP account from your service provider. This would allow you to run other client programs that could draw still more functionality out of the **WAIS** system.

Figure 5.2
The opening **WAIS**
screen at
quake.think.com.

```
SWAIS                              Source Selection                    Sources:  1
    #          Server                              Source                     Cost
001:   [       quake.think.com]  directory-of-servers                         Free
```

```
Keywords:

<space> selects, w for keywords, arrows move, <return> searches, q quits, or ?
```

Let's go back to that initial screen. **swais** works by asking us to select a server to search. We do this by pressing the **SPACEBAR**. With only one directory on screen, it may seem unnecessary to do this, but the system demands it. Therefore, with the screen highlight sitting atop the Directory of Servers entry, press the **SPACEBAR**. The immediate result will be an asterisk appearing next to that item, which tells you that the server has been selected for searching.

Because many **WAIS** databases exist that contain information about the Internet itself, let's run a quick search using **internet** as a keyword. To run the search, we press the **w** key after selecting our server. Doing so produces an immediate result at the bottom of the screen: The basic help information has been replaced with the keyword entry field, as shown here; I have already entered our search term, **internet**:

```
Keywords: internet
Enter keywords with spaces between them; <return> to search; ^C to cancel
```

You can enter more than one search term; for now, however, we will keep things simple. We press a **RETURN** to begin the search. **swais** queries the server and produces a screen full of hits, as shown in Figure 5.3.

Examine this screen with some care. You are looking at a listing of **WAIS** servers that specifically address themselves to Internet issues. There are actually several screens, as can be seen from the top right-hand corner of the figure, where the following appears:

```
Items:  40
```

Figure 5.3
A list of hits using the search term "internet."

```
SWAIS                           Search Results              Items: 40
  #     Score    Source            Title                      Lines
001:   [1000] (directory-of-se) ANU-Internet-Voyager-Guide        79
002:   [ 955] (directory-of-se) internet_services                 24
003:   [ 910] (directory-of-se) internet-mail                    131
004:   [ 864] (directory-of-se) Internet-user-glossary            29
005:   [ 819] (directory-of-se) internic-internet-drafts          63
006:   [ 819] (directory-of-se) ripe-internet-drafts              16
007:   [ 773] (directory-of-se) comp.internet.library             14
008:   [ 773] (directory-of-se) internet-intros                   13
009:   [ 773] (directory-of-se) internet-standards-merit          15
010:   [ 773] (directory-of-se) internet_info                     15
011:   [ 728] (directory-of-se) internet-rfcs-europe              13
012:   [ 728] (directory-of-se) internet-standards                64
013:   [ 455] (directory-of-se) fidonet-nodelist                  74
014:   [ 455] (directory-of-se) irtf-rd                          112
015:   [ 409] (directory-of-se) kidsnet                           53
016:   [ 364] (directory-of-se) internic-infosource               36
017:   [ 318] (directory-of-se) UCSC_directory_of_servers         55
018:   [ 318] (directory-of-se) conf.announce                     64


<space> selects, arrows move, w for keywords, s for sources, ? for help
```

We can move between the screens using a variety of possible keys, which I'll discuss in a moment; for now, we'll simply pick a source on this screen. Let's assume we are interested in searching the server called **internet_services**. To do so, we move the highlight down using the arrow keys. At this point, the going gets more difficult. If you press a **RETURN** here, you get background information about the server, as shown in Figure 5.4.

This is helpful information if we want to know more about what is available at this server. But there is no way that we can search the server from this screen. Instead, we have to go back to the original screen by entering a **q** command.

swais, remember, isn't always helpful. In this case, the command we need isn't listed on the bottom of the screen, so when we choose a server for searching we must mark it by putting the highlight over it and then press the **u** key (unlike the initial search, where we placed the highlight over the directory of servers entry and then ran our search). Doing so selects it and places it on a separate list of servers that you have designated for searching. You can then view the list of selected servers by pressing the **s** key, which at this point in our search, produces this result:

```
SWAIS                   Source Selection              Sources:  2
  #            Server                    Source                    Cost
001: * [   quake.think.com]  directory-of-servers                 Free
002:   [   munin.ub2.lu.se]  internet_services                    Free
```

As you can see, the original **directory-of-servers** is still selected; the **internet_services** server is not. Naturally, we want to search **internet_services** rather than the **directory-of-servers** a second time. So we can press the

Figure 5.4
Generating
background
information about a
server in **WAIS**.

```
SWAIS                       Document Display                  Page:  1
(:source
    :version  3
    :ip-address "130.235.162.11"
    :ip-name "munin.ub2.lu.se"
    :tcp-port 210
    :database-name "internet_services"
    :cost 0.00
    :cost-unit :free
    :maintainer "anders@munin.ub2.lu.se"
    :description "Server created with WAIS release 8 b5 on Aug 19 11:38:54 1992 b
y anders@munin.ub2.lu.se

Various documents describing services available on the internet:
* INTERNET DATABASES By Billy Barron,
  University of North Texas VAX System Manager
* Internet mailservers
* The Internet Resources Guide is compiled by the
  NSF Network Service Center (nnsc@nnsc.nsf.net) at BBN Systems
* NOT JUST COWS - A Guide to Internet/Bitnet Resources in Agriculture
  and Related Sciences
  Written and compiled by Wilfred Drew, May 8, 1992

Press any key to continue, 'q' to quit. _
```

SPACEBAR with the highlight on the **directory-of-servers** entry, which will deselect it. We then move the highlight to the **internet_services** server and press the **SPACEBAR** again, to select it. Now, we are ready to run our search.

> **Hint:**
>
> Although I've selected only one server to search in this example, we'll soon see that the ability of **WAIS** to search multiple servers at once is a key to its power. The idea is to use a single interface for a wide variety of distributed information. In this area, **WAIS** is like no other search engine.

The **w** key is always our keyword command. Pressing it calls up the keyword field, which still contains our original search statement: **internet**. Let's extend that now by including the word **library**, assuming we are looking for servers that deal with library materials available over the Internet. Thus, we now have two search words in action: **internet** and **library**. When we press the **RETURN** key to run this search, we produce the results shown in Figure 5.5.

All of these are library-related items maintained at the **internet_services WAIS** server. We can move the highlight bar between them to choose the ones we want to view. Pressing the **SPACEBAR** with an item highlighted causes that item to be chosen, and its contents displayed on the screen. We can use the **SPACEBAR** repeatedly to page through the file. Or, if we decide to read no more of this particular document, we can use a **q** to leave the pager program.

Figure 5.5
Results of a search using the terms "internet" and "library."

```
SWAIS                              Search Results            Items: 40
  #    Score     Source                      Title                Lines
001:  [1000] (internet_servic) NOT JUST COWS - A Guide to Internet/Bitn  2704
002:  [ 729] (internet_servic) ------------------------------------------  435
003:  [ 339] (internet_servic) INTERNET/BITNET ONLINE HEALTH SCIENCES R  1124
004:  [ 296] (internet_servic)   -Library Catalogs      ftp dla.ucop.edu     8
005:  [ 288] (internet_servic) Chapter 2: Library Catalogs               118
006:  [ 203] (internet_servic) University of Utah Library Card Catalog     61
007:  [ 195] (internet_servic) Boston University Library Catalog (TOMUS   121
008:  [ 195] (internet_servic) Cleveland Public Library Catalog           61
009:  [ 195] (internet_servic) Harvard Online Library Information Syste   121
010:  [ 186] (internet_servic) Penn State University Library Informatio   121
011:  [ 186] (internet_servic) POLYCAT, The Cal Poly, SLO, Kennedy Libr    61
012:  [ 178] (internet_servic) Gopher                                    168
013:  [ 178] (internet_servic) URSUS, University of Maine System Librar   121
014:  [ 169] (internet_servic) *   Bibliographical Databases -- Dozens      5
015:  [ 169] (internet_servic) SprintMail X.400 Gateway                  182
016:  [ 161] (internet_servic) Cataloging from Library of Congress       121
017:  [ 152] (internet_servic) Emory University Libraries Online Public  121
018:  [ 152] (internet_servic) University of Wisconsin                   181

<space> selects, arrows move, w for keywords, s for sources, ? for help
```

The **q** command is pesky. Not only does it get us out of the pager program, it also is used when we want to leave **swais** at the end of a search. More than a few times I've hit the **q** at the wrong moment, only to have **swais** end my session abruptly. There is no remedy but to be careful.

Let's run through the procedure one more time. We're using the directory of servers initially to search for **WAIS** servers that pertain to our topic. Once we have determined what they are, we can select one or more of them in which to search. We deselect the **directory-of-servers** so that we don't run a redundant search including it, and then proceed to search the other servers. We can then view any of our results by pressing the **SPACEBAR** with the highlight over the item we wish to see.

Hint:

The nature of the **swais** interface is perhaps the least important part of a **WAIS** discussion. You should be aware that interface design is in constant flux as new ways of approaching Internet resources are realized. The underlying **WAIS** engine is what drives your research, not the particular interface you are using at the time. Indeed, going from one Telnet accessible site to another may result in your seeing differences between the way **swais** is handled. While **quake.think.com** uses the lean, channeled interface we examined previously, the National Science Foundation site at **nnsc.nsf.net** displays the entire list of available servers on the opening screen. To search a directory, you must first locate the **directory-of-servers** within this list.

However the interface is presented, **swais** will ask that you select a source, provide one or more keywords, and then press a **RETURN** to search it. As with so many things on the Internet, your own ingenuity will frequently be called into play as modifications to the various interfaces are made. But the time you spend mastering the underlying system, and understanding basic **WAIS** concepts, will result in better and more efficient searching no matter what display you see.

THE NATURE OF CONTENT NAVIGATION

The simple search just shown tells us much about how **WAIS** handles information, and also reveals the differences between it and more conventional methods of database retrieval. Brewster Kahle calls the **WAIS** methodology *content navigation*, a method of searching that allows us to move between large collections of documents and search them using simple English questions. Rather than working with complex Boolean search strategies, as is common with database searches, the user simply enters words that seem germane as the search terms, and then examines a list of resulting documents (Boolean searching remains possible and, in some databases, preferable).

Now the method becomes interesting and innovative. The documents thus retrieved are themselves the user's key to finding further, still more applicable documents. **WAIS** examines the number of words that the documents have in common with the search terms. Those with many hits appear at the top of the list; they have the highest score. If you examine the screen in Figure 5.5 again, you will see that all these items have been given a ranking, beginning with the number 1000 as the highest rank. This ordered list of documents represents stage 1 of our search. We can now use it to refine the search for stage 2.

How? By choosing from among this list those documents that most nearly meet our criteria. Although **WAIS** has identified numerous documents that contain our search words, it has no way of knowing at this point which of these are most apropos. We can, however, select documents that we like and then ask **WAIS** to run the search again (provided both server and search engine support the process). Through the technique known as *relevance feedback*, **WAIS** will apply itself to locating other documents more nearly like the ones we've chosen. In an ideal world, this would result in a progressive process narrowing each search until the documents we retrieve are precisely what we want. As we'll see, however, the relevance feedback process is limited by the design of the database and the search engine itself.

Dow Jones News/Retrieval implemented relevance feedback technology when it established its DowQuest service, although DowQuest uses a different search engine than **WAIS**. Dow Jones users typically place a call by modem to the DJN/R computers, running the search there. Over the Internet, of course, **WAIS** takes a different approach. Here, the client/server structure of networking comes to the fore. The most exciting aspect of **WAIS** is that it can query, through its protocols, servers of information at diverse sites, established as data repositories by virtually anyone.

The Basic WAIS Commands

The **swais** interface we have been dealing with so far provides basic **WAIS** features, and is your route into the **WAIS** database environment. Clearly, an expanded network connection through SLIP, PPP, or a full-fledged Internet connection at work would allow you to use a variety of client software, incorporating pull-down menus, mouse-driven commands, and other graphical features. But **swais** is what dial-up users have available when they contact **WAIS** through a Telnet connection, and a great deal can be done with it.

The basic **swais** commands follow. Note that **swais** works in what is known as *cbreak mode*, which means that, when using a single character command, you don't have to press the **RETURN** key to activate the command. Look through these commands, and then we'll go onto the network to run some sample **swais** searches.

swais Movement Commands

Down arrow	Moves the highlight down to the next source (this can also be achieved through a **j** or a **Ctrl-N** command).
Up arrow	Moves up one source (or you can use **k** or **Ctrl-p**).
Ctrl-D	Moves down one screen at a time. You can also use **J** or **Ctrl-V**.
Ctrl-U	Moves up one screen at a time. You can also use **K**.

number	By entering a number, you can move directly to the source number you've specified.
/pattern	Allows you to move directly to the source that begins with your pattern. Thus, you could go directly to **eff.documents.src** by typing **/eff**, etc.

swais Search Commands

SPACEBAR	Selects or deselects the current source for use in a search. At the article level, displays the current item.
=	Deselects all sources. This is handy when you want to begin a new search and choose your sources from scratch.
r	Marks the current item as a relevant document. Used in relevance feedback sweeps.
R	Shows you a list of documents you have marked as relevant.
s	Shows you the list of sources and allows you to select new ones.
u	Marks an item to be added to the list of sources for your search.
v	Enables you to view information about the current source or article.
w	Lets you select keywords.
RETURN	Performs the search (after you enter keywords). Or, at the article level, displays the current item. Also can also be used after selecting your sources to ask for a new keyword.

Miscellaneous swais Commands

m	Mails the current item. This is a handy command; you can mail **swais** results to yourself or to any Internet address.
o	Sets **swais** options.
h	Produces a basic help display. You can also use the **?** command.
H	Shows the history of the program.
q	Quits the article you are reading. Or, at the main menu, quits **swais**.
S	If you are using a **WAIS** client on your own computer, this command saves the text you are reading to a file. But you can't use this command on a public **WAIS** host. Dial-up users should use **m** instead.

WAIS KEYWORD LIMITATIONS

As powerful as it is, **WAIS** imposes a structure upon database searching which you must keep in mind; otherwise, your results may be startling. Most database searchers are familiar with Boolean logic, which we looked at briefly in Chapter 4. Boolean logic allows you to use a series of terms like AND or OR in a search statement. The search term **shortstop AND ozzie**, for example, sets off a search looking for documents containing both statements. The term **shortstop OR ozzie** searches for documents containing one or the other of the terms, and so on. Boolean logic can become quite complicated, which is why information brokers exist and how they earn their fees.

Not all **WAIS** servers support Boolean logic. If you enter **shortstop AND ozzie** as your **WAIS** keywords, these servers will find documents containing the term **shortstop**, documents containing the term **ozzie**, and documents containing both. Bear this in mind when you run a search with multiple terms and retrieve hits that don't include one of your terms.

WAIS also precludes searching with wild cards, which is to say, terms like **financ*** used to locate documents containing keywords like **finance**, **financial**, and so forth won't work. You can do this with Boolean searching but not with **WAIS**. You are also prevented from excluding words. A search for **baseball NOT mets** won't work; in Boolean terms, it would have retrieved any documents with the word **baseball** but not the word **mets**.

A WAIS SEARCH USING RELEVANCE FEEDBACK

To examine how relevance feedback can change **WAIS'** output of information, let's run a sample search using it. I'm interested in learning more about issues of privacy and network communications. One of the great boons of the network environment is our ability to move quickly between widely distributed sites of data. But of course the counterweight is the question of how much information we are making available about ourselves and our businesses in the network environment. Certain **WAIS** databases seem likely to contain information that could help us understand these issues, and what current thinking about them is.

For this search, we will use four **WAIS** servers: **comp.risks.src** compiles the postings on the USENET group **comp.risks**, which discusses the problems and dangers associated with computing technology; **com-priv.src** does the same for the **com-priv** mailing list, on which network theoreticians analyze current developments in the growth of the Internet and its relationship to the so-called "information highway;" **eff.documents.src** compiles materials from the Electronic Frontier Foundation, the activist organization that is attempting to establish basic principles of law as they apply to computer networking; finally, the **computers-freedom-and-privacy.src** server contains the text of the proceedings from the Conference on Computers, Freedom and Privacy II, courtesy of the Association of Computing Machinery in New York.

Step 1: Selecting Our Sources

We can't search **WAIS** without specifying which sources we want to examine. I have begun this session by using Telnet to the address **quake.think.com**, where I have logged in using the **wais** login. There, I am presented with the **directory-of-servers.src** as my primary database. Two approaches are possible at this point. First, I could simply search the directory of servers, using terms like **privacy** or **freedom**. This would generate a list of possible servers which I could then query. This is the least effective way to search; it is better that I do some research and then opt for the second possibility.

The second option is to specify exactly which servers I want to contact. In this case, because I have examined a list of **WAIS** servers and know which ones I want, I need to tell the Directory of Servers to locate each in turn, and then to use it as part of my overall search. To do so, I search the **directory-of-servers.src** database, using in each case the name of the server I want to examine as my keyword. Thus, I would enter the **w** command and place **eff.documents.src** in the search field to retrieve a list of hits containing that server. I would do the same for each of the four servers I want to contact.

Step 2: Telling swais to Search a Particular Server

swais is not a friendly program. Although there is a list of basic commands at the bottom of the screen, it is far from complete, and often fails to suggest the most useful command for the situation in which you find yourself. When you have generated a list of servers containing one of the ones you want to search, for example, you must now invoke the **u** command to *use* the server. **swais** will deliberate for a moment (actually, the server is being placed on a list of sources that are going to be made available for your search). You must then repeat this process for each of the servers you want to access.

How do you know when your list is complete? Pressing an **s** will cause a list of selected servers to appear, as below. But here again, **swais** is counter-intuitive; when you call up this list, even though you have already selected the servers, you must press the **SPACEBAR** once again to select each. You also must press the **SPACEBAR** with the highlight on the **directory-of-servers.src** to cause that server to drop off your list. Otherwise, you would wind up once again searching the Directory of Servers, which is counter-productive; you've already run that search. Here is what the list of selected servers looks like once I've run through and selected my targets with the **SPACEBAR**:

```
SWAIS                           Source Selection              Sources:  5
    #         Server                      Source                      Cost
001:  * [     archive.orst.edu]  com-priv                            Free
002:  * [     quake.think.com]   computers-freedom-and-privacy       Free
003:    [     quake.think.com]   directory-of-servers                Free
004:  * [        wais.eff.org]   eff-documents                       Free
005:  * [ cmns-moon.think.com]   risks-digest                        Free
```

Remember, the asterisk tells you the source is now ready to be searched. The absence of an asterisk at the third entry says I have now removed it from my search list.

Step 3: Running the Initial Search

We now are ready to select a keyword and run our search. To do so, we must press the **w** key, which takes us once again to the keyword list. **swais** preserves our last search statement there in case we want to use it again. Assuming we do not, we can erase that statement and put in a new one by using one of several possible keys. Try the **BACKSPACE** key first; it should work, erasing the former entry. If it does not, try **Ctrl-H** or **Ctrl-BACKSPACE**. If neither of these works, try the **DELETE** key. The one that tuns out to be effective depends on how you've set up your communications software, but one of them should function.

Now we can enter our search term. Let's use **privacy** and see what we get. Entering that term, we then press the **RETURN** key to run the search. One screen of the result, after **swais** consults with the relevant servers, is shown in Figure 5.6

We actually have retrieved several screens, with a total of 31 items that meet our search criteria in some way. Three of these show the optimum score of 1000. We must now hunt through the rest of the list looking for items that are close to what we want. We will then use these items to run a revised search using relevance feedback.

Step 4: Marking Items for Our Next Sweep

Using the list of documents we have retrieved, we have several options. By pressing the **SPACEBAR** with the highlight on any entry, we can call up that entry for examination. A **RETURN** does the same thing. In most cases, this is how we will use **swais**—we'll run a single search and then examine the results.

However, we want to use relevance feedback this time around to make our list of hits still closer to what we want. To do so, we must mark those items on our initial list of hits that most closely match what we are after. We do this by moving the highlight bar to the item in question and then pressing the **r** key. This selects that document as a relevant document, and adds it to the list for the subsequent sweep through the data using relevance feedback.

Figure 5.6
Searching under the term "privacy."

```
SWAIS                              Search Results                  Items: 31
   #    Score    Source                        Title                    Lines
 001:   [1000] (omns-moon.think)  RISKS DIGEST 13.69.  CPSR Recommends NRE   62
 002:   [1000] (  eff-documents)  ees_fips.comments    /serv/ftp/pub/EFF/Is 19337
 003:   [1000] (computers-freed)  7.  PRIVATE COLLECTION OF PERSONAL INFOR  1931
 004:   [ 980] (omns-moon.think)  RISKS DIGEST 11.70:  Re: SCIENTIFIC AMER    54
 005:   [ 980] (omns-moon.think)  RISKS in mainstream entertainment (Missi   136
 006:   [ 960] (omns-moon.think)  RISKS DIGEST 14.83:  Privacy Digests  Da    47
 007:   [ 960] (omns-moon.think)  RISKS DIGEST 14.34:  Privacy Digests  Da    47
 008:   [ 960] (omns-moon.think)  RISKS DIGEST 14.02:  Privacy Digests  Da    46
 009:   [ 960] (omns-moon.think)  RISKS DIGEST 11.57:  CPSR Washington Sem    35
 010:   [ 960] (omns-moon.think)  RISKS DIGEST 10.48:  Government routine1    37
 011:   [ 960] (omns-moon.think)  RISKS-LIST: On Risks of Running RISKS:      39
 012:   [ 957] (  eff-documents)  ees_fips.comments    /serv/ftp/pub/EFF/Is 19337
 013:   [ 957] (computers-freed)  6.  WHO'S IN YOUR GENES?                   1105
 014:   [ 848] (computers-freed)  8.  PRIVACY AND INTELLECTUAL FREEDOM IN    1523
 015:   [ 784] (  eff-documents)  ees_fips.comments    /serv/ftp/pub/EFF/Po 19337
 016:   [ 784] (  eff-documents)  ees_fips.comments    /serv/ftp/pub/EFF/Po 19337
 017:   [ 784] (  eff-documents)  ees_fips.comments    /serv/ftp/pub/EFF/Po 19337
 018:   [ 784] (  eff-documents)  ees_fips.comments    /serv/ftp/pub/EFF/Is 19337


<space> selects, arrows move, w for keywords, s for sources, ? for help
```

Hint:

To repeat, **swais** is anything but friendly. In this case, when you select a particular item as relevant by pressing the **r** key, **swais** won't acknowledge your choice with any visual feedback. Therefore, be sure to place the highlight over the correct item before pressing the **r** key.

For the purposes of our search, I have selected certain items from the list of hits that I think are particularly useful. I have moved through the list and used the **r** command with the highlight over each item I want to use. I think we're ready to run the revised search, but first, it's important to verify that our list of relevant documents is what we want it to be. Therefore, I will use the **R** command (note the uppercase) to generate a list of relevant documents. The result is shown here:

```
SWAIS                             Rel. Documents                  Items:  6
  #    Score     Source                        Title Lines
001:  [ 304] (computers-freed) 11.  PUBLIC POLICY FOR THE 21st CENTURY    1205
002:  [ 739] (computers-freed) 1.   KEYNOTE ADDRESS: "Freedom in Cybersp   755
003:  [ 960] (cmns-moon.think) RISKS DIGEST 14.02:  Privacy Digests  Da     46
004:  [ 960] (cmns-moon.think) RISKS DIGEST 14.34:  Privacy Digests  Da     47
005:  [ 960] (cmns-moon.think) RISKS DIGEST 14.83:  Privacy Digests  Da     47
006:  [1000] (computers-freed) 7.   PRIVATE COLLECTION OF PERSONAL INFOR   1931
```

Examine this list for a moment. It shows six items that I have selected as useful. Let's now use these to make a second search, using them as our key examples.

Step 5: Putting Relevance Feedback to Work

To run the second search, we press the **w** key to call up the keywords field. Our original search terms are still there and we will leave them there. What we are doing, after all, is running the same search, but this time we have specified to **swais** that certain items are more like what we want than others. **swais** will take this information into account as it goes to work on our behalf. All we need do, then, is to press the **RETURN** key to run the revised search. The result is shown in Figure 5.7.

Again, we have a list of hits. But compare this list to the previous one and you will see that the two are not the same. Using the information we supplied it, **swais** has searched again for documents that are closer to those we want. The second list is, theoretically, a more accurate search result.

I say "theoretically" because in this case, the **WAIS** server behind the **swais** client is not a terribly powerful implementation of **WAIS**. Yes, we can run relevance feedback searches with it, but in practice, the results turn out to be not much different from our initial screen of results (and remember, not all servers support relevance feedback). More sophisticated **WAIS** servers and clients, however, can perform exceedingly focused searches using the **WAIS** techniques. **swais** gives us a glimpse of what is possible, but only hints at the power of more robust programs interacting with the **WAIS** protocol.

Figure 5.7
Results of the revised
search using relevance
feedback.

```
SWAIS                           Search Results               Items: 31
  #    Score    Source                   Title                    Lines
 001:  [1000] (cmns-moon.think) RISKS DIGEST 14.02: Privacy Digests  Da    46
 002:  [1000] (  eff-documents) ees_fips.comments   /serv/ftp/pub/EFF/Is 19337
 003:  [1000] (computers-freed) 7.  PRIVATE COLLECTION OF PERSONAL INFOR 1931
 004:  [ 966] (cmns-moon.think) RISKS DIGEST 14.34: Privacy Digests  Da    47
 005:  [ 957] (  eff-documents) ees_fips.comments   /serv/ftp/pub/EFF/Is 19337
 006:  [ 940] (cmns-moon.think) RISKS DIGEST 14.83: Privacy Digests  Da    47
 007:  [ 866] (cmns-moon.think) RISKS DIGEST 15.39: Privacy Digests  Da    47
 008:  [ 856] (computers-freed) 11. PUBLIC POLICY FOR THE 21st CENTURY  1205
 009:  [ 784] (  eff-documents) ees_fips.comments   /serv/ftp/pub/EFF/Po 19337
 010:  [ 784] (  eff-documents) ees_fips.comments   /serv/ftp/pub/EFF/Po 19337
 011:  [ 784] (  eff-documents) ees_fips.comments   /serv/ftp/pub/EFF/Po 19337
 012:  [ 784] (  eff-documents) ees_fips.comments   /serv/ftp/pub/EFF/Is 19337
 013:  [ 730] (computers-freed) 9.  COMPUTERS IN THE WORKPLACE: ELYSIUM o 1400
 014:  [ 728] (computers-freed) 3.  ETHICS, MORALITY, AND CRIMINALITY   1717
 015:  [ 715] (computers-freed) 8.  PRIVACY AND INTELLECTUAL FREEDOM IN  1523
 016:  [ 688] (computers-freed) 4.  FOR SALE: GOVERNMENT INFORMATION    1574
 017:  [ 659] (computers-freed) 2.  WHO LOGS ON?                        1472
 018:  [ 658] (computers-freed) 1.  KEYNOTE ADDRESS: "Freedom in Cybersp  755


  <space> selects, arrows move, w for keywords, s for sources, ? for help_
```

Hint:

How many relevance feedback searches should you run? Theoretically, by continuing to use relevance feedback until the results you are generating stay roughly the same, you will have exhausted the system's ability to refine the search any further. In practice, and given the inherent difficulties of using **swais** itself, your search will most likely include only a single relevance feedback sweep. To do more will be counterproductive, using up valuable search time for little in the way of significant results.

A ROUTINE WAIS STRATEGY

As with other Internet search tools, you should consider developing a strategy you will use whenever you approach **WAIS**. By keeping a particular format of searching in mind, you ensure that your search remains focused. Moreover, given the fact that each of the search tools we've examined makes particular demands upon your memory and patience, it's helpful to have a strategy blocked out no matter what your search's subject matter may be. Later in the search, you can depart from the canned approach to refine and tweak your strategy as the need arises.

Here, then, are the basic components of a suggested **swais** strategy, which we'll then use on a sample search:

1. **Download and use a list of WAIS servers**. We've already examined how to get two different text files listing current **WAIS** servers, and you should keep updating these files as new servers come on-line.

    But wait? Can't you just jump into **WAIS** and search the Directory of Servers? The answer is yes, but experience using the system has proven to me that there is no substitute for a methodical, off-line survey of available servers before you attempt your search. As good as **WAIS** is—and at times it is quite good—it won't always find the best servers for the topic you need. When I ran the previous search past the Directory of Servers, for example, and searched it under the term **privacy**, it came up with exactly one hit: the **computers-freedom-and-privacy.src** server. The other sites, so useful in our search, did not appear.

    The reason is obvious: The **computers-freedom-and-privacy.src** server is the only one that contained the search term **privacy** in its title, or as a keyword in the **.src** file. The lack of effective indexing, then, keeps us from making optimum use of the Directory of Servers. To keep up with **WAIS** events and to stay on top of new server sites as they come on-line, download and use the text files listing these sites. And periodically browse through one of the Telnet sites, like that at **sunsite.unc.edu**, which lists all the servers. Alternatively, you can do the same thing with **WAIS** via **Gopher**, as I'll discuss shortly. Believe me, there is nothing more frustrating than realizing *after* a lengthy search that there was a different server you could have included in your search that contained exactly what you needed.

2. **Use as few servers as you can.** True, one of the beauties of **WAIS** is that you can search multiple servers; in fact, this ability is crucial for some kinds of searches. But highly focused searches may only require one server; adding others only limits the number of hits from the one most likely to meet your requirements. Suppose, for example, that I were searching for the meaning of the acronym IEEE. The server **acronyms.src** would be all I would need to solve this search puzzle, quickly giving me the result (Institute of Electrical and Electronics Engineers).

3. **Think on your feet about which server to use.** The choice of servers is by no means intuitive; I could have found the above information as well, for example, in the **internet-user-glossary.src** server. **WAIS** often requires experimentation and a hefty dose of common sense to generate what you need. After a while, you will learn to stop looking for an immediately obvious solution and start casting about for more subtle ways to solve your problem.

4. **Begin your search with broad terms; narrow as necessary.** You might think that the quickest way to run a search is to be extremely precise. But all too often, the results of such an approach are hits that seem to have no bearing on what you need. Examine, for instance, what happens when I search the directory of servers for **WAIS** sites dealing with cooking. An amateur chef, I want to find out what recipes my fellow network denizens have been contributing to the gastronomic world. I set up a **WAIS** search under a series of keywords, reasoning that the more terms I use, the more precise the result

will be. Thus my search terms are **recipes**, **food**, **cooking**, and **online**. The result is shown in Figure 5.8.

At first glance, I seem to have hit paydirt; after all, I've retrieved 34 hits, 18 of which are shown in the figure. But actually, most of these items are inconsequential for my search, as **WAIS** itself attests by giving them low rankings. Nonetheless, I know by now that whatever ranking **WAIS** has assigned, I must go through the list with care to ensure that something doesn't slip past that I can use. And all this takes up time.

Examine now the list that I generate by going to a single search term, and keeping it broad enough to take in my topic. The term is **recipes**. The result is a mere two servers, each of them precise hits (although it's annoying that **WAIS** assigns one a value of 1000, while the other receives a mere 353!):

```
SWAIS                             Search Results              Items:   2
    #    Score      Source              Title                      Lines
  001:   [1000]  (directory-of-se)    recipes                         15
  002:   [ 353]  (directory-of-se)    usenet-cookbook                 21
```

Remember: Your time is valuable; anything you can do that both keeps your search targeted and relieves you of the obligation to sift through long lists of irrelevant material is all to the good. Stay flexible, and think of single concepts that encapsulate your search needs.

1. **Use relevance feedback sparingly.** We've already seen that relevance feedback can produce a reordered list of documents, with some items that were ranked low on the scale now given higher ranking, and vice versa. But in its

Figure 5.8
Using multiple search terms for precise results.

```
SWAIS                             Search Results              Items: 34
    #    Score      Source              Title                      Lines
 001:   [1000]  (directory-of-se)    recipes                         15
 002:   [ 655]  (directory-of-se)    online@uunet.ca                 23
 003:   [ 621]  (directory-of-se)    usenet-cookbook                 21
 004:   [ 586]  (directory-of-se)    online-mendelian-inheritance-in-man   60
 005:   [ 414]  (directory-of-se)    cool                           108
 006:   [ 276]  (directory-of-se)    San_Diego_Super_Computer_Center_Docs  67
 007:   [ 276]  (directory-of-se)    eros-data-center                94
 008:   [ 241]  (directory-of-se)    ANU-Internet-Voyager-Guide      79
 009:   [ 241]  (directory-of-se)    cool-directory-of-servers       58
 010:   [ 241]  (directory-of-se)    eos-ncsu                        14
 011:   [ 241]  (directory-of-se)    internet-mail                  131
 012:   [ 207]  (directory-of-se)    ANU-Tropical-Archaeobotany      86
 013:   [ 207]  (directory-of-se)    NeXT-Managers                  120
 014:   [ 207]  (directory-of-se)    Omni-Cultural-Academic-Resource 33
 015:   [ 207]  (directory-of-se)    bit.listserv.pacs-l             42
 016:   [ 207]  (directory-of-se)    cool-bib                        39
 017:   [ 207]  (directory-of-se)    cool-cdr                        45
 018:   [ 207]  (directory-of-se)    cool-cfl                        55

<space> selects, arrows move, w for keywords, s for sources, ? for help_
```

present state of development, the **swais** client makes relevance feedback comparatively awkward to use, while the benefits of using it are relatively minor. We still have to work through each screen of information to be sure that **WAIS** hasn't misassigned a document that we really do want to read. In terms of conserving our search time, then, relevance feedback adds little value. Refinements of the **WAIS** model and an ever-widening pool of servers will eventually change this; for now, however, consider relevance feedback no more than an option.

2. **Mail documents to yourself**. Having found a set of documents from a search that meet your criteria, the next step is to mail them to yourself. Use the **m** command to do so. The documents can then be printed out at your leisure.

USING GOPHER TO ACCESS WAIS

Using **WAIS** with a client program like **WAIStation** can be a joy, as the client takes much of the difficulty out of our navigation. The dial-up community, however, at least the vast majority of those who dial up a service provider and have no SLIP connection, is limited to the **swais** interface to do their work. **swais** can be a powerful tool, but no one would accuse it of elegance or ease of use.

My view is that you should master **swais** to acquire a thorough grounding in **WAIS** fundamentals. From there on, though, you may want to consider using **WAIS** through **Gopher**'s interface if your searching needs are relatively simple. I restrict this statement to simple searches because unlike **swais**, **Gopher** does not allow you to select multiple **WAIS** servers to search with a single sweep through the data. This means you must accurately target your databases one at a time, adding to your search time if you are trying to cover much ground. On the other hand, many of the databases we'd like to examine are unique; perhaps half of my own search time is concentrated within a single database at a time. For these searches, **Gopher** allows me to use a familiar interface and run my searches quickly.

For this example, I am going to use the **Gopher** at the University of North Carolina at Chapel Hill. The address is **sunsite.unc.edu**. And because I am using a **Gopher** client on my system, I will use the command **gopher sunsite.unc.edu**. Alternatively, I could find this **Gopher** by going through a menu of other **Gophers** at a Telnet-accessible site. At the opening screen, I'll look for a relevant item:

```
-->  3.  Surf the Net! - Archie, Libraries, Gophers, FTP Sites./
```

This one seems the most likely, as it points to a wide range of services. Taking it, I move to an item on the submenu:

```
-->  8.  Search WAIS Based Information /
```

Here, I press a **RETURN** to generate the screen shown in Figure 5.9. We are looking at a long list of **WAIS** servers. If you examine the bottom right hand side of the screen, you will see that this is 1 screen out of 37 possibilities. In fact, some 652 **WAIS** servers are listed here, which may explain why the popular site at **quake.think.com** recently changed its interface, as explained earlier. With so many servers, the problem is to track down which servers you need without spending half the day doing it.

Figure 5.9
Using **WAIS** through
Gopher.

```
                     ┌─────────────────────────────────────────┐
                     │ Internet Gopher Information Client v1.11 │
                     └─────────────────────────────────────────┘
                            Search WAIS Based Information

           -->_ 1.   AAS_jobs.src <?>
                2.   AAS_meeting.src <?>
                3.   AAtDB.src <?>
                4.   ANU-Aboriginal-EconPolicies.src <?>
                5.   ANU-Aboriginal-Studies.src <?>
                6.   ANU-Ancient-DNA-L.src <?>
                7.   ANU-Ancient-DNA-Studies.src <?>
                8.   ANU-Asian-Computing.src <?>
                9.   ANU-Asian-Religions.src <?>
               10.   ANU-AustPhilosophyForum-L.src <?>
               11.   ANU-Australia-NZ-History-L.src <?>
               12.   ANU-Australian-Economics.src <?>
               13.   ANU-Buddhist-Electrn-Rsrces.src <?>
               14.   ANU-CAUT-Academics.src <?>
               15.   ANU-CAUT-Projects.src <?>
               16.   ANU-CanbAnthropology-Index.src <?>
               17.   ANU-Cheng-Tao-Ko-Verses.src <?>
               18.   ANU-Coombseminars-Listserv.src <?>


           Press ▊ for Help, ▊ to Quit, ▊ to go up a menu        Page: 1/37
```

As we did at **quake.think.com**, then, we need to consult the Directory of Servers. And, in fact, there are numerous server directories from a number of sites. The one I urge you to use is **directory-of-servers.src**, which is likely to be the most up-to-date and comprehensive. As of this writing, it was found on the menu at **sunsite.unc.edu**'s **Gopher** as item 347:

```
-->   347.  directory-of-servers.src <?> p 20 of 37
```

Of course, these numbers will change (on the Internet, change is a daily and even hourly phenomenon). But to shorten your search, you can always use the **Gopher** search function from the main screen. To do so, we use this command:

```
/ directory-of-servers
```

The slash tells **Gopher** that we're searching; we could, of course, have searched under **directory**, or even **dir**, but this search takes us precisely to where we need to be.

I'm interested in tracking down a poem by William Butler Yeats. I know that it had something to do with the sea and with white birds. To find it, I will need to locate a server that specializes in literature. Thus, with the arrow pointing to the **directory-of-servers.src** server, I press the **RETURN** key to set **WAIS** to work. Soon I have a list of servers that fit my search term **literature**, as shown in Figure 5.10.

From here, I choose the most likely candidate, which is called **poetry.src**. Putting the arrow on it, I press the **RETURN** key again, calling up the search

Figure 5.10
Servers found
searching under the
term "literature."

```
┌─────────────────────────────────────────────────────┐
│         Internet Gopher Information Client v1.11      │
└─────────────────────────────────────────────────────┘

          directory-of-servers.src: literature

     --> 1.  queueing-literature-database.src <?>
         2.  ANU-Radiocarbon-Abstracts.src <?>
         3.  Medicine_Books_Lund_Pre1800.src <?>
         4.  ANU-Dhammapada-Verses.src <?>
         5.  ASK-SISY-Software-Information.src <?>
         6.  IAT-Documents.src <?>
         7.  NOAA_National_Environmental_Referral_Service.src <?>
         8.  POETRY-index.src <?>
         9.  Tantric-News.src <?>
        10.  poetry.src <?>
        11.  proj-gutenberg.src <?>
        12.  prosite.src <?>
        13.  stsci-preprint-db.src <?>




     Press ? for Help, q to Quit, u to go up a menu          Page: 1/1
```

screen. Now I enter my term; I'll use **white birds**, since I remember the term from the poem I read so long ago. **WAIS** ponders this request and then generates a sceen of hits, as shown in Figure 5.11.

Figure 5.11
Searching the works of
Yeats for the term
"white birds."

```
┌─────────────────────────────────────────────────────┐
│         Internet Gopher Information Client v1.11      │
└─────────────────────────────────────────────────────┘

              poetry.src: white birds

     --> 1.  WanderingsOfOisin    /mas/library/Poetry/currently-waised/Yeats/.
         2.  The_Rape_of_Lucrece  ../currently-waised/Shakespeare/Various_Poems/.
         3.  DramaticPoem  /mas/library/Poetry/currently-waised/Yeats/.
         4.  Venus_and_Adonis  ..try/currently-waised/Shakespeare/Various_Poems/.
         5.  WhiteBirds  /mas/library/Poetry/currently-waised/Yeats/.
         6.  FatherOHart  /mas/library/Poetry/currently-waised/Yeats/.
         7.  BaileAndAillinn  /mas/library/Poetry/currently-waised/Yeats/.
         8.  QueenMaeve  /mas/library/Poetry/currently-waised/Yeats/.
         9.  The Snowman on the Moor          Sylvia Plath.
        10.  Sonnet-98   ..s/library/Poetry/currently-waised/Shakespeare/Sonnets/.
        11.  Commendatory_Poems_and_Prefaces  ..aised/Shakespeare/Various_Poems/.
        12.  The_Phoenix_and_the_Turtle   ..tly-waised/Shakespeare/Various_Poems/.
        13.  CivilWar  /mas/library/Poetry/currently-waised/Yeats/.
        14.  GiftOfHarun  /mas/library/Poetry/currently-waised/Yeats/.
        15.  Dream with Clam-Diggers          Sylvia Plath.
        16.  Spinster          Sylvia Plath.
        17.  Sonnet-A_Lovers_Complaint  ../currently-waised/Shakespeare/Sonnets/.
        18.  Silences                      Gilbert Sorrentino.

     Press ? for Help, q to Quit, u to go up a menu          Page: 1/3
```

In this screen, we find that Yeats used the term in other poems, most particularly in the early "Wanderings of Oisin" (a lovely poem laced with Celtic echoes); we also see hits from Shakespeare and Sylvia Plath. But my poem is found as item 5, where it is listed as **WhiteBirds**. I move the pointer to this item and press another **RETURN** to see the poem. Figure 5.12 shows the result.

If you find this kind of literary excavation as exciting as I do, ponder both the implications of the technology and the current liabilities it possesses. Yes, we can find poetry by keyword searches using a distributed database; we have no idea where the server for **poetry.src** is and it really doesn't affect our search. You can imagine a future in which vast quantities of library information are made available in similar fashion, extending literacy and opening opportunities for research throughout the world.

On the other hand, we run up against the fact that the Internet in its present form contains only the smallest smattering of such information. We're out of luck, for example, if we're searching for most poets; we've got Yeats and Shakespeare, but where are Milton and Elliot, Herrick and Wyatt, Hopkins and Tennyson? What we need is further growth of the basic **WAIS** infrastructure. More libraries need to be built along the information highway.

Hint:

Gopher is an easy way to use **WAIS**, especially after we've dealt with the relatively unintuitive **swais** interface. But **Gopher** does possess two major drawbacks. Using it, you can't tap more than a single **WAIS** database at a time; nor can you use relevance feedback techniques to refine your search. Since both of these are among the most powerful **WAIS** features, it's clear that a **Gopher** search is best when your needs are highly targeted. Even then, you must be willing to sift through the resultant screens with great care to find what you need. **WAIS** will be unable to reshape the output through subsequent searching and relevance techniques.

USING WAISSEARCH FOR SPECIFIC SERVERS

What do you do if you know about a specific **WAIS** server that you'd like to search? As we've seen, you have several options. The first is to query a directory of servers, like the one at **quake.think.com**, using the name of your server as the search term to call it up; you then add it to your list of sources and search. The second is to use **Gopher**, which presents you with a list of servers. But there is a third alternative, which allows you to go directly to a server. It is a handy, text-based client program called **waissearch**.

The command structure of **waissearch** is simple enough. You enter the **waissearch** command and follow it with this information: the **WAIS** host server, the **WAIS** source you want to access, the port number (if it is other than 210, which is the standard port for **WAIS**), the **WAIS** database you are trying to reach, and the keyword for your search. The syntax, then, is as follows:

```
waissearch -h source -p portnumber -d database keyword
```

Figure 5.12
Yeats' poem "The
White Birds" displayed
on screen. Note that
the search terms are
highlighted.

```
cap{THE WHITE BIRDS}

I WOULD that we were, my beloved, white birds on the
foam of the sea!
We tire of the flame of the meteor, before it can fade
and flee;
And the flame of the blue star of twilight, hung low
on the rim of the sky,
Has awaked in our hearts, my beloved, a sadness that
may not die.
A weariness comes from those dreamers, dew-dabbled,
the lily and rose;
Ah, dream not of them, my beloved, the flame of the
meteor that goes,
Or the flame of the blue star that lingers hung low in
the fall of the dew;
For I would we were changed to white birds on the
wandering foam:  I and you!
I am haunted by numberless islands, and many a
Danaan shore,
Where Time would surely forget us, and Sorrow come
near us no more;
--More--(82%)[Press space to continue, 'q' to quit.]
```

This is clumsy, but it works. I'll search the **weather.src** server to see if I can get today's weather forecast as an example. To do so, I enter the following command at my system's command prompt:

```
% waissearch -h quake.think.com -d weather weather
```

Note the form this request takes. I've specified the **quake.think.com** site for my search. I haven't entered a port number, because **waissearch** will default to port 210, which is standard for **WAIS** servers. I've entered **-d weather** to name my database (I can leave off the **.src** suffix and **waissearch** will understand). I've followed the database name with my search word, which is itself **weather**.

The response comes through quickly; here's a sample:

```
Search Response:
  NumberOfRecordsReturned: 40
   1: Score: 1000, lines: 473 'WX-TALK.INFO'
   2: Score:  885, lines:  39 'weather.help'
   3: Score:  500, lines: 335 'Interior-British-Columbia.txt'
   4: Score:  346, lines: 137 'US-National-Summary.txt'
   5: Score:  308, lines:  31 'Atlanta-GA.txt'
   6: Score:  308, lines: 125 'Austin-TX.txt'
   7: Score:  308, lines:  34 'Baltimore-MD.txt'
   8: Score:  308, lines:  31 'Boston-MA.txt'
   9: Score:  308, lines:  44 'Charlotte-NC.txt'
  10: Score:  308, lines:  40 'Chicago-IL.txt'
  11: Score:  308, lines:  34 'Cincinnati-OH.txt'
  12: Score:  308, lines:  32 'Cleveland-OH.txt'
  13: Score:  308, lines: 160 'Coastal-British-Columbia.txt'
  14: Score:  308, lines:  65 'Detroit-MI.txt'
```

```
15: Score:  308, lines: 125 'Houston-TX.txt'
16: Score:  308, lines:  32 'Knoxville-TN.txt'
```

waissearch lets me choose which forecast I want by selecting its number and then pressing the **RETURN** key. I choose item 4, which seems to be a summary of weather across the United States. The message scrolls across my screen, as shown in Figure 5.13, which is only part of the lengthy forecast.

Hint:

waissearch can be helpful if you have a specific site you'd like to query and want to go right to it, without going through the rigamarole of dealing with a directory of servers first. But be sure to turn on your capture buffer when you're dealing with this program, or the results of your search may scroll past you before you know it.

INTERESTING WAIS SITES

I wouldn't even try to give you a comprehensive list of **WAIS** servers in this book. The medium is changing so fast that any such listing becomes obsolete almost immediately. If you do want to see a list of currently available sources, the best procedure is to download server site information in a text file from the address given earlier, or to study it online.

Figure 5.13
Checking the weather
with the help of **WAIS**.

```
NATIONAL WEATHER SUMMARY
NATIONAL WEATHER SERVICE KANSAS CITY MO
800 PM CST SAT JAN 29 1994



SNOW ASSOCIATED WITH THE MOST RECENT SURGE OF ARCTIC AIR INTO THE
NORTH CENTRAL U.S. HAS BEEN FALLING HEAVILY OVER PARTS OF WYOMING
AND WESTERN SOUTH DAKOTA SINCE LAST NIGHT.

SIX TO EIGHT INCHES OF NEW SNOW HAD BLANKETED THE LEAD AND
DEADWOOD AREA IN THE BLACK HILLS OF WESTERN SOUTH DAKOTA BY LATE
THIS AFTERNOON.  THE TOWN OF STURGIS HAD RECEIVED FIVE INCHES.
A WINTER STORM WARNING REMAINS IN EFFECT THE REST OF THE EVENING
FOR NORTHERN SECTIONS OF BLACK HILLS AREA.

MORE THAN A FOOT AND A HALF OF SNOW BLANKETED SOME PARTS OF THE
BIG HORN MOUNTAIN RANGE OF NORTHERN WYOMING LAST NIGHT AND TODAY.
A WINTER STORM WARNING CONTINUES IN EFFECT THROUGH TONIGHT FOR
THE BIG HORN MOUNTAINS AND WEST CENTRAL SECTIONS OF WYOMING.

A SNOW ADVISORY IS IN EFFECT TONIGHT FOR PARTS OF CENTRAL AND
NORTHEASTERN WYOMING.  AN ADVISORY FOR SNOW AND BLOWING SNOW
```

Certain **WAIS** servers are, however, of more than passing interest to the generalist. I found myself building a list of servers that I regularly consulted, because although it is possible to search a directory of servers, many of my own searches wound up being run on servers that I stumbled upon by chance. And as my list grew, I realized that tailoring such a list for my own use was a good idea. If you become an active **WAIS** searcher, I would advise you to maintain a list of sites that particularly meet your own needs, or pique your interest. Be sure to keep your list updated! To get you started, the following are some sites that have proven useful to me.

acronyms.src

A database of acronyms and abbreviations.

alt.wais.src

News from the **alt.wais** newsgroup. A handy way to check the archives of an active USENET newsgroup dealing with **WAIS**.

anu-socsci-netlore.src

This server is a good one to know about. It contains information about network resources of particular interest to academic researchers in the social sciences, arts, and humanities. New material is added every two weeks.

bit.listserv.pacs-l.src

The archives of the PACS-L list established by the University Libraries and the Information Technology Division of the University of Houston. PACS-L deals with computer systems in libraries, including CD-ROM databases, computer-assisted instruction, expert systems, hypermedia programs, library microcomputer facilities, locally mounted databases, on-line catalogs, and remote end-user search systems.

bryn-mawr-classical-review.src

Archives of the *Bryn Mawr Classical Review.*

cica-win3.src

Provides an index to the Microsoft Windows archive at the Center for Innovative Computing Applications (**ftp.cica.indiana.edu**), which contains thousands of Windows programs.

cicnet-directory-of-servers.src

A directory of servers at CICNet—The Committee on Institutional Cooperation Network in Ann Arbor, MI. This site contains a mirror of the **quake.think.com** directory of servers, and also information about servers at CICnet and elsewhere.

cnidr-directory-of-servers.src

A Directory of Servers is operated by CNIDR—The Clearinghouse for Networked Information Discovery and Retrieval.

college-email.src

Information on finding e-mail addresses for university students.

com-priv.src

Contains the **com-priv** mailing list archive. Updated nightly. **com-priv** discusses issues related to the commercialization and privatization of the Internet.

comp.archives.src

Archives of the **comp.archives** newsgroup.

comp.internet.library.src

An index for the newsgroup **comp.internet.library**, which focuses on issues involving the computerization of library resources.

comp.risks.src

Archives of the **comp.risks** newsgroup, discussing issues related to computer security and the impact of technology on society.

cool-directory-of-servers.src

A top level directory for Conservation OnLine (COOL), a collection of **WAIS** databases containing information on the conservation of library, archives, and museum materials. Users should query the **cool-directory-of-servers.src** to determine which COOL database will best meet their needs. To see a list of all the COOL databases, use the word "source" as your search term. New databases will be added to COOL so it will be a good idea to search this server regularly.

cs-journal-titles.src

Contains an index of article titles and authors from some 600 journals, books, and other publications relating to computing.

current.cites.src

Current Cites is a monthly publication of the Library Technology Watch Program—The Library, University of California at Berkeley. Over 30 journals in librarianship and computer technology are scanned for selected articles on electronic publishing, optical disk technologies, computer networks and networking, information transfer, expert systems and artificial intelligence, and hypermedia and multimedia. Brief annotations accompany most of the citations.

cwis_list.src

Judy Hallman's list of **Campus Wide Information Systems (CWIS)**.

disco-mm-zenon-inria-fr.src

A database of compact discs, containing ASCII text descriptions and graphics files of their covers, along with audio sampler files.

educom.src

EDUCOM documents, including archives, project updates, summaries, and a calendar of events.

eff-documents.src

Documents from the Electronic Frontier Foundation, including the EFF newsletter. This site mirrors the EFF ftp archives at **ftp.eff.org**.

elec_journ_newslett.src

Information on electronic journals, a fast growing area of Internet development.

ftp-list.src

A list of anonymous FTP sites.

fyis.src

The For Your Information documents (a subset of RFCs that provides general background information about Internet topics).

homebrew.src

Indexed archives of the BITNET homebrew mailing list and the **rec.crafts.-homebrew** newsgroup from USENET. Files date from 1989, and are reindexed weekly.

hst-weekly-summary.src

Weekly summary of Hubble Space Telescope (HST) completed observations.

hytelnet.src

All the information that is stored in the **HYTELNET** package by Peter Scott, of the University of Saskatchewan. This includes library OPACs, BBSes, CWISs, and any other TELNET accessible sites.

inet-libraries.src

Internet access to library catalogs is the subject, with information from a variety of directories and lists.

info-mac.src

Information from the **info-mac** newsgroup from USENET.

internet_info.src

Introductory material and guides for using the Internet.

internet-mail.src

Contains Scott Yanoff's internetwork mail guide, which provides information on addressing e-mail to networks connecting to the Internet.

internet_services.src

Various documents describing services available on the internet. Includes Billy Barron's list of Internet Databases, a list of Internet mailservers, The Internet Resources Guide, and "Not Just Cows—A Guide to Internet/Bitnet Resources in Agriculture and Related Sciences."

internet-user-glossary.src

Based on the FYI document called the Internet Users' Glossary, this server includes basic terms and acronyms you'll encounter around the network. Produced by the User Glossary Working Group of the User Services Area of the Internet Engineering Task Force, which is itself known by its acronym: IETF.

internic-whois.src

A **WAIS** implementation of the **whois** database on **rs.internic.net**. **whois** is composed of root level domains, networks, DNS servers, autonomous system numbers, organizations, and points of contact for the domains, networks, servers, and autonomous system numbers. Updated daily from the **whois** database maintained at **rs.internic.net** by InterNIC Registration Services.

isoc.src

Documents from the Internet Society.

journalism.periodicals.src

A **WAIS**-accessible version of the Journalism Periodicals Index, made available at no charge as an experiment by the Graduate School of Journalism at The University of Western Ontario. The Index to Journalism Periodicals is a cross-referenced subject index produced on microfiche. It contains more than 10,000 citations to articles from about 40 trade, professional, and academic journals related to journalism and mass communication. Most of the titles indexed are from Canada or the U.S.A., but some international journals are also indexed. References cover subjects such as business aspects of the media, ethics, freedom of information, government regulation, labor relations, medicine coverage, technology, and women in the media. Practical topics such as editing, investigative reporting, photo-journalism and reporting are also included.

lawrence-obrien-interview.src

I include this one as a demonstration of what **WAIS** can do. This server provides a focused look at former Democratic Party leader Lawrence O'Brien, with much information about his work in the Johnson and Kennedy administrations. We can envision future databases, equally focused, containing the memoirs of people in the news, a wonderful resource for scholarship.

macintosh-news.src

Publications of interest to Macintosh users. Includes the **info-mac** digest (**info-mac@sumex-aim.stanford.edu**), Michael Kelly's **comp.sys.mac.programmer** digest, and Adam Engst's TidBITS, an electronic magazine for the Macintosh.

mailing-lists.src

Listings of Internet and BITNET mailing lists, along with electronic serials and journals and USENET newsgroups.

matrix_news.src

Articles, columns, and more from *Matrix News,* a monthly electronic newsletter on networking.

midwest-weather.src

National Weather Service forecasts for the states of Michigan, Ohio, Indiana, Illinois, Wisconsin, Iowa, and Minnesota. Updated hourly from the **Gopher** weather server at the University of Minnesota.

movie-lists.src

Contains the latest releases of the USENET **rec.arts.movies** lists. The lists provide current references to TV and film credits. Includes lists of actors, actresses, cinematographers, composers, directors and writers.

nafta.src

The full text of the North American Free Trade Agreement, which eliminates most restrictions on trade, export, and import among the North American countries of Canada, the United States, and Mexico.

network-bibliography.src

Network-related bibliographies, including: Computer Networking Bibliography, Libraries and Information Resources, and the Networks bibliography compiled by Deidre E. Stanton.

news.answers-faqs.src

Contains all Frequently Asked Questions (FAQs) from the Usenet newsgroup **news.answers**. It is updated daily.

omni-cultural-academic-resource.src

Internationally oriented materials drawn from a variety of sources including databases and newsgroups.

online@uunet.ca.src

If you search on-line databases like DIALOG or Dow Jones News/Retrieval, you'll find much of interest here. This is a compilation of material from a mailing list that focuses on information brokering.

poetry.src

The intention of this server, its compilers say, is to collect as many poems as possible. Contains the complete poems of Shakespeare and Yeats, as well as a smattering of other poets.

proj-gutenberg.src

Mirrors the documents produced by Project Gutenberg. The documents themselves are at **mrcnext.cso.uiuc.edu:etext/***. The purpose of Project Gutenberg is to encourage the creation and distribution of English language electronic texts.

rec.gardens.src

Articles from the USENET newsgroup **rec.gardens**.

rfcs.src

Contains the Internet Request for Comments documents. Very handy for those in need of technical information.

roget-thesaurus.src

An on-line version of *Roget's Thesaurus*, provided by Project Gutenberg. This database is also available in the **Gopher** at **gopher.micro.umn.edu**, and for anonymous FTP from **mrcnext.cso.uiuc.edu**. The directory is *pub/etext*.

sample-books.src

Various on-line electronic texts.

sf-reviews.src

An archive of the USENET newsgroup **rec.arts.sf.reviews**, which is a forum for reviews of works of interest to fans of science fiction, as well as related genres like fantasy and horror.

smithsonian-pictures.src

Image files produced by the Smithsonian Institution's Office of Printing & Photographic Services, made available through a grant from the Apple Library of Tomorrow Program. These images cover topics ranging from air and space to science, technology, history, and current events. Photographs from Smithsonian museums on the Mall in Washington, D.C., plus other Smithsonian bureaus such as the National Zoo and the Smithsonian Astrophysical Observatory.

sunsite-ftp.src

An index of all the index and "readme" files in the anonymous FTP directory of Sunsite at the University of North Carolina in Chapel Hill.

us-congress-phone-fax.src

Telephone and fax numbers for members of the U.S. Senate and House of Representatives.

us-state-department-travel-advisories.src

The U.S. State Department Counsular Information Sheets and Travel Warnings. This can be a handy server to know about, and you can couple it with the CIA

World Factbook server discussed below to obtain an overview of a particular country for travel purposes.

usenet-addresses.src

One-line entries consisting of names and e-mail addresses culled from the **Reply To** or **From** lines of USENET postings, as well as a last-seen date associated with each address.

usenet-cookbook.src

The USENET Cookbook (Copyright 1991 USENET Community Trust).

usenet.src

Periodic informational postings (including FAQ postings) from various USENET newsgroups. Contains all entries that are cross-posted to ***.answers** newsgroups, as well as all postings (except those in **comp.mail.maps**) included in the "List of Periodic Informational Postings," which appears monthly in **news.announce.newusers**.

wais-discussion-archives.src

Access to the **wais-discussion** mailing list's archives.

wais-docs.src

Contains the text of all the current documentation for **WAIS**.

weather.src

A weather information server. Search for weather, and you will get the day's satellite weather maps. You can also retrieve textual weather forecasts.

world-factbook93.src

The CIA World Factbook 1993; this document has been slightly modified (table of contents removed, dashed lines placed between countries, etc.) from Project Gutenberg.

zipcodes.src

A **WAIS** index of U.S.A. Zip Code database.

KEEPING UP WITH WAIS

Like most moving targets, **WAIS** can be tracked through a USENET newsgroup. Its name is **comp.infosystems.wais**. This newsgroup's Frequently Asked Questions document is valuable, and can be downloaded by anonymous FTP from the following address:

```
rtfm.mit.edu
```

The directory is *pub/usenet/news-answers/wais.faq*. The file is **getting-started**.

And there is a mailing list called **wais-discussion** regarding **WAIS** and related issues. To subscribe, send e-mail to **wais-discussion-request@think.com** asking to be added to the list (your message might read **subscribe** *your_name* **wais-discussion**). That's all that's necessary.

Finally, if you want the latest on commercial **WAIS** client and server software, contact WAIS Inc. The address is:

WAIS Inc.
1040 Noel Drive
Menlo Park, CA 94025
415-327-WAIS
415-327-6513 (fax)

For information on freely available **WAIS** implementations, contact the Clearinghouse for Networked Information Discovery and Retrieval (CNIDR) at **info@cdnir.org**. Chapter 10 of this book focuses on the work of CNIDR.

6

World Wide Web: Hypertext As Browsing Tool

Most searching proceeds in a linear fashion. There is a particular path to follow, starting with entering a request for information or making a choice from a menu. The steps you take during the search are defined by the program you interact with, which uses its own protocols to consult one or more databases of information. Sometimes this information is local, that is, available on the computer you're using to search; and sometimes it's broadly distributed throughout the Internet, so that your search program moves from one location to another in its work. Whatever the case, the search has its own logic, and you learn to work within parameters laid down by the programmers who originally developed the tools you are using.

Hypertext and hypermedia are ways to transcend at least some of these limitations. Using them, you move through a set of structured information—not sequentially, but by making jumps between the various kinds of data you need. Rather than being forced to choose between gradually narrowing choices on fixed screens of menus, you have the ability to move between items that have been linked to each other by the person who set up the hyper connections. If that person did a good job, then your information hunt proceeds more quickly and certainly more intuitively than it would using many other search tools. If the hyper links are less than optimum, then your browsing runs into the same frustrations inherent in any browsing process: No one can anticipate every possible link; and search methods, while ingenious, are limited by the vision of those who construct the tools.

THE NATURE OF HYPERTEXT

Despite its information-age pedigree, hypertext as an information retrieval model has a long history. The index of any book is, in a sense, a hypertext tool, just as a judicious footnote pointing to further information on the bottom of the page or in the endnotes is a way of linking one set of data to another, which you can pursue at your discretion. The idea is simple: One set of ideas may be closely related to others. If we can find a way to show these associations within the document, and make it possible for the reader, or user of information, to move between them, then we have expanded the intellectual process by making knowledge more available. This is the intention of the project known as the **World Wide Web**, which we examine here. Chapter 7 will look at another hypertext project called **HYTELNET**.

What the computer does is hardly revolutionary—Chesterton would have understood hypertext in seconds, and doubtless produced an aphorism about it. But computer power makes it easier to access hypertextual information. Rather than noting a footnote number following a sentence, then checking the back of the book for the right reference, you are able to press a key at the marked place and instantly retrieve the linked data. And instead of setting up a single link, it's possible to create a document with numerous connections, each of which opens to other documents containing numerous connections, so that reading this material now loses its sequential nature entirely and becomes a pursuit of ideas through a forest of data.

You will understand hypertext if you realize that there is no single way to read a hypertext document. Open a textbook on physics and you read text, refer to illustrations and equations, and consult notes at the end of the chapter. Read through a hypertext book on physics and your route will be determined largely by what you need to know. Perhaps I have a weakness in understanding inertia. My reading through the relevant section would have me examining background information, choosing links that pointed to the basic concepts. Your reading might involve a hunt through the same textbook's links to mass. In an ideal world, even though we would both be using the same textbook, we would be optimizing our separate learning experiences.

The proponents of hypertext believe it is a new medium, one that transcends the limitations of standard printed books and opens up information in ways suited to the individual learner. Let's examine hypertext as it's available over the Internet now, to see how truly these ideals are realized. After all, there is no better example of unstructured information than the Internet itself.

THE WEB'S RESOURCES

The **World Wide Web** is the outstanding Internet implementation of hypertext, one that gains new adherents daily as information searchers discover its power. The **Web**'s project leaders like to refer to the **Web** as containing a "virtual library," an electronic Alexandria of information. The concept is visionary; certainly the translation of intellectual archives into digital form has hardly begun in many fields of knowledge. But browse through the list of topics available through the **Web** and I think you'll agree that it has made the data resources of the Internet available in a useful, structured way. Table 6.1 presents a consolidated list of offerings. The table is drawn from the **Web** itself, which allows you to search by subject as well as by server type and other criteria.

Table 6.1 The **World Wide Web**'s Information Holdings

The World-Wide **Web** Virtual Library: Subject Catalogue
THE WWW VIRTUAL LIBRARY

This is a distributed subject catalogue. See also arrangement by service type[1]., and other subject catalogues of network information[2].

Mail www-request@info.cern.ch to add pointers to this list, or if you would like to contibute to administration of a subject area.

Aeronautics	Mailing list archive index[3] . See also NASA LaRC[4]
Agriculture[5]	Separate list, see also Almanac mail servers[6] .
Archaeology	Classics and Mediterranean Archaeology[7]
Astronomy and Astrophysics[8]	Separate list.
Bio Sciences[9]	Separate list.
Computing[10]	Separate list.
Earth Science	US Geological Survey[11]. See also geography[12].
Economics	Newsgroups on economics[13] and research[14].
Education	See the Education Policy Analysis Archives[15] (EPAA), an analysis of education policy at all levels; ANU educational materials[16]; Esperanto HyperCourse[17]; the Department of Education[18] of the Universitat Jaume I (Castello, Spain), Computational Phonology[19]. The "English Server" Languages and Linguistics [20].
Engineering[21]	Separate list.
Environment	HOLIT[22] (Israel Ecological & Environmental Information System), ANU biodiversity services[23], FireNet[24], Hurricane and other disasters preparation[25], The Purdue - ES-USDA Water Quality[26] Information Management Project, the Australian Environmental Resources Information Network[27].
Finance	Financial Executive Journal[28].
Fortune-telling	Tarot Cards[29], I-Ching[30], Biorhythm[31].
Geography	World maps[32]. CIA World Fact Book[33], India: Miscellaneous information[34], Thai-Yunnan: Davis collection[35], ANU landscape ecology services[36], Manual of Federal Geographic Data Products[37], SUNY/Buffalo[38] list of resources; the University of North Carolina Institute for Transportation Research and Education[39].

(continued)

Table 6.1 The **World Wide Web**'s Information Holdings *(continued)*

History[40]	Separate list. See also Literature & Art[41], Newsgroup, soc.history[42].
Languages	Some Esperanto information[43]; Computational Phonology[44].
Law[45]	US Copyright law[46], Uniform Commercial Code[47], etc., NASDAQ Finance Executive Journal[48]; the "English Server" Judiciary[49].
Libraries[50]	Lists of online catalogues etc.
Literature & Art[51]	Separate list.
Mathematics[52]	Separate list.
Meteorology	US weather[53], state by state. Satelite Images [54]. Weather index[55]. ANU weather services[56].
Movies	Movie database browser[57], the "English Server" Film and Television[58].
Music	MIDI interfacing[59], Song lyrics[60] (apparently disabled for copyright reasons), UK Independant Music[61], The "English Server" Music[62].
Philosophy	Americal Philosophical Association[63]; the "English Server" Philosophy[64].
Psychology	"Psycoloquy[65]" electronic journal. Yale Psychology[66].
Physics	See High Energy Physics[67], Space Science[68], astrophysics[69], Complex systems[70], Univ. of Washington Nuclear Physics Laboratory[71], LANL Physics Information Service[72] (primarily devoted to electronic preprints); Physics Departments[73]
Politics and Economics	US politics[74], report of the National Performance Review[75] (aka Reinventing Government). Economics Working Papers[76] (NetEc provides bibliographic information & links to PostScript papers). The Queer Resources Directory[77]; White House[78] Files; the "English Server" Economics[79].
Recipes	The Recipes Folder[80].
Reference	Roget's Thesaurus[81]. English and technical dictionary[82]. Experimental English dictionary[83]; the "English Server" Reference[84].
Religion	The Bible[85] (King James version), The Book of Mormon[86], The Holy Qur'an[87], Dead Sea Scrolls[88] (part of EXPO[89]); Catholic source documents[90]
	Working Papers[76] (NetEc provides bibliographic information & links to PostScript papers). The Queer Resources Directory[77]; White House[78] Files; the "English Server" Economics[79].
Social Sciences	Coombs papers archive[91]. Journals of the scholarly communications project[92]. Nursing[93] Information System. The Queer Resources Directory[94]. The "English Server" Government, Law and Politics[95].

Other virtual libraries[96]
1-96, Back, Up, Quit, or Help:

The information available here can be viewed through various filters, for the **Web** makes it possible not only to read connected documents, but to tap resources like **Gopher** and **WAIS**. In fact, the first menu you see when you log on to the **Web** presents a basic choice: You can choose to search for information *by subject* (the list that results is shown in Table 6.1), or you can search *by type*. Types include **World Wide Web** servers, **WAIS** servers, USENET network news, **Gopher**, Telnet, anonymous FTP, X.500, **WHOIS**, and the TechInfo system from MIT. But the **Web** can also house other forms of data. Expect additional references to make their way on-line, including expanded **Web** access to **archie**, on-line journals, library systems, mailing lists, the UNIX manual pages and a host of other information.

Realize, too, that when you access **World Wide Web**, your hypertext jumps move not only between documents but between server sites. Although the interface suggests that you have reached a single repository of information which you are now exploring, in fact you are tapping a worldwide system of linked data whose connections have been rendered transparent to the user. Perhaps there is a server in London that could be useful to you. You could always reach it by a direct Telnet connection, but by using the **Web** instead, you can read the necessary document without ever realizing the underlying connection has been made. Making the retrieval process intuitive, then, includes doing the busy work for you behind the scenes, a job at which the **Web** excels.

ACCESSING THE WORLD WIDE WEB

There are three ways to gain access to the **World Wide Web**.

- Use Telnet to connect to a server. A list of public **World Wide Web** servers is provided in Table 6.2.

- Use a local client program. In **World Wide Web** parlance, these programs are known as *browsers*, and as with many other Internet search tools, a wide variety of clients are available.
- Use a graphical user interface like NCSA's **Mosaic** on your desktop computer. This requires, at minimum, a SLIP connection to work.

Table 6.2 World Wide Web Servers Available by Telnet

Server Address	Location	Country
fatty.law.cornell.edu	Legal Information Institute, Cornell Law School, Ithaca, NY	USA
fserv.kfki.hu	KFKI Computer Network Center, Budapest	Hungary
info.cern.ch	CERN (European Laboratory for Particle Physics)	Switzerland
info.funet.fi	Finnish University and Research Network FUNET	Finland
sun.uakom.cs	Institute of Automation and Communication, Banska Bystrica	Slovakia
ukanaix.cc.ukans.edu	University of Kansas, Lawrence	USA
vms.huji.ac.il	Hebrew University of Jerusalem	Israel
www.njit.edu	New Jersey Institute of Technology	USA

If you are asked for a login name at any of these sites, enter **www**. Not all sites require a login.

EXPLORING THE WEB

There is no one correct way to find information on the **Web**. In fact, the nature of its hypertext links implies that there will be multiple paths to the same information. This is both a plus and a minus: a plus in that your explorations often uncover links to information you hadn't realized were available; a minus in that finding a specific item you need often requires working through several layers of linked information, when a more targeted search could call up your data more quickly. The **Web** is, above all, an exploration tool, a kind of interactive library you browse at your leisure and with an eye open to discoveries. Some search tools require an analytical frame of mind, some a knack for detail. The **Web** requires curiosity—and patience.

Reading a Document On-Line with the Web

The deeply interlinked nature of hypertext becomes apparent with a quick browse through a text file. In Figure 6.1, I have opened a hypertext document called "The Big Dummy's Guide to the Internet," published and made available on-line by the Electronic Freedom Foundation. The section I am reading involves electronic mail. And as you can see, various items are followed by numbers inside brackets. Each of these points to a hypertext link.

I might, for example, enter a number **8** to reach the section called *E-Mail to other Networks*. Doing so produces the screen shown in Figure 6.2.

The result is another page of linkages, allowing me to choose the kind of system I want to move mail between. I choose number 25 to find out how to send mail to GEnie. Figure 6.3 shows the result. The hypertext link has taken

Figure 6.1
Examining a text file through **World Wide Web**.

```
                          Big Dummy's Guide to the Internet - Electronic Mail
          Go to the previous[1], next[2] chapter.

                          ELECTRONIC MAIL[3]

     ELM[4]: Hints on using ELM.

     PINE[5]: Hints on using PINE and PICO.

     Smileys[6]: Using emoticons to express yourself ;-)

     Seven UNIX Commands[7]: MS-DOS users can't live without.

     E-Mail to other Networks[8]: How to reach someone at...

     When things go wrong[9]: Some useful hints for the case of cases.

     E-Mail FYI[10]: Suggested further reading.

     Electronic mail, or e-mail, is your personal connection to the world of the
     Net.

     Every one of the millions of people around the world who use the Net have
                Big Dummy's Guide to the Internet - Electronic Mail (707/865)
```

Figure 6.2
Moving deeper into
the **Web** by following
a link.

                                    Big Dummy's Guide to the Internet - Electronic Mail (638/865)
                    For example,

ls man?

        would find a file called mane, but not one called manual.

    E-Mail to other Networks[18]

            America Online[19]

            ATTMail[20]

            Bitnet[21]

            CompuServe[22]

            Delphi[23]

            Fidonet[24]

            GEnie[25]
    1-45, Back, Up, <RETURN> for more, Quit, or Help:

Figure 6.3
Learning how to send
e-mail to GEnie
addresses.

                            Big Dummy's Guide to the Internet - Electronic Mail (773/865)
                message to be delivered in either direction. Also, because many Fidonet
        systems are run as hobbies, it is considered good form to ask   the gateway
        sysop's permission if you intend to pass large amounts of mail back and
        forth. Messages of a commercial nature are strictly forbidden (even if it's
        something the other person asked for). Also, consider it very likely that
        somebody other than the recipient will read your messages.

    GENIE[35]

        To send mail to a GEnie user, add '@genie.geis.com' to the end of their
        GEnie user name, for example: <valt@genie.geis.com>.   Unlike users of
        other networks, however, GEnie users can receive mail from Internet only if
        they pay an extra monthly charge.

    MCIMAIL[36]

        To send mail to somebody with an MCIMail account, add   '@mcimail.com' to the
        end of their name or numerical address. For example:

    555-1212@mcimail.com

    1-45, Back, Up, <RETURN> for more, Quit, or Help:

me directly to that place in the text that addresses GEnie. No index, no squinting at footnotes, the information pops up by pressing a key.

In a nutshell, this is how hypertext works. One link leads you to another; you work your way through a document not sequentially, but by a series of leaps. Remember, though, the process is heavily dependent upon the links established by a human being using a hypertext editor. Usually the links this person creates are effective; sometimes they go awry. Look, for example, at what "The Big Dummy's Guide to the Internet" shows as its link to e-mail information about CompuServe:

```
COMPUSERVE[23]

    Our forum on CompuServe is also open. 'GO EFFSIG' to join. Many of the files
    on ftp.eff.org, as well as other items of interest, are mirrored in the
    EFFSIG Libraries.
```

Clearly, we have been taken to the wrong item, an oversight that may be fixed by the time you read this. The point is, we can't expect perfection from any cataloging method, and the number of such mistaken links is relatively small on the **Web**. And navigating is not difficult, especially with the help of a software interface called a *browser*.

Using a Local Client with the World Wide Web

A *browser* is simply a client program that helps you work with the **World Wide Web**. Its function is to display documents and to make the links between items of information available. You can then choose which links you'd like to follow as you pursue your course through the **Web**. Bear in mind that a browser must be a powerful tool; it is designed to tap into almost all the resources available on the Internet, from **Gopher** to **WAIS** to Telnet, from NNTP (the Internet news protocol) to file retrieval by FTP. In fact, the diverse nature of these links means we are not necessarily limited to text as we use **World Wide Web**. *Hypermedia* refers to linking resources that are not the same, such as text to audio, images to text, or text to data. Depending on the browser you use, you might be able to display, for example, images or sound along with standard text files.

Why are these interfaces called browsers? Because the nature of working with the **World Wide Web** (**W3** as it's known to its friends) precludes your considering it a static information medium. Any movement through it involves making judgment calls about the kind of information you need. By necessity, your path through a series of data linkages is a kind of exploration; you don't always know where you will wind up. The concept of browsing, then, makes sense. A good browser program will enhance your **Web** explorations by making it easy to examine resources and move from link to link.

Many browsers are available on the Internet for a wide variety of platforms; the programs exist both in source code and in executable form. A direct TCP/IP connection to the Internet, or dial-up account with SLIP or PPP, makes browsers available that display graphics, typefaces, and complex page formats along with the basic text. Browsers like these, created for the Macintosh, Microsoft Windows, the X Window System and others, are becoming more powerful thanks to the rapid strides in the development of Internet search tools at places like CNIDR; they point to a future rich in audio and video links from or to text documents. Later in this chapter we will examine a graphical interface to the **World Wide Web**.

Dial-up users, however, can't use such tools unless they're using a SLIP or PPP connection. A regular dial-up connection through a modem session with an Internet service provider requires you to use a character-based browser.

We'll be looking at the simplest browser, a character-based tool called **www**, available to anyone using VT-100 emulation, and hence the one most likely to be used by people accessing the Internet via modem. **lynx**, a full-screen browser for VT-100 terminals that uses highlighting and other features, is also available to dial-up users, as is the browser from the New Jersey Institute of Technology. (We'll look at both **lynx** and the NJIT browser in our discussion of using Telnet to access the **Web**.) Although a graphical interface is the optimal way to go, the character-based browser described in this section is powerful and should be considered a full-fledged browsing tool. We will focus on one called **www**.

To determine whether **www** is available on your system, type **www** at the prompt. If the browser isn't available from your service provider, you'll see something like the following:

```
www: Command not found.
```

If you do not have a local **Web** browser, you'll need to use a **Web** browser through a Telnet connection, as demonstrated later in this chapter. However, most of the resources available over the **Web** will still be accessible to you. If you Telnet to **info.cern.ch** to get in, you'll find the same browser available that is discussed in the following material. No password or login is required.

If the browser is available, you'll see a screen like the one shown in Figure 6.4. Examine this screen with care. You're looking at the browser's *home page*,

Figure 6.4
Using the home page at **info.cern.ch**.

```
                                                      Overview of the Web
                          GENERAL OVERVIEW OF THE WEB

      There is no "top" to the World-Wide Web. You can look at it from many points
      of view. Here are some places to start.

      by Subject[1]          The Virtual Library organises information by subject
                             matter.

      List of servers[2]     All registered HTTP servers by country

      by Service Type[3]     The Web includes data accessible by many other
                             protocols. The lists by access protocol may help if
                             you know what kind of service you are looking for.

      If you find a useful starting point for you personally, you can configure
      your WWW browser to start there by default.

      See also: About the W3 project[4] .
        [End]




      1-4, Back, Up. Quit, or Help:
```

the basic entry point into the **Web**. The beauty of the **World Wide Web** is that it is entirely self-referential, and easy to use because it talks you through the browsing process. Notice that the first four items of information—*by Subject*, *List of servers*, *by Service Type*, and *About the W3 project*—all are followed by numbers in brackets. These numbers reveal the presence of hypertext links. Therefore, all that's needed to examine that link is to enter the number, followed by a **RETURN**.

Thus, we look at choice 2, *List of Servers*. The link takes us to a list of **World Wide Web** servers along with their location. The number of such machines has been growing rapidly, with servers devoted to special projects and other, more general information sources being made available through the technology. You can access a server at the Principia Cybernetica Project in Brussels, which declares its intent to organize all human knowledge in a universal framework. Or tap an Irish literary archive in Dublin, or a database rich with linkages about music at Nottingham University in the United Kingdom, not to mention abundant information on physics, biology, chemistry, and the other sciences. The InterNIC, too, maintains a server stuffed with Internet-related data.

Figure 6.5 shows a small section of the servers available in the United States. As you can see from the link numbers following each, this alphabetical list is preceded by a long list of servers in many other countries. This is also revealed by the number in the upper right corner: **444/939**. This means that we are examining a 939-line document, and that we have reached line 444.

The basic method remains the same: Each entry is followed by a number in brackets. Choose the number, and you move to the server in question. In Figure 6.6, I have entered the number **141** and followed it with a **RETURN** to move to the library server at Berkeley. **World Wide Web** has taken me directly to the server, which I can now explore with the same methods.

Figure 6.5
A page of **Web** servers in the United States.

```
                                          World-Wide Web Servers (444/939)
    Arizona

   CCIT Arizona[138]      University of Arizona information

   NOAO[139]              National Optical Astronomy Observatories
                          (experimental in sep 93)

    California

   BSDI[140]              Berkeley Software Design Incorporated.

   Berkeley               Library server [141]including "Current Cites"
                          journal. See also the Museum of Paleontology[142] :
                          currently contains an exhibit of pictures from a shark
                          research project.

   Caltech high energy theoretical physics group[143]
                          under construction in oct 93

   Digital Equipment Corporation
                          Product information[144] -- technical overviews,
                          performance summaries, software product descriptions
   1-276, Back, Up, <RETURN> for more, Quit, or Help:
```

Figure 6.6
Moving directly to the
Web server at Berkeley.

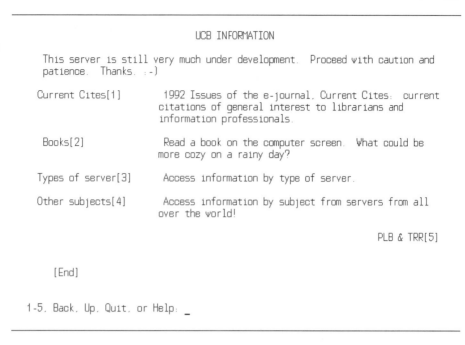

```
                              UCB INFORMATION

   This server is still very much under development.  Proceed with caution and
   patience.  Thanks.  :-)

   Current Cites[1]           1992 Issues of the e-journal, Current Cites:  current
                              citations of general interest to librarians and
                              information professionals.

   Books[2]                   Read a book on the computer screen.  What could be
                              more cozy on a rainy day?

   Types of server[3]         Access information by type of server.

   Other subjects[4]          Access information by subject from servers from all
                              over the world!

                                                                  PLB & TRR[5]


       [End]


   1-5, Back, Up, Quit, or Help: _
```

World Wide Web Terminology

As Internet browsing tools go, the premise of the **World Wide Web** is not particularly difficult to understand. This is unexpected, given its background as a tool for physicists, who needed some way to examine resources at the European Laboratory for Particle Physics (CERN) in Geneva, Switzerland. As we'll see later, a major Telnet address for the **Web** is **info.cern.ch**, the site of the original **Web** project, and a locus of continuing development. In fact, if you prowl through the list of available **Web** connections discussed previously, you'll find the following:

```
WorldWideWeb support[97]
                      information about W3 itself,  CERN entry point, and
                  Web overviews.
```

Scouting through the information here is an excellent way to learn more about the **Web**. Accessing it from this particular page, as you can see, simply involves entering the correct number: **97**. But there are many ways to reach any **Web** destination, as the following discussion will make clear.

Remember that the **Web** links to documents—which can actually be many different kinds of resources—and links between those documents. A **Web** cruise is, therefore, a process of following from one "document" to another, link by link, the exact route being chosen by you as you determine what is relevant and what isn't. The fact that the **Web** can access so many different kinds of information in so many places means, naturally, that it must have some way of linking its data.

This is where *Uniform Resource Locators*, or URLs, come in. A URL is a way of specifying where something is on the Internet. Anything available over the Internet can be described with a URL, which shows you not only the kind of resource that is involved, but also the address of that resource. Following, for example, is a listing of URLs, showing a variety of Internet objects including files and Telnet addresses:

```
[371]  http://www.ucla.edu/htbin/finger?buckmr@rpi.edu
[372]  file://ftp.nevada.edu/
[373]  file://ftp.uwp.edu/pub/music
[374]  file:ftp.iastate.edu/pub/lyrics
[375]  gopher://gopher.cic.net/
[376]  http://www.ucla.edu/htbin/finger?nichol@stavanger.sgp.slb.com
```

Let's examine this list. The information to the left is the link number for the item on the **World Wide Web**. Following this is the type of resource we're examining. Item 371 uses the unfamiliar **http** designation, which stands for a hypertext document (**http** refers to *HyperText Transport Protocol*, which is what the **Web** functions with). In this case, the **Web** is taking us to the address **www.ucla.edu**, from which we use a **finger** server to draw information from the site **buckmr@rpi.edu**. You'll notice yet another resource, **Gopher**, in the above list, in this case the **Gopher** server at **gopher.cic.net**.

Not only does the **Web** possess a broad reach, it also hides the complexities of these operations from you. You can generate a list of Uniform Resource Locators from any screen on the **Web**, simply by entering the command **list** (and this, of course, is how I generated the list above). But there is no reason for you to do so unless you're curious.

Creating hypermedia is no trivial matter. The links between information must be chosen with care, and the skills of the person making these critical choices will determine how useful a given hypertext document will be. The *Hypertext Markup Language*, or HTML, is used to produce documents in this format, using a hypertext or plain text editor that encodes the links to other documents. The result is a potpourri of hypertext materials in varying degrees of usefulness. Some are linked sparingly; you'd like to be able to follow up leads that aren't provided. Others contain a multiplicity of links to a wide range of data.

A Sampling of the Web's Reach

Let me illustrate how the **Web** reaches out to a diverse group of information sources. One of the most widely circulated, and certainly most appreciated, documents on the Internet is Scott Yanoff's "Special Internet Connections." The list, regularly updated and distributed through the USENET newsgroup **news.answers**, is a compilation of interesting Internet sites available through various means. The Yanoff list can be read sequentially, but the **Web** makes it available in a hypertext form that shows off the medium.

Examine Figure 6.7, and you'll see a screen showing some of the types of services available over the **Web**, and various destinations of interest within each. The Yanoff list is shown as item 14; entering a **14** calls it up.

Because the Yanoff list is packed with information, there are abundant hypertext links within it to the resources described. Figure 6.8 shows one screen

Figure 6.7
Finding Scott Yanoff's list
(item 14) with the **Web**.

```
                          Data sources classified by access protocol (37/48)
Network News[9]           Available directly in all www browsers. See also this
                          list of FAQs[10] .

Gopher[11]                Campus-wide information systems, etc. listed
                          geographically. See also: about Gopher[12] .

Telnet access[13]         Hypertext  catalogues by Peter Scott. See also: list
                          by Scott Yanoff[14] . Also, Art St George's index[15]
                          (yet to be hyperized) etc.

VAX/VMS HELP              Warning: this is no longer working with http 1.0 .
                          This is a known bug . Try it[16] ; Available using the
                          help gateway[17] to WWW.

Anonymous FTP[18]         Tom Czarnik's list of (almost) all sites. Search them
                          all with full hypertext archie gateways[19] (or telnet
                          to ARCHIE[20] )-- An index of almost everything
                          available by anonymous FTP.

TechInfo[21]              A CWIS system from MIT. Gateway access thanks to
                          Linda Murphy/Upenn. See also more about techinfo[22]

1-26, Back, Up, <RETURN> for more, Quit, or Help: _
```

from the list. I have paged well down into the document and have found some
items about music that have caught my interest. As you can see, each has its
own set of numbered links.

Figure 6.8
A screen from the Yanoff
list of resources.

```
                   Special Internet Connections: Last update 11/15/93 (1252/1778)
        finger buckmr@rpi.edu[371]

GUITAR CHORDS/TAB

     Tablature/Chords for guitar in /pub/guitar. Also at ftp.uu.net.

     ftp ftp.nevada.edu[372] [131.216.1.11]

LYRIC/MUSIC SERVER

     Lyrics, chords/tablature, and music pictures.

     ftp ftp.uwp.edu[373] in /pub/music

     ftp ftp.iastate.edu[374] in /pub/lyrics

MUSIC NEWSLETTER

     Reviews, interviews. (Body: SUBSCRIBE UPNEWS your full name)

     mail listserv@vm.marist.edu (internet)

1-481, Back, Up, <RETURN> for more, Quit, or Help:
```

Let me remind you of our list of URLs in the previous section. The items shown on it correspond to what Figure 6.5 shows; in other words, they represent the resources behind the hypertext links. The fourth URL on the list,

```
[373]   file://ftp.uwp.edu/pub/music
```

gives us the following information: The resource, a file, is reached through an FTP session; the address of same is **ftp.uwp.edu**, and the directory is *pub/music*. And if you examine the page from the Yanoff list, you'll see that this resource is a set of lyrics and information about tablature and chords, as well as musically related pictures. We also see from Yanoff's material that there is another site, **ftp.iastate.edu**, that contains similar material. Its link is numbered **374**, and the directory there is *pub/lyrics*.

Now remember this: The **Web** is a dynamic medium. The information it has just given us shows that there is a link between the hypertext list and the site in question. What happens if we enter the number, **373**, of the link? We engage in an FTP session with the site, as shown in Figure 6.9.

Here we see a listing of what is available in the directory, a set of files and subdirectories. Notice that each of these items is followed by a number, revealing a hypertextual link to the file or directory in question. Enter one of these numbers and you will be able to access the information, either by reading a text file or by seeing a list of the files available in a directory. As you can see, making the **Web** work involves creating better and better links to useful information.

Figure 6.9
An FTP session as run through the **Web**.

```
                                              FTP Directory of //ftp.uwp.edu/pub/music
                                         /PUB/MUSIC

            Up to Parent Directory[1]

                              folk[2]              .desc.pag[3]
            .cache[4]         classical[5]         guitar[6]
            misc[7]           CHANGES[8]            .desc.dir[9]
            releases[10]      lyrics[11]            info[12]
            database[13]      .cache+[14]           SITES[15]
            pictures[16]      sizes[17]             programs[18]
            faqs[19]          reviews[20]           lists[21]
            artists[22]       GOPHER.README[23]     midi[24]
            uap[25]           composition[26]       kurzweil[27]
            README.CORRUPT[28] contest[29]

               [End]

            1-29, Back, Up, Quit, or Help:
```

A Typical Search on the Web

No one journey through the **Web** is exactly like any other; I am reduced, therefore, to showing you examples of possible destinations. The following is a typical search, starting with a question and ending with more information than I realized was available, not an uncommon phenomenon when using the **Web**. After the search, I will illustrate some of the things you can find with determined browsing. You'll quickly find your own list of favorites, for the **Web** is anything but static, and the list changes constantly.

One of my favorite films of the past few years is *Local Hero*, the story of an oil company executive who is sent to Scotland in search of land for a new project his company wants to build. Along the way, he is subtly and charmingly changed by the people he meets at a small Scottish village. I recall that Burt Lancaster played a wonderful role as the oil company's CEO, but the rest of the cast escapes me, as does the name of the director. To remedy this, I turn to the **Web** by invoking the **www** command (again, if you don't have **www** on your system, a Telnet session to **info.cern.ch** will do).

The first task is to look for any resources involving the cinema. From the **Web**'s introductory screen, I look for the most appropriate choice and settle upon this one:

```
The Virtual Library[1]
                        A classification by information by subject. Includes
                        links to other known virtual libraries.
```

The list of information types generated by entering **1** at this prompt is the same one I showed you in Table 6.1. Paging through it, I come upon one that looks promising:

```
Movies                  Movie database browser[57] , the "English Server"
                        Film and Television[58].
```

Let's begin with **57**, a database browser, to see if we can locate *Local Hero*. Figure 6.10 shows the screen that results when I opt for this choice and follow the links to a database of movie information.

Entering the command **f local hero**, I pull up a solid bank of information, with hypertext links scattered throughout. Figure 6.11 shows the answers to many of my questions: The name of the film's star is Peter Riegert, who played the bemused Mac MacIntyre; much of the rest of the cast is listed as well. Burt Lancaster played oil industry tycoon Felix Happer.

If we press the **RETURN** key, as shown at the bottom of the screen, we will see the rest of the information. Included are the names of the people who made the film:

```
Directed by         Forsyth, Bill[17]

Music by            Knopfler, Mark[18]

Written by          Forsyth, Bill[19]

Cinematography by   Menges, Chris[20]
```

Figure 6.10
Finding a database of
movie information.

```
                                                                    Movie Info
                              TITLE SUBSTRINGS.

Enter a movie title or substring.

    Example, to search for movies with the word ``alien'' in their title,  type
    ``alien''.

    This will return details on several movies, including Aliens

    Note: if the title begins with A or The, leave it out. If you're determined
    to include it, then put  ', A' or ', The' at the end of the of the substring
    e.g.

        Enforcer, The

        Gauntlet, The

    Searching is case insensitive.

      Search.[1]  COMMA home.[2]  Fun & Games.[3]  Info.[4]


FIND <keywords>, 1-5, Back, Up, <RETURN> for more, or Help:
```

Figure 6.11
Results of a search for
"Local Hero."

```
                                                                    Movie Info
                              MOVIE DETAILS.

                              LOCAL HERO

          Review(s)..  [1]

    1983

        Cast                   Ammerman, Dan[2] ......Donaldson
                               Asante, Christopher[3] ......Reverend Macpherson
                               Black, Jennifer[4] ......Stella
                               Capaldi, Peter[5] ......Danny Oldsen
                               Chancer, Norman[6] ......Moritz
                               Fulton, Rikki[7] ......Geddes
                               Jackson, John[8] ......Cal
                               Jackson, John M.[9]  ......
                               Lancaster, Burt[10] ......Felix Happer
                               Lawson, Denis[11] ......Gordon Urquhart
                               MacKay, Fulton[12] ......Ben Knox
                               Norton, Alex[13] ......Watt
                               Riegert, Peter[14] ......Mac MacIntyre
                               Rozycki, Christopher[15] ......Victor
      1-39, Back, Up, <RETURN> for more, Quit, or Help:
```

Note that we have still more hypertext links. I could explore the films of Bill Forsyth, the brilliant Scottish director, by entering number **17** at the prompt. I would learn he also directed the low-budget but successful *Gregory's Girl*, among other films. As for star Peter Riegert, I could enter a **14** to learn about his other credits, such as the TV movie *Barbarians at the Gate*, where he played Peter Cohen, or the theatrical release *Crossing Delancey*, where he played Sam Posner. Because each of these items has its own links, I could call up information about his films as well.

But perhaps we'd like a review of *Local Hero*. The **Web** is obliging. Recall Figure 6.11: The first hypertext link on that screen was to a database of movie reviews. By following that link, I can generate the screen shown in Figure 6.12, paging through it with the **RETURN** key to read the entire text. This figure shows a review that originally appeared in one of the USENET newsgroups, and is now maintained in an archive with its own hypertext links, as we would find if we backed out of the document and examined the screens immediately before it:

```
USENET Review Archives[26]
USENET Review Archives Search[27]
```

Now the multiplicity of **Web** search paths becomes apparent; actually, we could have begun our search for a review here, opting for item **58** instead of **57** when originally presented with the choice:

```
Movies                    Movie database browser[57] , the "English Server"
                          Film and Television[58] .
```

Figure 6.12
Reading a review of "Local Hero" by following a hypertext link.

```
           fun/Movies/1992/Apr/LOCAL HERO  :  From: acbonin@amherst.edu (Adam B
From: acbonin@amherst.edu (Adam Bonin)
Subject: REVIEW: LOCAL HERO
Keywords: author=Bonin

                     LOCAL HERO
               A film review by Adam Bonin
                Copyright 1992 Adam Bonin

Written and directed by Bill Forsyth
Starring Peter Riegert, Burt Lancaster, Denis Lawson and Peter Capaldi.
MPAA Rating: PG

     Bill Forsyth's LOCAL HERO is one of the most "real" films I have
ever seen.  While it is fictional, the film's pacing and technical
aspects give it a sense of authenticity that one does not see in most
mainstream films.  What Forsyth is able to do in LOCAL HERO is create a
world that is only bent slightly from our own, a sort of "magical
realism", in a way that is much more credible than the typical
manipulative Hollywood fare.  But more than being realistic in its
characters and movements, it is extremely warm and entertaining as well,
providing the viewer with 110 minutes of pure cinematic pleasure.

Back, Up, <RETURN> for more, Quit, or Help:
```

This would have taken us directly to the review database. But of course, we didn't know that when we began. In any case, we found what we were after, even if we did take the long way around. You can see that searching the **Web** is often fruitful, just as it often takes a circuitous route.

A PANOPLY OF DIVERSE INFORMATION

The **World Wide Web** does not yet have its **Veronica**, the all-purpose search tool for **Gopher** that scours a database of collected resources to simplify the search process. The best word to describe the **Web** in its current form is "unwieldy," a gigantic bazaar of information, which is both fascinating and frustrating to use. Rather than making quick, targeted searches into the **Web**, you may find yourself drawn into extended sessions of exploration. Here, then, are some intriguing way stations along the search path. They are presented to hint at the **Web**'s richness.

The *I Ching*

In ancient times, people cast sticks upon the ground to provide the numerical references by which to query the *I Ching*, the Chinese book of prophecy. Like its counterpart in Delphi, the *I Ching* is an oracle of unusually cryptic language, one that requires reflection and, perhaps, the powers of the subconscious mind to untangle. The telecommunications age version of the *I Ching* is accessed via the Internet, as shown in Figure 6.13, where the **Web** is using a Telnet connection to bring you information.

I found this under the listing of information by subject on the **Web**'s home page, under a Fortune Telling category that also includes links to electronic Tarot

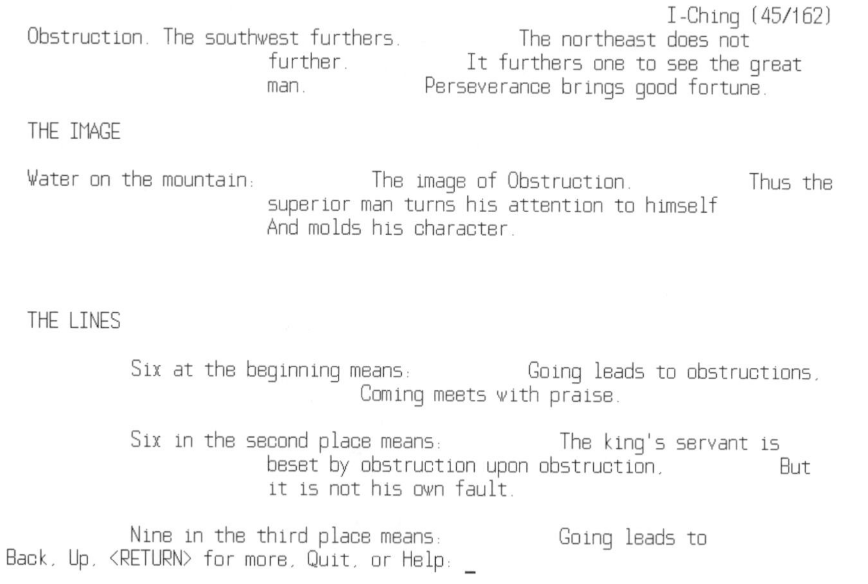

Figure 6.13
Running an electronic version of the *I Ching* through Telnet as mediated by the **Web**.

```
                                                              I-Ching (45/162)
Obstruction. The southwest furthers.          The northeast does not
                          further.          It furthers one to see the great
                          man.              Perseverance brings good fortune.

THE IMAGE

Water on the mountain:          The image of Obstruction.          Thus the
                        superior man turns his attention to himself
                        And molds his character.



    THE LINES

            Six at the beginning means:          Going leads to obstructions.
                          Coming meets with praise.

            Six in the second place means:          The king's servant is
                          beset by obstruction upon obstruction.          But
                          it is not his own fault.

            Nine in the third place means:          Going leads to
    Back, Up, <RETURN> for more, Quit, or Help: _
```

cards and a cyberspace reading of your current biorhythms. Hint: those in the know tell me that when using the *I Ching*, you should place your hands upon the keyboard and concentrate on your current situation before pressing the **RETURN** key, which rolls the digital dice. As for understanding what the *I Ching* tells you, you're on your own.

Black Beans and Other Recipes

Recipes pop up all over the Internet, most of them catalogued in the archives of various USENET newsgroups. You can home in on these archives by letting the **Web** handle the FTP connection for you. Figure 6.14 shows what the **Web** found at the site **ftp.halcyon.com** in the directory */pub/recipes/general/*. I reached this point first by choosing *Recipes* in the information-by-category listing from the home page, and then exploring the options presented. It's quite a list, and remember, this is just one directory listing vegetarian dishes; there are numerous other archives available. Don't miss the Cuban Black Beans.

The Dead Sea Scrolls at the Library of Congress

The Ancient Library of Qumran and Modern Scholarship is an exhibit that brings specimens of the famous Dead Sea Scrolls to the Internet, by way of their temporary home at the Library of Congress. Protected by desert conditions in caves for over 2,000 years, these scrolls are some of the earliest Biblical materials extant, and have provided numerous insights into the customs of their day, as well as into the collection of sacred texts assembled into the Old Testament as

Figure 6.14
Looking through
recipes at an FTP site.

```
FTP Directory of /ftp.halcyon.com/pub/recipes/general/
                /PUB/RECIPES/GENERAL/

       Up to Parent Directory[1]

                            couscous-croquettes[2]   spicy-bean-spread[3]
hummus-4[4]                 apple-quinoa[5]           hummus-3[6]
pizza[7]                    skillet-dinner[8]         easy-applesauce[9]
applesauce[10]              chestnut-seaweed-rice[11]
marinated-carrots[12]       stuffed-peppers[13]       kuri-gohan[14]
chickpeas-sundried-tomatoes[15]                       bhabha-ghanoush[16]
crockpot-beans[17]          millet-split-peas[18]     ghana-bhajee[19]
white-beans-pasta[20]       indian-chick-peas[21]     tabbouli[22]
apple-barley[23]            mustard-buckwheat[24]     basil-oats[25]
shiitake-spelt[26]          pumpkin-millet[27]        pasta-sundried-tomatoes[28]
grilled-veggies-capers[29]                            millet-mashed-potatoes[30]
baked-cranberry-squash[31]                            artichokes-curry-sauce[32]
eggplant-pancakes[33]   balsamic-strawberries[34]
mexican-lentil-stew[35] quick-bahji[36]               channa-daal[37]
scalloped-potatoes[38]  refried-beans-2[39]           quinoa-leek-currants[40]
cuban-black-beans[41]   lobia[42]                     lasagna-2[43]
seitan[44]              mu-shu-vegetables-2[45] vegetable-hash[46]
melon-lassi[47]         lefse[48]                      corn-tomato-linguini[49]
1-261, Back, Up, <RETURN> for more, Quit, or Help: _
```

we know it today. The original exhibition included over 100 scrolls and artifacts from the Qumran site, all loaned by the Israel Antiquities Authority.

The on-line version of the exhibition provides a glimpse of the electronic future. Twelve scroll fragments and 29 other objects collected for the exhibition are available in various formats, depending upon your browser. Figure 6.15 provides information about one of the exhibits, a scroll showing material from the Biblical book of Leviticus. As you can see, complete information about the scroll is presented, along with a hypertext link at the top of the figure. If we were using a graphical browser, choosing this link would then display the scroll.

Exploring a University

Because of its numerous links to **WAIS** indices, the **Web** can be a handy way to run through the on-line systems at various universities. PennInfo is a menu-based **CWIS**, or Campus Wide Information System. It contains more than 3,500 documents produced by some 70 providers of information. The entire course register, timetable, and final exam schedule are included, as are academic and cultural calendars, directories of campus facilities, and a variety of imagery available through GIF (Graphics Interchange Format) files. The **WAIS** index for PennInfo is shown in Figure 6.16.

A variety of other campus systems can be found by choosing the *TechInfo* option under the *Servers by type* item on the home page. TechInfo is a public information service that MIT has developed and uses to manage its own CWIS; use of the system has spread to a growing number of sites.

Figure 6.15
A look at part of a historical exhibit, the Ancient Library of Qumran and Modern Scholarship available on-line.

```
                                                    Dead Sea Scrolls -- Leviticus
                                    LEVITICUS

Va-Yikrah

    [1]


11Q1(PaleoLev)
Parchment
Copied late second century -  early first century B.C.E.
Height 10.9 cm (4 1/4 in.), length 100.2 cm (39 1/2 in.)
Courtesy of the Israel Antiquities Authority (4)

    This scroll was discovered in 1956, when a group of Ta'amireh Bedouin
    happened on Cave 11, but it was first unrolled fourteen years later, at the
    Israel Museum in Jerusalem.  Inscribed in the scroll are parts of the final
    chapters (22-27) of Leviticus, the third book in the Pentateuch, which
    expounds laws of sacrifice, atonement, and holiness.  This is the lowermost
    portion (approximately one-fifth of the original height) of the final six
    columns of the original manuscript.  Eighteen small fragments also belong to
    this scroll.  The additional fragments of this manuscript are from preceding
    chapters: Lev. 4, 10, 11, 13, 14, 16, 18-22.
1-2, Back, Up, <RETURN> for more, Quit, or Help: _
```

Figure 6.16
A Campus Wide
Information System
with hypertext links.

```
1-7, Back, Up, Quit, or Help: 6
 Judith Rodin Nominated for U. of Penn Presidency[1]
 About PennInfo[2]
 About the University of Pennsylvania[3]
 Academic Support[4]
 Calendars and Events (Penn Campus)[5]
 Computing and Networking[6]
 Delaware Valley Events[7]
 Directories (on campus)[8]
 Faculty and Staff Facilities and Services [9]
 Graduate Studies (Ph.D., A.M., and M.S.) [10]
 Interdisciplinary Programs[11]
 Libraries[12]
 Policies and Procedures[13]
 Schools[14]
 Student Activities and Services[15]
 University Life[16]
 How to Find "What's New" in PennInfo[17]

    Supply keywords to search all information at this TechInfo server (This
       [End]is at penninfo-srv.upenn.edu on port 9000.)

 FIND <keywords>, 1-17, Back, Quit, or Help: _
```

Software for Astronomy

By browsing through the various **World Wide Web** servers (do this by choosing *List of servers* on the home page), you can move in on collections of useful information and software. In Figure 6.17, for example, I have used the **Web** to travel to Cambridge University in the United Kingdom, where astronomy information from all over the world is assembled.

Here, I am examining software from the Cambridge collection; there are also astronomical databases as well as abstracts from meetings of astronomical societies and a collection of images, both from satellite photographs and telescope work.

Reading USENET News with the Web

Figure 6.18 shows an entry point from the **Web** into the massive collection of USENET newsgroups. The groups have been broken down by category—**comp**, **alt**, **rec**, and so on. The hypertext links make it easy to move into the category you choose.

Choose a link, and you are taken to a selection screen, from which you can pick an item you want to read. The point here is not that you should read USENET using the **Web**; the interface isn't optimum for that kind of ongoing flow of discussion. But the presence of the newsgroups points to the **Web**'s broad reach, providing diverse sources with internal links. Taming so unwieldy an enterprise as a USENET newsgroup, however, may be beyond even the **Web**'s capabilities.

Figure 6.17
Via the **Web** to
Cambridge University,
where abundant materials
on astronomy are
maintained.

```
                                                                Spectroscopy
  [1] [2]   [3]     Previous: Image analysis & photometry[4]    Up: ADAM Applica
tions[5]        Next: Specific wavelengths[6]


Spectroscopy



   FIGARO                    --- General data analysis

   FIGARO                  [SUN/86]

 A  general data reduction system written by Keith Shortridge at Caltech and
                      the AAO. Although many people find it of greatest use
                      in the reduction of spectroscopic data, it also has
                      powerful image and data cube manipulation facilities
                      and a photometry package. In many ways it is a
                      descendant of SPICA, possessing virtually all SPICA's
                      reduction facilities, but its different methods of
                      operation and data storage offer significant
                      improvements in features and performance. Starlink
                      recommends FIGARO as the most complete spectroscopic
1-6, Back, <RETURN> for more, Quit, or Help:
```

Figure 6.18
Using the **Web** to reach
USENET newsgroups.

```
                                                                   Usenet
                             USENET

   The Usenet is a collection of thousands of e-mail newsgroups grouped by
   category, each devoted to a particular interest, which together compose a
   massive information site.

   alt [1] (groups which discuss alternative viewpoints)
   bionet [2] (groups of interest to biologists and life scientists)
   bit [3] (items from the most popular of the Bitnet "LISTSERV" discussion
   groups)
   biz [4] (items relevant to business; advertising)
   comp [5] (groups discussing questions about computer hardware, software, and
   subcultures)
   k12 [6] (the kindergarten-through-twelfth-grade network)
   misc [7] (groups on various miscellaneous topics)
   news [8] (discussion and reporting of current events)
   rec [9] (creative works, discussions about hobbies and recreational
   activities)
   sci [10] (groups discussing scientific issues)
   soc [11] (social groups for special-interest and ethnic communities)
   talk [12] (groups of people babbling)

   1-12, Back, Up, Quit, or Help: _
```

By Gopher to the National Institutes of Health

Figure 6.19 shows how the **Web** handles a **Gopher**, in this case one of several at the National Institutes of Health. Internet access is provided to NIH clinical and health issues, funded grants, and research projects and research resources.

As you can see, the **Web** adds hypertext links to the normal interface of **Gopher**; otherwise, the **Gopher** menu structure remains intact. This **Gopher** was also modified and enhanced by the NIH's Convex Systems Staff and Computational Molecular Biology Section.

COMMANDS FOR THE WWW BROWSER

As for your own explorations, the commands at the bottom left of the **Web**'s screens of information are all you need to know to begin. Indeed, the best way to begin learning about the **Web** is to access it and simply experiment; its intuitive nature will readily become apparent. The numbers at the bottom of each screen represent the possible choices at the level you have reached; press one of them and you are taken to the information that number represents.

Following are the basic commands; some of them have not yet been displayed in the preceding examples, but we will examine how to use them as we move through the **Web**. Although the list seems to imply otherwise, case is not significant. The letters in caps are those that must be entered for the command to be effective. You could enter a solitary **b** to launch the **back** command, for example, but to go to the bottom of the screen, you would have to use the **bo** command (thus distinguishing that command from **back**).

Figure 6.19
The **Web** can also contact **Gophers**, as shown at the National Institutes of Health.

```
                                                    gopher://gopher.nih.gov:70/11/
Select one of:

        Announcements [December  3, 1993][1]
        About This and other Gophers at NIH[2]
        Health and Clinical Information[3]
        Grants and Research Information [4]
        Molecular Biology Databases[5]
        Library and Literature Sources[6]
        NIH Campus Info[7]
        NIH Computer and Network Resources[8]
        Weather and Area Information[9]
        Gopher Tunnels (To Other Gopher and WAIS Sites)[10]
        E-mail and Directory Services[11]
        Search NIH Phone Book[12]
        Search Menus at this Gopher Site by Keyword[13]


    [End]




1-13, Back, Quit, or Help: _
```

number   Moves to the specified link in the document. With the www browser, the links are always set off in brackets. Enter **14**, followed by a **RETURN**, to access the link shown in the statement **Physics[14]**, etc.

<RETURN>   Takes you to the next page of the document you are reading.

Back   Moves you back to the document you were reading before the current one. (Remember: You can just enter the first letter and it will be effective.) The effect is to return to the previous menu level. In the previous case, entering a b at the prompt while at the Berkeley library server takes me back to the list of **World Wide Web** servers worldwide. Another **b** would return me to the home menu.

BOttom   Typing **bo** at the prompt takes you to the last page of the current document. This command requires you to type the first two letters, to avoid confusion with the **b** command (for back).

Find *keywords* Searches the current index using the keyword selected. As we've seen, the **World Wide Web** contains not only text documents but also indices that can be searched.

Go *address*   Takes you to the document at the given address.

For example, I might want to access the document whose URL is:

```
http://info.cern.ch/hypertext/WWW/DesignIssues/Overview.html
```

at the server site at **info.cern.ch** in Switzerland. To do so, I would enter the command:

```
go http://info.cern.ch/hypertext/WWW/DesignIssues/Overview.html
```

To determine the address of the document, I would use the **list** command, as discussed in the upcoming list. The result of the **go** command for this document is shown in Figure 6.20.

As you can see, I have been taken directly to the document.

Help   The help command is dependent on context, meaning that what you see by way of available commands will be determined by what you are doing. Typing an **h** will generate a list of applicable commands.

HOme   Takes you straight to the starting document.

List   Displays the references for the displayed document. This refers to the linked documents (i.e., resources) that can be accessed through the page in question. The addresses given are frequently long and complex, as seen in the example under the **go** command.

Manual   Takes you directly to the on-line manual for the browser.

Figure 6.20
Going directly to a **Web**
document using a URL.

```
                                                      The World Wide Web project
                              WORLD WIDE WEB

   The WorldWideWeb (W3) is a wide-area hypermedia[1] information retrieval
   initiative aiming to give universal access to a large universe of documents.

   Everything there is online about W3 is linked directly or indirectly to this
   document, including an executive summary[2] of the project, an illustrated
   talk[3] , Policy[4] and Conditions[5] , May's W3 news[6] , Frequently Asked
   Questions[7] .

   What's out there?[8]    Pointers to the world's online information,
                           subjects[9] , W3 servers[10] , etc.

   WWW Software Products[11]
                           What there is and how to get it: clients[12] ,
                           servers[13] , gateways[14] , libwww[15] and tools[16]


   Discussion              Newsgroup comp.infosystems.www[17] , other groups[18]
                           , specialised mailing lists[19]

   Technical[20]           Details of protocols, formats, program internals etc
   1-27, Back, Up, <RETURN> for more, Quit, or Help: b
```

Next	When reading a sequence of documents, you can use the **next** command to move to the next document. If you were, for example, reading a document whose link was numbered 3, you could enter **n** to move to item 4.
Previous	Takes you back to the previous document in a sequence. If you were reading item 4, the previous command would take you to 3.
Print	Prints the current document. Note: This works only if you are using a full TCP/IP network connection. Dial-up users aren't able to use this feature.
QUIT	Exits the World Wide Web. Note that you must enter the entire word, not just a **q**, to make this command work.
Recall	Generates a list of the documents you have already looked at. You can then return to a particular one by typing its number. The following, for example, are the results of a **recall** command after a brief search on the **Web**:

```
   Documents you have visited:-

   R  1)   in Overview of the Web
   R  2)   in The World Wide Web project
   R  3)   in Newgroups relevant to the WorldWideWeb project
   R  4)   in Newsgroup bit.listserv.pacs-l,  Articles 7729-7767
   R  5)    Comment re: Denial of Internet Access in School Libraries

   1, Back, Up, <RETURN> for more, Quit, or Help:
```

To move back to one of these levels, I would simply enter the number in question, preceded by the **recall** command. Thus, to go back to the newsgroup **bit.listserv.pacs-l**, I would enter **recall 4**.

Top   Moves you to the first page of the current document.

Up   Moves you back to the previous screen. Contrast this with the
                 back command, which takes you to the next higher menu level.

> *filename*   This is an extremely important command. Using it, you can
                 capture the output of a document in a file for subsequent use.
                 Entering **> servers.txt**, for example, saves the current
                 document in a file called **servers.txt**.

> *filename*   A related command that appends the text of the current
                 document to a given file.

SEARCHING AN INDEX WITH THE WWW BROWSER

An index is searchable, making the **World Wide Web** an ideal way to scour a large database. When you encounter an index, you will be presented with a description of it and given the chance to enter keywords to begin a search. Many of the indices are based on **WAIS** sources. Therefore, we are using one tool, the **Web**, to access another, **WAIS**, to sift through information in a database that might be anywhere in the world. Nowhere is the interlocked nature of Internet search tools more apparent.

A simple search will demonstrate how useful these indices can be. Perhaps we'd like to find out which **WAIS** databases are available on the subject of literature. We can use the **Web** to do this, choosing the option

```
Servers by type[3]    if you know what sort of server you are looking for.
```

from the first **Web** screen, and following the trail it provides. The first fork, for example, will be:

```
WAIS servers[4]        Find WAIS index servers using the directory of
                       servers[5] , or lists by name[6] or domain[7] . See
                       also: about WAIS[8] .
```

Here, we can choose **5**, which allows us to search for **WAIS** servers using the master index.

The screen that results from this choice, illustrated in Figure 6.21, tells us much about how an index works when using the **Web**. First, we're given basic **WAIS** information, including material on where to look for more, with the relevant addresses provided. Then, we're prompted to add new information to the **WAIS** directory. Finally, at the bottom of the screen, the all important search field is provided:

```
FIND <keywords>, Back, Up, Quit, or Help:
```

Figure 6.21
The **WAIS** Directory of Servers as displayed (and searchable) through the **Web**.

```
                                              directory-of-servers index
                    DIRECTORY-OF-SERVERS

Server created with WAIS-8 on Fri Mar  8 14:30:57 1991 by
 brewster@think.com
This is a White Pages listing of WAIS servers.  For more information on
WAIS, use the WAIS system on the wais-docs server, or add yourself to the
wais-discussion@think.com mailing list, or get the newest software from
think.com:/public/wais.

To server makers: Please make new servers of text, pictures, music
whatever.  We will try to list all servers in the directory that get sent
in to: directory-of-servers@quake.think.com (use the -register option on
the command waisindex), but I reserve the right to take servers out if they
are not consistently available.  I will send notice to the maintainer
before doing so.

To get a list of all available sources, search for 'source'.  This may
limited by the maximum number of results allowed by a client.

Bugs and comments to bug-wais@think.com.
 -brewster@think.com

FIND <keywords>, Back, Up, Quit, or Help: _
```

The regular commands, **back**, **up**, **quit**, and **help**, are available, but we'll use the **find** command. Entering **find literature**, we generate the screen shown in Figure 6.22.

Figure 6.22
Running a **WAIS** search using the term "literature" through the **Web**.

```
                                           literature (in directory-of-servers)
                    LITERATURE

Index directory-of-servers contains the following 13 items relevant to
'literature'. The first figure for each entry is its relative score, the
second the number of lines in the item.

1000   158  queueing-literature-database.src[1]

 286    95  ANU-Radiocarbon-Abstracts.src[2]

 238    91  ANU-Dhammapada-Verses.src[3]

 238    34  ASK-SISY-Software-Information.src[4]

 238    33  IAT-Documents.src[5]

 238    97  NOAA_National_Environmental_Referral_Service.src[6]

 238    28  POETRY-index.src[7]

 238   120  Tantric-News.src[8]

FIND <keywords>, 1-13, Back, Up, <RETURN> for more, or Help:
```

Each of these entries is linked to further information. We'll choose **POETRY-index.src** by entering the number **7** to read a description of the **WAIS** source in question, as shown in Figure 6.23.

Now we are presented with links to the **WAIS** database itself:

```
Access links              Direct access[1] or through CERN gateway[2]
```

The database, of course, offers the same **find** commands, along with the usual **Web back**, **up**, **quit**, and **help** commands. The poetry database here is an index of all poems and reviews published in *POETRY Magazine* since volume 151, October, 1987. *POETRY* itself is a well-regarded source, founded in 1912; it quickly became a forum for the best poets of its time. Obviously, since the index only dates back to 1987, we can't search this early period, but more recent publications will appear. Searching for work published by Joyce Carol Oates in *POETRY*, for example, I used the command **find oates** and retrieved the following:

```
Joyce Carol Oates - Volume 151     October 1987-March 1988 Page 109
        Waiting on Elvis, 1956
        Motive, Metaphor
Joyce Carol Oates - Volume 151     October 1987-March 1988 Page 207
        Comment
Joyce Carol Oates - Volume 153     October 1988-March 1989 Page 159
        Late December, New Jersey


    [End]
```

Figure 6.23
Description of a **WAIS** server.

```
                                    /home3/wais/POETRY-index WAIS source file
                        /HOME3/WAIS/POETRY-INDEX DESCRIPTION

        Access links        Direct access[1] or through CERN gateway[2]

        Maintainer          paul_jones@unc.edu

        Host                sunsite.unc.edu

    Server created with WAIS release 8 b5
    on Apr  2 22:27:41 1993 by wais@calypso
    This is an index of all the poems and reviews published
    since volume 151 October 1987 in POETRY magazine of Chicago.
    POETRY was founded in 1912 by Harriet Monroe
    and quickly became a major publication venue for poets world-wide.
    Joseph Parisi - Editor
    Helen Lothrop Kaviter - Managing Editor
    60 West Walton Street
    Chicago Illinois 60610
    (312) 280-4870
    Useful words: literature american translation translations poet poets
    poetry poem poems writing creative verse lyric sonnet stanza
    review reviews english prose author authors
    1-2, Back, Up, <RETURN> for more, Quit, or Help:
```

USING TELNET TO SEARCH THE WORLD WIDE WEB

The sites given in Table 6.1 can be accessed through Telnet. As with many Internet search tools, the preferable method of access is to use a client program (or, in **WWW** terminology, a browser). These are less demanding on system resources and generally easier to use. But if you have no browser available, then the Telnet option remains. Remember to consider which of the sites is best to use. The site at CERN in Geneva, Switzerland is the birthplace of the **WWW** project and merits a look, but for regular access, it makes sense to choose a site close to your own location. If you're in the United States, there are three currently available for public access. Each has its own particular interface, as you'll see in the next section.

Using The Lynx Browser

Let's begin by using Telnet to reach the **WWW** server at the University of Kansas in Lawrence. The command is **telnet ukanaix.cc.ukans.edu**. Log in as **www**. Here is the first thing we see:

```
               The University of Kansas
           IBM AIX Version 3 for RISC System/6000
         (C) Copyrights by IBM and by others 1982, 1990.

 For assistance call 864-0110 or to report network problems call 864-0200

 Login as 'kufacts' for  access to the Campus Wide Information System.
          'history' for history network resources
          'ex-ussr' for former Soviet Union info
login:
```

Next we are presented with an interesting opening screen, as shown in Figure 6.24. This immediately clues us in to the fact that we are dealing with a different kind of interface, and therefore a different **World Wide Web** browser. The browser we used earlier (which is also used by some Telnet sites, such as the **info.cern.ch** server where **World Wide Web** originated) is a line-oriented tool, which simply means it sends output one line at a time, a relatively undemanding chore and one that is not dependent on the type of terminal being used to do its job.

The browser at the University of Kansas is called **lynx**, and it is the result of the university's attempts to build its own campus-wide information system, or **CWIS**. Think of **lynx** as just another way of using the **World Wide Web**'s resources, and as you'll see, in some respects it is a better one than the standard **www** browser. **lynx** is a full-screen tool that uses highlighting, reverse video (or underlining), and cursor-movement keys to display what's available. Examine the screen shown in Figure 6.24, and the differences should be readily apparent.

First of all, **lynx** doesn't provide bracketed numbers to show you the hypertext links that are available, which makes the opening screen far less cluttered than the comparable **www** screen. So, how do we know where the links are? Notice that, at the top of the screen, the term **WWW** is highlighted, indicating that a link is present and available by pressing the **RETURN** key. Further entries on this screen are also available, but rather than being shown as numbers, they're set off by blue highlighting. "About Lynx" is highlighted, as is

Figure 6.24
Logging in with **lynx** at
the University of Kansas.

```
                                                       Lynx default home page
                  WELCOME TO LYNX AND THE WORLD OF THE WEB

       You are using a WWW Product called Lynx. For more information about
       obtaining and installing Lynx please choose About Lynx

       The current version of Lynx is 2.0.12. If you are running an earlier
       version PLEASE UPGRADE!

     WWW INFORMATION SOURCES
        * For a description of WWW choose Web Overview
        * About the WWW Information Sharing project
        * WWW Information By Subject
        * WWW Information By Type

     OTHER INFO SOURCES
        * University of Kansas CWIS
        * Nova-Links at Nova University
        * O'Reilly & Ass. Global Network Navigator
        * NCSA Network Starting Points
        * NCSA Information Resource Meta-Index
        * All the Gopher servers in the world
   Commands: Use arrow keys to move, '?' for help, 'q' to quit, '<-' to go back
```

"About the WWW." And everything under the heading "Other Info Sources" is highlighted as well.

Consequently, instead of entering numbers with **lynx** we use the arrow keys to move between the items in question, and the **RETURN** key to choose the one we want. An important key is the left arrow (**<-**), which takes us back to the document's previous page. So the model is, **Up** and **Down Arrow** keys to move further into the **Web**, **Left Arrow** key to back out, one step at a time. And, as should be clear, the system of highlighted links persists throughout the **lynx** interface. In Figure 6.25, for example, I have moved to a screen offering information about the people behind the **World Wide Web**, and have begun paging through it.

Tim Berners-Lee, whose biography is presented in this figure, started the **Web** project at CERN in 1989. Here, too, we're shown links from within the document, to *WorldWideWeb*, *application on the NeXT*, and *bio*, *disclaimer*. Moving between these fields with the arrow keys will take us through the **Web** to these linked documents. Using the **Left Arrow** key will take us back.

You should be aware of an important **lynx** command, the one used to mail documents to yourself. By entering **p** within a particular document, you will be given the opportunity to enter your address, and the document in question will soon appear in your mailbox. In Figure 6.26, I have done this with the document about people on the **Web**.

As you can see, I have highlighted the option *Mail the file to yourself* and have been prompted for an address, which I have already entered. The file soon appears in my mailbox.

Figure 6.25
Highlighting its linkages
makes **lynx** the easiest of
the VT-100 **Web**
browsers to use.

```
                      People involved in the WorldWideWeb project (p2 of 12)
         Carl was at CERN for a six month period during his degree course at
         Brunel University, UK. Carl worked on the server side, on client
         authentication and multiple format handling.

      Eric Bina

         [IMAGE] Worked on NCSA Mosaic and the HTMLWidget. ( more )

      Tim Berners-Lee

         [IMAGE] Currently in CN division. Before coming to CERN, Tim worked
         on, among other things, document production and text processing. He
         developed his first hypertext system, "Enquire", in 1980 for his own
         use (although unaware of the existence of the term HyperText). With a
         background in text processing, real-time software and communications,
         Tim decided that high energy physics needed a networked hypertext
         system and CERN was an ideal site for the development of wide-area
         hypertext ideas. Tim started the WorldWideWeb project at CERN in 1989.
         He wrote the application on the NeXT along with most of the
         communications software. Phone: 3755, Email: timbl@info.cern.ch. See
         bio , disclaimer

      -- press space for next page --                                       -
```

Figure 6.26
Mailing a document to
yourself with **lynx**.

```
                      Printing Options

         There are 253 lines, or approximately 4 pages, to print.

            Some print functions have been disabled!!!
            You have the following print choices
                      please select one

         Mail the file to yourself

         Print to the screen
```

```
         Please enter a valid internet mail address: gilster@rock.concert.net
```

The following are the basic commands you'll need to use **lynx**:

DownArrow	Moves to the next topic.
UpArrow	Moves to previous topic.
RightArrow	Moves to highlighted topic.
LeftArrow	Returns to previous topic.
SPACEBAR	Goes to next page. You can also use the plus symbol **(+)** to do this.
-	Goes to previous page. You can also do this with the **b** command.
g	Goes to the file you specify. This is equivalent to the go command with the **www** browser. You must specify a URL address to make it work.
i	Displays an index of documents.
m	Returns to the main screen.
p	Allows you to mail a document to yourself.
q	Quits the **lynx** browser.
/	Searches for a string of characters. You can also use the s command to do this.
n	Goes to the next instance of the search string in question.

Using **lynx** is not difficult, but as with any Internet search tool, you should procure the complete set of commands. The preceding list shows the major ones you will need to move around in and use the system. By entering a question mark (**?**) at the prompt, you can generate a complete set for your files, and then use the **p** command to mail this command list to yourself.

What You Need: A Complete Command List for the **lynx** Browser

How to Get It: Telnet to **ukanaix.cc.ukans.edu**. Use the **?** command at the prompt. When the help document is displayed, enter the **p** command. When prompted, enter your mailing address. The document will be sent to your mailbox.

Using the NJIT Browser

There is no point in going through all the browsers available, though generating information about them is easy enough to do on the **Web**. But if you are limited to a Telnet connection to do your work, then getting to know the differences between the various remote browsers can be helpful. At the New Jersey Institute of Technology there is a different browser implementation. The entry screen for this site, **www.njit.edu** (login as **www**) is shown in Figure 6.27.

Note the local information, including faculty and staff phone numbers for Rutgers University, where the NJIT is housed, as well as numbers for fire and local police.

You can move between items with either the cursor keys or by selecting the number of the link you want to follow. Choosing item 2, "WORLD WIDE WEB," takes you into the **Web**. Figure 6.28 gives you an idea of how the NJIT interface overlays the basic **Web** structure. Note the help function, which is invoked with the ? command.

WORLD WIDE WEB TIPS

The **Web** can be frustrating to use, depending on the kind of information you need. It would be nice, for example, to be able to log on and simply enter a structured query, letting the system race off and deliver hypertext choices leading to our destination. But it is the very size and complexity of the Internet, and the **Web**'s remarkable power, that makes this alternative unavailable. The **Web**

Figure 6.27
Logging in at the New Jersey Institute of Technology.

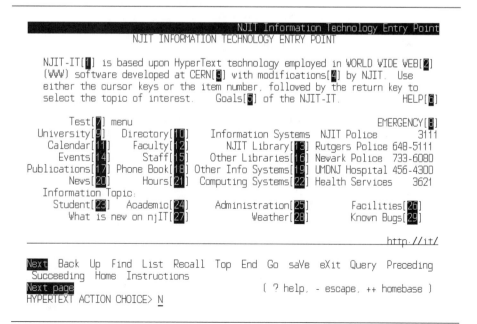

Figure 6.28
The NJIT interface,
highlighting the hypertext
links.

```
                                                    The World Wide Web project
                              WORLD WIDE WEB

     The WorldWideWeb (W3) is a wide-area hypermedia[1] information retrieval
     initiative aiming to give universal access to a large universe of documents.

     Everything there is online about W3 is linked directly or indirectly to this
     document, including an executive summary[2] of the project, an illustrated
     talk[3] , Policy[4] and Conditions[5] , May's W3 news[6] , Frequently Asked
     Questions[7] .

     What's out there?[8]      Pointers to the world's online information.
                         subjects[9] , W3 servers[10] , etc.

     WWW Software Products[11]
                         What there is and how to get it: clients[12] ,
                         servers[13] , gateways[14] , libwww[15] and tools[16]

                            http://info.cern.ch/hypertext/WWW/TheProject.html


     Next  Back  Up  Find  List  Recall  Top  End  Go  saVe  eXit  Query  Preceding
      Succeeding  Home  Instructions
     Next page                              ( ? help, - escape, ++ homebase )
     HYPERTEXT ACTION CHOICE> N
```

accesses so many tools across such a broad spectrum of technologies that your
search, of necessity, proceeds step by step, from one link to another. If there is
one truth that will become apparent the more you use the **Web**, it is that no two
searches are ever the same. And you will probably discover something new each
time you use this tool.

This being the case, consider the following when you embark upon your own
explorations:

Think in broad terms: If you enter the **Web** with the notion that you are
going to find every reference to Aeneas' father Anchises in Vergil's *The Aeneid*,
you will be frustrated by your inability to go directly to the text. But if you
think in terms of literature, classics, the ancient world, and so forth, you can
perform a subject search by following links to the source. You might begin
like this:

```
Archaeology              Classics and Mediterranean Archaeology[7]
```

and then proceed to a particular text project:

```
Internet Wiretap: Selected Texts[7]
```

Soon you would be reading the Dryden translation of *The Aeneid*, as shown in
Figure 6.29.

If you're using the **www** browser, you won't be able to search for a specific
term, like *anchises*, but other browsers, like **lynx**, allow you to enter a search
term, which makes it possible to pull up the references desired quickly.

Figure 6.29
The Dryden translation
of the *Aeneid* on-line.

```
                              Vergil: Aeneid (Dryden Translation) (46/13895)
         This text is in the public domain, released August 1993.


         THE FIRST BOOK OF THE AENEIS

         THE ARGUMENT. -- The Trojans, after a seven years' voyage, set
         sail for Italy, but are overtaken by a dreadful storm, which AEolus
         raises at Juno's request. The tempest sinks one, and scatters the
         rest. Neptune drives off the Winds, and calms the sea. AEneas,
         with his own ship, and six more, arrives safe at an African port.
         Venus complains to Jupiter of her son's misfortunes. Jupiter com-
         forts her, and sends Mercury to procure him a kind reception among
         the Carthaginians. AEneas, going out to discover the country, meets
         his mother in the shape of an huntress, who conveys him in a cloud
         to Carthage, where he sees his friends whom he thought lost, and
         receives a kind entertainment from the queen. Dido, by a device
         of Venus, begins to have a passion for him, and, after some dis-
         course with him, desires the history of his adventures since the
         siege of Troy, which is the subject of the two following books.


         ARMS, and the man I sing, who, forc'd by fate,
         And haughty Juno's unrelenting hate,
         Back, Up, <RETURN> for more, Quit, or Help: _
```

Slow down: A search through the **Web** takes time because the hypertext is reflecting your own mental processes, or at least, attempting to do so. The problem with this is, despite the best intentions of hypertext programmers, no two people think alike, and the links between information that seem apparent to one person may not be optimum for another. This is why, in the previous search, we had to look under the topic of archaeology to find Vergil's *Aeneid*, while another topic that would seem to be germane—literature—did not reference Vergil's work. Always remember that we are walking down data paths set by other people at their whim.

Use an index wherever possible: An index can take some of the effort out of a complicated search by allowing you to enter keywords, as we saw when we looked for information about the film *Local Hero*. Because some **Web** connections are to **WAIS** sources, it makes sense to find out whether there is a **WAIS** index for the material you need to find. You can look at **WAIS** information by searching the **WAIS** database of directories. Go directly to the top screen entry for type searching:

```
Servers by type[3]
```

if you know what sort of server you are looking for. There you can find out if any **WAIS** servers can help.

Before you search, determine whether the Web is the appropriate tool: Each Internet application has its own strengths and weaknesses. Among the **Web**'s strong points is its ability to access information from a wide variety of resources, and applications from **WAIS** to **archie** to **Gopher**. But this very diversity can also be a drawback. If, for example, the information you need is only to be found in a **WAIS** server, and you already know the address of the **WAIS** site, then going through the **Web** to get it may be needlessly time-consuming. Wading through the **Web**'s information is in one sense like browsing through a good library; you find resources you didn't realize existed. On the other hand, it can be a phenomenal time-waster if you're in a hurry.

The kind of search for which the **Web** is ideal is a search in which you have a sound idea of what you need but no clear direction as to how to find it. Perhaps a search of **WAIS** servers has turned up nothing, and a run through **archie** has left you without a file or a direction. In such a case, browsing the **Web**'s virtual library allows you to select categories of information, gradually narrowing down your chase until you have isolated a server, somewhere, that contains the resources you need. The **Web** is also ideal for broad information gathering; each journey into it results in a different set of paths, and each time you follow them, you are exposed to new Internet possibilities.

MOSAIC: THE WEB GOES TECHNICOLOR

We have already learned that the **World Wide Web** functions through software tools called *browsers*, which allow you to move between collections of data involving various media. **Mosaic** is such a browser. But its impact on the Internet community is likely to be far wider than that description suggests. **Mosaic**, by offering perhaps the most elegant interface solution for any Internet tool, has captured the imagination of the computer press. Its widespread acceptance and the growing interest among those just learning about the Internet suggests that its principle—displaying imagery, fonts and text in a superb supportive environment—will become the benchmark for all subsequent client programs.

It is important to be clear on one point. **Mosaic** is an interface; the underlying application remains **World Wide Web**. It is a measure of the success of **Mosaic** that it is commonly discussed as an all-purpose Internet tool rather than as a **Web** browser. That emphasis acknowledges the fact that **Mosaic**, through its graphical hooks to the **Web**, offers access to everything from full-motion video to straight ASCII text. You can use the **Web** to examine an FTP site or to create a Telnet connection, with **Mosaic** as the overlay. And what you read on-screen is supported by full-color graphics and an audio-visual environment determined by the people who designed the particular **Mosaic** site you're visiting.

You have already seen that the client you use can have a profound impact upon how you search. Indeed, the **swais** client we used with **WAIS** is a lowest common denominator tool which is readily replaced, once SLIP becomes available, by intuitive clients like **WAIS-for-Mac**, **WAIS Manager for Windows** and their ilk. So, too, the useful **Gopher** interface running under VT-100 readily yields to the persuasions of **HGopher for Windows**, or **TurboGopher**. My point throughout this book is that you should understand the underlying system; the choice of clients will evolve as you go.

Consider **Mosaic** as an example of the kinds of choices you will have to make. This book has focused largely upon the VT-100 character-based world that the dial-up user encounters through a UNIX service provider. At some point, such a user will need to consider a SLIP connection if the use of advanced clients like **Mosaic** becomes an issue. Indeed, **Mosaic** will probably be the fulcrum of this choice; therefore, examine it with an eye to determining whether its advantages justify the move into a SLIP account, which is harder to set up than a regular dial-up account and which can be slow on anything but the fastest modems. The day will come when dial-up network access evolves into the use of true network connections through high-speed fiber-optic lines into the home. At that point, **Mosaic** and its like will control how you use the resources built by the pioneer searchers.

WHAT IS MOSAIC?

Mosaic was created at the National Center for Supercomputing Applications (NCSA) at the University of Illinois in Urbana-Champaign. Marc Andreessen and Eric Bina were its original authors; today, some 30 programmers are developing the program in its various versions. The software is a graphical interface that allows you to access networked information. Specifically, **Mosaic** is a browser for **World Wide Web** data in hypermedia format; as such, it takes its place alongside other graphical user interfaces (GUIs) such as **Viola** (for XWindows), **cello** (for Microsoft Windows), and **Mac WWW** (for the Macintosh). Because the **World Wide Web** itself is able to access a variety of data types, **Mosaic** can be used to read text, view images, listen to audio, and even to examine full-motion video files, which are becoming increasingly common.

The difference between **Mosaic** and a standard, character-based browser like **www** could not be more startling. **Mosaic**, for example, can use colors to highlight information links. It can help you navigate through the **Web**, tracking your journeys and alerting you when you are about to retrace your footsteps (an occupational hazard when using the **Web**, and one of its drawbacks). And while character-based browsers like **lynx** are full-featured and relatively simple to use, **Mosaic's** ability to display graphics works to its advantage when you're dealing with some of the cutting edge exhibits now featured on the Internet. Figure 6.30, for example, shows information about an exhibit of art and documents on the life of Columbus, which was produced at the Library of Congress and made available over the Internet. Let's examine it first through the standard **www** browser, then turn to **Mosaic**.

This is the **Web** as we have come to know it. Note the familiar information at the bottom of the screen, containing the available commands. We can page through this material using the **RETURN** key, and the factual data we retrieve provides a good background to Columbus and the exhibit.

Now examine Figure 6.31, which shows the same **World Wide Web** page through **Mosaic**. Using its graphical features, we are now able to view not only an image that appears above the first document, but also to use windows to view more than a single source at a time; it is also possible to view any text formatting, such as boldfacing, underlining, and font changes, which are made available in the document. These, of course, are lost in the VT-100 version.

In this figure, we are examining **Mosaic** on a Macintosh (UNIX and Microsoft Windows versions are also available). As you can see, the interface is child's play to use. **www** is not difficult either, but we can certainly draw a comparison between **Mosaic** and, say, the **swais** browser for **WAIS**, that points up the general ease of use of graphical browsers. And obviously, the introduction of graphical screen elements adds to our reading experience and conveys additional information.

Figure 6.30
The Library of Congress
Exhibit on Columbus
using a VT-100 browser.

```
Welcome to                                                    1492 Exhibit


                       1492: AN ONGOING VOYAGE



        AN EXHIBIT OF THE LIBRARY OF CONGRESS, WASHINGTON, DC

        1492. Columbus.  The date and the name provoke many questions related to
        the linking of very different parts of the world, the Western Hemisphere and
        the Mediterranean.  What was life like in those areas before 1492?  What
        spurred European expansion?  How did European, African and American peoples
        react to each other?  What were some of the immediate results of these
        contacts?

           1492: AN ONGOING VOYAGE addresses such questions by examining the rich
        mixture of societies coexisting in five areas of this hemisphere before
        European arrival.  It then surveys the polyglot Mediterranean world at a
        dynamic turning point in its development.

           The exhibition examines the first sustained contacts between American
        people and European explorers, conquerors and settlers from 1492 to 1600.
        1-14, Back, Up, <RETURN> for more, Quit, or Help: _
```

Figure 6.31
The Columbus exhibit as
seen through **Mosaic**.

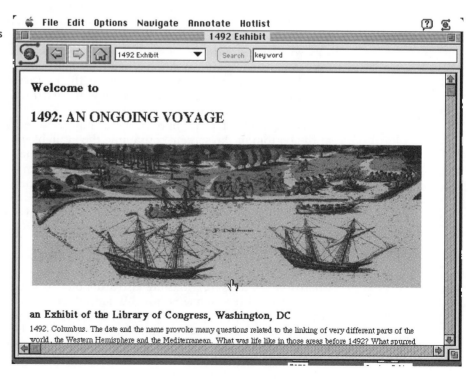

Now let's examine a familiar site as seen through **Mosaic**. In Figure 6.32, we are looking at the home page at CERN, the physics laboratory in Switzerland where Tim Berners-Lee developed the **Web**'s architecture in 1989; here we are using the Microsoft Windows version of **Mosaic**, where the graphical elements are interesting in a different way. The large letter W in the box at the top of the screen is static; it contains no links to other information. However, the small figure of a book at the lower left is actually a link to remote data. Were we to move the cursor to it, the arrow would turn into a hand with a pointing finger. A click on the left mouse button would then take us to a different page of the document, listing Internet resources by topic.

The book metaphor is important in understanding how the **World Wide Web** functions. We have trouble seeing this in a text-based environment, but **Mosaic** demonstrates the paradigm with ease. Text, graphics, and sound are integrated into "pages" of information in this model, the "home page" at a given site being the introductory screen(s) which lead to nested hypermedia information. Graphical **Gopher** and **WAIS** client programs (available through full network connections like SLIP) can also display different types of data, although they must set them up in separate on-screen windows. With **Mosaic**, the page is an integration of the various media elements. And the beauty of such pages is that they can be composed of sources from all over the Internet—a text file from down the street, an image from Japan, an audio file from California.

Mosaic and SLIP

Given the obvious advantages of browsers like **Mosaic**, why doesn't everyone use them? Some accounts in the popular press have suggested that **Mosaic** is the breakthrough browsing tool of the '90s, the interface that will make the

Figure 6.32
The CERN Home Page as seen through the Windows version of **Mosaic**.

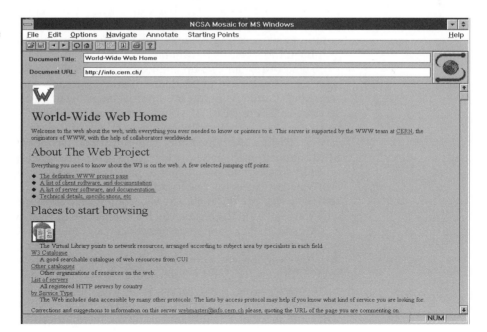

Internet finally accessible to the vast majority of people who would like to use it more but are intimidated by its spartan interface. This view, an easy one to understand, misses a critical point about **Mosaic**. To run the software, a SLIP connection is required, or else PPP; a low-speed dial-up link using VT-100 emulation can't do the job.

Mosaic, you see, requires direct network access to perform its magic; it counts on manipulating that connection so that, working with the hardware resources on your desktop, it can bring you the graphical features we've discussed. There are two ways to make such a connection. The first is to be part of a network that already connects directly to the Internet rather than through a standard dial-up connection. The second is to use your modem to call a server computer that allows SLIP (Serial Line Internet Protocol) or PPP (Point-to-Point Protocol) connections. Using the latter, your computer now acquires capabilities denied to the average dial-up user.

Think about what happens when you place a dial-up call. You are calling a computer at the site of your service provider. *Your* machine is not on the network; rather, it is using the services of a computer that is. You can run client programs on your service provider's machine, but cannot run clients on your own computer because you lack the necessary TCP/IP connection. Only your service provider's computer can run clients, sending the results to you through the telephone line. Your computer then emulates a terminal and connects through a character-oriented mode like VT-100. All of which works fine, but allows you no graphical features.

Both SLIP and PPP adopt a different model. Yes, each begins with your establishing a telephone connection through your modem to a service pro-vider's site. But by using SLIP or PPP software on your own machine, the connection you make enables you to use TCP/IP features on your own. The result: Your computer can be an Internet host—you can have your own Internet address, rather than piggybacking through the computer at your service provider's site. In addition, you can run any client software that your own computer's operating system will allow. Programs like **Mosaic** and other graphical tools become available for use.

Think of regular dial-up connectivity, then (as opposed to SLIP and PPP), as offering a lowest common denominator approach to Internet browsing and searching. Certainly, if you are approaching the Internet through a commercial service like BIX or DELPHI, your interface will be basic VT-100 and **Mosaic** cannot be run on your computer. If you have a standard dial-up account with an Internet service provider, the same holds true. But if you have paid the extra money for a SLIP connection, then the world of graphical software is open. And because prices on SLIP connections have fallen so greatly (and show every sign of continuing to fall), you can expect interest in both SLIP and PPP to grow. Add to this the fact that setting up the necessary software is becoming an easier proposition and you can see why you may want to consider such a connection in your own network activities.

Mosaic makes enough demands on your equipment that you should be sure you have enough horsepower to run it. Its minimum requirements for the Windows version, for example, include a 386SX computer with at least 4MB of RAM, although the developers recommend a 486 with 8MB of RAM for optimum performance. And don't forget your modem; a 2400 bps modem is simply inadequate to the task of running **Mosaic** over your SLIP connection. In a time when the price of 28,800 baud modems has plunged below $300, it would be senseless not to upgrade. I wouldn't recommend running **Mosaic** on anything less than a 14,400 baud modem.

How to Get Mosaic

Like so many good things on the Internet, **Mosaic** is free, although commercial products are also available. Versions exist for UNIX (running the graphical XWindows system), Microsoft Windows, and the Macintosh. You can access **Mosaic** through anonymous FTP. The site:

```
ftp.ncsa.uiuc.edu
```

Note that **ftp** is part of the address; in other words your complete command will be **ftp ftp.ncsa.uiuc.edu**. Here, you will find the directories that contain the latest versions of the program for the different platforms.

The *PC/Mosaic* directory contains the Windows version of **Mosaic**. The filename is **wmos20a4.zip** (the numbers may have changed by the time you read this). The file is stored in "zipped" format to save disk space. Download it using a binary setting (that is, type **binary** at the **ftp>** prompt before proceeding with the retrieval command, which is **get wmos20a4.zip**). Once you have the zipped file on your own system, you will need PKUNZIP to unpack it. Use version 2.04 of the software, which is the current release. You can find it at numerous sites; try **oak.oakland.edu**, where it can be found as **pkz204g.exe** in the *pub/msdos/zip* directory.

The Macintosh version of **Mosaic** is found in the */Mac/Mosaic* directory at the NCSA site. The filename is **NCSAMosaicMac.103.sit.hqx**. This file is compressed with StuffIt and then BinHexed to save disk space. To unpack it, you will need StuffIt Expander or a comparable decoding program. Download the program as an ASCII, rather than binary, file. Again, the program name may have been changed by the time you try this as new versions are released.

The XWindows version of **Mosaic**, along with supporting files, is found in the */Mosaic* directory. Versions for various UNIX platforms are available.

Mosaic and Internet Tools

Gopher through Mosaic

Because it is capable of accessing so many different kinds of information, **Mosaic** is almost an all-purpose tool. It is possible, for example, to move into a **Gopher** menu and read the results, which brings the benefits of the menu-driven environment to **Gopher**'s lean interface. The range of **Mosaic** is shown by a few trips through its resources. Let's take a look at an interesting **Gopher** to show how **Mosaic** displays its information. The screens are different from what we are used to, but the underlying engine is familiar.

Figure 6.33 shows the **Gopher** at the University of Minnesota. Note that the **Gopher** menu items are underlined, which shows us that we can click on any of them to call up the underlying information. **Gopher**'s menu structure, of course, is intact, with everything that implies about finding information. We move up and down menu trees to do so.

Figure 6.33
Using **Gopher** through
Mosaic.

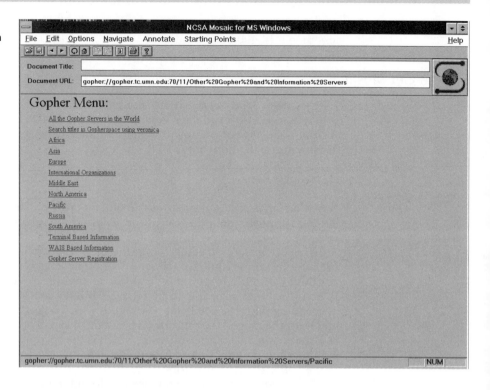

To go directly to a **Gopher** site, the following method will work. From the
File menu, click on the *Open URL* option. Enter the URL of the **Gopher** you want
to visit in this format:

```
gopher://address/
```

For example, to see the **Gopher** at The World, we enter the URL this way:

```
gopher://world.std.com/
```

Mosaic takes us directly to the site, as soon as we clicked on the **OK** button.

Figure 6.34 shows the beginning of Tennyson's "Ulysses," as presented on
The World's **Gopher** and viewed through **Mosaic**. Notice the lengthy URL in the
Document URL box. Every step of the retrieval process is encapsulated here, from
the **World's Gopher** address down to the exact path to the file.

FTP the Mosaic Way

And what about FTP? In Figure 6.35, we are looking at a list of FTP sites. Note
that the title of the current document, a list of sites, is shown at the top of the
screen; below it is the URL, which lays out the full path to the resource. Each of
the sites is underlined; clicking on any one of them opens the FTP connection
to the site. It is possible to move about in the directories of FTP sites looking for
information and reading files that interest you.

Figure 6.34
Tennyson's *Ulysses* viewed through **Mosaic** on The World's **Gopher**.

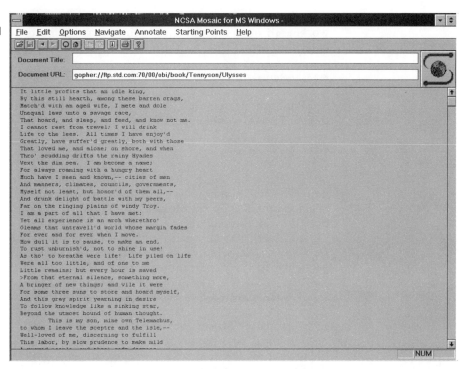

Figure 6.35
Examining a List of FTP Sites with **Mosaic**.

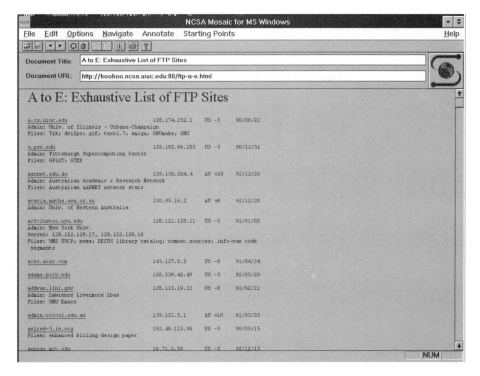

Perhaps you would like to go directly to a known FTP site, rather than working through a list of sites to find what you need. **Mosaic** can oblige if you enter the correct URL for the site. The URL should appear in this form:

```
file://address/
```

For example, to reach the **oak.oakland.edu** software repository by anonymous FTP, you would enter this as your URL:

```
file://oak.oakland.edu
```

Entering the URL is simple. Go to the *File* menu and click on the *Open URL* item. This will pop up a box within which you can enter the address. Then, by clicking on **OK**, you set **Mosaic** in motion to the destination. **Mosaic** will log onto the root directory at the FTP site.

You may now move through the directories at the site. As you do, the *Document URL* window will show the URL of each item you examine. A particular file may sport quite a lengthy URL. For example:

```
file://oak.oakland.edu/pub/msdos/compress/comp430s.zip
```

Fortunately, **Mosaic** handles the anonymous FTP login for you; there is no need to insert your password or enter **anonymous** at a prompt. Transferring a file to your own system is likewise easy. Bring down the *File* menu and click on the *Save As* option. Give the file the name of your choice.

Mosaic as USENET Reader

Reading USENET newsgroups is also a possibility, albeit a limited one, with **Mosaic**. Figure 6.36 shows a message from the USENET newsgroup **alt.architecture**. You can move among the various news hierarchies, reading messages as you please. **Mosaic** was not designed to be a news reader, and you will doubtless find that other ways of reading the news are more efficient, but this link to USENET demonstrates how widely the **Web** ranges, and how **Mosaic** presents the material thus discovered.

Running a Telnet Session

Activating a Telnet session through **Mosaic** is a workable proposition. To do so in the Microsoft Windows version of **Mosaic**, you must have a Windows Telnet product, and you need to specify the path to that program in you **mosaic.ini** file (which was created when you unpacked **Mosaic**). This file can be edited with any text editor; doing so allows you to tweak **Mosaic** to reflect your local system. Look for the last line in the *[Viewers]* section of the **mosaic.ini** file. You will find a line that looks like this:

```
telnet="c:\path\executable_name.exe"
```

This line must be edited to reflect the path to your own Telnet program. Once you have done so and saved the file, you can open a Telnet session.

Figure 6.36
Reading a USENET
newsgroup with **Mosaic**.

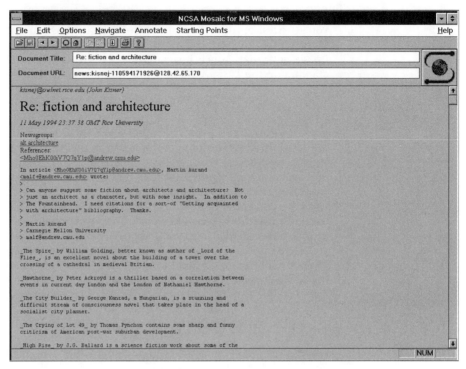

Go to the *File* menu and choose the *Open URL* item. When the dialog box pops up, enter a URL with information about the Telnet site you want to visit. The form is as follows:

```
telnet://address/
```

Assume, for example, that I would like to Telnet to the **sunsite.unc.edu** site. I would enter the URL this way:

```
telnet://sunsite.unc.edu/
```

Then, I would then click on the **OK** button, and the session would be activated.

Speeding Up Mosaic

Mosaic's graphical environment is a thing of beauty, particularly if you have long experience with the VT-100 interface. But using **Mosaic**'s images can be time-consuming as you wait for the graphics to load. Fortunately, there is a way to tell the program to bypass its screen images, and present you with icons in place of pictures.

With the Windows version of **Mosaic**, for example, you would bring down the *Options* menu, then choose the *Display Inline Images* item. This is a toggle switch. Click on it with the left mouse button and the check mark next to it will disappear, indicating you have told **Mosaic** not to display its images. Now, when you go to a site, you will get much quicker results. You can always see a particular image by clicking on the icon that represents it. And resetting **Mosaic** to display images automatically is just a matter of returning to the Options menu and again clicking on the *Display Inline Images* item.

Using the Hotlist

Uniform Resource Locators (URLs) allow us to specify the exact way to reach a particular Internet resource, no matter what the type. The downside of URLs is their length; these descriptors can be extensive, and you'd better enter them correctly or they won't work. To get around the problem, **Mosaic** includes a "hotlist" function. By pulling down the *Navigate* menu and clicking on the *Add Current to Hotlist* item, you have added the current document to your list. Now you can return to the page in question with a single mouse click. To do this in the Windows version, bring down the *File* menu and click on the *Open URL* item; a submenu will open with the items you have added to the hotlist displayed. Click on the items of your choice and **Mosaic** will create the connection. Your explorations on the net will uncover unexpected treasures, and the Hotlist is how you manage your finds.

MOSAIC AT WORK: GLOBAL NETWORK NAVIGATOR

O'Reilly & Associates, the Sebastopol, CA-based publisher and provider of network information, took an early lead in developing information services through the **World Wide Web** format. The company's *Global Network Navigator* is a **WWW**-based news and feature service that focuses on the Internet itself, with articles filled with background information, an on-line version of portions of Ed Krol's seminal *The Whole Internet User's Guide and Catalog*, and much more. GNN also contains a Marketplace section, where you will find a directory of commercial resources, products and services, as well as a Navigator's Forum, where ideas can be shared and questions answered.

The concept of an on-line magazine is hardly new; in fact, electronic journals have begun to proliferate on the Internet, in varying degrees of quality. But most of these are specialized publications, targeting researchers in particular academic fields. We are now seeing the beginning of a movement to bring electronic publishing into the mainstream. The obvious disadvantages of the medium—a screen is no substitute for the printed page, either in terms of comfort or the intangible quality of the reading experience—are at least ameliorated by the dynamic, interactive aspects of using a networked information tool.

Mosaic is obviously a major player in this; its page orientation is the closest thing going to the concept of a true electronic book. Watch what happens as we move beyond the limits of character-based interfaces. Figure 6.37, for example, shows us part of *Global Network Navigator* as seen by the VT-100 based **www** browser.

In this figure, we have moved past the entry menu and are examining the first page of *GNN Magazine*. This is the table of contents for the second issue, released in January, 1994. You can see that hypertext links have been established for each of these items. Simply pressing the number following each moves you directly to that article. Press a **RETURN** and you will see further possibilities. The interface is easy but pedestrian.

Figure 6.37
Global Network Navigator as shown through a VT-100 browser.

```
                                                    Table of Contents (22/42)
    GNN Magazine: Issue Two January 1994 (ISSN 1072-0413)

    The Internet -- An Education in Itself

      Remarks by Vice President Al Gore at National Press Club[1]

      Publishing for Professors [2] by Dale Dougherty

      Is the Surf Up?[3] by Mitchell Sprague

      Teaching and Learning in a Networked World[4] by Donna Donovan

      Environmental Education on the Net[5] by Laura Parker Roerden

      SchoolNet: Canada's Educational Networking Initiative[6] by Tyler Burns

      Academy One Introduces Classrooms to the Internet[7] by Linda Delzeit

      KIDLINK - Global Networking for Youth 10 - 15[8] by Odd de Presno

      Global Lab Project Cultivates Young Scientists[9] by Boris Berenfeld

    FIND <keywords>, 1-21, Back, <RETURN> for more, Quit, or Help:
```

Now examine the same interface as viewed with the help of **Mosaic**. Figure 6.38 shows the result. Here, underlining indicates links rather than text, and color is used as a tool to determine where the links exist. And, as you can see, we have also moved into the realm of graphical design, with handsome fonts setting off illustrations and text that reminds us more of a typical magazine as found on the newsstand than on a computerized information service. And, of course, we gain the advantages of hypertext—now we can move directly to the article we choose reading in a nonsequential but targeted manner. Note that we have place the marker (the little hand) on an article by Mitchell Sprague called "Is the Surf Up?"

Figure 6.39 takes the concept one step further. Here, as viewed with the **lynx** browser, is Sprague's feature. Obviously, we can read the text without great difficulty, but look at what we can do with **Mosaic**. In Figure 6.40, we see the article and a photograph of its author within a graphical format that is pleasing to the eye. Hands down, **Mosaic** wins the beauty contest.

MOSAIC'S FUTURE

With an on-line marketplace, a forum for Internet tips, and a thriving news-gathering and dissemination program, *Global Network Navigator* shows off **Mosaic** at its best, pointing to a networked future that taps pull-down menus, graphics, and other aids to simplify Internet exploration and bring the abundant resources of the network to more people. It will be intriguing to see how this journal fares, and whether it sets off a wave of interest in similar projects. For its part, O'Reilly & Associates, and Spry, a Seattle software firm, are following up with Internet-in-a-Box, a comprehensive package containing a subscription

Figure 6.38
*Global Network Navigator
as seen through* **Mosaic.**

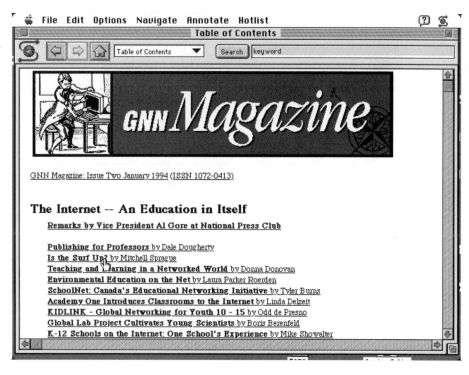

Figure 6.39
Viewing a GNN article
with the **lynx** browser.

```
                                                      Introduction (p1 of 2)

          Sponsored by O'Reilly & Associates: The Whole Internet Catalog




                                 IS THE SURF UP?

          by Mitchell Sprague




          _____


     Introduction



          I'd like to know who coined the term "Internet Surfing" and strap him
          to a surfboard going over Niagara Falls. It all sounded so glamorous.
          You dial in, push a few buttons, and information is at your
          fingertips. You crest on the wave of the information age, flawlessly
     --More-- This is a searchable index. Use 's' to search
          Arrow keys: Up and Down to move. Right to follow a link; Left to go back.
     H)elp O)ptions P)rint G)o M)ain screen Q)uit /=search [delete]=history list
```

Figure 6.40
The same article viewed through **Mosaic.**

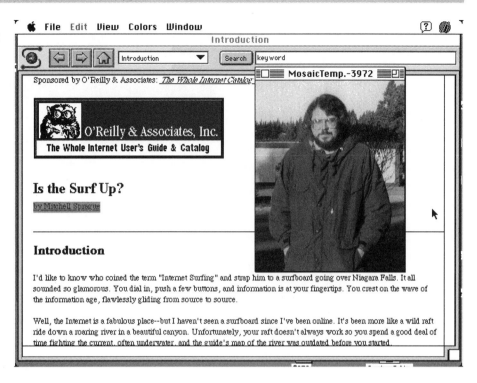

to GNN, a version of the **Mosaic** software, and other tools. The package includes a connection to NovX Interserve, a Seattle-based Internet service provider that uses SprintLink.

And in May 1994 came the announcement of Mosaic Communication Company, a firm launched with the notion of providing software and services for businesses and consumers on the Internet. Founded by Dr. James Clark, founder and former Chairman of Silicon Graphics, and Marc Andreessen, the originator of **Mosaic**, the company can also boast of a technical team that includes old **Mosaic** hands from the NCSA. In the cards from the Mosaic Communication Corp. is a "cyberspace mall," which will use **Mosaic** as the basis of an on-line "virtual" shopping place. The firm will also release a commercial **Mosaic** product and authoring tools.

7

HYTELNET:
The Database on Your
Computer

The **World Wide Web** is a powerful browsing tool, allowing us to wander through the Internet for hours at a time, exploring network connections and discovering new resources. But the **Web** is itself intimidating to the newcomer, who expects that somewhere a concise directory of Internet resources is to be found. Such a tool would allow the user to explore Internet connections off-line, thus avoiding the delays created by actually logging on at each site only to find that the information there isn't useful. But when the time came to log on to a given computer, the tool would make the process as painless as does the **Web**.

Couch these parameters within a hypertext context and you've described **HYTELNET**, a hypertext browser that charts many sites on the Internet that are accessible by Telnet, **Gopher**, and **WAIS**. Created by Peter Scott of the University of Saskatchewan Libraries, the earliest versions of the program were developed for MSDOS-compatible equipment, but subsequent versions have now appeared, the Macintosh adaptation created by Charles Burchill of the University of Manitoba, and a UNIX/VMS version prepared by Earl Fogel, of the Computing Services Department at the University of Saskatchewan.

If you plan to become an accomplished searcher of the Internet, **HYTELNET** needs to be in your bag of tricks. Like other search tools, the program offers its own particular slant on the navigation process. By downloading the software and running it on your own machine, any user (and this includes those dialing in to Internet connections) can take advantage of its useful index of resources. And while those without a direct network connection can't take advantage of **HYTELNET**'s ability to connect to the sites it displays, there are useful alternative ways to employ it.

Using HYTELNET

HYTELNET is useful to any category of Internet user. We can tap its resources in one of three ways:

- Using **HYTELNET** is easiest with a direct network connection. By downloading the software, we make available on our machines a directory which, with the pressing of a key, takes us directly to the sites it describes (this feature is available only on the Macintosh, UNIX, and VMS versions of **HYTELNET**). As opposed to the **World Wide Web**, the browsing process is completed on our own machines before a network connection is made. It is only when we have made the decision about a site we'd like to explore that we press the **RETURN** to begin the Telnet session. At that point, we use **HYTELNET**'s login information to begin our exploration of the remote computer.

- For those with dial-up connections only, **HYTELNET** is also useful, because the program not only describes Telnet sites but also provides login and instructions for each. Thus, tracking the addresses you need in your next Internet session becomes a trivial task, providing they are indexed by **HYTELNET**. You simply jot down what you need to know (or, if you're running a multitasking session, just keep **HYTELNET** running in a Window for easy reference) and then supply the necessary information to make the Telnet connection.

- Finally, **HYTELNET** is also available through Telnet. You can log on to a **HYTELNET** server and use the system on-line, checking the addresses you need for later Telnet sessions. Although the UNIX version accessible through Telnet is capable of making direct Telnet connections to remote sites, this feature is not available when you access the system through the **access.usask.ca** address we examine below. In the figures in this chapter, I use both a stand-alone implementation of **HYTELNET** as well as a Telnet connection to illustrate how the program works.

HYTELNET Servers

The following is a list of **HYTELNET** servers and their addresses.

Server	Address	Login
Columbia Law School	**lawnet.law.columbia.edu**	lawnet
El Paso Community College	**laguna.epcc.edu**	**library**

Server	Address	Login
Manchester Computing Centre, UK	**info.mcc.ac.uk**	**hytelnet**
National Chiao Tung University, Taiwan	**nctuccca.edu.tw**	**hytelnet**
Oxford University, UK	**rsl.ox.ac.uk**	**hytelnet**
University of Adelaide, Australia	**library.adelaide.edu.au**	**access**
University of Arizona	**info.ccit.arizona.edu**	**hytelnet**
University of California, San Diego	**infopath.ucsd.edu**	Log in as **infopath**. Select "Computing Services" from main menu. Select "HYTELNET" from next menu.
University of Saskatchewan, Canada	**access.usask.ca**	**hytelnet**
University of Denver	**du.edu**	Log in as **atdu**. Select "internet" from main menu. Select <program> to access HYTELNET.

Downloading HYTELNET

HYTELNET is frequently updated as Telnet addresses change and new ones are added, which makes keeping up with new versions a critical matter. You can always find the latest version of the program at the University of Saskatchewan. The address is **ftp.usask.ca**. Use anonymous FTP to connect and download the software. The directory to look in is *pub/HYTELNET*, where you will find a listing of the subdirectories for the various operating platforms, as shown here. Note that there is even an Amiga implementation of **HYTELNET**.

```
drwxr-xr-x  2 1033    system     512 Aug 27 17:00 amiga
drwxr-xr-x  3 1033    system     512 Oct 15 15:02 mac
drwxr-xr-x  3 1340    system    3584 Jan  6 18:39 pc
drwxr-xr-x  3 1033    system     512 Oct 25 14:29 unix
drwxr-xr-x  3 1033    system     512 Oct 19 10:45 vms
```

To reach any of these directories, enter **cd *directory_name***. In other words, to get the PC version, you would type **cd pc**. To get the Macintosh version, it's **cd mac**, and so on.

The archival file for **HYTELNET** is located within each directory. At the time of this writing, the software had reached version 6.6. The filename for the PC was **hyteln66.zip**, a zipped file containing the necessary executable program and support files. While the version number will change as **HYTELNET** undergoes its frequent updates (the software is made available in new versions every two months), the format isn't likely to vary, so look for **hytelnxx.zip**, where *xx* stands for version numbers. If you're a Mac user, the file is **HYTELNET6.6.sea.hqx**.

Hint:

Don't forget that whatever platform you're going to use **HYTELNET** on, the program you're downloading is a compressed file. To download it correctly, you must enter the **binary** command at the **ftp>** prompt before you start the actual download. After logging in at **ftp.usask.ca**, enter **binary** followed by a **RETURN** before changing directories. Doing so will ensure an accurate download. The file transfer command itself is standard FTP— **get hyteln66.zip** (for MS-DOS machines). Once unpacked and installed, the program creates numerous subdirectories and individual files.

If you intend to use **HYTELNET** through a Telnet session, choosing, for whatever reason, not to run it on your PC, you certainly can, and we'll see in a moment how to invoke the program through Telnet. But I recommend that you consider downloading this admittedly gigantic database anyway. Having a wealth of Internet destinations available for your off-line browsing can be extremely useful, and it is guaranteed to give you ideas about future sessions you'd like to try. At the very least, consider downloading the software, unpacking it, and running it just to get the feel of the interface. Like the **World Wide Web**, it's an easy program to master.

Hint:

Although versions of **HYTELNET** exist for various platforms, the Mac, UNIX, and VMS versions of the database all use the information files included in the PC version. This means that if you plan to download one of the other versions, you will need to also download these text files. Further information is available at the FTP site.

PUTTING HYTELNET TO WORK

Now let's make a Telnet connection to **HYTELNET** to examine how the system works. If you were to use the **HYTELNET** software on your own computer, you would see something very similar to the UNIX version that I'm showing here (I'm accessing this through a Telnet session). The basic principles of moving around the system and retrieving information remain the same no matter what the platform.

There are a variety of sites that now make **HYTELNET** available through Telnet, all of them accessible through the **HYTELNET** program itself. To find out what they are, you need to first access the University of Saskatchewan's **HYTELNET** server. To do so, Telnet to the address **access.usask.ca**. Your command, in other words, should be **telnet access.usask.ca**. When prompted, log in as **hytelnet**.

When you have performed the login, you will see the screen shown in Figure 7.1. As you can see, there is a menu of items, each with a bracketed abbreviation to its right. A highlight sits atop *<WHATIS>*, which is the abbreviation for *What is HYTELNET?*

Figure 7.1
Logging in to use
HYTELNET at
access.usask.ca.

```
              Welcome to HYTELNET version 6.6.x
                 Last Update: January 6, 1994

          What is HYTELNET?              <WHATIS>
          Library catalogs              <SITES1>
          Other resources              <SITES2>
          Help files for catalogs      <OPOOO>
          Catalog interfaces           <SYSOOO>
          Internet Glossary            <GLOSSARY>
          Telnet tips                  <TELNET>
          Telnet/TN3270 escape keys    <ESCAPE.KEY>
          Key-stroke commands          <HELP>


   Up/Down arrows MOVE     Left/Right arrows SELECT     ? for HELP anytime

       m  returns here     i  searches the index     q  quits


            HYTELNET 6.6 was written by Peter Scott
          E-mail address: aa375@freenet.carleton.ca
             Unix and VMS software by Earl Fogel
```

Like **Gopher**, **HYTELNET** poses few conceptual difficulties. You move about the screen by using the **Up** and **Down Arrow** keys, just as it says on the screen. To select an item after you have moved to it, there are several options. You can push either the **Right** or **Left Arrow** key, or else enter a **RETURN** at this point. The item you have selected will then appear on the screen. Figure 7.2 shows what happened when I pushed the **RETURN** key with the arrow over the *<WHATIS>* item.

The range of **HYTELNET** information is also suggested, though imperfectly, by the opening menu (Figure 7.1). Library catalogs are certainly a major feature of **HYTELNET**'s listings (remember that **HYTELNET**'s developer is a library specialist). You should also be aware that the program is based on the University of North Texas' directory of Telnet-accessible library catalogs, maintained by Billy Barron. The *raison d'etre* of the UNT list is to serve as a directory of on-line bibliographic databases with accompanying Telnet site information, so the library-oriented slant of **HYTELNET** is understandable.

Browse down the list. There are items marked *Other resources <SITES2>* and *Catalog interfaces <SYS000>*. A world of information can lurk behind the simplest menu entry. Pressing the **RETURN** key with the highlight on *<SITES2>*, for example, reveals a powerful submenu:

```
Other Telnet-accessible resources

            <ARC000>  Archie: Archive Server Listing Service
            <CWI000>  Campus-wide Information systems
            <FUL000>  Databases and bibliographies

            <DIS000>  Distributed File Servers (Gopher/WAIS/WWW)
            <BOOKS>   Electronic books
            <FEE000>  Fee-Based Services
```

Figure 7.2
Moving into
HYTELNET's linkages
to look at information
about the program.

```
                        HYTELNET version 6.6....

        Is designed to assist users in reaching all of the
        INTERNET-accessible libraries, Free-nets, CWISs, BBSs, &
        other information sites by Telnet, specifically those
        users who access Telnet via a modem, serial line, or
        direct network connection.

        HYTELNET is available on IBM PC, Unix, VMS and Macintosh
        systems.  You are now using the Unix version.


        For information on customizing the program   <CUSTOM>
        For accessible Library on-line catalogs       <SITES1>
        For other information sites                   <SITES2>
        For more information on the program           <READ.ME>
```

```
        <FRE000>   FREE-NETs & Community Computing Systems
        <BBS000>   General Bulletin Boards
        <HYT000>   HYTELNET On-line versions

        <NAS000>   NASA databases
        <NET000>   Network Information Services
        <DIR000>   Whois/White Pages/Directory Services

        <OTH000>   Miscellaneous resources
```

Notice the range here. We have links to everything from **archie**, our FTP file finder, to **CWIS** systems of university personnel and students. We also have major entries such as *<FUL000>*, which points to databases, and *<FRE000>*, pointing at Free-Net systems worldwide. *<DIR000>* covers various white pages directory systems, while *<HYT000>*shows us the location of other on-line versions of **HYTELNET**.

Let's take the *<HYT000>* option for a moment. Here, we find where other **HYTELNET** sites are:

```
On-Line versions of HYTELNET

<HYT006> Columbia Law School
<HYT005> El Paso Community College
<HYT008> Manchester Computing Centre
<HYT002> National Chiao Tung University (CCCA)
<HYT009> Oxford University
<HYT010> University of Adelaide
<HYT011> University of Arizona
<HYT007> University of California, San Diego
<HYT001> University of Saskatchewan
<HYT003> University of Denver
```

By pressing the **RETURN** key with the highlight on any one of these items, we can learn more about it. Figure 7.3, for example, shows us the opening screen at the National Chiao Tung University in Taiwan.

Figure 7.3
Gathering sign-on
information for a Telnet
session to a distant site.

```
                    National Chiao Tung University (CCCA)

TELNET NCTUCCCA.EDU.TW or 140.111.3.21
login: hytelnet

        Campus Computer Communication Association (CCCA)        NCTUCCCA.edu.tw
        National Chiao Tung University, Taiwan, R.O.C.          HYTELNET Version 6.5


                                                        Public Access HYTELNET
        What Is HYTELNET?              <WHATIS>
        Taiwan (TANet) Resources      <TAIWAN>          Univ of Saskatchewan
        Internet Library Catalogs     <SITES1>             Access.USask.CA
        Other Internet Resources      <SITES2>              (128.233.3.1)
        Help File For Catalogs        <OP000>          Natl Chiao Tung Univ
        Catalog Interfaces            <SYS000>             NCTUCCCA.edu.tw
        Internet Glossary             <GLOSSARY>           (140.111.3.21)


                                                           SPECIAL COLUMN
    H  MOVEMENT            SELECT
    E  DownArrow,j:Down    RightArrow,l:Next Topic         <CCCA> What's CCCA?
    L  UpArrow,k:Up        LeftArrow,h:Previous Topic      <AUTHOR> Orig. Author
    -- press space for more --
```

Hint:

If we are using **HYTELNET** as a stand-alone reference program, we could press the **RETURN** key with the highlight on this item to retrieve the information we need to log in. In this case, because we're not on-line, **HYTELNET** can't make the connection, but it can provide us the necessary data. We learn, for example, that the address for this **HYTELNET** server is **nctuccca.edu.tw**. We also learn that the login here is identical to that in Saskatchewan: **hytelnet**. If we were so inclined, then, we could access this server through a direct Telnet connection rather than routing ourselves through Canada.

As you move from one **HYTELNET** server to another, you won't necessarily see the identical set of information or, depending on your access method, even the same interface. But the underlying program is **HYTELNET**. Check into **HYTELNET** at the University of Arizona and you get the basic **HYTELNET** package, as at Saskatchewan. Try Columbia Law School and you get this menu:

```
CU-LawNet Info System
------------------------------------------------------------------
  1 - Law Library Catalog PEGASUS
  2 - University Catalog  CLIO
  3 - Project JANUS experimental textual search interface
  4 - Law School Academic Services
  5 - Law School Career Services
```

```
6 - ColumbiaNet
7 - Advanced World wide library access (HYTELNET)
h - Help message

-----------------------------------------------------------------

Please make a selection or enter Q to quit.
```

Don't expect every **HYTELNET** implementation to look the same then; certainly as **Gopher** has spread around the Internet, the variety of individual **Gopher**s has become more and more apparent. The same thing seems to be happening with **HYTELNET**, although the process hasn't gone nearly as far.

THE HYTELNET COMMANDS

There are few commands to master with **HYTELNET**, and here they are, along with their variations.

Down arrow	Selects the next menu item.
Up arrow	Selects the previous menu item.
Right arrow	Moves to the next menu page (this is the same as pressing the **RETURN** key).
Left arrow	Moves back to the previous menu page.
+	Scrolls down to the next menu page.
-	Scrolls up to the previous menu page.
m	Returns you to the main screen.
?	Produces a help screen.
q	Quits HYTELNET.

HYTELNET AS SEARCH TOOL

HYTELNET's resemblance to the **World Wide Web** is the result of its hypertext linkages. Using its browser, you move about a database by choosing items, delving deeper into subjects that interest you. The same positive aspects of **World Wide Web** that we have already discussed—its ability to let you discover information by following your nose down virtual pathways, its excellence as a browsing tool—apply to **HYTELNET**. And so, of course, do its defects. We can't readily search **HYTELNET**, for example, by entering a keyword and letting a search engine go to work. Instead, we must manage the process ourselves, by choosing menu item after menu item and checking out what we find.

Hint:

Assuming you are a dial-up user, you can save the network considerable traffic if you download **HYTELNET** and run your search on it off-line before trying anything else. This way, you can explore the pathways to the information you need without tying up network resources. You can then access your service provider and run the necessary Telnet session to reach the site you require. Using Telnet to access the **HYTELNET** servers is helpful in understanding how the program works, but if you keep the program on your system, you minimize network workload.

Searching for the WELL

Established in Sausalito, CA in 1985, The WELL has established itself as one of the on-line world's more interesting destinations. Its ancestry as a resource of the *Whole Earth Catalog* community has ensured it an active base of users and system operators who are concerned with using technology to advance the social welfare. Having heard interesting things about this system, I decided to find it on-line to learn more. **HYTELNET** can help with this search.

The most obvious place to begin such a search is under the *Other resources* <*SITES2*> heading from the main menu (Figure 7.1). Highlighting it, I press a **RETURN** to access the list of Internet destinations previously shown. I'm interested in checking several of these. <*FEE000*> *Fee-Based Services* is a possibility; without knowing whether a fee is involved in accessing The WELL, it would be wise to put this on our list for future reference. <*FRE000*> *FREE-NETs & Community Computing Systems* is also a possibility; after all, The WELL has made quite a name for itself as a community service system, bringing the benefits of worldwide networking to an active local as well as international community.

And then there's <*BBS000*> *General Bulletin Boards*; again, it's a possibility, depending on how we stretch the definition of bulletin board. <*NET000*> *Network Information Services* may have something on The WELL, but it doesn't seem likely; these tend to be network-affiliated sites such as NICs (Network Information Centers); the InterNIC is a good example. Let's go ahead and check <*NET000*> just to be on the safe side. What we retrieve is a multipage list:

```
Network Information Services

<NET001> ASK: German Universities' Online Information
<NET002> BASUN: Information System for the Swedish University Network
<NET003> CONCISE: COSINE Network's Central Information Service for Europe
<NET016> DATAPAC Information System
<NET004> DFN-Informationssytem
<NET005> INFO und Softserver (Information & Software Server)(Stuttgart)
<NET006> Internet Resource Guide
<NET018> InterNIC Registration Services Center
<NET015> Inter-Network Mail Guide
<NET007> JANET News (Joint Academic Network)(United Kingdom)
<NET008> JvNCnet Network Information Center On-Line (NICOL)
<NET020> Korea Network Information Center
<NET014> Merit Net Mail Sites Database
<NET009> MichNet Online Help System
<NET010> Network Information Center On-Line Aid System (NICOLAS)
```

```
<NET011> NYSERView (Network Information Interface)
<NET021> ONet (Ontario Network)/Internet Instruction
<NET012> RIPE Network Coordination Centre (NCC)
<NET017> TENET (information and application)
<NET019> University of Colorado Fremont demo login
<NET013> Usenet News
```

You can see at a glance that **HYTELNET** has gathered a great deal of useful information about various network connections. It's helpful, for example, to know that you have quick access to the InterNIC and RIPE, the European Network Information Centre in Amsterdam. No mention of The WELL, however; we're in the wrong category of material.

<BBS000> General Bulletin Boards is another possibility. Here, we generate a second multipage list containing bulletin board systems accessible on the Internet. Some examples follow:

```
<BBS052> CAPPnet: California Academic Partnership Program
<BBS071> Classroom Earth!
<BBS005> Cosy at Victoria, British Columbia, Canada
<BBS007> Delft University Bulletin Board System (Netherlands)
<BBS038> Edinburgh University Computing Service - EUCS
<BBS058> European Southern Observatory Bulletin Board
<BBS068> FedWorld: National Technical Information Service
<BBS008> Florida Atlantic University
<BBS041> Grants Bulletin Board (CALSTATE)
<BBS009> Hewlett-Packard Calculator Bulletin Board
<BBS036> Humanities Communication Bulletin Board Project (HUMBUL)
<BBS066> ICU BBS : Informatik Club Der Universataet Zuerich
<BBS048> International Education Bulletin Board
<BBS059> IRIS Data Management Center Electronic Bulletin Board
<BBS046> Karl's Cafe / AKCS Public Access Site
```

It's an interesting list, to be sure; these are bulletin board systems that contain Internet hooks to allow users to log on via Telnet. Public access UNIX sites are available, as are a number of specialized bulletin boards like Classroom Earth! and the Humanities Communication Bulletin Board Project. But The WELL doesn't make the list; it's much more of a full-service system as well as an Internet access provider than a bulletin board per se.

<FRE000> FREE-NETs & Community Computing Systems is next on our list. Here we're looking at regional and community-based systems. Free-Nets in particular are interesting; they're public-access computer systems created by local activists whose vision of socially conscious telecommunications has extended many benefits of the Internet to people who would otherwise not have them. The WELL isn't exactly a Free-Net, but let's see what else is on this menu. Here's a snippet:

```
<FRE013> Big Sky Telegraph
<FRE012> Buffalo FREE-NET
<FRE022> CapAccess: National Capital Area Public Access Network
<FRE001> Cleveland FREE-NET
<FRE023> Columbia Online Information Network (COIN)
<FRE029> Dayton FREE-NET
<FRE011> Denver FREE-NET
<FRE002> Heartland FREE-NET
<FRE008> Lorain County FREE-NET
<FRE026> Milwaukee FREE-NET
<FRE017> National Capital Freenet, Ottawa, Canada
<FRE028> Rio Grande FREE-NET
```

There are plenty of interesting systems here (Big Sky Telegraph in Montana, in particular, is one of the most creative networking projects in the US), but no WELL.

We fall back on our final possiblity: *<FEE000> Fee-Based Services*. Pressing **RETURN** with the highlight on the item takes us to a multipage listing of systems that charge for access. Here's a sample of what we find there:

```
<FEE019> PORTAL Online Communications Service
<FEE023> STN (Scientific and Technical Information Network)
<FEE057> Techbook
<FEE022> Telerama
<FEE063> TelLink Networking - An Internet access service
<FEE028> Texas Department of Commerce Bulletin Board
<FEE064> Texas Innovation Network
<FEE032> Texas Metronet
<FEE045> Universal Access Online Communications Service
<FEE036> Vnet Internet Access - Charlotte North Carolina
<FEE027> Web - The Network for social change
<FEE007> The WELL, Sausalito, California
<FEE015> The World
<FEE033> Wyvern Technologies, Inc.
```

The WELL is listed as *<FEE007>*. In a stand-alone implementation of **HYTELNET**, I can now press the **RETURN** key on this item to see the necessary Telnet information:

```
The WELL, Sausalito, California

TELNET WELL.SF.CA.US or 192.132.30.2
Type your userid or   newuser   to register
```

Also presented are two screens of information about the system, which allow us to make the Telnet connection, log on and, if we choose, establish an account. And remember, with the UNIX/VMS implementation of **HYTELNET** we can make the actual connection by pressing the **RETURN** key.

Hint:

You can see from the preceding search that **HYTELNET** lacks an ability to search across its menu structure; it could use its own equivalent of **Veronica**. In the absence of such a tool, PC users could search across directories with an external program like Magellan. Mac users could use Gofer. On the other hand, no search tool is devoid of context. **HYTELNET** exists to provide as comprehensive as possible a directory of Internet-wide resources, as opposed to **Gopher**, which attempts to establish a local menu structure with links to the rest of the Internet. **HYTELNET** is thus a valuable resource because it compresses a wide range of information in a small space. I often turn to it first when I'm browsing for good sources on particular subjects.

HYTELNET AND LIBRARY RESOURCES

Library catalogs are the reason why **HYTELNET** was created; it shouldn't surprise us that they remain its strongest suit. The main menu item, *Library Catalogs <SITES1>*, takes us to a submenu offering a choice of libraries in the Americas, Europe and Scandinavia, and Asia, Pacific, and South Africa. Within each, the library listings are broken down by country, as shown:

```
Europe/Scandinavia


    <AT000>    Austria
    <BE000>    Belgium
    <DK000>    Denmark
    <FI000>    Finland
    <FR000>    France
    <DE000>    Germany
    <HU000>    Hungary
    <IS000>    Iceland
    <IE000>    Ireland
    <IL000>    Israel
    <IT000>    Italy
    <NL000>    Netherlands
    <NO000>    Norway
    <ES000>    Spain
    <SE000>    Sweden
    <CH000>    Switzerland
    <UK000>    United Kingdom
```

Pressing a **RETURN** on one of these items produces site information for various systems. Here, for example, is the listing for the University of Budapest:

```
Technical University of Budapest

TELNET TULIBB.KKT.BME.HU or 152.66.114.1
Username: aleph
At the CCL> prompt, type  ?/eng for English version

To exit, hit the Telnet escape key
```

Now, all this is well and good, but isn't this what **HYTELNET** does with all its resources? The answer is yes, but there's more to the story. The great profusion of searchable library catalogs on the Internet presents us with a useful tool, but library systems abound in utter profusion. Sure, we can use Telnet to get into a particular site, but what do we do when we're there? Perhaps the library in question is running software called CLSI, or DOBIS/LIBIS, or DYNIX, or GALAXY. Then again, maybe its librarians work with GEAC, GEAC ADVANCE, GvB, or INLEX. The list can be extended quite a way, to NOTIS systems, to the OCLC interface, to PALS. Each of these systems provides access to a library catalog, but with its own interface and command structure. What's a user to do?

HYTELNET is a handy tool for addressing this problem; if your needs include library searching, you should have it in your arsenal. From the main menu, take the item marked *Help files for catalogs <OP000>*; a press of the **RETURN** key leads you to a listing of all the above-mentioned library software systems. Pressing the **RETURN** on NOTIS, for example, calls up several screens, such as the following:

```
Using NOTIS

Title searches:      To search for a particular title, use the t= search
                     command followed by the title.
                     Example:  t=foundation

Author searches:     To search for a particular author, use the a= search
                     command followed by the author's name.
                     Example:  a=asimov

Subject searches:    To search for a particular subject, use the s=
                     search command followed by the subject.
                     Example:  s=tennis

Keyword searches:    To search for a particular keyword, use the k=
                     search command followed by a string.
                     Example:  k=cry wolf

                     You may use the logical operator (AND, OR, NOT) and
                     parenthesis to group the operators.
                     Also, $ is a wildcard  character.
                     Examples: k=car and fast
                               k=computer and not ibm
                               k=comp$ and (toy or game)
```

As you can see, **HYTELNET** has delivered the basic tools for getting around the system. Keeping **HYTELNET** ready for use as you engage in a Telnet session with a remote library may be one of the best moves you can make. It's hard to imagine taking full advantage of the Internet's library resources without it.

Using HYTELNET through Gopher

A helpful implementation of **HYTELNET** through **Gopher** is available at Washington and Lee University. The address is **liberty.us.wlu.edu**. Your command, assuming you have a **Gopher** client accessible, would therefore be **gopher liberty.us.wlu.edu**. Alternatively, you could find this **Gopher** by using Telnet to one of the **Gopher** sites available thusly, and then follow menus to access remote **Gopher** sites from there. But the client approach is easier.

At the Washington and Lee **Gopher**, look for a menu item like the following:

```
-->  4. Explore Internet Resources/
```

From there, the following submenu will take you to the **HYTELNET** options:

```
-->  5. HYTELNET (Telnet Login to Sites)/
```

The **Gopher** implementation of **HYTELNET** is helpful because it brings a search capability into play that **HYTELNET** would otherwise lack. Examine the following screen to see what I mean. The **Gopher** has broken down **HYTELNET**'s menued information into separate branches, and includes a search option under item 1.

```
Internet Gopher Information Client v1.11

                        HYTELNET (Telnet Login to Sites)
 -->  1. HYTELNET (word search) <?>
      2. Library Catalogs /
      3. Library Catalogs, By System Type /
      4. Library Catalogs, Help Files /
      5. New or Revised HYTELNET Entries        [updated: Monday 9:52]/
      6. Other Resources /
```

By pressing a **RETURN** at this point, we call up a search screen in the usual **Gopher** format. I tried out this feature by entering the term **nasa** in the search field and pressing another **RETURN**. I retrieved the list below:

```
Internet Gopher Information Client v1.11

                     HYTELNET (word search): nasa

 -->  1. NASA Goddard Space Flight Center.
      2. NASA Goddard Space Flight Center <TEL>
      3. NASA Mid-continent regional technology transfer center BBS.
      4. NASA Mid-continent regional technology transfer center BBS <TEL>
      5. NASA Science Internet (NSI) Online Network Data.
      6. NASA Science Internet (NSI) Online Network Data <TEL>
      7. NASA Spacelink <TEL>
      8. NASA Spacelink.
      9. NASA/IPAC Extragalactic Database.
     10. NASA/IPAC Extragalactic Database <TEL>
```

By allowing you to cluster various references from **HYTELNET** and to search across its menu structure, **Gopher** thus provides a **Veronica**-style boost to the program. Of course, the actual boost is provided by **WAIS**, which underlies the **Gopher** engine in this case. It's an example of how integrated search engines change the way we work on the Internet, often functioning behind the scenes to do so.

KEEPING UP WITH HYTELNET

HYTELNET is expanding rapidly, with frequent new versions and ever-widening coverage. With over 1,400 Internet sites, the system now includes Campus Wide Information Systems (**CWIS**), **Gopher** and **WAIS** sites, **World Wide Web** sites, and more. You should make it a point to keep up with **HYTELNET** and update your software as frequently as possible. To do so, consider joining the **HYTELNET** mailing list, which is simple. Send mail to the following address:

listserv@kentvm.bitnet

or

listserv@kentvm.kent.edu

In your message, include the following line:

```
subscribe hytel-l firstname lastname
```

Insert your own name in the above statement, and leave the message field blank.

The archive site for the **HYTELNET** list is at **listserv@kentvm.bitnet**. Send the command **INDEX HYTEL-L** to retrieve the index. You can search for material by using the methods outlined in Chapter 9 on BITNET archives.

LIBTEL—AN ON-LINE LIBRARY RESOURCE

Two other menu-driven systems exist to provide access to library materials, as well as BBS systems, **CWIS** implementations, databases, and other resources. Both provide active links to Telnet so that you can find what you need and access it immediately. **LIBTEL** was developed by Dan Mahone, of the University of New Mexico in Albuquerque; it is available in UNIX and VMS versions, as well as through a Telnet connection. **LIBS** comes from Mark Mesmer at Sonoma State University in California. Let's take a quick look at both.

LIBTEL was designed to provide access through menus to libraries and public access database sites around the world. Once you've found the resource you're interested in, **LIBTEL** proceeds to make the connection for you. An inherent problem in library searching remains, however—namely, that you can easily move between library collections in a wide variety of areas, but you don't necessarily know which is the most likely site for what you need. Fortunately, **Gopher** once again springs to the rescue, as we'll see shortly. For now, we'll use **LIBTEL** to make the connection.

To access **LIBTEL**, use Telnet to connect to the following site:

```
bbs.oit.unc.edu
```

Log in as **bbs**. You will be greeted with a menu and asked to set up a new account, which you can do by entering your name and choosing a password. From this point, follow the menu structure to reach **LIBTEL**. The software currently appears as menu item 3.

```
3. On-line Information Systems (LIBTEL)
```

Choose this item and you will be taken to the primary **LIBTEL** menu:

```
Internet Accessible Libraries and Information Systems
_____

(NA)    North American Region    (MISC) Miscellaneous Services

(EUR)   European Region          (BBS)  Other Bulletin Boards

(ANZ)   Pacifica Region          (NOT)  Notes on LIBTEL (Please Read)

(ASA)   Asian Region             (CTP)  Contemporary Poetry
```

```
(ME)   Middle-Eastern Region      (EXIT) Go Back to the BBS

To return to this screen during search press 'ctrl G'
Where would you like to go?
```

The beauty of **LIBTEL** is similar to that of **HYTELNET**; both are easy to use. In this case, the idea is to choose one of the terms in parentheses, which will take you to a submenu for the particular library region you are interested in. I will choose (NA) for North American libraries, and retrieve the following menu:

```
North American Region Libraries and Information Systems
----------------------------------------------------------------
(AL)Alabama             (ME)Maine           (OH)Ohio
(AK)Alaska              (MB)Manitoba        (OK)Oklahoma
(AB)Alberta             (MD)Maryland        (ON)Ontario
(AZ)Arizona             (MA)Massachusetts   (OR)Oregon
(AR)Arkansas            (MI)Michigan        (PA)Pennsylvania
(BC)British Columbia    (MN)Minnesota       (PE)Prince Edward I.
(CA)California          (MS)Mississippi     (QB)Quebec
(CO)Colorado            (MO)Missouri        (RI)Rhode Island
(CT)Connecticut         (MT)Montana         (SA)Saskatchewan
(DE)Delaware            (MX)MEXICO          (SC)South Carolina
(DC)Washington DC       (NE)Nebraska        (SD)South Dakota
(FL)Florida             (NV)Nevada          (TN)Tennessee
(GA)Georgia             (NB)New Brunswick   (TX)Texas
(HI)Hawaii              (NF)Newfoundland    (UT)Utah
(ID)Idaho               (NH)New Hampshire   (VT)Vermont
(IL)Illinois            (NJ)New Jersey      (VA)Virginia
(IN)Indiana             (NM)New Mexico      (WA)Washington
(IA)Iowa                (NY)New York        (WV)West Virginia
(KS)Kansas              (NC)North Carolina  (WI)Wisconsin
(KY)Kentucky            (ND)North Dakota    (WY)Wyoming
(LA)Loisiana            (NS)Nova Scotia
Where would you like to go? [RETURN to exit]
```

All of the available areas are shown with the necessary commands in parentheses. A native of Missouri, I'll choose that state by entering **MO** followed by a **RETURN**. I am then presented with a submenu of possible sites there:

```
Missouri


             University of Missouri

             1. Columbia Campus

             2. Rolla Campus

             3. St. Louis campus

          4. Washington University in St. Louis


Pick a number [RETURN exits]
```

When I choose item number 1, for the University of Missouri at Columbia, something interesting happens. I am presented with the necessary login information to get me into the system there, a sequence I wouldn't have been able to duplicate without this helpful screen:

```
Columbia Campus

                Press TAB to get to the COMMAND prompt and type
                DIAL VTAM. At the next prompt, type LUMIN
                To quit, type #LOGOFF and then UNDIAL.
Connect?  [y]
```

Note the last item. By entering a **y**, followed by a **RETURN**, at this point, I tell **LIBTEL** to make the Telnet connection for me. Like the Macintosh, UNIX, and VMS versions of **HYTELNET**, **LIBTEL** can take you directly to the site. Here is the result, the login screen at the University of Missouri at Columbia:

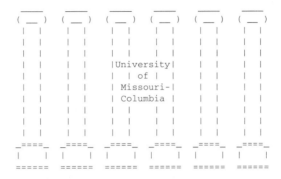

```
VM/ESA ONLINE
              ____     ____     ____   ____     ____     ____
            ( __ )  ( __ )  ( __ )  ( __ )  ( __ )  ( __ )
             |   |    |   |    |   |    |   |    |   |    |   |
             |   |    |   |    |   |    |   |    |   |    |   |
             |   |    |   |    |   |    |   |    |   |    |   |
             |   |    |   |    |University|    |   |    |   |
             |   |    |   |    |  | of |  |    |   |    |   |
             |   |    |   |    | Missouri-|    |   |    |   |
             |   |    |   |    | Columbia |    |   |    |   |
             |   |    |   |    |   |    |   |    |   |    |   |
             |   |    |   |    |   |    |   |    |   |    |   |
             |   |    |   |    |   |    |   |    |   |    |   |
             _====_   _====_   _====_  _====_   _====_   _====_
             |  |  |   |  |  |   |  |  |  |  |  |   |  |  |   |  |  |
             ======   ======   ======  ======   ======   ======

   Fill in your USERID and PASSWORD and press ENTER                    >
   PASSWORD ===>

   COMMAND  ===>

                                                        RUNNING   MIZZOU1
```

LIBTEL is clearly a simple and accessible system. Given the large number of library catalogs now on the Internet, having a concentration of possible sites in one place is extremely useful, as is the sign-on information. **LIBTEL's** disadvantage at present is that it is available only through the overworked UNC site. Were such tools to spread to numerous additional sites, using library catalogs would become much easier.

Hint:

As with all Internet tools, you must be wary of generalizations. **LIBTEL** occasionally blips; in fact, when running a recent session, I discovered that the login information required had been changed at the remote site I was trying to access. If this happens to you, consider changing sites for your search, and be aware that some libraries are beginning to restrict access to their catalogs. Or, if the site in question is important to you, wait a day or two for **LIBTEL** to be updated to reflect the change.

USING LIBS TO SEARCH REMOTE LIBRARIES

LIBS (**L**ibrary **I**nternet **B**rowsing **S**oftware) is a Telnet-based network access tool that helps users find and log on to library catalog systems. The program became available in June, 1991, reaching what creator Mark Mesmer considered a stable version 1.0 in July of that year. Originally crafted to run under the VMS operating system, **LIBS** became available in 1992 in a UNIX version. The system also grew in size, connecting to numerous on-line library catalogs as well as campus wide information systems (**CWIS**), information services, and a variety of databases. Mesmer, who is Director of Computing, Media and Telecommunications at Sonoma State University in California, continues to refine and extend the software.

How can you use **LIBS**? If your site does not make it available locally, you can evaluate the program through a Telnet session. The Telnet connections available for **LIBS** are shown in the following list.

Address	Site	Login
nic.csu.net	California State University	**libs**
nessie.cc.wwu.edu	Western Washington University	**libs**
rsl.ox.ac.uk	Menuegesteuerter hierarchischer Bibliothekszugang	**libs**
garam.kreonet.re.kr	KREONet, Republic of Korea	**nic**
info.anu.edu.au,	Electronic Library Information Service at Australian National University	**library**
oavax.csuchico.edu	CSU Chico LIBS Information Service	**libs**

As you can see, the standard login for a **LIBS** system is **libs**. After using Telnet to reach one of these sites, and entering **libs** at the login prompt, you will see a menu like this one:

```
          LIBS - Internet Access Software v2.0
     Mark Resmer, Sonoma State University, Dec 1992
                   WWU rev. 10/11/93
     On-line services available through the Internet:
     1 United States Library Catalogs
     2 Library Catalogs in other countries
     3 Campus-wide Information Systems
     4 Databases and Information Services
     5 Wide-area Information Services
     6 Information for first time users
     7 Special Internet Connection List

     Press RETURN alone to exit now or
     press Control-C Q <return> to exit at any time

     Enter the number of your choice:
```

The menu is straightforward. Note that, like **HYTELNET**, **LIBS** includes links to a wide variety of information. We'll begin our examination by asking to see library catalogs in the United States (menu item 1). The menu of states gives us the ability to pick one. Let's choose Hawaii.

```
University of Hawaii

Note the following instructions carefully
Once you are connected:

The UH Computing Center greeting will display, which concludes with the prompt:
"enter class". Then type LIB.

Select VT100 as your terminal type from the menu (option 5)
To exit the system, simply type //EXIT,
or press Control-Z Q <return> to exit at any time

Do you want to connect now? (Y or N):
```

We have all the information we need to log on at the University of Hawaii, and a prompt asking whether we want to proceed with the connection.

LIBS also provides a handy menu for **CWIS** systems. These come in handy when we are trying to locate people in a university setting.

```
Campus-wide Information Systems are accessible in the following places:
      1 Arizona                        2 Arkansas
      3 Colorado                       4 Connecticut
      5 Germany                        6 Indiana
      7 Illinois                       8 Iowa
      9 Massachusetts                 10 Michigan
     11 Minnesota                     12 Mississippi
     13 Texas                         14 Washington
     15 Nebraska                      16 New Brunswick
     17 New Hampshire                 18 New Jersey
     19 New Mexico                    20 New York
     21 North Carolina                22 Ohio
     23 Pennsylvania                  24 Quebec
     25 South Carolina                26 Switzerland
     27 United Kingdom                28 Vermont

          Press RETURN alone to see previous menu
          Press Control-C Q <return> to exit at any time

          Enter the number of your choice:
```

And a glimpse at **LIBS'** range is shown by its menu of miscellaneous resources, all of them accessible by Telnet:

```
          1 BUBL Library Information System
          2 CHAT Information System
          3 DUATS aviation weather
          4 FEDIX/MOLIS
          5 Geographic Name Server
          6 Ham Radio Callsign Server
          7 HP Calculator BBS
          8 Library of Congress
          9 UMD Database
```

BUBL is a network aid for those interested in the services available on the British network called JANET. *CHAT* is an intriguing information retrieval technology developed by Communications Canada (one part of which lets you engage in conversation with a computer), while the *UMD Database* contains a variety of information about computer, government, and eceonomic data. **LIBS** clearly boasts quite a range; it even includes *DUATS aviation weather!*

GOPHER AS LIBRARY TOOL

We have already seen that **Gopher** includes library catalogs; it's possible to tap into holdings from Singapore to Sacramento using its powers. But several **Gophers** deserve special mention for anyone interested in exploring libraries. They are the sites containing the most current lists of library catalogs available on the Internet. Connections were originally drawn from the data files of **HYTELNET** and converted to **Gopher** format by Michigan State University. The list was then checked against Billy Barron's University of North Texas' *Accessing On-line Bibliography Databases* document, as well as the list published by Art St. George at the University of New Mexico and Ron Larsen at the University of Maryland.

The result? Useful **Gopher** information about libraries that can help us answer the fundamental library problem. It's very useful, of course, to be able to search a **HYTELNET** or a **LIBTEL** to find the information we need to log in at a given library. But what do we do when we know the nature of the collection we're interested in examining, but don't know where it is? Suppose, for example, that I wanted to track down libraries with a stronger than usual emphasis on a particular subject, such as southern historical literature?

Gopher, you'll recall, allows connections to databases. Let's see what we can find at the University of Texas at Dallas **Gopher**. Figure 7.4 gives you an idea. We find a **Gopher** menu full of library catalog items. You can see that the third item, *Catalogs Search by Keyword <?>* is a database, because of the **?** in brackets following it.

By pressing a **RETURN** with the arrow on this item, I call up a search field, where I can enter my search term. Entering **southern historical**, I generate the list of libraries shown in Figure 7.5.

Figure 7.4
The **Gopher** at the University of Texas at Dallas is a useful library resource.

```
                        Internet Gopher Information Client v1.11

                           Library On-Line Catalogs

              1.  About-Library-Catalogs.
              2.  Catalogs Listed by Location/
        -->   3.  Catalogs Search by Keyword <?>
              4.  Instructions for different catalog types/
              5.  Library Bulletin Boards/
              6.  Library Gophers/
              7.  Manuscript and Archives Repositories - at Johns Hopkins/
              8.  Updates made recently to the list of libraries.
```

```
        Press ? for Help, q to Quit, u to go up a menu              Page: 1/1
```

Figure 7.5
A list of libraries that specialize in southern historical literature.

```
┌──────────────────────────────────────────────┐
│ Internet Gopher Information Client v1.11       │
└──────────────────────────────────────────────┘

       Catalogs Search by Keyword: southern historical

 -->  1.  University of Southern Colorado.
      2.  Georgia Southern University.
      3.  Southern Oregon State College.
      4.  Southern Utah University.
      5.  Stanford University - Martin Luther King Jr Bibliography.
      6.  University of California (MELVYL).
      7.  .links   /export/Libraries/by.place/Americas/US/Colorado/.
      8.  .links   /export/Libraries/by.place/Americas/US/Georgia/.
      9.  .links   /export/Libraries/by.place/Americas/US/Illinois/.
     10.  Southern Illinois University Law Library.
     11.  University of Maine System.
     12.  Minnesota State University System.
     13.  Nevada Academic Libraries Information System (NALIS).
     14.  .links   /export/Libraries/by.place/Americas/US/Oregon/.
     15.  Southern Methodist University.
     16.  .links   /export/Libraries/by.place/Americas/US/Texas/.
     17.  .links   /export/Libraries/by.place/Americas/US/Utah/.
     18.  Institute for Research in Social Science Data Services.


  Press ? for Help, Q to Quit, U to go up a menu          Page: 1/2
```

Now I have all the information I need to home in on libraries that can help me, and I can use **Gopher**'s links to data to move to them automatically.

There are three **Gophers** you should be aware of:

gopher.utdallas.edu — enter **gopher gopher.utdallas.edu** with your client program or, in the absence of a client program, work through **Gopher** menus to reach it.

yaleinfo.edu — gopher yaleinfo.edu is the command.

gopher.sunet.se — **gopher gopher.sunet.se** is the command.

Hint:

You can also retrieve Billy Barron's guide by FTP, if you prefer to have it in paper format. The address is **ftp.utdallas.edu**. The directory is *pub/staff/billy/libguide*.

And, if you're interested in the document prepared by Art St. George and Ron Larsen called *Internet—Accessible Library Catalogs & Databases*, you can retrieve it via anonymous ftp at the address **ariel.unm.edu**. The directory is *library*, and the filename is **internet.library**.

USING CATALIST AS AN ON-DISK LIBRARY SOURCE

One other resource needs mentioning, although with some qualifications. Like **LIBTEL**, **CATALIST** aims at making your life easier by providing easy directional information to on-line catalogs. But the tool is more like **HYTELNET**, for **CATALIST** is a program that you can download and use on your own computer. Those interested in exploring library resources will find it a handy guide to what's available, and a means of searching through potential sites off-line.

They'll also find it out of date. Program author Richard Duggan at the University of Delaware hasn't been able to update his work and now says that it's too old to use. Why include it in our list of tools, then? Because **CATALIST** is the kind of resource, independently crafted and meeting a particular need, that we need to encourage. Anyone interested in the design of off-line Internet browsers should take a look at **CATALIST**, and perhaps someday it will be updated and brought back to full speed.

The program can be found by using anonymous FTP to reach the following address: **zebra.acs.udel.edu**. The directory is *pub/library*. The file **readme.txt** provides information about the program, and you should retrieve and read it before proceeding.

CATALIST runs as a ToolBook book, which means it requires the program Asymetrix ToolBook to run. Users without ToolBook need to retrieve the file **FULLCAT.EXE** from the directory; it contains a run-time version of ToolBook 1.5 that allows any Windows user to get the program up quickly. The install routine is included in the program. The archive is self-extracting; entering **fullcat** at the DOS prompt will unpack it, after which running the install program will set up a Windows directory and icons.

Users who already own Asymetrix ToolBook can download the file **CAT10.EXE**, a much smaller file that contains only the **CATALIST** book and icon. Either way, you'll soon have the program and its exceptionally clean interface on-screen. The basic search screen appears as a choice between geographic options and alphabetical searching. You click on either option with the mouse and you're off. Figure 7.6 shows this screen.

By clicking on Mexico from this menu and then moving in on my target progressively, I can call up a screen full of information about a particular library. In Figure 7.7, you are looking at **CATALIST**'s help screen for the Monterey Institute of Technology.

Note that we have complete Telnet address information, along with the user name that we'll need to log in. But **CATALIST** also provides other useful features, including the Telnet and tn3270 escape keys (handy information when you get stuck in a remote computer!) and a notepad, which allows you to jot down pertinent facts. The program's inability to cut and paste between the library screen and the notebook, however, limits the notebook's utility. The shape of a helpful search tool is here; who will refine it?

Figure 7.6
The basic screen from **CATALIST**, a program in need of an update.

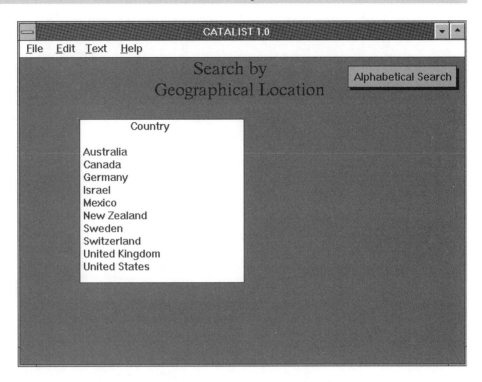

Figure 7.7
Gathering information about the library at the Monterey Institute of Technology using **CATALIST**.

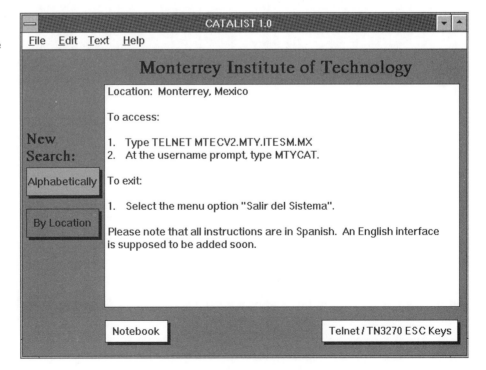

8

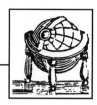

WHOIS, netfind, X.500: Finding People

Electronic mail is the most widely used resource on the Internet. That it should be is no surprise; one-to-one communication, whether global or local, is quick and easy to manage using even the simplest mail programs, like UNIX **mail** or more adaptive readers like **elm** and **pine**. Nor does mastering the addressing scheme behind TCP/IP present any problem, because an Internet address can be typed in as is—the routers on the network are responsible for making the necessary conversions into IP (Internet Protocol) numbers and seeing to it that the message is delivered.

Where we run into problems is in finding the address in the first place. Newcomers find themselves in the awkward position of having access to a powerful communications medium without knowing to whom they can talk. Typically, they begin their mail excursions by sending messages to people on their local network or other users of their dial-up service provider, perhaps responding to a welcome message or to a posting they think relevant. Their list of potential correspondents increases as they begin signing on to mailing lists and reading the postings on USENET.

Inevitably, though, the day comes when you know the name of a person but don't know how to reach them. In this chapter, we will discuss how to address this dilemma. It is, perhaps, the most widely asked question on the Internet: How do I find a particular mailing address? And surprisingly, the Internet's directory tools make the job an extremely difficult proposition. We'll take a look at present directory schemes and show how they can help; their limitations may surprise you. We'll then examine the range of options to try when your first search doesn't work. In no other area of Internet research is the finding process more accumulative than here. It may take numerous tools and multiple searches with each to find the address you need. And even with all that firepower, you may still come up empty.

X.500 AND THE SEARCH FOR ADDRESSING STANDARDS

We'd like to have something on the order of a telephone book, albeit an electronic one: Insert the name in the specified place, and out comes a list of possible people; choose the one you want, and the address appears. The analogy to telephone directories is so obvious that Internet directory tools are often referred to as "yellow pages" and "white pages," with the same distinction as between the paper versions. Yellow pages are the directories to search for business addresses; the white pages contain the names of individuals. But, as we'll see, the two areas frequently overlap, and in many cases, a white pages search will require a business or organization name to make it work. In addition, the multiplicity of directory options makes any Internet name search more complicated than searching through standardized telephone directories.

X.500 is an attempt to create directories in a format useful to the Internet. Because there is no central site running the Internet, the information available on it is distributed widely throughout the world. A directory system that hopes to reach people will have to be able to extend into many different locations, searching throughout a broad spectrum of possibilities. To do this, X.500 uses a so-called *distinguished name*, which allows the system to search flexibly for a given person and, having found him or her, map that person's name into a standard format called X.400.

Let's untangle the terminology. Terms like X.400 and X.500 refer to standards developed by the International Organization for Standardization (known by its French acronym, ISO). ISO was founded in 1947 as a voluntary organization (which means no treaties are involved) that would come to international agreements on standards for many different technologies. The representative standards organizations of participating countries comprise the membership of ISO, which, in turn, certifies them to carry out standards-making activities. Each of these bodies can participate in ISO discussions and vote on any ISO technical committee. Membership now includes some 90 different countries. The organization is currently divided into over 160 technical committees.

As you wade into the Internet, you've doubtless come across the term Open Systems Integration (OSI). OSI is a reference model, a set of protocols, used for making sure that the various data communications functions that have to work together to make a worldwide network operate do indeed function as planned. After all, with thousands of networks feeding into the Internet, the variety of equipment passing packets of data is immense. OSI, then, is designed to help these different machines work together; its goal is open systems, keeping the products of a multitude of manufacturers transparent to each other and working.

If this sounds familiar, it's because open systems and the integration of varied resources are what the Internet's TCP/IP protocols are all about. The present-day Internet has been largely defined by TCP/IP, but OSI still has its adherents, particularly in Europe. Its problem thus far has been the glacial pace of its implementation. Nonetheless, after 1989, OSI began to be more of a presence on the network, as the idea of multiprotocol networking began to gather steam. Still, OSI remains more a goal than a working environment, far outstripped by TCP/IP as its adherents have focused on developing their protocols by committee.

But in the area of search tools, ISO's work is making itself felt, largely because this is one area where existing Internet tools have failed to coalesce. ISO has had collateral success in the area of electronic mail.

X.400: WHAT IT IS AND HOW IT WORKS

X.400 is a mail transfer standard that can serve as a gateway protocol between different kinds of mail systems. Think of X.400 as an alternative way to specify a network address. The method was developed by another group with a French acronym, the Comite Consultatif Internationale de Telegraphique et Telephonique (International Telephone and Telegraph Consultative Committee). This group, known as the CCITT is, in turn, an organ of the International Telecommunications Union (ITU), which formulates recommended standards and procedures. Out of this bureaucratic swirl came a new set of e-mail standards, X.400, which would be incorporated into OSI.

How X.400 Differs From TCP/IP Electronic Mail

X.400 addresses are different from standard Internet addresses. Recall that the addressing strategy used by TCP/IP works with names and domains. A computer on the Internet can be referred to by a name or a number. In fact, its address can be presented as a sequence of either. Thus, **library.dartmouth.edu** can also be expressed as **129.170.16.11**, while **info.ccit.arizona.edu** can also be written as **129.196.76.201**. Each level of the address is called a *domain*. When the network address is expressed numerically, it is called an IP (Internet Procotol) address. Type in the name of the computer you hope to reach, and the translation of that name into the appropriate IP address is handled for you by a computer within the domain in question. The transaction is thus transparent to the end user.

X.400 addresses consist of more than a name and a domain. They are constructed from a list of attributes, allowing them to be broken down in great detail and making them much more specific than any TCP/IP address. When you construct an X.400 address, you specify the attributes to create the entire address. Each attribute is given along with an equal sign (+) and a value; slashes separate one attribute from the next. Unwieldy? Indeed. Consider the following example of an X.400 address:

```
/G=John/S=Dryden/O=Whitehall/C=UK/ADMD=TELEMAIL/@sprint.com
```

Here's how to untangle these elements:

G	Given name. The recipient's first name.
S	Surname. The recipient's last name.
O	The organization at which the recipient works or is affiliated.
C	Country code.
ADMD	The name of the mail system the recipient is using.

You can add a huge number of qualifiers to your field of attributes, including the following:

DDA   Domain defined attribute. This is a code that identifies the recipient. It could be an account name or any other number specific to the individual.

I   An initial, as in /G=William/I=F/S=Buckley/.

PRMD   A private system with a gateway into the public mail system.

Because there are so many possible attributes, and because you won't necessarily know which attributes you need to specify in a given address, piecing together an X.400 address from information you know is probably pointless. The very complexity of the X.400 address conventions makes it necessary for us to fall back on some kind of organizing structure—which is precisely what X.500 is all about.

X.500 As a Directory Service

Think of X.500 as a directory service that organizes the information tied up inside unwieldy X.400 addresses. Rather than needing to know an entire X.400 address, we're able to feed the directory a few of the terms we do know and it will accomplish the search for us. But we have to specify where we're looking. Using Telnet to reach a specific X.500 site, for example, I could type in a name, but in the absence of an organization, the system would simply search its local directories for the person in question. But because X.500 searches are interactive, I can then narrow the search with further specifications.

X.500 searches are generally run through a software system called **fred**. An acronym for **Fr**ont **E**nd to **D**irectories, **fred** is the gateway through which you use X.500. Unfortunately, it's an evolving system that is as likely to crash as not, so be prepared to be patient as you explore it. One way to check out X.500 operations is through Telnet. The command is **telnet wp.psi.com** or **telnet wp1.psi.com**, either of which logs you into the experimental directory service at Performance Systems International. Log in as **fred**; no password is required. What you'll see when you sign on is shown in Figure 8.1.

Searching with **fred**'s help is fairly basic. You type **whois** followed by the name you're looking for and, assuming the person is not at Performance Systems International (PSI), the name of the organization where the person is employed. (**WHOIS**, by the way, is a separate protocol. It's not part of X.500). A typical search, then, might appear in this form:

```
whois dryden -org whitehall
```

There are numerous commands to use with **fred**, and be warned, they are by no means easy to remember. In fact, the manual page for **fred** makes this comment: "The command syntax, while meant to be intuitive, is tedious." In my part of the country, this is known as an understatement.

Some of the commands that **fred** will accept are shown here:

Figure 8.1
Logging on at the PSI
White Pages Pilot Project
using **fred**.

```
SunOS UNIX (wp1.psi.net)

login: fred
Last login: Tue Nov 16 08:37:32 from nysernet.org
SunOS Release 4.0.3c (WP_PSI_BOOTBOX) #3: Mon Mar 8 12:14:31 EST 1993
You have new mail.


Welcome to the PSI White Pages Pilot Project

Try  "help" for a list of commands
     "whois" for information on how to find people
    "manual" for detailed documentation
    "report" to send a report to the white pages manager

To find out about participating organizations, try
    "whois -org *"

  accessing service, please wait...

fred> _
```

whois *name*	Searches for entries with this name in the default area. The "area" is set by the system administrator at the directory site. Thus, searching with the command **whois jones** pulls up anyone named Jones at, in this case, the PSI site.
whois surname *name*	Allows you to specify a particular surname. This can be different from the command above, because **fred** uses a namesearch variable that will match either surnames or full names depending on how it's set. **whois surname jones** searches only for a surname of **jones**.
whois *name* -org *organization*	Now we are specifying a particular organization along with a name. I could, for example, search using **whois jones -org abc** to specify a search for someone named **jones** at ABC Corporation, presuming ABC Corp. was participating in the X.500 project. Alternatively, searching under **whois jones -org a*** would cause **fred** to run through all the organizations beginning with **a** one at a time, asking whether I wanted to search in each one.
whois -org *	Presents the registered organizations in the default geographical area.
whois -org * -geo @ *countrycode*	Generates a report of all registered organizations in a particular country. For example, the command **whois -org * -geo @c=gb** will generate a list of organizations in Great Britain. A sample of this list is shown in Figure 8.2.

The limitations of using X.500 for searching should by now be obvious. Your search will be successful only if the organization to which the person is

Figure 8.2
Using **fred** to generate a
list of searchable
organizations in Great
Britain.

```
fred> whois -org * -geo @c=gb
100 matches found.
 11. Aberdeen University                         +44 224 27-0000
 12. Anglia Polytechnic University               +44 245 493131
 13. Aston University                            +44 21-359-3611
 14. Bell-Northern Research                      +1 613-763-2211
 15. Boldon James Limited                        +44 270-883880
 16. Bournemouth University                      +44 202-524111
 17. Bradford University                         +44 274 733466
 18. Brunel University                           +44 895 274000
 19. BT Plc                                      +44 71-356-5000
 20. Cambridge University                        +44 223-33-7733
 21. City University                             +44 71 477 8000
 22. Combined Higher Education Software Team      +44 225 826042
 23. Commonwealth Secretariat                    +44 71 839 3411
 24. Concurrent Computer Corporation             +44 753 534511
 25. Courtauld Institute of Art                  +44 71-872-0220
 26. Coventry University                         +44 203-631313
 27. Cranfield Institute of Technology           +44 234 750111
 28. DANTE                                       + 44 223 302992
 29. Data General                               +44 223-67600
 30. De Montfort University                      +44 533-551551
 31. Edinburgh University
 32. Fulcrum Communications                      +44 21771-2001_
```

affiliated is using X.500. You can, of course, check this by using the **whois -org** * command, but that adds another step to your search method; in any case, it frequently results in your finding that your target's firm isn't involved in X.500. Until such time as X.500 becomes a universally accepted standard, using it will be a hit or miss proposition. Nonetheless, it has the potential of developing into the kind of directory tool we need.

fred does provide help functions, although they're about as intuitive as **fred** itself. Nevertheless, the help system does let you focus in on the major commands. Enter **help** and you'll receive a list of commands. But a better idea is to enter **manual**, which will produce the manual page for **fred**, along with the great variety of command options available. I recommend you capture this material and print it for future reference.

THE PARADISE PROJECT: A DIFFERENT INTERFACE

X.500 services are often available through interfaces other than **fred**'s. The PARADISE Project at University College London is a case in point. There, an X.500 directory is provided through a more intuitive interface called **Directory Enquiries**, or **DE**, which was developed by Paul Barker at University College under the auspices of the European Commission's COSINE PARADISE Project funding. Directory Enquiries draws the same information—electronic mail addresses, postal addresses, telephone and fax numbers—out of the database as **fred** does: You provide information and the directory service then searches both local and remote databases to try to match it.

To reach the PARADISE Project, enter the following command:

```
telnet paradise.ulcc.ac.uk
```

Log on as **de**. You will see the screen shown in Figure 8.3.

Space does not permit a thorough explication of the PARADISE Project's commands. But note that entering an **i** will produce several pages of instructions, while using the **?** key will take you into the system's help functions.

The system works by asking you a sequence of questions. You are prompted for NAME, DEPARTMENT, ORGANIZATION, and COUNTRY. You need not answer them all, of course, and outcomes vary depending upon how you approach the search. Entering a single name, even a surname alone, will get the program started trying to match entries with similar names. It even attempts to handle common misspellings (don't ask **fred** to do that). Entering precise information about an organization or department will help you home in on the person you need. Entering an asterisk (*) will cause the system to list all people in the selected department or organization.

You can even leave the name field blank and search for broader information about the people in various departments and organizations. To produce the results shown in Figure 8.4, I entered an asterisk instead of a name, doing the same under the department field. When prompted for an organization, I entered **ulc**, for University College London. I was then prompted for which group within the University of London Computer Centre I would like to search. Choosing the User Services Group from a short menu, I retrieved the information shown.

Although easier to work with than **fred**, the PARADISE Project's interface remains daunting, and you'll have to practice to get the hang of it. The system's initial menu offers simple look-ups, by which it means searches for a specific person, department, or organization. Entering an **s** at the command prompt sets

Figure 8.3
Using **de** at the
PARADISE Project.

```
Connecting to the Directory - wait just a moment please ...
You can use this directory service to look up telephone numbers and electronic
mail addresses of people and organisations participating in the Pilot
Directory Service.

Select the mode you would like:

S Simple queries - if you know the name of the organisation you want to search
  (this is how the interface always used to behave)

P Power Search - to search many organisations simultaneously

B  Browser - best suited for exploring the Directory

Y Yellow Pages - power searching but allows user to search for an entry
  based on criteria other than the entry name

I Brief instructions explaining the program modes and how to use the program

? The help facility - usage and topics

Q To quit the program

Enter option:
```

Figure 8.4
A search at the PARADISE
Project for names at
University College,
London.

```
Found the following entries.  Please select one from the list
by typing the number corresponding to the entry you want.

United Kingdom
  University of London Computer Centre
    User Services Group
          1   Julie Altmann        +44-71-405-8400 x 358   J.Altmann@ulcc.ac.uk
          2   Margaret Barfield    +44-71-405-8400 x 403   M.Barfield@ulcc.ac.uk
          3   Group Manager        +44-71-405-8400 x 357
          4   Linda Hawkins        +44-71-405-8400 x 366   L.Hawkins@ulcc.ac.uk
          5   James Henderson      +44-71-405-8400 x 359   J.Henderson@ulcc.ac.uk
          6   Chris Howarth        +44-71-405-8400 x 362   C.Howarth@ulcc.ac.uk
          7   Allan Hume           +44-71-405-8400 x 367   A.Hume@ulcc.ac.uk
          8   Malcolm Keech        +44-71-405-8400 x 357   M.Keech@ulcc.ac.uk
          9   Minaz Punjani        +44-71-405-8400 x 330   M.Punjani@ulcc.ac.uk
         10   Andy Quick           +44-71-405-8400 x 438   A.Quick@ulcc.ac.uk
         11   Rosa Quick           +44-71-405-8400 x 342   R.Quick@ulcc.ac.uk
         12   Steven Self          +44-71-405-8400 x 372   S.Self@ulcc.ac.uk
         13   David Winstanley     +44-71-405-8400 x 397   D.Winstanley@ulcc.ac.uk

Simple query mode selected
Person's name, q to quit, * to browse, ? for help
```

this mode. Another route is a multiple organization search, which should be chosen when you know the name of a person and the country in which they work but don't know the name of the organization. The command for this mode is **p** (it stands for "power search"). A **q** quits the program entirely.

USING GOPHER TO RUN AN X.500 SEARCH

Gopher provides perhaps the most intuitive and widespread access route to X.500. Using the **Gopher** at MCNC, the research institution between Raleigh and Durham, NC, I was able to access X.500 directories by moving through the menus. Most **Gopher**s will have an entry something like the one I have found labeled for *Phone Books/* (remember that the slash following the entry tells you there is another directory following that menu choice). I then found a menu choice for *X.500 Gateway/* which took me to the screen shown in Figure 8.5.

Note that, with the exception of items 1 and 2, the rest of the entries show individual countries or organizations. Choosing one of these allows you to browse through a list of organizations participating in X.500 directories. Figure 8.6 illustrates the information I retrieved by choosing item 6, *Austria (country)/*. As you see, I can now choose to search an individual organization, or I can take the broader search option to search within the entire country.

X.500 differentiates between the levels you choose to search on. At its upper levels, which means when you search from the root or country level, searches are assumed to be for organizations or localities; at the lower levels (searching within an individual organization), searches are assumed to be for people. The **Gopher** implementation isn't perfect, but it is thus far the most intuitive of the X.500 gateways, and the widespread acceptance of **Gopher** probably means we'll be seeing more refined X.500 search tools coming from this quarter.

Figure 8.5
Gopher provides easy
access to X.500
directories.

```
              Internet Gopher Information Client v1.11

                             X.500 Gateway

        --> 1.  About the Gopher to X.500 Gateway.
            2.  Search root <?>
            3.  Internet (organization)/
            4.  North Atlantic Treaty Organization (organization)/
            5.  Europe (locality)/
            6.  Austria (country)/
            7.  Australia (country)/
            8.  Belgium (country)/
            9.  Brazil (country)/
            10. Canada (country)/
            11. Switzerland (country)/
            12. Germany (country)/
            13. Denmark (country)/
            14. Spain (country)/
            15. Finland (country)/
            16. France (country)/
            17. Great Britain (country)/
            18. Greece (country)/

        Press ? for Help, q to Quit, u to go up a menu          Page: 1/3
```

Figure 8.6
Using X.500 through
Gopher to search for
information in Austria.

```
              Internet Gopher Information Client v1.11

              Akademie der bildenden Kuenste (organization)

            1.  Read Akademie der bildenden Kuenste entry.
        --> 2.  Search Akademie der bildenden Kuenste <?>
            3.  DS-Manager (alias).

        +---------------Search Akademie der bildenden Kuenste--------------+
        |                                                                  |
        |  Words to search for                                             |
        |                                                                  |
        |                          [Cancel ^G] [Accept - Enter]            |
        |                                                                  |
        +------------------------------------------------------------------+




        Press ? for Help, q to Quit, u to go up a menu          Page: 1/1
```

WHOIS as a Search Tool

Let's return now to the concept of white pages which we discussed earlier. A white pages directory works by letting you insert a name; the information contained in the directory that is associated with that name then appears. By offering a variety of search commands, the X.500 system we studied fits this description. But so do other Internet search tools, perhaps the most prominent of which is **WHOIS**. Servers around the Internet make **WHOIS** available to their users, and there are a variety of ways of using this tool.

But again we run into the organization trap. The average **WHOIS** server lets you run your queries past a database of names and addresses for a particular organization. You can move easily between different organizations and their respective **WHOIS** servers, but the result is typical of the Internet's problems with individual name searches: We need to know something about the person in question *before* we can mount the search.

Another problem with **WHOIS** is its scope. The best estimates on the number of people contained within **WHOIS** databases converge at around 70,000. Considering that the Internet is now reputed to be home to over 20 million users, this is a tiny fraction of the available population. **WHOIS**, then, is a limited tool, and you should consider it within the larger context of other directory tools; any search for a given person has a limited chance of success with directories in their current state of development. You must register to be in a **WHOIS** or X.500 database, and not many **WHOIS** or X.500 servers exist. It may be necessary for you to use several directory tools to find the person you need. And after using them all, you may still come up short.

Accessing WHOIS

As with other Internet search tools, there are a variety of ways to tap into a **WHOIS** server.

- Using Telnet. You can reach a **WHOIS** server with a simple command: **telnet *server-name***. Thus **telnet indiana.edu**, or **telnet whois.ade-laide.edu.au**. Log in as **whois**.
- Using a local client. The command is **whois**.
- Using electronic mail. The mail address is **mailserv@ds.internic.net**.

Using WHOIS Through Telnet

The first thing to do when you want to use **WHOIS** with Telnet is to locate a public access server. For purposes of illustration, I'll use the server at the InterNIC, which is reachable by giving the command **telnet whois.internic.net**. However, a wide variety of servers are out there; in fact, the latest list, which is collected and compiled by Matt Power of M.I.T., shows some 153 sites, ranging from the Royal Institute of Technology in Sweden to the Institute of Automatic Control at Warsaw University, although the great majority of the sites are in the US. Power's list does not include sites that provide directory services exclusively through **finger** or by electronic mail, so the actual number of directory sites is higher still. Here's a snippet of Power's list:

`indiana.edu`	Indiana University C=US
`kean.edu`	Kean College C=US
`acad.csv.kutztown.edu`	Kutztown University C=US
`whois.rsmas.miami.edu`	University of Miami, Rosentiel School of Marine and Atmospheric Sciences C=US
`mit.edu`	Massachusetts Institute of Technology C=US
`whois.msstate.edu`	Mississippi State University C=US
`vax2.winona.msus.edu`	Minnesota State University - Winona C=US
`nau.edu`	Northern Arizona University C=US
`whois.ncsu.edu`	North Carolina State University C=US
`nd.edu`	University of Notre Dame C=US
`earth.njit.edu`	New Jersey Institute of Technology C=US
`acfcluster.nyu.edu`	New York University, Courant Institute C=US
`sun1.mcsr.olemiss.edu`	University of Mississippi C=US

Don't be misled by naming conventions. Although it is common to choose **WHOIS** as the first part of the domain name, as in **whois.msstate.edu**, many sites don't do this. M.I.T., in fact, runs its **WHOIS** service from the host **mit.edu**, reflecting the fact that some sites have chosen to put their **WHOIS** servers high up in the organization's domain hierarchy. The thing to do, then, is to retrieve Power's complete list of **WHOIS** servers and proceed from there.

Use FTP to **sipb.mit.edu** to get Power's list. The directory is *pub/whois*. The filename is **whois-servers.list**.

As we'll see in a moment, there are differences between the way servers handle the user interface for **WHOIS**. For now, our practice will involve the InterNIC **WHOIS** server. Later, I'll show you how to log on to other servers on the list.

Using **WHOIS** is relatively simple. Having given your Telnet command, you'll encounter a prompt, at which point you type in the search information you need. The system default is to run a broad search which attempts to match your search term in a variety of fields, from name to net address. The results are then displayed; in the case of a single hit, you get the detailed information: in the case of multiple hits, you'll receive short summaries. Figure 8.7 shows the login screen at the InterNIC's **WHOIS** server.

Typing **whois** then takes us to the system prompt.

```
Whois:
```

To proceed from this prompt, we simply type in the name we are looking for. Figure 8.8 shows what happens when we type the name **bradley** at the prompt.

As you can see, we've retrieved a number of bradleys; the system has paused partway through the list to ask if we want to see the rest of the hits.

Most records in a **WHOIS** database include a name field. If you're trying to find a particular person, bear in mind that the name field is presented last name first. Searching for Bill Bradley, then, let's type **bradley, bill** as our search term. Entering **bradley, b** would include anyone with a first initial of **B**.

Any part of a name up to a space or a comma can be specified as the search term. You can also run a *partial search*, which lets you search for everything starting with the target term. Putting a period (.) after the text indicates the partial search is in effect. Thus, **john.** will retrieve not only people whose last

Figure 8.7
Logging in at the
WHOIS server at
the InterNIC.

```
Escape character is '^]'.


SunOS UNIX (rs) (ttyr3)

*******************************************************************************
* -- InterNIC Registration Services Center  --
*
* For gopher, type:                  GOPHER <return>
* For wais, type:                    WAIS <search string> <return>
* For the *original* whois type:     WHOIS [search string] <return>
* For the X.500 whois DUA, type:     X500WHOIS <return>
* For registration status:          STATUS <ticket number> <return>
*
* For user assistance call (800) 444-4345 | (619) 455-4600 or (703) 742-4777
* Please report system problems to ACTION@rs.internic.net
*******************************************************************************
Please be advised that the InterNIC Registration host contains INTERNET
Domains, IP Network Numbers, ASNs, and Points of Contacts ONLY. Please
refer to rfc1400.txt for details (available via anonymous ftp at
either nic.ddn.mil [/rfc/rfc1400.txt]  or ftp.rs.internic.net
[/policy/rfc1400.txt]).
Cmdinter Ver 1.3 Wed Nov 17 10:22:43 1993 EST
[vt100] InterNIC >
```

Figure 8.8
A **WHOIS** search using
the name **bradley**.

```
Bradley Forthware (FORTHWARE-DOM)                          FORTHWARE.COM
Bradley University (BRADLEY)    BRADLEY.BRADLEY.EDU         136.176.10.11
Bradley University (NET-BRADLEY1) BRADLEY-NET               136.176.0.0
Bradley University (BRADLEY-DOM)                            BRADLEY.EDU
There are 16 more matches.  Show them? y
Bradley, Bob (BB44)             bbradley@UTMARTN.BITNET     (901) 587-7890
Bradley, Dale M. (DB1032)       BRADLEYD@EGLIN.AF.MIL
                                        (904) 882-3189 (DSN) 872-3189
Bradley, David (DB46)           ddave@FORUM.VA.GOV          (301) 427-3700
Bradley, Jim (JB410)            FNA104@URIACC.URI.EDU       (401) 792-2501
Bradley, John (JB59)            jbradley@CYBERSTORE.CA      +1 604 430-8600
Bradley, Ken (KB87)             bradley@ULTRYX.COM          (614) 885-8799
Bradley, Kevin (KB188)          SREPAC@NCTSEMH-WASH.NAVY.MIL
                                        (808) 653-5559 (DSN) 453-5559
Bradley, Kevin (KB205)          bradley@ETN.COM            (216) 523-4894
Bradley, Kevin (KB11)                (804) 273-0033 (FAX) (804) 273-9024
Bradley, Kit (KB10)             kbradley@ITRON.COM   (509) 924-9900 ext. 475
Bradley, Larry (LB164)          larry@VM.NRC.CA            (613) 993-0240
Bradley, Mark (MB12)            mbradley@MICROSERVE.COM    (717) 779-4430
Bradley, Mitch (MB361)          wmb@FORTHWARE.COM          (415) 961-1302
Bradley, Randy (RB683)          MARCO03@UNLVM.UNL.EDU      (402) 762-4156
Bradley, Richard M. (RMB)       richardb@SPIDER.CO.UK      +44 31-554-9424
Bradley, Seth J. (SJB4)         sbradley@SCIC.INTEL.COM    (503) 531-5045
Whois:
```

name is John, but also Johns, Johnson, Johnston, and so on. When we try this at the InterNIC, this is what we get:

```
Whois: john.
[No name] (JOHN-HST)         JOHN.DENVER.SSDS.COM              134.127.16.1
Ackley, John (JA188)         john@SOFTSPACE.COM             (614) 873-3907
Addie, John (JA285)          john@wrq.com                   (206) 324-0405
Aspden, John (JA16)          John.Aspden@CCI.CCINET.AB.CA  +1 403 450 6787
Babbitt, John E., Jr. (JEB122) John@Cutler.COM              (503) 770-9000
There are 454 more matches. Show them?
```

The system has flagged several people whose name matches our specifications. Faced with displaying over 450 matches, it asks us whether we want to continue.

We should, however, be able to narrow our search down further than this. When there is only a single match found for our search term, we will get the full record. Thus, a search on the name **Kosters** brings the following record of InterNIC employee Mark Kosters:

```
Whois: kosters
Kosters, Mark A. (MAK21)           markk@INTERNIC.NET
   Network Solutions, Inc.
   505 Huntmar Park Drive
   Herndon, VA 22070
   (703) 742-4795

   Record last updated on 10-Mar-93.
```

Here the record includes postal address, phone number, electronic mail address, and the date of last update.

Sometimes, though, you will have to search broadly and then tell the system which name you need. Let's assume we're searching for someone with the surname Jones; we know the first name begins with a **c**, but that is all. We can set up such a search using the search term **jones, c***. The results are shown below.

```
Whois: jones, c*
Jones, Captain (CJ)                       (301) 771-3580 (DSN) 797-7018
Jones, Carl (CJ94)        carljs@IDS.NET                  (401) 846-2738
Jones, Chris (CJ458)      jcj@visual.com                     508 836-4400
Jones, Clay (CJ153)       clay@telos.com                  (719) 632-4004
Jones, Cliff (CJ12)       root@ECRAAA.ARMY.MIL
                                          (410) 787-1188 (DSN) 923-7742/7743
Jones, Cory A. (CAJ)      cory_jones@VORTEX.VDT.COM       (503) 754-2806
Jones, Curtis (CJ41)                      (714) 736-5240 (DSN) 933-5240
```

Examine the list closely. At the left, each name is followed by an expression in parentheses. Look at the entry for Carl Jones, for example. It is followed by the term **CJ94**. This is a field in the database called the *handle*; it's a unique identifier to the person in question. We can now tell the system which of these entries we want to see in detail by specifying the handle. Here is what happens:

```
Whois: !cj94
Jones, Carl (CJ94)           carljs@IDS.NET
   Salve Regina University
   100 Ochere Point Avenue
   Newport, RI 02840

   (401) 846-2738

   Record last updated on 18-Feb-93.
```

Using an exclamation point (!) before the handle, and following it with the handle itself (with no space in between) has retrieved the record we need. As we'll see shortly, we can do the same thing with a client-based search of a **WHOIS** server.

Tips on Using WHOIS by Telnet

As illustrated, asking **WHOIS** for a broad search term like **john**. is asking for plenty of responses, and in the process, stressing the system (as well as the user's patience). It would make more sense, then, to work out a search strategy to minimize time and system resources. Fortunately, there are ways of doing so. Perhaps the most significant of these is the ability to search by field.

Each record in a **WHOIS** database contains a field specifying the kind of record it is. Because the main database holds records for individuals, domains, groups, hosts, networks, and organizations, you can search by these criteria. The result is fewer matches than **WHOIS**, and matches that more closely meet your search terms. An additional bonus is that this method of searching allows you to perform searches on fields not normally searched during a general query, like the one we just did for names beginning with **john**.

Searching by Domain

To search a database by domain, you simply use the keyword **do** before your search term. For example, entering **do std** at the **WHOIS** prompt produces the following description of Software Tool and Die:

```
Whois: do std
Software Tool and Die (STD-DOM)
   1330 Beacon Street
   Brookline, MA 02146

   Domain Name: STD.COM

   Administrative Contact, Technical Contact, Zone Contact:
      Shein, Barry  (BS25)  BZS@SKULD.STD.COM
      (617) 739-0202

   Record last updated on 05-Mar-91.

   Domain servers in listed order:

   SKULD.STD.COM               192.74.137.1
   WORLD.STD.COM               192.74.137.5
   NS.UU.NET                   137.39.1.3

Whois:
```

This list includes not only the usual address information, but also the server machines within the **std** domain.

Searching by Host

Perhaps you'd like to see what hosts, or computers, are available at a specific site or within a given area. To do so, use the **ho** keyword, followed by your search term. To list hosts in Indiana, for example, you could use **ho indiana** as my search statement.

```
Whois: ho indiana
Indiana Cooperative Library Services Authority (OAK3-HST) OAK.PALNI.EDU
                                                               198.62.84.36
Indiana Higher Education Telecommunications Systems (JEFFERSON-HST) JEFFERSON.IT
                                                               157.91.128.2
Indiana Higher Education Telecommunications Systems (WASHINGTON-HST) WASHINGTONT
                                                               157.91.128.1
Indiana Sports Corporation (DNS29-HST) DNS1.INSPORTSCORP.COM   198.133.236.4
Indiana University (UIVAX)      IUVAX.CS.INDIANA.EDU           129.79.254.192
Indiana University (VITA1)      IUGATE.UCS.INDIANA.EDU         129.79.1.9
Indiana University of Pennsylvania (ACORN-IUP) ACORN.GROVE.IUP.EDU144.80.128.8
Indiana University-Purdue University at Indianapolis (HUMMER) HUMMER.IUPUI.EDU
                                                               134.68.1.9
Indiana Wesleyan University (BARNABUS-HST) BARNABUS.INDWES.EDU 198.51.158.2
Indiana Wesleyan University (DORCAS-HST) DORCAS.INDWES.EDU     198.51.158.1
Whois:
```

This retrieves records of host computers with the word **indiana** somewhere in their records. Note that the search term does not have to appear in the actual computer name. It does in a record like **iuvax.cs.indiana.edu**, but the hosts at Indiana Wesleyan University appear despite the fact that the term **indiana** does not show up in the machine name.

If you wanted to get more specific, you could ask for computers at a particular location by specifying a unique search term. Thus, **ho university of montana** would produce the following result:

```
Whois: ho university of montana
University of Montana (SELWAY)   SELWAY.UMT.EDU             150.131.14.2
University of Montana (UMT)      UMT.UMT.EDU                150.131.14.1
```

Searching by Network

You can also use **WHOIS** to search by network records, using the **ne** keyword. Here, I've asked the **WHOIS** server for information about Infonet, a major packet switching network.

```
Whois: ne infonet
INFONET (NET-INFOLAN-C)         INFOLAN-C                  192.92.20.0
INFONET (NET-INFOLAN-C1)        INFOLAN-C1                 192.92.21.0
INFONET (NET-INFOLAN-C10)       INFOLAN-C10                192.92.30.0
INFONET (NET-INFOLAN-C11)       INFOLAN-C11                192.92.31.0
INFONET (NET-INFOLAN-C12)       INFOLAN-C12                192.92.32.0
There are 122 more matches. Show them?
```

Again, because of the length of the reply, I'm asked whether I want to see the entire list. Although I've searched for Infonet by using the network name, it's also possible to search by network number. Thus, **ne 192.92** would also retrieve the Infonet information, along with a great deal more, as shown in the following result:

```
Whois: ne 192.92
A.B. Dick Company (NET-ABDCPREPRESS) ABDCPREPRESS          192.92.84.0
```

```
AMCAST Industrial Corporation (NET-AMCAST) AMCAST              192.92.98.0
Abekas Video Systems (NET-ABEKRD) ABEKRD                      192.92.109.0
Allegheny Ludlum Corporation (NET-ALCNET) ALCNET             192.92.159.0
Applied Computing Systems (NET-ACS) ACS                      192.92.123.0
There are 168 more matches. Show them?
```

Searching by Individual Name

To search by person, you can simply use the **pe** keyword. The effect is the same as if you had entered the name directly at the **WHOIS** prompt. Here, I'm searching for anyone with the name **holland**.

```
Whois: pe holland
Holland, Anthony R. (TONY)     TONY@KL.SRI.COM                    (415) 859-4246
Holland, Barry (BH285)                                     +44- [081]-562-4150
Holland, Carl D. (CDH10)               301-826-4908 (DSN) 312-326-4908
Holland, Frank T. (FH4)        frank@INR.COM                      (617) 275-7440
Holland, Jim (JH438)           hollanjh%snyplava.bitnet@CUNYVM.CUNY.EDU
                                                                  (518) 564-3013
Holland, Joe E. (JH399)        HOLLANDJ@S5.INFO.WPAFB.AF.MIL (DSN) 787-2034
Holland, Martin (MH58)         hollandm@PRL.PHILIPS.CO.UK   +44 293 815911
Holland, Mike (MH61)                                            803-734-3813
Holland, William H. (WHH19)    william.H.Holland@ATT.COM     (614) 860-4906
```

Searching by Mailbox

A general **WHOIS** search checks the mailbox field for matches. You can also home in on mailboxes by using a set of further keywords.

user@   Specifies that the system should search the username part of mail addresses for your target. You could, for example, use a search term of **@billg**, if you knew that your target's username was **billg**.

@host   Pulls in all mailboxes on a given host. This is what I retrieved when I used **@unc** as my search term:

```
Whois: @unc
Beil, Bill (BB2)              beil@UNCECS.EDU             (919) 841-9196
Cancro, Art (AC11)           ajc@UNCNSRD.ORG             (914) 761-0632
Caston, David (DC17)         dcaston@UNCECS.EDU          (919) 770-3315
Givens, Hosea (HG14)         edwards@UNCECS.EDU          (919) 486-1531
Graves, William H. (WG88)    bill_graves@UNC.EDU
                                  (919) 962-7155 (FAX) (919) 962-1593
There are 12 more matches. Show them?
```

user@*host*   Searches for an exact mailbox address. This would be useful is you knew the mailing address but wanted further information, such as a phone number, about the person.

Searching Other Servers

As you've seen, Matt Power's list contains quite a few **WHOIS** servers that can be accessed by Telnet. However, many of these machines are not set up as public access **WHOIS** servers, and they're often not easy to use. When you set up a Telnet connection to the address listed on Power's list, you may be asked to log in and provide a password. To prevent this, be advised that **WHOIS** servers usually run on port 43 of the computer. When you Telnet directly to the machine, in other words, you should use the port number in your address. Thus, if you want to use the **WHOIS** server at Indiana University, you would enter the command **telnet indiana.edu 43**, rather than just **telnet indiana.edu**.

This is an important fact to keep in mind. If I try to reach the **WHOIS** server at North Carolina State University, using the **whois.ncsu.edu** address given by Power, I wind up being asked to log in. But if I add the port number, I can enter the system. It is not, however, set up to make use easy. Note in the following login that once I am accepted into the system, I am given no prompt. The system is simply waiting for me to enter a search term, as I do here.

```
% telnet whois.ncsu.edu 43
Trying 152.1.10.46 ...
Connected to infopoint.cc.ncsu.edu.
Escape character is '^]'.
willis, william
Name             : Willis, William E.
Campus address   : M-2 Hillsborough Bldg., Box 7109
Campus phone     : 5-2516     5-3787
Department       : Computing Center
Position         : Associate Provost/Academic Computing
E-mail address   : BILL_WILLIS@NCSU.EDU
Connection closed by foreign host.
```

Using WHOIS with a Client Program

With a local client on your system, you can quickly search a **WHOIS** database with a few simple commands. The basic strategy is to use the command **whois [-h *host*] '*name*'** (note that the name in question should be surrounded by single quotation marks). Here again, it's necessary to have the list of **WHOIS** servers that we retrieved earlier in this chapter. Setting up a search at the InterNIC, for example, I would enter the following command:

```
whois -h whois.internic.net 'johnson'
```

to find anyone named Johnson in the InterNIC database (there are quite a few). Likewise, to search the server at **whois.ncsu.edu**, I would proceed with this command:

```
whois -h whois.ncsu.edu 'johnson'
```

By using a client, I don't need to specify the port address, as I would have to do if I was trying to reach this site by Telnet. Here is an example: I'm searching the **WHOIS** server at North Carolina State University for network guru William Willis. The result follows:

```
% whois -h whois.ncsu.edu 'willis, william'
Name             : Willis, William E.
Campus address   : M-2 Hillsborough Bldg., Box 7109
Campus phone     : 5-2516     5-3787
Department       : Computing Center
Position         : Associate Provost/Academic Computing
E-mail address   : BILL_WILLIS@NCSU.EDU
```

Note several things about this search. First, I'm using a full name, and have entered the last name first, followed by the first name. Second, I enclosed the name with quotation marks. Without them, the search may not work.

If you fail to specify a host site, the system defaults to whichever **WHOIS** server your system administrator has specified. It may well be the InterNIC server, because it contains so many major Internet figures. Otherwise, it may be a server within your own organization, or one that is geographically close to you. For European users, it is likely to be the server at RIPE, the Reseaux IP Europeens, in Amsterdam. To perform searches comparable to those we've been running with the InterNIC, then, Europeans should use the address **whois.ripe.net**.

Bear in mind as you search that the **WHOIS** databases may contain different references to the same person. In the preceding example, I found Dr. Willis at North Carolina State University's **WHOIS** server; using the **WHOIS** server at the InterNIC, also located him, but with a different result:

```
Whois: whois -h whois.internic.net 'willis, william'
Willis, William E. (WEW)                    willis@EOS.NCSU.EDU
   X Engineering Software Systems Corporation
   1001 Brothwell Court
   Raleigh, NC 27606
   (919) 859-2466
   Record last updated on 10-Sep-91.
```

Same person, but a different reference, this time to a company he is involved in rather than to the university (and note how old the information is). The InterNIC's **WHOIS** server is, in fact, a good place to begin a **WHOIS** search. Its database contains many of the major figures in the Internet community. The **WHOIS** server at **nic.ddn.mil**, which used to contain civilian as well as military addresses, is now reduced to MILNET people only, and won't help you if you're looking for a civilian. It is, obviously, the place to go for military people.

When a search retrieves more than a single name, you are presented with a list of possibilities, just as you are when using a Telnet connection to a **WHOIS** server. The following output resulted from my search for someone whose last name is **Smith**, with a first name beginning with the letter **s**.

```
% whois -h whois.internic.net 'smith, s*'
Smith, Scott (SS374)           netadmin@WORMS-GIIS.ARMY.MIL011-49-6241-487003
Smith, Scott (SS48)                                      (602) 287-4977
Smith, Stanfield (SS110)       STAN@SEADOG.CNS.COM       (516) 737-2238
Smith, Stephan (SS438)         steve@COMCO3.AKCESS.COM   (615) 546-3664
Smith, Stephen (SS214)         smith@AMPERSAND.COM       (508) 392-1171
Smith, Stephen A. (SAS36)                                (907) 459-1476
Smith, Steven (SS2186)                                   212-216-8701

The InterNIC Registration Services Host ONLY contains Internet Information
(Networks, ASN's, Domains, and POC's).
Please use the whois server at nic.ddn.mil for MILNET Information.
```

To choose one of these entries, I must send another **whois** command. This time I specify the handle:

```
% whois -h whois.internic.net 'ss110'
Smith, Stanfield (SS110)             STAN@SEADOG.CNS.COM
```

```
CNS Enterprises
P.O. Box 1127
Lake Ronkonkoma, NY 11779
(516) 737-2238

Record last updated on 29-Mar-90.
```

The InterNIC Registration Services Host ONLY contains Internet Information (Networks, ASN's, Domains, and POC's).
Please use the whois server at nic.ddn.mil for MILNET Information.

As you can see, using a Telnet connection is in this case easier than working with a client; there is less to type.

NETFIND: FINGERING THE RIGHT PERSON

A **WHOIS** search is specific; you choose the database to examine and then use the **WHOIS** program to find your target. Obviously, this involves knowledge of, or at least an educated guess about, where your person is located. The **netfind** program suffers from the same limitation. You enter a name and any other information you have, such as organization or location, and turn **netfind** loose. The program then scours the network looking for what you need. It can turn up a name and mailing address, as well as **finger** information about the person you're trying to find. What it can't do is to search comprehensively for a name alone; it must have a reasonable description of where the target person works to be successful. Within those admittedly narrow parameters, however, **netfind** can be a useful tool.

Accessing netfind

There are two ways to run a **netfind** search:

- **Using Telnet to log onto a remote computer.** The current list of **netfind** servers is shown in Table 8.1. As always, remember that, by the time you read this, the list will likely have been expanded. The best way to keep up with new server sites is to log on to the server at **bruno.cs.-colorado.edu** (log in as **netfind**); alternate servers are listed on the opening screen.

- **Using a client program.** To determine whether you have one available on your system, type **netfind** at the system prompt. **netfind** is available only on UNIX systems.

Table 8.1 netfind Servers

Server Address	Location	Country
archie.au	AARNet, Melbourne	Australia
bruno.cs.colorado.edu	University of Boulder, CO	USA
dino.conicit.ve	Consejo Nacional de Investigaciones Cientificas y Technologicas, Caracas	Venezuela

(continued)

Table 8.1 netfind Servers *continued*

Server Address	Location	Country
ds.internic.net	InterNIC Directory and Database Services, South Plainfield, NJ	USA
lincoln.technet.sg	Technet Unit, Singapore	Singapore
malloco.ing.puc.cl	Catholic University of Chile, Santiago	Chile
monolith.cc.ic.ac.uk	Imperial College, London	United Kingdom
mudhoney.micro.umn.edu	University of Minnesota, MN	USA
netfind.anu.edu.au	Australian National University, Canberra	Australia
netfind.ee.mcgill.ca	McGill University, Montreal, Quebec	Canada
netfind.oc.com	OpenConnect Systems, Dallas, TX	United States
netfind.vslib.cz	Liberec University of Technology	Czech Republic
nic.nm.kr	Korea Network Information Center, Taejon	Korea
nic.uakom.sk	Academy of Sciences, Banska Bystrica	Slovakia
redmont.cis.uab.edu	University of Alabama at Birmingham	USA

Accessing netfind with Telnet

Let's use **netfind** to run a basic search routine. Out of curiosity, I decided to hunt for a known target: myself. Let's see if **netfind** can track me down.

We'll use Telnet to reach the **netfind** server at the University of Colorado in Boulder. The command is **telnet bruno.cs.colorado.edu**. The login is **netfind**.

When the connection is established, you'll see a screen of alternate server information (if too many people are using **netfind** at the same time, you may be given instructions to try one of the other sites). This is followed by the login prompt:

```
I think that your terminal can display 24 lines. If this is wrong,
please enter the "Options" menu and set the correct number of lines.

Top level choices:
      1. Help
      2. Search
      3. Seed database lookup
      4. Options
      5. Quit (exit server)
-->
```

The help system for **netfind** is relatively comprehensive, and I recommend that you work your way through it with your capture buffer on so that you can print it for later reference. But for now, let's work our way through the system doing a sample search. We enter **2** to tell the system we want to search, and the following prompt appears. Note how I've answered it:

```
Enter person and keys (blank to exit) --> gilster concert north carolina
```

I've given **netfind** some basic information about myself—my last name, the name of the network I used when preparing this chapter, and a geographical location. Remember, **netfind** needs—at minimum—a name and a rough description of where the search target works; that is, where he or she is likely to have an account from which to access the Internet. The information you give

netfind can consist of a state, a city, a company, an educational institution, or a domain from a DNS address.

In this case, we get a quick response:

```
MAIL IS FORWARDED TO gilster@jazz.concert.net
NOTE:    this is a domain mail forwarding arrangement - so mail
         for "gilster" should be addressed to "gilster@concert.net"
         rather than "gilster@jazz.concert.net".

------
Search of domains completed. Proceeding to search of hosts.

SYSTEM: rock.concert.net
        Login name: gilster                In real life: Paul A Gilster --s
        Directory: /home/gilster           Shell: /bin/csh
        On since Nov 22 17:42:32 on ttyq1 from nb1.concert.net
        New mail received Mon Nov 22 17:49:04 1993;
          unread since Mon Nov 22 17:42:38 1993
        No Plan.


SUMMARY:
- "gilster" is currently logged in from
  nb1.concert.net, since Nov 22 17:42:32.
- The most promising email address for "gilster"
  based on the above search is
  gilster@concert.net.

Continue the search ([n]/y) ? -->
```

We've retrieved quite a lot of information. **netfind** has determined that the system I use forwards my mail to the appropriate host in the CONCERT network in North Carolina (this address has changed, incidentally; **netfind** will now locate me as **gilster@interpath.net**). We also learn information from using **finger** at this site, which is one tool **netfind** uses to find me. My full name is listed, the name of the host computer (**rock**) that I was using when I wrote this, and the fact that I was currently logged on, not to mention when I last received mail. The suggested address, according to **netfind**, is **gilster@concert.net**.

This *looks* great, but if you had tried to send me mail at this address, it would have bounced, even during the period when I maintained my account at CONCERT. In fact, the address you need incorporates the name of the host computer: **gilster@rock.concert.net**. **netfind** has brought you into the system I used, and even found the name of the host, but its best guess at the address fell short. The moral: When you retrieve a **netfind** result, examine it carefully and be willing to experiment. The correct address is included in the **finger** information above, but **netfind** can't unravel every possible forwarding arrangement.

How netfind Works

netfind works with several different search tools. First, it maintains its own "seed database" of sites, including information on the names of computers, organizations, and Internet domains. **netfind** determines the best matches for your search terms there and then checks into these sites using tools like **finger**

and **WHOIS** to find a match. When you are given a list of domains to choose from, **netfind** will search the domain(s) you select, looking for *nameservers*, which are the computers that manage machine addresses. Having done this, it searches all computers in the domain. **netfind** looks for the last time the user logged in and the computer on which he or she last read mail in an attempt to isolate the most likely address. Many people, after all, have multiple accounts.

Your keywords should include a name and one or more locations. A name can be a first or last name; it can even be a user ID. A location can be a geographical place or a domain from an Internet address, which is why we were able to use **concert** in the preceding search, as well as **north carolina**, as our search terms. But think geography rather than domain names. Although you can use a domain name in your search, you must specify it without the dots. **std.com**, for example, would be entered as **std com** in a **netfind** search. In fact, running the search using **std com** as the search term generates the following possiblities:

```
Please select at most 3 of the following domains to search:
     0. std.com (software tool and die, brookline, massachusetts)
     1. std.comsat.com (communications satellite corporation, clarksburg, ma)
     2. std.teradyne.com (teradyne, inc, agoura hills, california)
     3. world.std.com (software tool and die, brookline, massachusetts)
```

When it receives your search terms, **netfind** returns a list of the domains it has found. If there are more than 100 such domains, the system will list some of these and ask you to create a more specific search. The following, for example, is what happened when I was trying to find a particular address in Palo Alto. I knew that my friend, Paul Pease, lived in the city, and I also knew that he had an account with a service provider called CR Laboratories. But I had forgotten his specific address. What to do?

First, I tried a purely geographical search, coupled with his last name, as follows:

```
Enter person and keys (blank to exit) --> pease palo alto
Netfind: your search covers more than 100 domains
Partial list of domains that matched your search:
     3do.com (the 3do company, palo alto, california)
     admin.stanford.edu (administration office, stanford university, palo al)
     advice.com (advice marketing communications, palo alto, california)
     affymax.com (affymax research institute, palo alto, california)
     affymetrix.com (affymetrix, inc, palo alto, california)
     ahi.com (artificial horizons, inc, palo alto, california)
     ako.dec.com (digital equipment corporation, western research laboratory)
     al.org (atlantean league, palo alto, california)
```

The list of domains went on for several screens, and I was asked to come up with a better strategy. Using a tool like **netfind**, you have to think on your feet. My previous search generated plenty of sites in Palo Alto, but of course, my target's service provider might not be physically located in that city; he could be accessing the Internet through a packet connection to the server site. So I looked up CR Laboratories in Peter Kaminski's PDIAL list, which tracks dial-up service providers for the Internet, and found that the domain name for the firm is **crl.com**. I incorporated that information into the search as follows (note that no periods separate the domain names):

```
Please form a more specific query.
Enter person and keys (blank to exit) --> pease crl com
Please select at most 3 of the following domains to search:
          0. cico.com (crl user slip, larkspur, california)
          1. crl.com (cr laboratories, larkspur, california)
          2. kirksmith.com (crl user slip, larkspur, california)
          3. merlot.com (crl user slip, larkspur, california)
          4. ness.com (crl user slip, larkspur, california)
          5. ssnet.com (crl network affiliate, larkspur, california)
          6. crl.dec.com (cambridge research laboratory, digital equipment corpor)
          7. crl.mobil.com (mrdc cent

Enter selection (e.g., 2 0 1) --> 1
```

Now I'm getting somewhere. The list of domains contains only one that's relevant, which I have selected; I now see that CR Laboratories is located in Larkspur, California. Having entered the number (1) for the search to focus there, I let **netfind** generate a new set of information:

```
( 1) check_name: checking domain crl.com. Level = 0
MAIL FOR Paul Pease IS FORWARDED TO pease@crl.com
NOTE:   this is a domain mail forwarding arrangement - so mail intended
        for "pease" should be addressed to "pease@crl.com".

------
Search of domains completed. Proceeding to search of hosts.
------
( 1) check_name: checking host nntp.crl.com. Level = 0
( 2) check_name: checking host crl2.crl.com. Level = 0
( 3) check_name: checking host nfs.crl.com. Level = 0
( 1) do_connect: Finger service not available on host nntp.crl.com -> cannot dop
( 3) do_connect: Finger service not available on host nfs.crl.com -> cannot do p
( 2) connect timed out

SUMMARY:
- The most promising email address for "pease"
  based on the above search is
  pease@crl.com.

Enter person and keys (blank to exit) -->
```

And indeed, the address **pease@crl.com** turns out to be correct.

netfind actually searches in two waves. First, it searches into the domain in question, looking for mail-forwarding information; it will then try to use **finger** to retrieve data about the search target at whatever hosts it finds. In its second phase, the system performs **finger** searches into other host computers in its main database. It then summarizes its search results, generating screensful of information tracking its progress. Entering **Ctrl-C** will interrupt any search in progress and cause **netfind** to summarize what it has found so far.

netfind Search Strategies

By now, you can see that **netfind** is at its best when you already have most of the information you need. Let me illustrate this with one more search, and conclude with some general thoughts on **netfind** search strategies.

Our target in this case is Michael March, president of a firm called Internet Direct, Inc. in Phoenix. To home in on Mr. March, I have asked **netfind** to search for **michael internet direct**. I retrieve a list of people whose first name is Michael, a snippet of which is shown here:

```
Login name: berak                     In real life: Michael Miller
       Directory: /home/u/berak           Shell: /usr/bin/bash
       On since Nov 23 06:44:52 on pts013    from phx-ts0.indirect.com
       15 seconds Idle Time
       New mail received Tue Nov 23 06:47:00 1993;
          unread since Tue Nov 23 06:47:01 1993
       No Plan.


       Login name: makins                    In real life: Michael Akins
       Directory: /home/u/makins
       Last login Mon Nov 22 16:26 on pts014 from phx-ts0.indirect23Michael Aks
       No unread mail
       No Plan.


       ~~~~~~~~~~~~~~~~~~~~~~~~~~~~~~~~~~~~~~~~~~~~~~~~~~~~~~~~~~~~~~~~~~~~~~
             Internet Direct, Inc. ---   Arizona's Internet Connection!
                 Phoenix: (602)274-0100   TuCSOn: (602)324-0100
             For more information, please write "info@indirect.com".
       ~~~~~~~~~~~~~~~~~~~~~~~~~~~~~~~~~~~~~~~~~~~~~~~~~~~~~~~~~~~~~~~~~~~~~~
```

This material is followed by **netfind**'s search into various hosts:

```
( 1) check_name: indirect.com leads us to 12 other machines
( 2) check_name: checking host phx-ts0.indirect.com. Level = 1
( 4) check_name: checking host phx-ts1.indirect.com. Level = 1
( 2) do_connect: Finger service not available on host phx-ts0.indirect.com -> cp
( 4) do_connect: Finger service not available on host phx-ts1.indirect.com -> cp


SUMMARY:
- Found multiple matches for "michael", so unable to determine most
  recent/last login information,
  or most promising electronic mail information.
  Please look at the above search history and decide for yourself which is best.

Continue the search ([n]/y) ? -->

above is michael indirect com

Searching indirect.com
( 1) check_name: checking domain indirect.com. Level = 0
SYSTEM: indirect.com
       Login name: march                     In real life: Michael March
       Directory: /home/march                Shell: /bin/bash
       Last login Mon Nov 22 19:10 on pts036 from veggie.indirect.h<23Michael h
       New mail received Tue Nov 23 06:44:47 1993;
          unread since Mon Nov 22 19:10:51 1993
       Plan:
       Slewpy..
```

As you can see, we've found the person we're after. And we've reiterated these core principles about **netfind**:

• You can search for a person's first, last, or user name.

- You can specify one or more locations, which can be geographical names or domain names from an Internet address.

- **netfind** works best the more you know. The optimum search occurs when you can specify the bulk of a mailing address; in other words, when what you lack is the user name at the site.

- **netfind** may take you close to your target but fail to go the last mile. Its attempt to determine which is the best address will rely on such factors as when and how many times the person has logged onto multiple accounts, and so forth. As with any Internet search tool, you have to think on your feet to use **netfind**.

netfind is an evolving tool; future plans call for it to support **WHOIS**, X.500 and other directory information, so you should plan to keep up with it if finding people on the network is important to you. As of late 1993, **netfind** could track down people at over 17,000 sites, and the numbers were about to increase as **netfind** became able to query X.500 sites and **CSO** servers. Its creator, Michael F. Schwartz, estimates that it can reach over 10 million individuals. I verified this by checking with Schwartz, after running a **netfind** search to get his e-mail address. The search strategy **schwartz boulder colorado** turned it up: **schwartz@cs.colorado.edu**.

WHAT IS FINGER INFORMATION?

netfind, as we've seen, works with **finger** information to tell you something about the person in question. Let's refresh our memories about what this involves. **finger** is a program that will display public information about a user on an Internet host computer. A growing number of sites restrict **finger** searches, but most do not. The service generates a user ID for the person you're asking about, the person's full name, and more. Here's an example, taken by fingering my own address (which has subsequently changed):

```
% finger gilster
Login name: gilster               In real life: Paul A Gilster—Computes
Directory: /home/gilster          Shell: /bin/csh
On since Nov 23 09:11:47 on ttyp1 from nb1.concert.net
New mail received Tue Nov 23 10:11:08 1993;
  unread since Tue Nov 23 10:08:14 1993
Project: Freelance Technology Writer
Plan:
Available 8:00 AM to 6:00 PM EST weekdays.
```

We've retrieved my home directory, the UNIX shell I use (**csh**), and information about when I was last logged on, and when I've received new mail. Also listed are two other categories. *Project* and *plan* are both fields established to allow users to communicate something about themselves. Both are based on files: The *project* field contains the contents of the file **.project**, and the *plan* field contains whatever is in **.plan**. Both these files can be created and are maintained in the user's home directory. Mine show my occupation and a snippet of information about when I work.

Because of the availability of project and plan fields, **finger** information can be very interesting. Here, for example, is what you would retrieve if you fingered **netfind**'s creator, Michael F. Schwartz:

```
% finger schwartz@cs.colorado.edu
[cs.colorado.edu]

To access the campus directory service, telnet cs.colorado.edu
and login as "da." On-campus may use the "da" or "411" commands.

Fingering schwartz@latour.cs.colorado.edu
------------------------------------------

[latour.cs.colorado.edu]
Login name: schwartz                 In real life: Mike Schwartz
Directory: /home/latour/schwartz     Shell: /bin/tcsh
Last login Mon Nov 22 14:10 on ttyp0 from netblazer.cs.col
No unread mail
Project: Resource Discovery and WAN measurement
Plan:
Department of Computer Science
University of Colorado
Boulder, CO  80309-0430
Voice: +1 303 492 3902
Email: schwartz@cs.colorado.edu

Fall Office Hours: Tues. 3:00-4:30 PM, Thurs. 1:30-3:00 PM.
Office: ECOT 7-11

Research efforts:
        - space-efficient and non-textual indexing
        - managing incompleteness and inconsistency in discovered data
        - interoperable information systems
        - data access and movement measurement studies
        - data distribution and caching algorithms
        - resource discovery applied to network management
        - measurements of Internet scope and service connectivity

Travel:
        Nov 19          Oregon Graduate Institute, Portland, OR
        Nov 22          Intel, Portland, OR
        Nov 24          University of Washington, Seattle, WA
        Nov 25-28       Seattle, WA
        Dec 6-8         SOSP conference, Asheville, NC
        - 1994 -
        Jan 7-8         IRTF-RD meeting, Boulder, CO
        Jan 21          Northeastern University, Boston, MA
        Jan 24-25       ComNet panel, NASA, NSF, and ARPA, Washington, DC
        Feb 17-20       INSNA conference, New Orleans, LA
        Mar 15-18       ARPA HPCC Symposium, Alexandria, VA
        Mar 28-Apr 1    IETF, Seattle, WA
        Apr 14-17       Boston, MA
        Aug 16-30       Hungary, Italy
        Aug 31-Sep 2    SIGCOMM Conference, London, England
%
```

Note that, the project information is limited to a single line, but the plan information is comprehensive; it can contain whatever you choose to put in its file. All of this is by way of illustrating that **finger** can hold plenty of information if the person in question has chosen to add such information to his or her **.plan** and **.project** files. What you will see, then, depends on the site in question and the person's own preferences. You may want to consider manipulating your own **.plan** and **.project** files to update them or, if they don't yet exist, creating them with a text editor like **pico** or **vi**.

KNOWBOTS AND INTELLIGENT SEARCHING

A Knowbot is the sort of creation science fiction tempted us with, an automated program that not only searches for information but does so with a fair degree of intelligence. Given the complexity of the Internet, this is exactly the sort of tool we'd like to employ. Rather than having to figure out every possible job in the data highway, we want to specify our needs and then do something else while our intelligent agent scours the data paths. We haven't yet reached that goal, but the first Knowbot, created by the Corporation for National Research Initiatives, is available, providing a tantalizing glimpse of what future developments may bring.

Using the Knowbot by Telnet

To access the Knowbot, use Telnet. The command is **telnet info.cnri.reston.va.us 185**; 185 is the port number, a software specification that routes traffic to the right destination (it has nothing to do with hardware, like serial ports.). No login is required. Here is what you will see when you log in:

```
% telnet info.cnri.reston.va.us 185
Trying 132.151.1.15 ...
Connected to info.cnri.reston.va.us.
Escape character is '^]'.
                  Knowbot Information Service
KIS Client (V2.0).   Copyright CNRI 1990.   All Rights Reserved.

The KIS system is undergoing some changes.
Type 'news' at the prompt for more information
Type 'help' for a quick reference to commands.
Backspace characters are '^H' or DEL

Please enter your email address (or your name if no email)in our guest book...
(Your email address?) > gilster@rock.concert.net

>
```

The prompt is inscrutable, but the basic command is **query**. You use it in combination with the search term you're after. Let's use **query daniel dern** for this example. Dern is the former editor of *Internet World* and a highly regarded author of Internet books. Let's see if the Knowbot can find him.

```
> query daniel dern

Connected to KIS server (V1.0). Copyright CNRI 1990. All Rights Reserved.


The ds.internic.net whois server is being queried:

No match for "DERN and DANIEL"
*
```

```
The rs.internic.net whois server is being queried:

No match for name "DERN,DANIEL".

The nic.ddn.mil whois server is being queried:

No match for name "DERN,DANIEL".
Name:          Daniel Dern
City:          Belmont
State:         MA
Country:       US
E-Mail:        313-6878@mcimail.com
Source:        mcimail
Ident:         313-6878
Last Updated:  unknown
(Press RETURN to continue)
```

The results are interesting on several levels. First, notice what is happening as the search proceeds. The Knowbot is running a search through the InterNIC (**ds.internic.net** and **rs.internic.net**) before proceeding to the Defense Data Network's Network Information Center (now known as the DISA NIC, though still referred to here by its old title, the DDN NIC). Finding no matches there, the Knowbot suddenly pulls up a hit, an address at MCI Mail.

Clearly, the Knowbot can search far afield for information. In fact, the InterNIC and MCI Mail are just two of its possible sources; the Knowbot maintains no address lists of its own, but relies on others. To find out what other possibilities exist, enter **services** at the bracket (**>**) prompt. As of late 1993, the Knowbot was aware of the **WHOIS** server run by the InterNIC, MCI Mail, RIPE (Reseaux IP Europeens—in effect, the European InterNIC), **finger**, **WHOIS** (servers at various Internet sites), X.500, quipu-country (an X.500 listing of country abbreviations), quipu-org (an X.500 listing of known organizations, and site-contacts, allowing X.500 searches for Internet addresses).

Note: *When the Knowbot begins its work, only some of these sources are selected as defaults for searching.* The defaults are the InterNIC, MCI Mail, and RIPE. These services are defaults because the only thing they require is a name to search for. The other services require further information before they can be run. To provide such information, you can use a variety of commands. Here are the basic ones:

country   Allows you to specify a particular country.

help   Prints the basic commands.

man   Prints the manual page for the Knowbot.

news   Prints updated information about the Knowbot.

org   Allows you to specify an organization at which your target works. This is important for X.500, **finger**, and **WHOIS** searching, which must use a specified organization name. The organization name should be the title of the organization, or at least enough of it to provide a unique identifier for the Knowbot. You can use part of a hostname here; thus, **org ncsu.edu** could be used instead of **org north carolina state**.

print   Shows you the name, organizations and services you have set up.

query   Searches for the person in question. You can use a first, middle, or last name. When you enter two names, the Knowbot assumes they are first and last names, in that order.

quit   Leaves the service.

service Adds the specified service to the list of sources to check.

services Prints the services the Knowbot will examine.

These commands must be entered one to a line, but you can use as many commands as you wish. The **print** command will then remind you of the organizations and services you have chosen up to this point in the search.

The following, for example, is how I would search for Brewster Kahle, the man behind the creation of the Wide Area Information Servers concept, and now president of WAIS, Inc. Note that I give the commands on separate lines: **org wais.com** tells the server to look for this organization, and also enables it to search X.500, **WHOIS**, and **finger** services because we have been specific about the organization. I follow this with the query command:

```
> org wais.com
> query kahle
The ds.internic.net whois server is being queried:
---
Kahle, Brewster (BK28)          kahle@THINK.COM
    Thinking Machines Corporation
    245 First Street
    Cambridge, MA 02142-1264
    (617) 234-1000

    Record last updated on 15-Apr-91.
```

Using the Knowbot by Electronic Mail

You can also send mail to the Knowbot to generate the information you need. To do so, send to one of two possible addresses:

kis@cnri.reston.va.us

or

netaddress@sol.bucknell.edu

Place your search request in the body of the message, using the same format as for a Telnet session. This is a sample e-mail message I sent to the Knowbot to retrieve information about network figure Vinton Cerf:

```
% mail kis@cnri.reston.va.us
Subject:
org cnri
query vinton cerf
```

The results quickly appear in my mailbox:

```
The rs.internic.net whois server is being queried:

Cerf, Vinton G. (VGC)          CERF@NRI.RESTON.VA.US
   Corporation for National Research Initiatives
   1895 Preston White Drive, Suite 100
   Reston, VA 22091
   (703) 620-8990 (FAX)
```

The great benefit of the Knowbot is that it allows you to search a wide variety of white pages for information without learning the particular search syntax of each one. The same search terms that you use for MCI Mail, for example, are applicable to your search in the other databases. This alone makes the Knowbot a tool you'll want to keep an eye on. For additional information about this rapidly evolving search tool, you may want to join a mailing list where questions and problems are addressed. To subscribe to the Knowbot Information Service mailing list, send mail to **kis-users-request-@cnri.reston.va.us**. Leave the subject field blank. The message should read **subscribe kis-users** *your_name*.

CSO DIRECTORIES

Many of the search tools discussed in this chapter can be used through a variety of different interfaces. **WHOIS**, for example, can be tapped through **Gopher**, while **WAIS** provides a useful search tool for the USENET address server discussed in a moment. Generally, I've addressed the search tools themselves in this chapter, with reference to the capability of using them in other formats in the relevant chapters. But one tool deserves special treatment, because it is explicitly designed as a white pages directory front-end and can be used easily through the medium of **Gopher**.

This tool is the **CSO**. Unlike most Internet terms, this acronym doesn't explain much about itself when unravelled—**CSO** stands for *Computing Services Office*, and refers to the entity at the University of Illinois at Urbana-Champaign where this tool was first developed. You will find **Gopher** entries marked **CSO** at many academic sites, as a look at the burgeoning number of university **Gophers** will quickly reveal. Figure 8.9 displays the format of these entries.

As you can see, those entries marked **<CSO>** clue us to the location of **CSO** directories at their respective institutions. Other entries are also searchable, as shown by the **<?>** after each. Some of these directories are based on **WHOIS** servers, some on X.500 and various other search tools. We'll concentrate on **CSO**s by trying to find a person at Bucknell University, which is home to the developer of the Knowbot, Ralph Droms. Let's see if we can get the right address. Figure 8.10 shows what happens when I press **RETURN** at the entry for Bucknell.

Figure 8.9
How **Gopher** presents **CSO** entries.

```
           Internet Gopher Information Client v1.1

                        North America

 -->  1.  Albert Einstein College of Medicine <CSO>
      2.  American Mathematical Society Combined Membership List <?>
      3.  Arizona State University <?>
      4.  Auburn University <?>
      5.  Bates College <CSO>
      6.  Baylor College of Medicine <?>
      7.  Board of Governors Universities (Illinois) <CSO>
      8.  Boston University <CSO>
      9.  Bradley University <CSO>
     10.  Brigham Young University <CSO>
     11.  Brown University <CSO>
     12.  Bucknell University <CSO>
     13.  Bull HN Information Systems <?>
     14.  California Institute of Technology <?>
     15.  California Polytechnic Institute <CSO>
     16.  California State University - Fresno <?>
     17.  California State University - Hayward <?>
     18.  California State University - Sacramento <?>

 Press ? for Help, q to Quit, u to go up a menu        Page: 1/14
```

Figure 8.10
Using a **CSO** to find the developer of Knowbot.

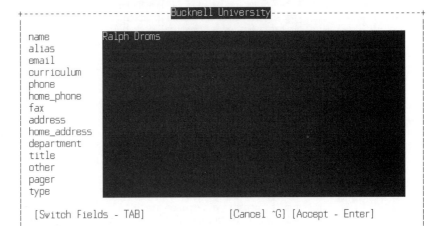

```
           Internet Gopher Information Client v1.11
+----------------------------Bucknell University----------------------------+
|                                                                            |
|   name          Ralph Droms                                                |
|   alias                                                                    |
|   email                                                                    |
|   curriculum                                                               |
|   phone                                                                    |
|   home_phone                                                               |
|   fax                                                                      |
|   address                                                                  |
|   home_address                                                             |
|   department                                                               |
|   title                                                                    |
|   other                                                                    |
|   pager                                                                    |
|   type                                                                     |
|                                                                            |
|   [Switch Fields - TAB]            [Cancel ^G] [Accept - Enter]             |
|                                                                            |
+----------------------------------------------------------------------------+

 Press ? for Help, q to Quit, u to go up a menu                      . . .
```

I am given a screen with fields of information. In Figure 8.10, I have entered the name and am about to press the **RETURN** key to proceed. When I do, the results are quickly displayed:

```
-------------------------------------------------------
       name: Droms, Ralph E
      email: droms@bucknell.edu
      phone: (717) 524-1801
    address: Bucknell University
          : Lewisburg PA  17837
 department: Comm & Info Tech
      title: Co-Director, Office of Comm & Info Tech
```

The **TAB** key allows me to move between the various fields to enter information. Notice that I used a full name, but I could also have used an asterisk to serve as a wild card in my searching. Thus, entering **r* droms** would have retrieved anyone whose last name was **droms** and whose first name began with an **r**.

SEARCHING THE USENET ARCHIVES

USENET, that worldwide assemblage of newsgroups on every conceivable topic, provides yet another database that can be searched for name and address information. Figure 8.11 shows a typical USENET message. You will notice at the top that the Internet address of the sender, along with a full name, is provided. Clearly, being able to search an archive of such material for a mailing address could provide a useful way to track someone down, provided he or she was known or likely to be a user of USENET newsgroups.

Figure 8.11
A USENET message, providing address and full name of the sender.

```
news.newusers.questions #16778 (0 + 0 more)           [1]
From: ts@chyde.uwasa.fi (Timo Salmi)
[1] The Weekly FAQ on test postings
Summary: Posted automatically each Thursday
Organization: University of Vaasa, Finland
Date: Thu Nov 25 16:21:02 EST 1993
Lines: 43

-From: garbo.uwasa.fi:/pc/ts/tsfaqn38.zip Frequently Asked Questions
-Subject: Where to put test postings

17. *****
Q: Where to put test postings?

 A: Let me try to give hopefully helpful information about how best
go about making test postings.
   Please don't take offense by this item. It is meant as a friendly
piece of advice, not as a flame. Novice users, and sometimes even
others, occasionally place these "A test, please ignore" messages in
discussion newsgroups. Please don't do this. It is wasteful of the
resources. These news reach tens of thousands of readers, so a very
wide distribution is involved. Furthermore, many users find the test
messages very annoying in the discussion newsgroups, and you have a
--MORE--(42%)
```

Jonathan Kamens is a major figure on USENET, perhaps best known for his updates of mailing lists accessible on the Internet. Kamens administers a computer at the Massachusetts Institute of Technology whose network address is **rtfm.mit.edu**; this machine serves as a repository of archives for USENET at large, where documents like Kamens' own list and the complete collection of Frequently Asked Questions (FAQs) for USENET newsgroups is stored. For our purposes, the most interesting thing about this machine is the white pages directory Kamens maintains on it, which stores the address information from USENET postings in a database. There is a strong likelihood that the name and address of a recent poster to USENET will be found here, making this a prime hunting ground for address searchers.

To reach the USENET address server, send electronic mail to the following address:

`mail-server@rtfm.mit.edu`

You can leave the subject field blank. The body of the letter should contain your search terms in the following format:

`send usenet-addresses/name`

Here is how I sent a request to the address server when I was checking to determine Jonathan Kamens' address:

```
% mail mail-server@rtfm.mit.edu
Subject:
send usenet-addresses/kamens
```

The result was quick to arrive, as shown:

```
Date: Fri, 26 Nov 1993 09:02:52 -0500
From: mail-server@rtfm.MIT.EDU
To: Paul A Gilster—Computer Focus <gilster@rock.concert.net>
Subject: mail-server: "send usenet-addresses/kamens"

-----cut here-----
jik@gza.COM (Jonathan I. Kamens)         (Aug 25 93)
news-answers-request@MIT.Edu (Jonathan I. Kamens)        (Aug 19 93)
jik@pit-manager.mit.edu (Jonathan I. Kamens)    (Dec 21 92)
jik@Aktis.COM (Jonathan I. Kamens)        (Mar 1 93)
HKAMENS@KENTVM.BITNET (Harry Kamens)        (Mar 21 93)
jik@aktis.COM (Jonathan I. Kamens)        (Mar 1 93)
jik@Athena.MIT.EDU (Jonathan I. Kamens)   (Nov 22 92)
jik@gza-client1.gza.com (Jonathan I. Kamens)      (Nov 19 93)
jik@security.ov.com (Jonathan I. Kamens)         (Nov 21 93)
snk@ctt.bellcore.com (Samuel Kamens)    (Nov 14 93)
jik@athena.mit.edu (Jonathan I. Kamens) (Nov 17 93)
jik@security.ov.COM (Jonathan I. Kamens)         (Nov 17 93)
snk@fork.uucp (Samuel Kamens)    (Oct 13 93)
snk@fork.bae.bellcore.com (Samuel Kamens)        (Oct 31 93)
"Lauren Kamens" <p00273@psilink.com>    (Oct 27 93)
jik@GZA.COM (Jonathan I. Kamens)         (Sep 21 93)
-----cut here-----
```

You may also be interested in another Kamens project, a document about finding people on the network. This text file includes a number of ingenious methods for tracking people down on the Internet. To get it, use anonymous FTP to **rtfm.mit.edu**. The directory is */pub/usenet/news.answers*. The file is **finding-addresses**. Still another helpful text file is David Lamb's study of finding people at academic sites. To retrieve it, use anonymous FTP to the same site, **rtfm.mit.edu**. The directory is *pub/usenet/news.answers/mail/college-email*. The file is broken into three parts: **part1**, **part2**, and **part3**.

CAMPUS WIDE INFORMATION SYSTEMS

If you know the object of your search works at a particular university, but that university does not maintain a **CSO**, you still have a good chance of finding him or her through a Campus Wide Information System, or **CWIS**. These depositories of campus information frequently include directories of faculty and students, along with information on campus events, class schedules, library information, job opportunities, and anything else related to campus life. Figure 8.12 shows the opening screen for a Campus Wide Information System at North Carolina State University in Raleigh. Notice item 3, the *Faculty/Staff Telephone Directory*, as well as item 4, a directory of students.

I am looking for a professor of Spanish named Gilbert Smith. Using this **CWIS**, I can search by last name to find him. In Figure 8.13, I have asked for information about anyone named Smith, using search instructions supplied on-screen.

The result is given in a series of screens, each listing the faculty members named Smith along with their telephone numbers. Choosing the number of the correct entry yields the information I need, as shown in Figure 8.14.

Obviously, Campus Wide Information Systems can zero in directly on our targets. But first, we have to know which systems are available; after all, despite their recent proliferation, **CWIS** services haven't spread into every campus, and certainly are more easily found at larger schools than small colleges. There are two ways around this dilemma. First, **CWIS** entries are available on many **Gophers**, which can take you right into the system in question. Second, there is a regularly updated list of **CWIS** servers maintained by Judy Hallman at the University of North Carolina at Chapel Hill. This list should be kept in your files if you plan to do frequent searching. You can retrieve Hallman's list by anonymous FTP. The address: **ftp.oit.unc.edu**. The directory is *pub/docs/about-the-net/CWIS*, and the file is **CWIS-l**.

Bear in mind, if you plan to do frequent searches with **CWIS** systems, that the search methods may vary from one site to another. These systems are maintained for on-campus use, which means that they are explicitly designed to be easy to use. So follow through with the commands suggested on-line, and you should be able to search the available directories.

MAIL TO THE SOURCE

As we've seen, finding a particular person on the Internet is no easy task, unless you already know a great deal about the person. Aware of the problem, researchers

Figure 8.12
North Carolina State
University's Campus Wide
Information System.

NCSU's

H a p p e n i n g s !
Your campuswide information system

1. University Datebook	9. Computing Information
2. NCSU Press Releases	10. NCSU Libraries Information
3. Faculty/Staff Telephone Directory	11. Visitor Information
4. Student Telephone Directory	12. Newsstand
5. Jobs Jobs Jobs !!!	13. Reach Out
6. Class/Course Listings	14. Newsletters & Journals
7. Crime Beat	15. University Surplus Items
8. University Infobook	16. NCSU Graduate Fellowships

99.   Help Using Happenings!

Suggestions? Contact Harry Nicholos, NCSU Computing Center,
Harry_Nicholos@ncsu.edu, or (919) 515-5497.

Enter Menu Choice or Exit and press RETURN

NCSU>

Figure 8.13
Searching for people
named Smith at NCSU.

NCSU FACULTY AND STAFF TELEPHONE DIRECTORY

The faculty and staff directory is updated monthly. For changes,
contact Telecommunications, 515-7986 or 4213. All on-campus numbers
begin with the 3 digits "515" unless otherwise noted. NCSU is in
the 919 area code.

To FIND an entry, choose f followed by the last name or
department you wish to locate. You may use an * to replace
characters you may not know. For example, you may search on
"stat*", and it would locate last names and departments whose
first four characters are "stat".

If more than one match is found, choose the number of the one you
want and press <return>. Finds can be done on any page in this
section.

Commands: Find   Main menu   Backup   Help   Exit

NCSU>f smith

Figure 8.14
A directory listing found through the NCSU **CWIS**.

```
                            Faculty/Staff Campus Directory




          Name:    Smith, Gilbert G.
          Work:    119 - 1911 Bldg., Box 8106
          Phone:   515-2475
          FAX:     515-6981
          Dept:    For. Lang.
          Pos:     Professor & Scheduling Officer
          E-Mail:  GSMITH@SOCIAL.CHASS.NCSU.EDU




               Information provided by NCSU Telecommunications




     NCSU>
```

and programmers are already working hard on the solution. In many respects, creating a satisfactory directory structure remains one of the greatest challenges of the Internet.

Today, even if you do know a few things about your target, it may still prove impossible to learn more. Some commercial on-line services, for example, don't make information about their members available. This will continue to be a problem, for the number of dial-up users coming into the Internet from sources like America Online and DELPHI is growing daily. Thus the odds increase that your Internet person hunt may come up short. There is, however, still one solution we haven't yet examined.

If you still can't find the person you're looking for, consider asking a live person. If you know the address of the machine your person uses but don't know his or her user name, you can always send a request to the administrator responsible for that machine. Every domain accepts the electronic mail address **postmaster**. Therefore, if you know that your contact uses the machine **chaos.sbh.edu**, you could send a message to the following address:

postmaster@chaos.sbh.edu

A polite request ought to get the e-mail name you need.

9

E-Mail:
Noninteractive
Searching

pproximately four million people use one or another of the commercial
on-line services like CompuServe or GEnie, and for many, this is their only
link to the Internet. While some services, notably DELPHI, BIX, and
America Online, have moved beyond electronic mail to offer other Internet
features, it is nonetheless true that huge numbers of modem users can reach the
Internet only by mail. We must factor in the growing number of local bulletin
board systems (BBS) with Internet links; with few exceptions, they provide
access to electronic mail and (sometimes) USENET newsgroups alone.

Clearly, an interactive Internet account is preferable, because it allows us to
use such crucial features as FTP and Telnet. But the people who use networks
are ever ingenious, and a wide (some would say wild) variety of fixes have
appeared, allowing users to tap most of the Internet search tools in some fashion
through mail. Some of these methods are efficient and relatively straightforward; others are complex and frequently unstable. But I think you will
be surprised at how many sources you can search through an electronic mail
connection. Let's examine them.

ARCHIE THROUGH ELECTRONIC MAIL

Without interactive FTP, **archie** would seem to be the kind of tool we could do without. After all, searching for files on the Internet will do us little good if we can't retrieve them. But a service called **ftpmail** has appeared that allows mail users to send requests for files to designated sites; the results are then mailed to the user in 7-bit ASCII format, according to standard Internet conventions regarding e-mail. Even executable files may be sent this way in **uuencoded** form. Decode the file using a software tool called **uudecode** and you have a working program. The intricacies of **ftpmail** are beyond the scope of this book (for a complete discussion of **ftpmail** and sample sessions showing how to use it, see my previous book *The Internet Navigator,* John Wiley & Sons, 1993).

For now, though, the question becomes, how do we activate **archie** and search FTP sites by electronic mail? Actually, those of us with fully interactive Internet connections frequently find that using the system by mail is beneficial, even if the methodology seems cumbersome. People accessing **archie** through Telnet sessions already know that the load on **archie** servers has become intense, enough so that it's frequently difficult to log on. An electronic mail message can save you the trouble of repeatedly trying the same server looking for an open slot.

For that matter, the timing of many **archie** searches isn't necessarily critical. When you don't have a pressing need to review the results immediately, why not consider the e-mail route? Your list of hits will appear in your mailbox in short order, and in the meantime, you can proceed with other work. Not all of **archie**'s search capabilities are available through mail, just as many of the advanced Telnet settings are unusable through a local UNIX client, but certainly the major commands can be driven through mail.

archie by E-Mail Commands

The way to use a mail server is to send a message to the site with your command inside. You can send mail to any of the **archie** server sites listed in Chapter 2. The address to use is:

`archie@server`

where *server* is the name of the **archie** site. This can result in an awkward-sounding address. For example, if I choose to send my e-mail request to the server at **archie.ans.net**, I would send to the address **archie@archie.ans.net**. As you can see, the idea is simply to prefix the **archie@** sequence to the server address.

The message you send should contain the appropriate **archie** commands and nothing else. You are not limited to a certain number of commands, but do note that: *each command must begin in the first column of a line, or it will not be processed correctly.* We'll see this principle applied when dealing with any mail server, so commit it to memory now.

The **archie** commands specific to using **mail** follow. Within your message, the basic **archie** by Telnet commands are available. (Note: Some servers may still be using older software. Alternative commands for using them are also listed here.)

compress   Causes **archie** to send your reply in compressed and encoded form.

find   The familiar search command, which has supplanted the **prog** command in **archie** version 3.0 (although you can still use **prog**). But note: Your electronic mail search presumes a search strategy based on UNIX regular expressions (*regex*). This is opposed to the line-oriented UNIX client program (which presumes an *exact* search unless you change its settings) and Telnet to **archie**, which defaults in version 3.0 to *sub* (substring). You will probably want to set a different search type before proceeding. Use the usual Telnet search type commands to do so.

help   Put this in your message and archie will return the basic help document, listing the e-mail commands and providing further information.

set mailto   You can set a path statement that tells archie to return your search results to an address different from the one on your e-mail. The older version of this command is **path**. Thus, **path plorre@casablanca.com** instructs the system to send results to that address,, as does set **mailto plorre@casablanca.com**. It's a good idea to include the path statement in any case to ensure accuracy.

quit   Closes your archie request.

servers   This is another way of generating an updated list of archie servers. The server site will return a list of all servers known to it at the time.

whatis   Allows you to supply a keyword for a search of the *Software Description Database*. This is another reason to use electronic mail. The UNIX client program for **archie** does not support **whatis** searches (although Telnet to **archie** does).

A Sample archie Search Using Electronic Mail

Assume I am interested in searching for files having to do with fax software. I can set up an **archie** search as shown in the following message (note that I've left the Subject: field blank).

```
% mail archie@archie.sura.net
Subject:
set mailto gilster@interpath.net
set search sub
set maxhits 50
find fax
whatis fax
quit
```

Let's take the search statement apart. I've begun with my electronic mail address, inserted here simply as a precaution against any mix-up in the header of my message. The next statement is familiar; it sets the search type as *sub*, so that my search will find any example of the search term, **fax**, within the file or directory name. I've limited the maximum number of hits to 50, and then inserted the **find** command, **find fax**. I've also included **whatis fax**, because I'd like to have a look at what's in the *Software Description Database* under this heading. I haven't sorted the output by time because I'm exploring in general for fax files; I'm not worried at this point about which is most recent. The **quit** command closes my request.

The message is then sent on its way. After a time that depends on how busy the server is, I will find the results waiting in my mailbox. Figure 9.1 shows one screen's worth of what I retrieved:

archie Courtesy

One final note about **archie**: Servers respond to requests made upon them by lining up the searches. The smaller requests are taken care of more quickly than the larger ones, which means that when you send a large query to **archie**, or make your queries frequent, you're creating a longer waiting period for everyone. The principle is to avoid asking for big jobs during busy times of day. If you're using an **archie** client program, setting the **-N** option for "niceness" reflects well upon your attitude toward your fellow on-line citizens. According to the **archie** manual page, an **-N** setting of 5000 ranks as "very nice." Surely we can all afford to wait a few extra minutes by being so.

WAIS by Electronic Mail

WAIS hardly suggests itself as a satisfactory vehicle for electronic mail. The nature of a **WAIS** search, after all, is to query an electronic database, receiving

Figure 9.1
archie search results as sent by e-mail.

```
Message 3/33  From archie-errors@forum.ans.net                    Page 3

Last updated 00:11 24 Jul 1993

      Location: /usenet
         DIRECTORY    drwxr-xr-x    1024 bytes  01:00  9 Nov 1992  comp.dcom.fax


Host ugle.unit.no    (129.241.1.97)
Last updated 17:39  9 Nov 1993

      Location: /faq/comp.answers
         FILE    -rw-rw-r--    63682 bytes  12:15  3 Nov 1993  fax-faq


Host ftp.uwo.ca    (129.100.2.12)
Last updated 14:07  8 Nov 1993

      Location: /doc/FAQ
         FILE    -rw-rw-r--    63667 bytes  01:22  4 Nov 1993  fax-faq


Host roxette.mty.itesm.mx    (131.178.17.100)
There are 259 lines left (20%). Press <space> for more, or 'i' to return.
```

a set of hits which we can then tune up with relevance feedback. But as we saw in Chapter 5, relevance feedback isn't always effective unless we have a sophisticated client program to run **WAIS**. And because we can do a great deal without using it, the ability to search through e-mail takes on a new interest. The **WAIS** mail server we are about to discuss isn't elegant, but it can return the results you need.

Once again, we can offer thanks to Thinking Machines Corp. in Cambridge, MA, where **WAIS** was initially developed. Jonny Goldman at Thinking Machines developed the mail server program now in use there, called **WAISmail**. The procedure is common to any mail server program. You send a message to the appropriate address specifying what you are looking for and where to look for it. **WAISmail** runs the search and sends back a list of hits. You can then examine the list, choosing items you'd like to see, and request them.

Hint:

There are times when the mail server approach to an Internet search seems very compelling. Perhaps it's late on a Friday afternoon and you're ready to head for a well-deserved weekend break. But you also need to track down a document or two on the Internet. You could stop packing your briefcase and do it now. Or you could send the search to **WAISmail** and let the mail server handle it for you. On Monday morning, presumably refreshed, you would return to your office to find the results of your search waiting.

Constructing a WAISmail Search

The address for **WAISmail** is **waismail@quake.think.com**. The vital thing about using the system is that the message must be formatted precisely as shown. Here is the format:

```
search source-name keywords
```

source-name, of course, refers to the **WAIS** database you wish to search. This can appear without the standard **.src** suffix with which **WAIS** databases are normally listed. To search the **world-factbook93.src** database, then, containing the CIA World Factbook, you would enter **world-factbook** as your source name. The keywords you specify should follow.

A Sample WAISmail Search

Let's search the CIA World Factbook looking for information about Zambia. World copper prices are depressed, and I have heard that Zambia is rich in copper. What more can we learn about Zambian ore deposits, in case we have an interest in investing at the bottom of the market cycle?

First, we construct a search statement:

```
search world-factbook zambia
```

Then we send the message to **waismail@quake.think.com**. The result, which soon arrives as a message in my mailbox, is shown in Figure 9.2.

The results are interesting. As you can see, **WAISmail** has restricted itself to ten responses. As with a standard, interactive **WAIS** search, the hits have been given numerical rankings. Thus, item 1 shows a ranking, or score, of 1000, while number 2 shows a score of 957. Clearly, **WAIS** has chosen correctly, because as we examine the list, we see that the first entry is indeed the main entry for

Figure 9.2
Results of a **WAISmail** search for information about Zambia.

```
Date: Thu, 3 Feb 94 05:34:46 PST
From: WAISmail@quake.quake.think.com
To: Paul A Gilster -- Computer Focus gilster@rock.concert.net
Subject: Your WAIS Request: WAIS Query

Searching: world-factbook
Keywords: zambia

Result # 1 Score:1000 lines:  0 bytes: 10625 Date:920120 Type: TEXT
Headline: Zambia  Geography Total area: 752,610 km2; land area: 740,720 km2
DocID: 0000000244CIA :cmns-moon.think.com@cmns-moon.think.com:210%TEXT

Result # 2 Score: 957 lines:  0 bytes: 11466 Date:920120 Type: TEXT
Headline: Namibia  Geography Total area: 824,290 km2; land area: 823,290 km2
DocID: 0000000153CIA :cmns-moon.think.com@cmns-moon.think.com:210%TEXT

Result # 3 Score: 957 lines:  0 bytes: 10988 Date:920120 Type: TEXT
Headline: Malawi  Geography Total area: 118,480 km2; land area: 94,080 km2
DocID: 0000000134CIA :cmns-moon.think.com@cmns-moon.think.com:210%TEXT
Result # 4 Score: 935 lines:  0 bytes: 151677 Date:920120 Type: TEXT
Headline:      Appendix C: International Organizations and Groups
DocID: 0000000250CIA :cmns-moon.think.com@cmns-moon.think.com:210%TEXT

Result # 5 Score: 935 lines:  0 bytes: 10992 Date:920120 Type: TEXT
Headline: Zimbabwe  Geography Total area: 390,580 km2; land area: 386,670
km2
DocID: 0000000245CIA :cmns-moon.think.com@cmns-moon.think.com:210%TEXT

Result # 6 Score: 935 lines:  0 bytes: 13174 Date:920120 Type: TEXT
Headline: Zaire  Geography Total area: 2,345,410 km2; land area: 2,267,600
km2
DocID: 0000000243CIA :cmns-moon.think.com@cmns-moon.think.com:210%TEXT

Result # 7 Score: 935 lines:  0 bytes:  8384 Date:920120 Type: TEXT
Headline: World  Geography Total area: 510,072,000 km2; 361,132,000 km2
(70.8%)
is water and
DocID: 0000000240CIA :cmns-moon.think.com@cmns-moon.think.com:210%TEXT
Result # 8 Score: 935 lines:  0 bytes: 10422 Date:920120 Type: TEXT
Headline: Botswana  Geography Total area: 600,370 km2; land area: 585,370
km2
DocID: 0000000028CIA :cmns-moon.think.com@cmns-moon.think.com:210%TEXT

Result # 9 Score: 914 lines:  0 bytes: 13224 Date:920120 Type: TEXT
Headline:    Appendix B: Abbreviations for International Organizations and
Groups
DocID: 0000000249CIA :cmns-moon.think.com@cmns-moon.think.com:210%TEXT

Result #10 Score:  1 lines:  0 bytes: 21384 Date:930616 Type: TEXT
Headline: *** HELP for the Public CM WAIS Server ***
DocID: 0000000000HELP:cmns-moon.think.com@cmns-moon.think.com:210%TEXT
```

Zambia. Other entries are the articles for other countries, in which Zambia is mentioned but probably doesn't play a major role.

We want to retrieve document 1. To do so, we consult the **WAISmail** information again. The procedure for requesting a document is to send another message to **waismail@quake.think.com**. This time, the message will have but a single line containing the word **retrieve** along with the identifier for the document we want. We can find this by examining the results in Figure 9.2 and looking for the line marked **DocID**. This is how the first of our hits appeared:

```
Result # 1 Score:1000 lines: 0 bytes: 10625 Date:920120 Type: TEXT
Headline: Zambia  Geography Total area: 752,610 km2; land area: 740,720 km2
DocID: 0000000244CIA :cmns-moon.think.com@cmns-moon.think.com:210%TEXT
```

The document identifier is lengthy:

```
0000000244CIA :cmns-moon.think.com@cmns-moon.think.com:210%TEXT
```

To request this document, then, we must send this message:

```
retrieve 0000000244CIA :cmns-moon.think.com@cmns-moon.think.com:210%TEXT
```

Before long, the document appears in my mailbox. Here is the first part of it, showing the retrieval mechanism at work:

```
Date: Thu, 3 Feb 94 06:08:32 PST
From: WAISmail@quake.quake.think.com
To: Paul A Gilster—Computer Focus gilster@interpath.net
Subject: Your WAIS Request: WAIS Request

Retrieving "0000000244CIA :cmns-moon.think.com@cmns-moon.think.com:210%TEXT"
 DocID: 0000000244CIA
 Database: cmns-moon.think.com
 Host: cmns-moon.think.com
 Port: 210
 Type: TEXT


0000244CIA
920120
CIA World Factbook 1991
Zambia
```

This material is followed by a lengthy document, with information about Zambia's natural resources, political leadership, population and more. Along with this potpourri of information comes the material we were seeking, relating the country's copper deposits to its economy:

```
Economy
Overview: The economy has been in decline for more than a decade
with falling imports and growing foreign debt. Economic difficulties
stem from a sustained drop in copper production and ineffective economic
policies. In 1990 real GDP stood only slightly higher than that of 10
years before, while an annual population growth of more than 3% has
brought a decline in per capita GDP of 25% during the same period. A
high inflation rate has also added to Zambia's economic woes in recent
years.
```

Clearly, if we plan to take a position in Zambian copper resources now, we're the adventurous kind of investor!

Hint:

The document identifiers for the **WAISmail** system are quite lengthy, and a single error in the request will cause the system to bounce your request entirely. Even the spaces between items must be accurately transcribed. Therefore, you may find it easier to simply use the reply function in your mail program when you request a document. By doing so, and including the text of the **WAISmail** document in your response, you can then edit the message to eliminate everything but your **retrieve** command and the document identifier itself. **WAISmail** will also accept and act on the DocID by itself (with no **retrieve** command). If you do this, be sure that there are nothing but blank spaces between the beginning of the line and the DocID keyword.

The WAISmail Commands

The following are the commands you can use to make **WAISmail** work. Notice that it is possible to change various parameters if you want, for example, to see more than the default number of responses. Invoke one command per line.

maxres *<number>*   Sets the number of hits returned by the number you select. This command should be set before you issue your search command.

search *<source-name> <keywords>*   The source name you insert in your search command is the name of the source as listed in the directory of servers; you don't need to include the **.src** suffix. Note: You can search through more than one source at a time if you wish. To do so, enclose the source names in quotations. For example, to search **usenet-cookbook.src** and **usenet.src** for messages involving Thai cuisine, you would enter the command **search "usenet-cookbook.src usenet.src" thai**.

retrieve *<DocID>*   Retrieves a document. Note that you must include the identifier for each item you wish to retrieve. Enter the identifier with great care.

Hint:

WAISmail makes it possible to retrieve more than one item at a time. To do so, separate your retrieval commands with a blank line. And note this statement in Jonny Goldman's help document for **WAIS**mail: "Most 'Bad DocID' errors are the result of lost spaces in transmission."

DocID: *<DocID>*   Also retrieves a document. Here, the DocID stands by
itself and generates the necessary retrieval.

To retrieve, for example, one of the Thai recipes I found in the multiple
source search I ran above, I would send this command:

```
DocID: 0000000417WWP :cmns-moon.think.com@cmns-moon.think.com:210%TEXT
```

I did this simply by using the reply function in my mail reader and editing out
all the other **WAISmail** DocIDs. Again, multiple retrievals are possible within a
single message; just separate the ID numbers with a blank line. Figure 9.3 shows
part of the resulting file as read through the **pine** mail reader program.

And, if you think the DocIDs we've been using are lengthy, you haven't seen
anything yet. Consider this one:

```
DocID: 0 1760
/proj/WAIS/db/weather/weather.help:/proj/WAIS/WAIS-sources/weather@quake.quake.t
hink.com:210%TEXT
```

I show you this to illustrate not only how unwieldy a DocID can be, but also to
point out that **WAISmail** can handle DocID statements that take up more than
a single line. When this happens, the important thing to remember is not to
insert any extra spaces into the DocID statement. Some mailers force you to use
80 character lines, which is where this problem may arise.

Figure 9.3
A Thai recipe retrieved
through **WAISmail**.

```
 PINE 3.89    MESSAGE TEXT            Folder: INBOX  Message 5 of 5  38%

VAGUELY-THAI SCALLOPS

    SCALLOPS-1 - Saut'eed scallops with snow peas in fish sauce

    This is something I invented with what I had around after  I
    bought  some scallops on impulse.  It's inspired partly by a
    recipe of Madeline Kamman's and partly by Thai  and  Chinese
    recipes, although scallop recipes are rare in my Asian cook-
    books.  It's not spicy and probably has very  little  to  do
    with  real Thai cooking, but the taste of Nam Pla (Thai fish
    sauce) is an interesting complement to the scallops.   Serve
    it with rice.

INGREDIENTS (4 servings)
     1 lb      scallops preferably  the  large  (sea)  kind, but
               small bay scallops should be ok
     1/2 lb    snow peas
     1/2 cup   white wine
     3 Tbsp    nam pla (Thai fish sauce)

? Help        M Main Menu  P PrevMsg     - PrevPage  D Delete    R Reply
O OTHER CMDS  V ViewAttch  N NextMsg   Spc NextPage  U Undelete  F Forward
```

Hint:

WAISmail is more than a little bit finicky! When using the **DocID** command to retrieve a document, you must type the word **DocID** exactly as shown. Case matters.

like *<DocID>*   Allows you to set up a relevance feedback search by telling **WAISmail** that a particular document is the kind you're looking for. While it is possible to use relevance feedback by mail (which is in itself intriguing), the results are not likely to be worth the time it takes to construct the query with multiple "like" documents. If you do use **like**, be aware that all **like** commands must go before the search command.

Binary Files Through WAISmail

If you're interested in retrieving nontextual information through **WAISmail**, you're in luck; such files will be sent to you in **uuencoded** form. The basic mail protocols used on the Internet specify that mail must travel as 7-bit ASCII characters, as we saw in the section on using **archie** by mail. A program called **uuencode** is used to translate a binary file, such as an executable program or a graphics file, into ASCII. On your end, you need a copy of the **uudecode** program, which can sort out the resulting ASCII tangle and make the file back into a program.

Hint:

uudecode can be run from the system prompt in a UNIX environment. Or, if you need to run it on your own computer, you can find the program all over the Internet, and there are various implementations of it. Run an **archie** search to find abundant listings. From the system prompt, enter the command **archie uudecode**. The site you choose will depend on your system. For MS-DOS users, for example, a major source is the huge FTP archive at **oak.oakland.edu** (the Oak Software Repository at Oakland University, Rochester Michigan). Look in the directory *pub/msdos/decode*. The filename is **uuexe525.zip** (although the number may have changed by the time you read this—software tools are always in a state of evolution). Macintosh users will want to check out sites like **mac.archive.umich.edu**.

Let's test the system by looking for a satellite image of today's weather. I'll search the **weather.src** server through **WAISmail** with the following command:

```
search weather gif
```

Figure 9.4
A satellite image retrieved through **WAISmail** and subsequently decoded.

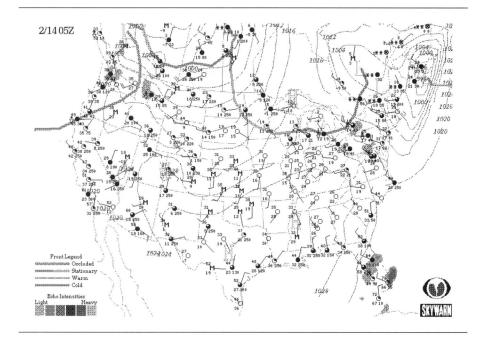

Here I am using gif as one of my keywords because I want to find images, which are often made available in so-called **G**raphics **I**nterchange **F**ormat. This is the quickest way to get recent satellite images through the **weather.src** server.

The file I receive looks like a mess, a sea of apparently random ASCII. But after turning the **uudecode** program loose on it, I retrieve the image shown in Figure 9.4.

GOPHER BY ELECTRONIC MAIL

Gopher by electronic mail? Surely I jest. In fact, there is a way to access **Gopher** through e-mail, believe it or not. **GopherMail**, created by Fred Bremmer (with help from Nick Hengeveld and Matt Ranney), does the trick. It's an ingenious solution to the problem of using **Gopher** by mail, although one that's byzantine enough to probably convince you of the virtues of getting a full Internet connection. Whereas **WAISmail** is comparatively straightforward—you run a search, identify one or more documents, and then request to see them— **GopherMail**'s challenge is to adapt to the e-mail format of the menued information structure that the underlying client uses.

This is no easy matter, but **Gopher** by mail is certainly better than no **Gopher** at all. To access **GopherMail**, send mail to one of these addresses: **gophermail@calvin.edu** or **gophermail@ncc.go.jp**. Clearly, your choice should be dictated by whichever is closest to you, under the principle that we always want to use the smallest number of system resources possible.

A GopherMail Query

Your first move with **GopherMail** is to take a look at the main **Gopher** menu at the site. To do so, send mail to one of the **GopherMail** addresses with no subject and no message. **GopherMail** will respond with a **Gopher** menu that will be the basis for everything that happens next. In Figure 9.5, we can see the basic response.

Examine this screen. Notice that it is structured as a standard **Gopher** menu, including local information about Calvin College and various campus resources, as well as menu links to worldwide information. Nothing, in other words, is unusual about the menu save for the way we'll access individual items. Also included in the returned document, along with the menu, is a list of the links to the various **Gopher** items. We discussed links in Chapter 3 on **Gopher**; they provide information about where each item is found, including address and port number.

You might, for example, choose to find out more about how this **Gopher** server operates. To do so, heed the instructions above the **Gopher** menu and place an **x** before the items you want to see. The easiest way to do this is to simply edit the incoming mail file in your mail reader. Tell your mail reader that you want to insert the original message in your reply. Then, place the **x** directly in front of item 2, *About Calvin's KnightLine Gopher Server*, and you have alerted the server to send you this document. The next step is simply to mail the entire message back to the original address.

Figure 9.5
GopherMail will return a document that you can use as a search template for your **Gopher** work by mail.

```
From gophermail@Calvin.EDU Mon Feb  7 08:29:18 1994
Date: Mon, 7 Feb 94 07:56:59 EST
From: GopherMail Server gophermail@Calvin.EDU
To: Paul A Gilster -- Computer Focus gilster@rock.concert.net
Subject: Calvin College Gopher Server

Mail this file back to gopher with an X before the menu items that you want.
If you don't mark any items, gopher will send all of them.


        1.  About Calvin College.
        2.  About Calvin's KnightLine Gopher Server.
        3.  Academic Divisions/
        4.  Administrative Departments/
        5.  Calvin Student Organizations/
        6.  Campus Committees/
        7.  Campus Publications (includes phone book)/
        8.  Library Resources/
        9.  Research/
        10. The World/
        11. Veronica (Search Titles of Gopherspace)/
        12. Weather Report for Grand Rapids.
        13. Ye new gopher stuff.
```

Hint:

When marking items with an **x**, remember to place the **x** at or near the beginning of the line. It should appear *before* the menu numbers for the options you choose. Figure 9.6 shows my request when I have told the **GopherMail** server that I want to see choice 2. I've also requested the first item, a backgrounder on Calvin College. The header information is from the **pine** mail program within which I have inserted the original message. Note: It is not necessary to edit out the rest of the original message; marking the items you need is sufficient.

Limiting GopherMail's Output

Some electronic mail gateways restrict the size of the messages they can handle; therefore, **GopherMail** provides two ways to break its output into several smaller messages when they become too big. First, you can tell **GopherMail** the maximum number of menu items it should send in a single message. Alternatively, you can specify the maximum size for incoming messages by including the necessary information in the **Subject:** field of your message.

For example, to restrict the number of menu items to 10, you would send the command **Menu=10** in the **Subject:** field. To restrict the size of incoming messages to 49,000 bytes, you would enter the command **Split=49000**. You can place either or both of these responses in the **Subject:** field.

The alternative is to place the same commands in the body of your message, although in that case they should appear on separate lines. This information is

Figure 9.6
Editing the **GopherMail** file. The Xs indicate what you want to retrieve.

```
 PINE 3.89    COMPOSE MESSAGE REPLY              Folder: INBOX  7 Messages

To      : GopherMail Server <gophermail@Calvin.EDU>
Cc      :
Attchmnt:
Subject : Re: Calvin College Gopher Server
----- Message Text -----
On Mon, 7 Feb 1994, GopherMail Server wrote:

> Mail this file back to gopher with an X before the menu items that you want.
> If you don't mark any items, gopher will send all of them.
>
>
X       1.  About Calvin College.
X_      2.  About Calvin's KnightLine Gopher Server.
>       3.  Academic Divisions/
>       4.  Administrative Departments/
>       5.  Calvin Student Organizations/
>       6.  Campus Committees/
>       7.  Campus Publications (includes phone book)/
>       8.  Library Resources/

^G Get Help  ^C Cancel    ^R Read File ^Y Prev Pg  ^K Cut Text  ^O Postpone
^X Send      ^J Justify   ^W Where is  ^V Next Pg  ^U UnCut Text^T To Spell
```

already included in the basic **GopherMail** reply to your initial query. It is placed after the menu items and before the link information that accompanies them. The material looks like this:

```
Split=27K bytes/message <- For text, bin, HQX messages (0 = No split)
Menu=100 items/message <- For menus and query responses (0 = No split)
```

To change any of these values, simply edit them in your mail program as a part of your response to the **GopherMail** server.

A GopherMail Search Using Veronica

To prove that **GopherMail** works, let me demonstrate how you can use it to search for information with **Veronica**. I am interested in tracking down **Gopher** sites with material on flying, hence my **Veronica** search term will be **aviation**. The first thing I need to do is to get the basic **GopherMail** menu; as previously, I do this by sending a blank message to **Gophermail@calvin.edu**. When I get the menu back, I put an **x** by the appropriate item. In this case, it is item 11:

```
11. Veronica (Search Titles of Gopherspace)/
```

I return the message marked in this way and soon receive a return message that allows me to access the **Veronica** servers. That message looks like this:

```
1. Search index of Gopher site names <? (Send keywords in Subject:)
2. Search Gopherspace Using Veronica (from U. Nevada, Reno)/
3. Search high-level menus in Gopherspace (via Washington & Lee Law
   Lib.) <?> (Send keywords in Subject:)
```

I return the message with an **x** in front of the 2, and get the response shown in Figure 9.7.

Figure 9.7
Veronica can be searched by electronic mail using **GopherMail**.

```
PINE 3.89   MESSAGE TEXT              Folder: INBOX  Message 10 of 14  13% ANS

Date: Mon, 7 Feb 94 09:05:53 EST
From: GopherMail Server <gophermail@Calvin.EDU>
To: Paul A Gilster -- Computer Focus <gilster@rock.concert.net>
Subject: Search Gopherspace Using Veronica (from U. Nevada, Reno)

Mail this file back to gopher with an X before the menu items that you want.
If you don't mark any items, gopher will send all of them.


     1.   Search gopherspace at PSINet <?> (Send keywords in Subject:)
     2.   Search gopherspace at PSINet <?> (Send keywords in Subject:)
     3.   Search gopherspace at U. of Manitoba <?> (Send keywords in Subject:)
     4.   Search gopherspace at University of Cologne <?> (Send keywords in
Subject:)
     5.   Search Gopher Directory Titles at PSINet <?> (Send keywords in
Subject:)
     6.   Search Gopher Directory Titles at PSINet <?> (Send keywords in
Subject:)
     7.   Search Gopher Directory Titles at U. of Manitoba <?> (Send keywords

? Help       M Main Menu   P PrevMsg     - PrevPage   D Delete     R Reply
O OTHER CMDS V ViewAttch   N NextMsg   Spc NextPage   U Undelete   F Forward
```

Note that this response includes the instruction, critical for our purposes, to search by putting our keywords in the **Subject:** field. I choose one of the **Veronica** sites by putting an **x** in front of it and then send the message, inserting the keyword **aviation** into the **Subject:** field.

The response is broken into two messages, each quite lengthy. A sample is shown in Figure 9.8. As you can see, the method now simply repeats what we have been doing. The basic **GopherMail** procedure remains the same at all levels. You select the menu item that you wish to see, place an **x** by it, and return the message to the **GopherMail** server. Keep this process going until you get the information you need.

Hint:

If you plan to use **GopherMail** with any regularity, keep the basic strategy in mind. Because everything is based on the original document that **GopherMail** sends you, you should keep a copy of that document at hand for subsequent use. If you use a mailer program like **pine**, you can save the document in a folder and reuse it whenever the need arises. If you are using **GopherMail** through a mail-only service like CompuServe (which is more likely, because if you had full Internet access you would be using **Gopher** interactively), then maintain a copy of the document as an ASCII file, which you can reedit for subsequent searches.

Figure 9.8
Response to **Veronica** search.

```
 PINE 3.89    MESSAGE TEXT          Folder: INBOX  Message 13 of 14  21%

Date: Mon, 7 Feb 94 09:09:57 EST
From: GopherMail Server <gophermail@Calvin.EDU>
To: Paul A Gilster -- Computer Focus <gilster@rock.concert.net>
Subject: Search gopherspace at U. of Manitoba (aviation) Part 3

Mail this file back to gopher with an X before the menu items that you want.
If you don't mark any items, gopher will send all of them.


      201.aviation-faq.gz.
      202.aviation-netiquette.gz.
      203.aviation-faq.gz.
      204.aviation-netiquette.gz.
      205.aviation-faq.gz.
      206.aviation-netiquette.gz.
      207.aviation/
      208.aviation/
      209.aviation/
      210.Civil Aviation Authority (organization)/

  ? Help        M Main Menu   P PrevMsg     - PrevPage   D Delete    R Reply
  O OTHER CMDS  V ViewAttch   N NextMsg    Spc NextPage  U Undelete  F Forward
```

A final note: You can ask to see a different host as the top level **Gopher** for your search. To do so, place its address as the subject of your message. For example, to see the **Gopher** at *WiReD Magazine* as the top level **Gopher**, I would send a blank message with the statement **gopher.wired.com** in the **Subject:** field of my message.

FINGER BY ELECTRONIC MAIL

finger is a useful Internet tool that allows us to access various information servers and to retrieve data about people connected to the net. As with **GopherMail** and **WAISmail**, it is also possible to use electronic mail to query a **finger** site. And, as before, the results are returned to you in the form of a mail document.

For fun, let's see if we can generate a list of trivia questions about movies and television. A **finger** server exists to provide just this service. The address is **cyndiw@magnus1.com**, and we would normally reach it using the command **finger cyndiw@magnus1.com**. In this case, however, we want to send mail to a different address: **b.liddicott@ic.ac.uk**. We'll send mail to this address with the following subject line: **#finger cyndiw@magnus1.com**. Note the numerical sign before the **finger** command; don't leave it out! Sending this message, I quickly receive a response, as shown in Figure 9.9.

Of course, **finger** can also be used to generate information about individuals, which is how the service evolved in the first place. To do so, we use the same technique. For example, if I want to **finger** my own user ID at my alternate account on The World, I would use the command **finger**

Figure 9.9
A mailed response to a **finger** request.

```
  PINE 3.89    MESSAGE TEXT              Folder: INBOX  Message 1 of 1   26%


                         TV / Movies
                         %%%%%%%%%%%


      1. What was the name of the fraternal order to which Ralph Kramden
         and Ed Norton belonged in "The Honeymooners"  ?

      2. Was it actually Anthony Perkins or a stand-in who stabbed Janet
         Leigh in "Psycho", 1960  ?

      3. In his confrontation with a bank robber In "Dirty Harry" (1971)
         how many shots did Harry Callahan fire ?

      4. Upon what street does Roseanne reside in Lanford, in the series by the
         same name ?

      5. What was the name of the brother which Ben searches for in the series
         "The Immortal" (1970-1971) ?


  ? Help        M Main Menu  P PrevMsg   - PrevPage   D Delete     R Reply
  O OTHER CMDS  V ViewAttch  N NextMsg  Spc NextPage  U Undelete   F Forward
```

#pag@world.std.com. As before, I would put this command in the **Subject:** field of my message and leave the message body blank. Soon I would receive a response:

```
Date: Tue, 8 Feb 94 13:03:51 gmt
From: b.liddicott@ic.ac.uk
To: gilster@interpath.net
Subject: Result of finger pag@world.std.com
Benhaha's Happy Mail Daemon

Syntax: #finger <user>@<machine name>

The Daemon received a subject line containing the following:
#finger pag@world.std.com
The Daemon attempted to finger the following user:
pag@world.std.com

Which generated the following output:
[world.std.com]
world-The World-Public Access UNIX-Solbourne 6E/900 OS/MP 4.1A.3
  8:03am  up 1 day, 11:20,  51 users,  load average: 4.07, 4.17, 4.01
```

This is followed by a list of users currently signed on at The World, along with their **.plan** and **.project** information, as discussed in Chapter 8.

WHOIS BY ELECTRONIC MAIL

Mail-only users of the Internet have the ability to conduct a **WHOIS** search. Some **WHOIS** servers will handle mail queries. To use the important server at the InterNIC, you would send mail to **mailserv@ds.internic.net**. Through this means, you can access the **WHOIS** databases of the InterNIC, including the MILNET server, the server at InterNIC Registration Services (for nonmilitary personnnel), and the local server at Directory and Database Services. The server at this addresses accesses all three of these databases.

Assuming I want to retrieve information about network writer Ed Krol, I could send the following mail to the mailserver:

```
% mail mailserv@ds.internic.net
Subject:
whois .krol
```

It's important to note the conventions for constructing the message here. First, no subject is necessary. Second, the mail server recognizes the leading period (.) I have placed before Krol's name; this tells it I am making a query for a person rather than an organization. Notice, too, that I have begun the message on the far left column. If I fail to do this, the automated mail server function won't work. Soon a message will appear with the result, as shown in Figure 9.10.

I could also use mail to look for organizations. Suppose I wanted to know which computers were on-line at the University of Wisconsin. Constructing a mail request would be simple. In this case, I would leave out the leading period (.), which would tell the server this is not a request for

Figure 9.10
The Results of a **WHOIS**
search by electronic mail.

```
Message 5/20   From AT&T-InterNIC Mail Server                    Page 2


The rs.internic.net whois server is being queried:

Krol, Ed (EK10)           Krol@UXC.CSO.UIUC.EDU
    University of Illinois
    Computing and Communications Service Office
    195 DCL
    1304 West Springfield Avenue
    Urbana, IL 61801-4399
    (217) 333-7886


The nic.ddn.mil whois server is being queried:

Krol, Ed (EK10)           Krol@UXC.CSO.UIUC.EDU
    University of Illinois
    Computing and Communications Service Office
    195 DCL
    1304 West Springfield Avenue
    Urbana, IL 61801-4399
    (217) 333-7886

There are 44 lines left (51%). Press <space> for more, or 'i' to return.
```

a person. The server will then search for any information regarding the university. Here is my command:

```
% mail mailserv@ds.internic.net
Subject:
whois university of wisconsin
```

A snippet of what I receive is shown in Figure 9.11. As you can see, this query generated quite a few hits.

If you use mail as your primary access to the Internet and need to find people, I would suggest you get the complete list of **WHOIS** mail server commands from the InterNIC. To do this, send mail to the same address, **mailserv@ds.internic.net**, with the command **whois help** as your message.

CHECKING INTERNET IP ADDRESSES

Perhaps you already know an Internet address and would like to know the IP address at that site. The difference between a Domain Name System (DNS) address like **world.std.com** and an IP address is that the DNS address, which uses words to describe computers, works in opposite fashion to the numerical IP addressing scheme. Whereas the DNS sets up addresses with the most specific information at the far left (as in **gilster@interpath.net**, where the most specific item, my name, is on the left, and the most general, **.net**, is on the right), IP addresses present their most general information at the left and work progressively to the right, ever tightening their specificity.

Figure 9.11
Searching for active
addresses at the
University of Wisconsin,
as found through
WHOIS.

```
Message 4/7   From AT&T-InterNIC Mail Server                              Page 2

     University of Wisconsin-Madison
     Department of Physics
     Sterling Hall, room 3417
     1150 University Avenue
     Madison, WI 53706
     (608) 262-4093

     Record last updated on 18-Apr-91.
     --------------------
Feng, Paul (PF89)                    PAUL.FENG@VMS.MACC.WISC.EDU
     University of Wisconsin-Madison
     Department of Physics
     Sterling Hall, room 3522
     1150 University Avenue
     Madison, WI 53706
     (608) 262-7555

     Record last updated on 08-Apr-91.
     --------------------
Walker, Thad G. (TGW9)           Walker%wiscnuc.bitnet@CUNYVM.CUNY.EDU
     University of Wisconsin-Madison
    There are 457 lines left (9%). Press <space> for more, or 'i' to return.
```

If you're wondering why you would need an IP address in the first place, given the fact that the Domain Name System has become so widespread, the answer is that IP numbers are how the network's computers do their work. A nameserver computer in the appropriate domain actually translates the names you use in your address into the corresponding IP numbers for routing. And there are times when a given site may have the IP numbers for various destinations but not the DNS names. This can occur particularly at military sites; many use IP addresses exclusively for their addressing. Persons at such a site might need the IP address for a computer for which they had only a DNS address.

To find it, it is possible to use an *IP Address Resolver*. As of this writing, there are two available. The addresses are **resolve@cs.widener.edu** and **dns@grasp-.insa-lyon.fr**. Use the first of these if you're based in North or South America; use the second if in Europe or Asia, to minimize network overhead.

The usage is straightforward. Send a mail message to either site with the query **site *address***. For example, if I want to find out the IP address for **interpath.net**, I can do so by sending this query: **site interpath.net**. Shortly, I receive a response:

```
Date: Tue, 8 Feb 94 08:51:05 EST
From: Address Resolver <resolve@cs.widener.edu>
Reply to: Resolve Maintainer <resolve-request@cs.widener.edu>
To: Paul A Gilster—Computer Focus <gilster@rock.concert.net>
Subject: Response for address(es)

The address(es) for your request:

        interpath.net                         128.109.131.2
--
Contact sven@cs.widener.edu with problems or comments.
Please note: no guarantees come with this, it's just a hack.
```

At the **dns@grasp.insa-lyon.fr** site, you can get a help file by sending the command **help** as the text of your message.

> **Hint:**
>
> Take note of the comment at the end of the message from the IP resolver. "No guarantees come with this," says the message, "it's just a hack." In a broader sense, you should bear in mind that many interesting network tools are like this; they grow out of the work of individuals and small groups at various network sites, and sometimes have a brief life. Others grow out of similar circumstances to become key network tools; **archie** is a case in point.
>
> So, as you use Internet tools and learn of new ones, you should realize that it is possible that some of them will have changed considerably by the time you try them out. If this is the case, be patient. The network is in a state of continuous evolution. Ultimately, changes to its tools can only occur through experimentation and a willingness to try, and to support, new ideas.

SEARCHING A LISTSERV ARCHIVE SITE

BITNET provides a mother lode of valuable information, which remains one of the most unexploited storehouses on the Internet. Because of its global connectivity to academic sites, BITNET mailing lists are often highly specific and sometimes arcane, but there are few subjects worthy of serious investigation that are not reflected in its mailing lists. These lists, heavily subscribed by the academic departments in whichever specialty is being discussed, often maintain archives of previous postings that can prove useful to the intellectually curious.

The reason BITNET list servers are not more commonly considered a part of Internet search strategies is that they are so difficult to use. Mailing lists are usually controlled by programs called LISTSERVs (although another automatic mailing list program, LISTPROC, is growing in use; LISTPROC runs on UNIX systems). LISTSERVs automate the mailing process and control what happens when you ask to search an archive site. The noninteractive nature of the connection—BITNET mail flows through gateways to and from the Internet, because the underlying computer protocols differ—means that searching is a multistep process. You can think in terms of **GopherMail** as a precedent, although even its complicated back and forth messaging is relatively straightforward compared to the demands of BITNET.

A BITNET Search Paradigm

If you keep in mind that BITNET did not evolve with ease of use in mind, you can face the LISTSERV *Command Job Language Interpreter* (CJLI) with equanimity. Just remember that each search must be run with exceeding care so as not to violate the conventions of the CJLI. Those conventions are based on a basic search template which is shown below. Your job is to fill out this template and send the result to the LISTSERV in question.

```
//
Database Search DD=Rules
//Rules DD  *
command 1
command 2
...
/*
```

We will insert our own commands into the relevant parts of the template to make our search work.

Targeting the Right Mailing List

Searching a LISTSERV is a highly targeted enterprise; you must know which LISTSERV and which mailing list you are going to search. The question is, how do you make that determination? Obviously, it's possible to sift through a directory of mailing lists, such as Eric Braun's *The Internet Directory* (Fawcett Columbine, 1994) or *netguide*, a compilation of network resources by Peter Rutten, Albert F. Bayers III and Kelly Maloni (Random House Electronic Publishing, 1994). *Internet World's on Internet 94* (Mecklermedia, 1994) is also a useful resource. Such directories can point you in the direction of the right mailing list for your needs.

On the other hand, you may want to consider automating this part of the search as well. It is possible to query the BITNET Network Information Center (BITNIC) to receive a list of mailing lists. To do so, send electronic mail to **listserv@bitnic.bitnet**. Your message should be **list global** (the **Subject:** field can be left blank), which will send a compilation of all lists known to BITNIC at the time.

There is another way, too. It is possible, even in noninteractive e-mail mode, to search BITNIC's list on-line. To do so, we need to send another command to **listserv@bitnic.bitnet**. The command should be **list global** */topic*. For example, let's assume I am trying to learn something about Admiral Nelson and the great naval engagements of the Napoleonic wars. It would interest me to hear what specialists in the field were saying, but I don't know which mailing lists to sign onto. I can send the command **list global /history** to BITNIC.

In response, I receive a message containing the desired information. In fact, there are numerous history mailing lists; each is shown with its name to the left, followed by the letter **L**. The results shown in Figure 9.12 represent only a

Figure 9.12
You can ask for BITNET mailing lists by topic by querying BITNIC.

```
HPSST-L       HPSST-L@QUCDN      History and Philosophy of Science and Sci
HTECH-L       HTECH-L@SIVM       History of Technology Discussion
IEAHCNET      IEAHCNET@UICVM     American Colonial History Discussion List
ISLAM-L       ISLAM-L@ULKYVM     History of Islam
KUHIST-L      KUHIST-L@UKANVM    History at KU
MEDIEV-L      MEDIEV-L@UKANVM    Medieval History
MILHST-L      MILHST-L@UKANVM    Military History
OHA-L         OHA-L@UKCC         Oral History Association Discussion List
PERSIA-L      PERSIA-L@EMUVM1    Jewish Literature and History in the Persian+
RENAIS-L      RENAIS-L@ULKYVM    Early Modern History - Renaissance
RUSHIST       RUSHIST@CSEARN     (Peered) RusHist - Russian History Forum
              RUSHIST@UMRVMB     (Peered) RusHist - Russian History Forum
SHARP-L       SHARP-L@IUBVM      SHARP-L Society for the History of Authorshi+
SHOTHC-L      SHOTHC-L@SIVM      History of Computing Issues
```

fraction of the output of this search command. But you can see that by searching the global list, we have quickly reduced our range of choices, and can now look among these lists for the ones most appropriate for our search.

For the purposes of our search, let's choose the Military History list (**MILHST-L**). We can always try another list if this one doesn't pay off.

Hint:

Not all sites can work with the **.bitnet** suffix in an address. If you try to reach BITNIC and your mail bounces, try the "percent hack," a solution named after one of the characters used to direct mail. For example, instead of sending to **listserv@bitnic.bitnet**, you could try this:

```
listserv%bitnic.bitnet@mitvma.mit.edu
```

We are routing our mail through a known BITNET gateway. Doing so should resolve the problem. The gateway's mail program will forward the message properly.

More than one BITNET/Internet gateway exists. You can try **cunyvm.cuny.edu**, for example, or **pucc.princeton.edu**. The format remains the same:

```
name%node.bitnet@gateway.address
```

Thus, I could route my BITNIC mail as follows:

```
listserv%bitnic.bitnet@pucc.princeton.edu
```

Sending for an Index

Having determined which mailing list we want to search, we now need to determine whether an archive is maintained by the mailing list in question. We already have an address for the Military History list; it's **milhst-l@ukanvm**. To make this work in the Internet environment, we add the **.bitnet** suffix to the address. And because we need to send our commands to the LISTSERV rather than the list itself, we must use **listserv** in the address. Consequently, the proper address will be **listserv@ukanvm.bitnet**.

Hint:

Note the principle here. When you have a BITNET mailing list address, substitute the term **listserv** for the name of the mailing list, and add the **.bitnet** suffix. Here's another example. Suppose I want to query a mailing list called **sharp-l@iubvm**. I substitute **listserv** for **sharp-l**, and add **.bitnet** to the end. Thus, my address for the query is **listserv@iubvm.bitnet**.

To retrieve any index at this site, we send the command **index milhst-l**, and send this message to the address we've already specified: **listserv@ukanvm.bitnet**. If there is an archive there, we will receive a return message giving us the news. And indeed, a message quickly appears. Figure 9.13 shows a sample of what it contains.

Figure 9.13
An archival index for the
Military History list.

```
From LISTSERV@UKANVM.CC.UKANS.EDU Fri Feb 11 08:26:16 1994
Date: Thu, 10 Feb 1994 07:54:30 -0600
From: BITNET list server at UKANVM <LISTSERV@UKANVM.CC.UKANS.EDU>
To: Paul Gilster <gilster@interpath.net>
Subject: File: "MILHST-L FILELIST"

*   MILHST-L FILELIST for LISTSERV@UKANVM.
*
*   Archives for list MILHST-L (Military History)
*
*   ::::::::::::::::::::::::::::::::::::::::::::::::::::::::::::::::::::::
*
*   The GET/PUT authorization codes shown with each file entry describe
*   who is authorized to GET or PUT the file:
*
*       ALL = Everybody
*       OWN = List owners
*
*   ::::::::::::::::::::::::::::::::::::::::::::::::::::::::::::::::::::::

*
*   NOTEBOOK archives for the list
*   (Monthly notebook)
*                                  rec            last - change
*  filename filetype   GET PUT -fm lrecl nrecs   date       time   Remarks
*  -------- --------   --- --- --- ----- -----   --------  -------- -----------
   ---------------
   MILHST-L LOG9301    ALL OWN V      87 13166   93/01/29 08:15:44 Started on Fri,
   1 Jan 1993 01:44:30 -0700
   MILHST-L LOG9302    ALL OWN V      80  3391   93/02/28 01:13:20 Started on Fri,
   29 Jan 1993 14:57:33 -0600
   MILHST-L LOG9303    ALL OWN V      80  1730   93/03/31 23:52:22 Started on Mon,
   1 Mar 1993 22:29:25 -0500
   MILHST-L LOG9304    ALL OWN V      80  1950   93/04/29 18:34:07 Started on Thu,
   1 Apr 1993 10:13:45 CST
   MILHST-L LOG9305    ALL OWN V      82  5217   93/05/31 19:58:17 Started on Mon,
   3 May 1993 10:27:51 -0700
   MILHST-L LOG9306    ALL OWN V      80  6056   93/06/30 23:15:43 Started on Tue,
   1 Jun 1993 14:00:00 EST
   MILHST-L LOG9307    ALL OWN V      80  3244   93/07/30 08:57:49 Started on Thu,
   1 Jul 1993 10:19:58 EDT
   MILHST-L LOG9308    ALL OWN V      80  2798   93/08/31 15:16:25 Started on Mon,
   2 Aug 1993 07:49:22 +0100
   MILHST-L LOG9309    ALL OWN V      85 10367   93/09/30 20:44:13 Started on Fri,
   3 Sep 1993 15:21:41 EDT
   MILHST-L LOG9310    ALL OWN V      86 15721   93/10/31 21:34:24 Started on Fri,
   1 Oct 1993 07:12:33 CET
   MILHST-L LOG9311    ALL OWN V      85 17791   93/11/30 22:02:30 Started on Mon,
   1 Nov 1993 00:43:34 CST
   MILHST-L LOG9312    ALL OWN V      86 22952   93/12/30 21:33:55 Started on Wed,
   1 Dec 1993 00:08:48 CSTf
```

Examine this figure for a moment, and you will see that the discussions of the Military History list have been broken down into monthly segments, each with a statement indicating who can access them. If we chose, we could retrieve any one (or more) of these monthly files. To retrieve the first one shown in the figure, for example, we would send the command **get milhst-l log9301**, and send it to the list address at **listserv@ukanvm.bitnet**.

Hint:

Why do we have to query an individual mailing list about whether it maintains an archive? Because many do not, and others restrict their use of their archives to members of the list. We can't assume that a given list maintains an archive. If you ever want to know which databases of information are available through a particular LISTSERV computer, send the command **database list** to that server. A given LISTSERV might make several different archives available for a variety of mailing lists.

If you attempt to query a mailing list whose archives are available only to its members, you may receive a message like the one I recently received from the Foodwine List (**listserv@cmuvm.csv.cmich.edu**):

```
> index foodwine
You are not authorized to GET file "FOODWINE FILELIST" from filelist
NOTEBOOK.
```

But we're after more specific game than a monthly collection of messages. We want to know what is being said about Admiral Nelson. So let's search across the collected archives for any messages referring to the hero of the Battle of Trafalgar, the man who said, before sailing into the engagement in which he would die, "England expects every man will do his duty."

Constructing the Search

We know now that to search this archive, we must establish a search template containing our search terms. Setting up the search is simple enough; we simply plug the term **nelson** into the template. We also include the command **index** so that we will have a list of the messages that meet our criterion (without this command, we would run the search but receive no results)! Here is what the search statement looks like:

```
//
Database Search DD=Rules
//Rules DD  *
Search Nelson in milhst-l
Index
/*
```

We send this message in the same manner we send any command to the LISTSERV; that is, we use no entry in the **Subject:** field and send the command as the subject of our message.

By return mail, we will receive the answers to our query. As you can see by consulting Figure 9.14, the list contains, on the far left, item numbers for each message in the archive, followed by other information, including the date and time of posting and the subject posted on the message itself. We will use the **Subject:** field here to help determine which of these messages we want to examine. We can request the LISTSERV to send one or more messages.

Requesting Messages from the LISTSERV

As always, we use mail to send our request to the LISTSERV. Again, we need to construct a workable template. But this time, we want to add a second command, which tells the LISTSERV the messages we want to see. Examining Figure 9.14, we might ask, for example, to look at messages 44, 364, and 452. Here is how I have structured the template, with a request to examine these messages.

```
//
Database Search DD=Rules
//Rules DD  *
Search Nelson in milhst-l
Print all of 44 364 452
/*
```

Notice that the template follows the identical format as before, but this time with a request to print (or send) the messages we want. Sending this template to the LISTSERV, we will soon receive the requested messages.

Figure 9.14
Results of a search of the Military History archive.

```
> Search Nelson in milhst-l
--> Database MILHST-L, 54 hits.

> Index
Item #   Date      Time   Recs   Subject
------   ----      ----   ----   -------
000044 93/01/04 15:57     33   Re: Generals out of synch.
000207 93/01/08 00:54     18   List Information.
000208 93/01/08 01:06    380   HISTLIST.BIB
000255 93/01/11 03:18     30   The United States' Army.
000331 93/01/14 23:30     52   America/Vietnam Conference
000364 93/01/19 09:21     26   changes in naval ranks over time
000389 93/01/20 04:36     63   Re: changes in naval ranks over time
000452 93/01/29 23:43     15   Naval, Military, Russian History.
```

Hint:

You don't always have to be a member of a mailing list to search its contents. These commands will work with many of the mailing lists that maintain an archive. If they do not, it may be necessary for you to join the list long enough to run the necessary search. To join a BITNET mailing list, send the command **subscribe listname** *firstname lastname*. Thus, to sign on to the **Media-L** list (a discussion of education and technology issues for people who work in media services), I would send the command **subscribe media-l paul gilster** to the relevant LISTSERV address, which happens to be **listserv@bingvmb.bitnet**.

The Typical BITNET Search

We have now established a search paradigm for BITNET:

- Find the right mailing list.
- Translate the mailing list address into the appropriate LISTSERV address, adding the **.bitnet** suffix.
- Query the LISTSERV to see if an archive is available. If necessary, join the mailing list to enable yourself to access its archives.
- Search the archive using keywords.
- Request the files you would like to see.

We will now put the paradigm to work on a quick practice search that involves further manipulation of the search commands, and thus, more refined searching.

The View from Middle Earth

The 1993 film "Shadowlands" created a new interest in the life and works of C. S. Lewis, the Oxford don whose works on medieval English literature defined our view of the era in the middle part of the twentieth century. But Lewis was best known to the popular audience as the author of numerous works of religious and spiritual reflection, along with the beloved Narnia books, fantasies for children set in a world that could be reached only by walking through a magical wardrobe. Among Lewis' numerous influential colleagues at Oxford was J. R. R. Tolkien, author of *The Lord of the Rings,* perhaps the greatest work of fantasy in the annals of literature.

We can use BITNET to learn more about these friends and their relationship to each other. I have heard that a mailing list has been established to consider the works of Tolkien, but I need an address. Let's implement this search with step one of our paradigm, by searching the LISTSERV at BITNIC to determine the list information. Let's see what happens when we send the **list global /tolkien** command to **listserv@bitnic.bitnet**. The BITNIC LISTSERV is fast, and I soon have a response:

```
Excerpt from the LISTSERV lists known to LISTSERV@BITNIC on 14 Feb 1994 10:05
Search string: TOLKIEN

Network-wide ID  Full address    List title
---------------  ------------    ----------
TOLKIEN          TOLKIEN@JHUVM   J.R.R.Tolkien's readers
```

From this information, we can construct an address. We have the BITNET address already: **tolkien@jhuvm**. To enable us to reach through our Internet gateway to the address, we need to add **.bitnet** to the end, and to address ourselves to the relevant LISTSERV. Thus, our address is **listserv@jhuvm-.bitnet**. It is to this address that we will direct all our traffic.

Now we need to find out if the list uses an archive. Our message to the LISTSERV is as follows: **index tolkien**. The result appears in partial form below:

```
*  NOTEBOOK archives for the list
*  (Monthly notebook)
*                          rec           last - change
* filename filetype  GET PUT -fm lrecl nrecs  date     time     Remarks
* -------- --------  --- --- --- ----- ----- -------- --------
-------------------------------
  TOLKIEN   LOG9210     ALL OWN V      87  4232 92/10/31 14:24:30 Started on Thu,
15 Oct 1992 13:58:37 EST
  TOLKIEN   LOG9211     ALL OWN V      87 15935 92/11/30 20:53:41 Started on Sun,
1 Nov 1992 13:48:24 IST
  TOLKIEN   LOG9212     ALL OWN V      82  9399 92/12/29 13:28:17 Started on Mon,
30 Nov 1992 23:01:24 CST
  TOLKIEN   LOG9301     ALL OWN V      87  9954 93/01/31 20:25:50 Started on Fri,
1 Jan 1993 03:59:23 CST
  TOLKIEN   LOG9302     ALL OWN V     157 26205 93/02/27 00:36:31 Started on Mon,
1 Feb 1993 14:15:04 +0100
```

The content of the entire list is immaterial; what we have done is verify that there is indeed an archive at this site. Our next step is to search it.

We are interested in the relationship between Tolkien and C. S. Lewis, so I will construct the following search template and send it:

```
//
Database Search DD = Rules
//Rules DD  *
Search lewis in tolkien-1
Index
/*
```

At this juncture we will learn whether we are given access to the archives; if not, we will have to join the mailing list by sending **a subscribe tolkien firstname lastname** to the listserv address. Instead, we quickly receive a list of hits:

```
> Search Lewis in tolkien
--> Database TOLKIEN, 156 hits.

> Index
Item #   Date     Time  Recs   Subject
------   ----     ----  ----   -------
000091 92/10/30 23:54    35    Apocrypha
000101 92/11/02 05:06   161    Various Lieutenants
000408 92/11/25 17:18   201    Many comments.
```

The list goes on; we have 156 hits all told, meaning that 156 messages on the Tolkien mailing list have used the search term **lewis** at least once. Paging through the hits, I find the following to be of interest:

```
001367 93/02/19 21:31    75    The purpose of literature
003497 93/11/29 11:59    27    CS Lewis Film
003498 93/11/29 07:09    21    Re: CS Lewis Film
003499 93/11/29 12:13    21    Re: CS Lewis Film
003559 93/12/02 22:24    23    Re: Narnia and Shakespear
003806 94/01/10 16:43   127    Mainly about C.S.Lewis.
```

We can now construct the final search paradigm including these numbers:

```
//
Database Search DD = Rules
//Rules DD  *
Search lewis in tolkien-l
Print all of 1367 3497 3498 3499 3559 3806
/*
```

The relevant messages will soon appear in our mailbox.

Reading More on BITNET Searching

A number of other search options are available to the dedicated BITNET searcher in a huge document that provides all the necessary commands. Searching BITNET mailing lists isn't for the timorous, but if you find that these lists contain information that is valuable to you, you'll want to acquire this document. It is called *Revised LISTSERV Database Functions*, and it is available through the BITNIC. To get it, send mail to **listserv@bitnic.bitnet**. In the body of your message, send the command **info database**.

FINDING AND USING OTHER MAIL SERVERS

We know now that a mail server is a computer that is programmed to accept e-mail requests for files, with greater or lesser human intervention depending on the system. A remarkable amount of information is available through such servers, much of it specialized in nature. We can break our use of mail servers into two parts. First, it pays to send for the mail server's help documents, which give you specific information about how to use it. Second, we'll send another message to the server requesting a specific file. Whether it's a text file or an executable program, the result will appear as an ASCII file in our mailbox.

What's available through such a mail server? Sid's Music Server is an example of a specialized site, offering lists of rare recordings. The USENET Oracle is a different kind of mail server; you send it questions about absolutely anything at all and receive Delphic replies, which are actually generated by networked individuals far and wide who are joining the fun. ACE, Americans Communicating Electronically, offers government documents by mail, while OSS-IS offers FTP lists, library and service lists, and other government information.

A Sample Mail Server Search

Let's run a sample query past a mail server. We'll choose the Amateur Radio mailserver at **info@arrl.org**. The first step, remember, is always to send for the help message. We do so by sending mail to the Amateur Radio address and enclosing the single command **help** in the body of the message. The response is shown in Figure 9.15.

We learn from the help message that we can retrieve an index of files by sending the command **index** to the mail server. The index soon appears, with a listing of files. The basic layout is shown below:

```
FILENAME         SIZE  DATE   DESCRIPTION
---------------- ---- ------ --------------------
#Note - If you are not yet an Amateur Radio operator retrieve the
#file prospect (send prospect) for information on how to easily get
#started in this fun hobby.

PROSPECT.TXT       2k 930514 How to get your Amateur Radio license
```

Figure 9.15
The **help** message from the Amateur Radio mail server.

```
HELP on using the ARRL's Automated Information Server (info@arrl.org)

    INFO is a service of ARRL HQ.  To use it, mail messages to:

     info@arrl.org

Each line of the message should contain a single command as shown
below.  You may place as many commands in a message as you want.
Each file you request will be sent to you in a separate message.
Only ASCII text files are supported at present.

Note to users with FTP capability:  All of these files are also
available by anonymous ftp to world.std.com in the
/pub/hamradio/ARRL/Server-files/info area.

Valid INFO email commands:

help             Sends this help file

index            Sends an index of the files available from INFO

reply address    Sends the response to the specified address. Put this
                 at the BEGINNING of your message if your From: address
                 is not a valid Internet address.

send <FILENAME>  Sends "FILENAME" example: send PROSPECT.TXT

quit             Terminates the transaction (use this if you have
                 a signature or other text at the end of the message.)

Note: your message will *not* be read by a human!  Do not include any
requests or questions except by way of the above commands.  Retrieve
the "USERS.TXT" file for a list of email addresses of ARRL HQ people.
```

```
EXAMS.TXT           52k 930629 Current exam schedule info - updated bi-weekly
EXAMINFO.TXT         9k 921020 Examinations - what to bring - requirements
USERS.TXT            6k 930119 List of HQ Email addresses
ARRLCAT.TXT         39k 930709 Catalog of ARRL Publications - commercial content
JOIN.TXT             2k 930621 How become an ARRL member
SERVICES.TXT         5k 930621 A condensed list of ARRL membership services
TOUR.TXT            28k 930621 An electronic tour of ARRL Headquarters
```

To retrieve one of these files, we need only to specify the filename, along with the **send** command. Thus, to receive the catalog of ARRL publications, we would use the command send **arrlcat.txt**. The method is simple; the only thing to bear in mind is that many mail servers implement their own variations on these methods, and you should always get the help file and read it before you try to use the server.

Interesting Mail Server Sites

The following are some mail servers that may pique your interest:

Almanac
USDA government news and information about the use of computers in agriculture. Sites:

almanac@esusda.gov
almanac@ecn.purdue.edu
almanac@oes.orst.edu
almanac@ces.ncsu.edu
almanac@silo.ucdavis.edu
almanac@joe.uwex.edu
almanac@wisplan.uwex.edu

Command: Use the command **send guide** in the body of your letter to get started.

Amateur Radio
Text files about amateur radio and shortwave subjects. Site:

info@ arrl.org

Command: Send mail with the **help** command to get started.

Career Centers Online
A resume service and jobs database offering search by location and other features. Site:

occ-info@mail.msen.com

Command: **help**

CancerNet
Cancer information available through electronic mail. Site:

cancernet@icicb.nci.nih.gov

Command: **help** or **Spanish**

Genetics Banks
A database of genetic material information. Sites:

gene-server@bchs.uh.edu
retrieve@ncbi.nlm.nih.gov
blast@ncbi.nlm.nih.gov
genmark@ford.gatech.edu
blocks@howard.fhcrc.org
mail cbrg@inf.ethz.ch
quick@embl-Heidelberg.DE
netserv@embl-Heidelberg.DE

Command: Send the **help** command in the **Subject:** field to all these addresses except **blast@ncbi.nlm.nih.gov** and **cbrg@inf.ethz.ch**; to these, send the **help** command in the body of the message.

Sid's Music Server
Lists of recordings and CDs for sale. Site:

mwilkenf@silver.ucs.indiana.edu

Command: Place the command **boothelp** in the **Subject:** field.

The USENET Oracle
Answers all questions about your life and fortunes. Site:

oracle@cs.indiana.edu

Command: Send mail with the command **help** in the subject field.

OSS-IS
Government documents, FTP lists, Frequently Asked Questions documents, and more. Site:

info@soaf1.ssa.gov

Command: Send **index** in the message field.

Americans Communicating Electronically
Government documents by e-mail. Site:

info@ace.esusda.gov

Command: Use **send help** command in body of message.

White House Press Releases
Releases on different topics. Site:

clinton-info@campaign92.org

Command: Send mail with the command **help** in the subject field.

White House Summaries
Summaries of daily White House press releases. Site:

almanac@esusda.gov

Command: Send **subscribe wh-summary** in body of message.

NetLib
Mathematical programs via e-mail. Sites:

netlib@ornl.gov
netlib@uunet.uu.net

Command: Place **send index** command in body of message.

StatLib Server
Statistical information and datasets for researchers. Site:

statlib@lib.stat.cmu.edu

Command: **send index** in body of message.

UUCP Map Entries
UUCP map information by mail. Site:

dns@grasp.insa-lyon.fr

Command: **help** in body of message.

10

CNIDR:
The Future of Internet
Searching

Curiously, the future of Internet searching may not consist of a completely new set of tools, at least not for the time being. The development of today's tools was not evolutionary but rather sudden and quirky. Four years ago, little was available that allowed you to run searches or browse effectively for Internet material. Then, after several years of concentrated activity at a number of sites, the key tools emerged: **Gopher**, **WAIS**, **archie**, **World Wide Web**, **Veronica**. The immediate future is likely to consist of numerous adjustments to these tools to make them more powerful.

Numerous enhancements to existing technology are now being addressed. **Gopher** is being tuned to handle a greater variety of file types and to work with clients that can understand which items they can access and which they cannot. **archie** is likewise in a state of flexibility and growth, as Bunyip Information Systems moves toward adding new data-gathering and front-end serving components beyond the current harvesting of FTP sites. Indeed, **archie** seems to be leaving its file-specific roots behind to grow into a general database maintenance engine. Meanwhile, a flurry of activity persists with **World Wide Web**, including the widespread acceptance of the powerful **Mosaic** client.

All this growth makes it clear that the paradigm for the development of navigation tools has undergone a sea change. **Gopher** and **archie** both grew out of the perceived need to organize large collections of data; essentially, they were responses to a problem whose dimensions were, at that time, only beginning to become clear. Today, these tools, developed within the academic community for university users, have become commercialized. Bunyip Information Systems provides **archie** to various sites under a subscription system, with discounts for qualified educational institutions and quantity purchases. **Gopher**, likewise, is moving to the commercial model (although free versions will remain available). **WAIS** continues its development under the auspices of **WAIS** Inc., while the Clearinghouse for Networked Information Discovery and Retrieval provides **freeWAIS**.

It was inevitable that the need for better navigation tools would become a money-making proposition, and only right that the people who had put in so much time and effort creating these tools would receive compensation for their work. Unfortunately, the effect of this today, in some quarters, is that rival camps are actively developing independent solutions to common problems. Is **World Wide Web** better than **Gopher**? Is **Veronica** superior to **WAIS**? Such questions are inevitable among partisans, but the nature of Internet data implies that these tools serve us best when they work together. No tool is an island, to paraphrase John Donne, in a worldwide distributed cyberspace.

Although it will be fascinating to observe developments in each of the search tools, not to mention the growth of additional software, it is gratifying to see a healthy move in the direction of user interface issues. **Gopher**, of course, grew into prominence because it addressed the need of the technologically unsophisticated to benefit from the computing resources of a university. By attaching itself to **Gopher**'s browsing engine, **Veronica** benefits from the same relatively undemanding interface, and **World Wide Web** offers an inherently nontaxing way to move about a wide cluster of information, jumping between items as the need arises.

With the growth of the Internet (estimates of 15 percent a month make good press, but the actual number is difficult to determine) into commercial environments and—through new service providers—into the home, we are likely to see this trend accelerate. Watch for providers to offer interfaces unique to their services, which make complex Internet tasks a matter of point-and-shoot mouse commands supplemented with drop-down menus. Watch too for search engines to evolve in the direction of more refined clients, programs that users can put to work immediately because the programs lead them through the search process step by step.

What will drive this growth? Surely it is the convergence between the demands of new users for solutions they can understand and the market reality of a burgeoning Internet industry dedicated to tapping the public dollar. Already, prices on SLIP accounts are dropping like a stone. SLIP allows the individual user to put client software to work beyond the limitations of the VT-100 model. The traditional dial-up user had no way to work with mice and pull-down menus in a graphical environment. SLIP will change all that as it becomes both more affordable and easier to implement. The appearance of new packages like O'Reilly's *Internet in a Box* points precisely in this direction. Look for this trend to accelerate.

THE EMERGENCE OF CNIDR

The Internet has always benefited from the tension between its underlying anarchy and the need to impose structure upon its operations. Consider that the worldwide metanetwork contains over 30,000 participating networks within its matrix, and you realize that an imposed organizational structure is both problematic and at the same time desirable. We revel in the net's wide open spaces and seemingly limitless freedom of expression, but we chafe when we can't find the file we want; we long for order.

Out of this tension has arisen the wide variety of search and browsing tools we have examined in this book. From **archie** to **Gopher** to **WAIS** and beyond, Internet search tools spring out of our need to organize cyberspace just enough to allow our computers to pass along information to each other. It should be no surprise, then, that the need to track down resources has prompted the growth of an organization whose charter is broad enough to encompass all our search tools: the Clearinghouse for Networked Information Discovery and Retrieval, or CNIDR. Located in Research Triangle Park, North Carolina, CNIDR exists to promote the use of these tools and to foster their future development.

Numerous organizations have contributed to the emergence of CNIDR as the primary center for the development of distributed discovery and retrieval tools. Early support came from the Center for Communications at MCNC in North Carolina; MCNC itself is a research consortium involved in microelectronics, communications and supercomputing in a nonprofit environment. Other early backers included Apple Computer, Inc., Digital Equipment Corporation, IBM, NeXT, and the University of North Carolina at Chapel Hill, whose Office of Information Technology has been an active player in the development of networked research tools.

CNIDR was conceived as a more specific institution than the one into which it has evolved. The notion was of a support center promoting the Wide Area Information Servers (**WAIS**) retrieval concept that we discussed in Chapter 5. Developers, implementers, and users of the initial public domain **WAIS** software were among its first participants, and the idea of a clearinghouse for Internet navigation and search and retrieval systems was what initially caught the eye of the National Science Foundation, a crucial funder of the center's projects.

The Clearinghouse was able to hold a **WAIS** workshop in February 1992, with the help of funding from a National Science Foundation grant, and the energetic efforts of CNIDR director George Brett and assistant director Jane Smith. Even before the workshop, both Brett and Smith had been active proponents of search and retrieval tools, speaking at numerous conferences and aligning their fledgling organization with such groups as the Internet Engineering Task Force (IETF), the Coalition for Networked Information (CNI) and the Reseaux Associes pour la Recherche Europeenne (RARE), which fosters network growth in Europe.

In October 1992, CNIDR received a three-year grant from the NSF, which it has used to increase its network activities. CNIDR's server was brought on-line to provide pointers to the various client and server implementations of **WAIS**, **Gopher**, and any other Internet search tools that have been developed for use in the public domain. By creating and promoting such a site, CNIDR thus simplifies the task for anyone who is hoping to establish a server or use a search tool for any kind of resource.

But such a site has broader implications as well. By providing a central focus, it encourages developers of new tools to work within established frameworks that will ensure compatibility and interoperability between their tools. As tools are created, CNIDR can play a key role in generating news of their existence on the network and promoting their use. The site also provides pointers to documentation and project information, ideally stimulating future growth in those areas that need development most.

"Our major focus," says CNIDR director George Brett, "is the research and education environment, but in that light, following the public library model, what we're trying to do is to create a level paying field, a baseline for the entry points of these tools. We have a tradition of building consensus, of bringing diverse communities together." Building such a consensus among developers, Brett believes, will ensure robust tools in the future.

A January 1992 meeting in Denver, attended by prominent members of the library and networking communities, makes Brett's point. Brett's focus was on the creation of a common vocabulary. Some people talk about *templates*, others talk about *records*; some database-oriented researchers discuss *fields*, others talk about *data elements*. How is it possible to be sure they are all talking about the same thing? The group spent three hours working out a consensus on a list of seven basic terms, and then went on to hammer out another 23. Similar meetings have occupied CNIDR's attention in the areas of medical networking and K-12 education.

The Global Schoolhouse Project is one such project. Sponsored by the National Science Foundation, the project showcases the convergence of technology and education. The tools: Internet-mediated communications, including videoconferencing and distance learning. In one session, CNIDR used Cornell University's **CU-SeeMe** software in conjunction with **MUSH** 2.0, a virtual environment conferencing system, to engage in a live dialog with students in several states.

BUILDING SEARCH ENGINES

Not many years ago, funding for network developments came from various agencies of the federal government. The mission was broad, but the notion of connecting significant resources, such as universities, research centers and laboratories, and defense establishments was critical. Underlying this expansion was the NSFNET, funded by the government, and aimed at furthering the expansion of regional networks.

We are now moving into a new era, one in which the old notion—George Brett calls it the "circle of gifts"—is giving way to the hard realities of the marketplace. Under the old paradigm, the academic user saw no real costs to networking. Hard cash was subsumed in taxes and federal grants; it took the eye of an accountant to follow the connection. "We built up this notion that everything is for free," Brett says. "It still gets a lot of play. As we move into the commercialized marketplace, increasingly, people realize there is financial value to be gained from various aspects of the network."

Case in point: **Gopher**. Call it a presentation tool, a browser; whatever the description, **Gopher** met the needs of a university computer science department that was simply overloaded with requests for information. The question is: How to keep end users connected and productive, without tying up every system administrator's time? Mark McCahill's answer at Minnesota was to create a menu structure that would be easy to understand yet powerful enough to house the primary tools needed by his users.

The success of **Gopher** brought with it a surprise. User demand for the resource outstripped the expectations of everyone on the original design team. A similar response happened with **archie** at McGill University, where an indexing concept designed to reduce search time took on a life of its own, and quickly began to spread across the network. A circle of gifts? Certainly, in the sense that voluntary effort produced a useful network tool out of thin air. But no matter how useful, such tools pushed hard against the charter granted their creators by their respective university administrations. Budgetary restrictions and heavy demand on the tools inevitably raised the question of whether they could continue to be supported at this level.

CNIDR grows out of such concerns, and the need to support and encourage continued development within the networking community. But it also runs headlong into a growing, and sharpening, sense of competition between the tool providers. In the early 1990s, the rush of technology was producing navigation tools that couldn't interoperate as efficiently as they should. The need for some kind of organizing structure was keen, but it has always been difficult to implement within the virtual anarchy of the Internet community.

"We were concerned that there be some kind of interoperability and protocol compliance," says CNIDR assistant director Jane Smith. "It was critical to get these guys talking to each other, because they were all doing good things but in very different ways." CNIDR can point to positive results in this regard, such as a standard description of the **Gopher** protocol that is published as a Request For Comment (RFC), and a similar description of **World Wide Web** that is close to becoming an RFC. The development of **whois++**, which will combine information from a variety of Internet resources into a searching system, points to an emerging consensus about how our tools should interoperate.

TAMING THE KUDZU PATCH

Kudzu is a vine, indigenous to Japan, that proliferated upon transplantation to the southeastern United States. Anyone driving the highways of North Carolina will find great thickets of the stuff growing uncontrollably over everything in its path. Throughout the South, kudzu is a blight, Dylan Thomas' "green fuse that drives the flower" in its elemental form. But in Japan, the root is carefully maintained, its leaves fed to cattle, its stems used for cloth making, its taproot used as a thickener in cooking. The difference could not be more obvious: The plant can be a pestiferous nuisance or a powerful natural resource.

It is said that kudzu can manage 12 to 18 inches of new growth every day, which may explain why CNIDR's logo has become an interlinked wreath of kudzu leaves. Like kudzu, the Internet is managing growth rates that boggle the imagination. Also like the prolific plant, the network, properly cultivated, offers the potential for resource development of the kind educators and intellectuals dream about. Think of CNIDR, then, as the overseer of a potential garden. "We consider NIDR tools promising cultivators and harvesters," says CNIDR's brochure, "and the developers of these tools among the master gardeners."

In George Brett's office at CNIDR, working quietly on a table at the side of the room, a Digital Equipment Corporation Alpha computer polls **Gopher** sites to build a **Veronica** database; Brett calls it "harvesting Gopherspace." The work is emblematic of CNIDR's presence in the network community. **Veronica**'s development team at the University of Nevada at Reno lacked the resources to bring the new server to bear, so CNIDR stepped in. Likewise, the Clearinghouse has made contributions that enable networkers to attend crucial meetings. Upcoming Internet gurus have been brought to standards meetings through CNIDR's largesse. These are the gardeners of tomorrow's network as we evolve toward gigabit datapaths.

There is much gardening to be done; indeed, pruning back the kudzu is an ongoing mission. Central to the forward movement of search tools is a broad conception of their interoperability. Is **WAIS** better than **Gopher**? Is **World Wide Web** the ultimate Internet engine? Can **Gopher** talk to **World Wide Web**? These issues become the stuff of long debate at networking meetings, where partisans of the rival camps engage in a kind of religious war, not so dissimilar in tone and content from the bitter exchange of religious tracts that swept Europe during the Reformation.

CNIDR's mission is to present an ecumenical approach. Brett recalls speaking at one meeting where the merits of the various tools were in sharp debate. "The **Web** client can go into **Gopher**, but the **Gopher** client can't go into the **Web**. I said, maybe we should think about the **Web** client. Everyone wanted to talk about **Mosaic**, but I talked about a nice VT-100 package called **lynx**. There's your text-based environment, your bridge. So you go with the **Web** clients for those things that need to be pretty, and those things that are quick and dirty can go into **Gopher**."

Interoperability? The idea is to get at resources through tools, not to promote the merits of a single approach in a network as diverse as the Internet. Jane Smith agrees: "With clients like **Mosaic** that use URLs, you have a way to describe the location of a resource. So within the **Mosaic** client you can get to FTP, Telnet, **Gopher**, and **Web** resources. With that single common element you begin to break out of the religious wars."

The Nature of the Internet Search

We would like to think of computer networks as tools that lighten our workload. But in the realm of searching, the Internet poses as many challenges as it solves. The level of knowledge that the user must attain to use the basic search tools is high. Only two automated systems currently exist: **archie**, which conducts automatic data harvesting, and **Veronica**, which indexes **Gopher** menu titles. With every other tool, you must go straight to the source and construct your own search on a case-by-case basis.

Even the automated tools offer a host of problems. For instance, suppose we would like to find **Gopher** servers that mention the word **music**. The search is straightforward enough; we move to the **Veronica** screen on our **Gopher** and enter the search term. We retrieve multiple pages of hits, seemingly an inexhaustible supply of information. But as we start going through the list, we begin to notice that many of the titles are duplicates, the same information posted on different **Gophers**. **Veronica** does not cross-check them for redundancy (although this problem is being worked on).

Gopher itself is a problem. Because there is no standard for **Gopher** menus, a system administrator can create a **Gopher** item and give it whatever name seems appropriate at the time. The same file may appear on 11 different

Gophers under 11 different names. How do you determine whether you're dealing with duplicate information or not? If you're thorough, the only way is to check each item. And that takes time.

The scope of this problem is staggering. One sweep of **Gopher** titles by CNIDR's **Veronica** machine turned up ten million items. Yet upon closer examination, those ten million files and connections showed a remarkable level of redundancy. According to George Brett, only 1.5 million unique items were actually available. And Jane Smith says, "There seems to be this notion that there's a whole lot more information out there now that we have electronic networks, but there probably really isn't."

Nor is the quality of information available over the Internet beyond reproach. Anyone can put information into a **Gopher**, for example, yet random checks at **Gopher** sites reveal a disturbing willingness to post items without attribution. Fortunately, there is movement on this issue. **World Wide Web** is moving in the direction of style guides, which include the last data a given page was updated, and the name of a person who is responsible for its presence. **Gopher**, too, is beginning to create link information about contact people at a site that is built into its links.

Surveying Internet sites, one comes to a reluctant conclusion: Many of the sources that appear so useful on the surface turn out to be examples of self-publishing, the electronic equivalent of the vanity press. The gap between those who are originating information and those who are making it available will have to be bridged. Information *maintenance* is an issue that is seldom considered. The updating of posted information is random and capricious, and there is no way to authenticate resources. The tools that allow us to describe the location of a resource are still in their infancy.

What are we looking for in terms of the quality of our information? Smith points to the current academic model. People get a Ph.D by finding specific information about a specific topic, a time-consuming process that advances their overall level of knowledge. "I don't see why we should consider that it's not going to take some special effort to get information into the electronic environment," she adds. "I still contend that's why we need the librarians. We need people with a mindset toward information management and information science. Technical people can build the structure underneath that allows that management to take place in the electronic environment."

Librarians? But aren't we living in the age of the so-called digital library? The press would have us believe so, but information professionals know better. In an eloquent article in *Internet World* magazine (Sept./Oct. 1993), Smith summed up her view: "If CNIDR's message has been so unclear as to promote the notion that the library as we know it is now extinct and that librarians are expendable, then we have failed in one of our critical missions."

And just as high-quality information must be available for the Internet to live up to its promise, so too must the technology of the network support that information's retrieval. **World Wide Web** experienced a 900,000 percent growth in access in 1993. Anyone who has worked with the network over the past several years will know how difficult it has become to reach certain sites by Telnet or FTP. Solving the problem of growing congestion awaits a broadening of the access pipe as we move toward gigabit networks capable of handling multimedia datastreams.

WHAT THE INTERNET NEEDS

Alan Blatecky is vice president of MCNC, whose Information Technologies Division houses and has provided financial support to the CNIDR team. Blatecky is concerned with how we process and filter information. An electronic mailbox, for example, might receive 200 messages on a given day. How does the user allocate time efficiently, answering significant mail, discarding the rest? How does a person search Internet information to avoid the time-killing redundancy of retrieving the same file 40 times? Of such issues is the life of an information specialist made.

Blatecky knows today's search tools backward and forward. Appreciative of their powers, he is, nonetheless, clear-eyed about what they lack. Consider the following:

Gopher: "If you know what you want and where you want to go, **Gopher** takes care of all the interim stuff for you; you don't have to type FTP or Telnet to get there. But it doesn't really let you surf the Internet. That's the biggest criticism I have of all the search tools. They're all aimed at someone who already knows where he or she is going."

Veronica: Because it harvests **Gopher** menu items, **Veronica** is dependent upon the perceptions of the people who built the **Gopher** menus in the first place. **Gopher** menus lack standardization, which is why menu items may not be usefully descriptive. "Descriptions are something we haven't done well. In libraries, there is a common way to mark and understand things; it can be arcane but at least it gives you a commonality. That's clearly missing in today's tools."

archie: The FTP site browser culls data without regard for its currency. Blatecky returns to the library analogy. You can quickly go to a volume in a library that is most current. Searching for files on the Internet is more problematic. We need to know more about what we can retrieve before we retrieve it.

World Wide Web: The **Web** grew so fantastically in 1993 because it solves a basic problem of data integration. It provides hypertext linking, handles images, and unites methods of data retrieval from Telnet to FTP. But the **Web**'s downside is likewise significant. "I'm being forced to deal with the **Web** as you have put it together," Blatecky says. "Somebody made the decision about where the links go, and what seems obvious to me may not be to you."

WAIS: Blatecky finds **WAIS** intriguing because it allows you to search thoroughly and retrieve hits ranked by relevance. What's needed next, in his opinion, is the addition of visual data. "If you were sitting at your desktop and had a photo album, you could flip through hundreds of images in minutes. But how can I do that over the net?"

What's needed to ensure a healthy growth of Internet search tools? Blatecky sees three major needs:

1. Authentication: How do you really know to whom you're talking on the Internet?

2. Security: How do you protect valuable proprietary data?

3. Data Integrity: How do you safeguard your data from alteration and misrepresentation?

No one who has "surfed" the Internet for long can miss the obvious—much of the material available over the network is freely available or in the public domain. The reason for this is obvious. The Internet lacks the kind of security barriers that would allow vendors of proprietary data to place their wares on-line safely. Not all information is free, and for networking to thrive, there must be provision for commercial growth as well as altruistically provided free materials. Making it possible for companies to make money over the network is critical.

Provisions for on-line billing, along with security to prevent unauthorized access, will make the Internet into a more useful repository of information. Right now, to search back issues of newspapers, the information professional turns to commercial database vendors like DIALOG, BRS, and Dow Jones News/Retrieval. These companies have implemented security measures by controlling access to their systems through passwords and by maintaining their services over dial-up packet providers like BT Tymnet and SprintNet. Why not move such operations onto the worldwide Internet, providing that the network evolves in the direction of Blatecky's big three?

Ultimately, we are talking about getting credit for information. "If we're going to do our job right, we need to continue to push the tools," said Blatecky. "So whether it's working with the **Mosaic** folks developing and pushing security or some other project with a different developer, we want to be pushing these issues so they're being addressed by somebody. We focus primarily on the public domain material, but there is no reason why industry can't take some of this, add their own value to it, and market it."

GROWING INTO A WORLDWIDE CYBERSPACE

The notion of an information highway is idle daydreaming without the development of our research tools. Make what you will of hundreds of video channels on demand, interactive games playing and all the rest; what will count is the ability of a person with a computer to access high-quality information in a variety of formats, from text to audio to video, and to translate acquired data into greater productivity. Too much current speculation about our high-tech future assumes that the Internet will become nothing more than a giant television screen with interactive push buttons, a prospect that chills the committed networker.

What we need is clear:

- A movement of genuinely useful data—including commercially available materials of unquestioned value—onto the network.

- A concomitant movement to ensure intellectual property rights. Before the best of our intellectual heritage can become available, there must be a way for people to get paid for their work. The availability of networked information may also require changes in copyright law.

- A new focus on data maintenance as the most crucial aspect of preserving the integrity of our on-line data centers.

- A solution to the problem of authentication, so that electronic transactions of any stripe can take place with unquestionable authority.

- The growth of network security systems to provide firewalls between data and those who are not supposed to have access.

- A means of securing the integrity of information so that electronic alteration cannot distort the intent of posted materials.

- Better search systems and tools, so that searchers can rely upon comprehensive databases of current materials as they run their sweeps through the data.

- Direct linkages between data and its creators, along with posted information on the contact person for the data in question and the date of the most recent updates.

People sometimes compare the Internet today to the telephone system as it grew into a nationwide communications service. But perhaps a better analogy is to the power companies. The nation's power grid eventually brought electricity to the farthest reaches of the United States, allowing the transformation that made high technology possible. Networking a planet requires similar infrastructure projects on a massive scale, the laying of fiber-optic cable to business and homes, the introduction of new tools in the workplace environment, and user training.

The Internet is a precursor of such a worldwide network. It will grow through expanded data pipes and increasingly powerful computing tools, but no one would imagine that transforming our intellectual base into the electronic environment will be easy. We have barely begun this process. The tools we have examined here remind us that we need a coalition of information professionals, librarians, computer scientists, and independent scholars to help us refine our model. We are creating the electronic counterpart to the Dewey decimal system, an information tool which, if we are prescient enough to build it right, may one day lay claim to the extravagant title of digital library.

Glossary

anonymous FTP
Entering **anonymous** as your login at an FTP site allows you to use resources that the system administrator has made available to the public. See FTP.

ANSI
American National Standards Institute. This body is responsible for standards like ASCII (q.v.).

archie
A system of distributed computers that tracks the holdings at FTP sites throughout the world. You can use **archie** to search for files.

ARPA
Advanced Research Projects Agency (formerly DARPA). This agency funded the original research that resulted in ARPANET, the network that validated the concept of packet switching through TCP/IP.

ARPANET
Funded by ARPA to study how to make computer networks secure in the event of nuclear war, this network later split its functions, with MILNET breaking off in 1983. ARPANET was retired in 1990.

ASCII
The American Standard Code for Information Interchange, which creates a standard for representing computer characters.

asynchronous
The transmission of information without reference to timing factors on the receiving end.

ATM	Asynchronous Transfer Mode. Perhaps the hottest news in network technology. Allows networks to move vast amounts of data, such as live video, on a switched, as opposed to a point-to-point, basis.
backbone	The system of high-speed connections that routes long-haul traffic, connecting to slower regional and local datapaths.
bandwidth	The size of the data pipeline. The higher the bandwidth, the faster information can flow.
BBS	A bulletin board system. The term usually refers to a small, dial-up system designed for local users, although some BBSs are now widely available over public data networks.
BITNET	An academic network containing mailing lists on a wide variety of subjects, often populated by scholars and experts in their various fields. Uses a different protocol than the Internet to move its data.
CCIRN	The Coordinating Committee for Intercontinental Research Networks, which focuses on the growth of research in the global arena. Membership includes networking organizations in numerous countries.
ClariNet	A commercial service offering news and features in the form of USENET newsgroups.
CNIDR	The Clearinghouse for Networked Information Discovery and Retrieval, in Research Triangle Park, NC. Its mission is to support the development of network search tools.
client	Software that requests services from another computer (called the server). This model is known as client/server computing.
CMC	Computer Mediated Communication, an acronym you will occasionally encounter that refers to the entire range of networking activities.
compression	The process of squeezing data to eliminate redundancies and allow files to be stored in less disk space.
CSO	An acronym (Computing Services Office) for a system that allows you to search for students and faculty members at a given school.
CWIS	Campus Wide Information Systems serve universities and colleges with local news, directories, library connections, and databases.

cyberspace	The universe of networked computers. Your electronic mail could be said to flow through cyberspace.
dial-up user	A person who accesses the Internet through a modem. This means the user connects to a machine that is on the Internet and uses its resources, rather than having his or her machine actually on the network. As used in this book, dial-up does not refer to SLIP accounts.
Domain Name System	The system that locates the IP addresses corresponding to named computers and domains. A DNS name consists of a sequence of information separated by dots. Thus, **mayer.hollywood.com**.
domain	A part of the DNS name. The domain to the far right is called the top-level domain. In the preceding example, this is **.com**.
downloading	Moving a file from one computer to another.
e-mail	Electronic mail involves sending and receiving messages over the network. You use a mail program like **mail** or **pine** to compose and read your messages.
emoticon	Another term for *smiley* (q.v.).
FARNET	The Federation of Advanced Research Networks, a non-profit corporation promoting networking in research and education.
FAQ	A Frequently Asked Questions list is a document that covers basic information from a particular USENET newsgroup or mailing list.
finger	A program that can display information about users on a particular system. Can also be used for other kinds of data.
flame	An angry response to a message posted on USENET or a mailing list. People get "flamed" for a variety of reasons, such as breaking Internet taboos against advertising over the network. Some newsgroups consist mostly of flames.
Free-Net	A community-based, volunteer-built network. Free-Nets are springing up in cities around the world, as citizens work to provide free access to selected network resources, and to make local information available on-line.
FSF	The Free Software Foundation is devoted to creating free software replacements for proprietary programs. Its operating system, GNU, is compatible with UNIX.

FTP	File Transfer Protocol is your tool for moving files from any one of thousands of computer sites to your service provider's machine. From there, you can download them to your own computer.
FYI	The acronym for For Your Information. Refers to a series of Internet documents containing basic material for beginners.
gateway	A computer that handles moving data from one network to another.
Gopher	A tool developed at the University of Minnesota that creates menus that allow you to access network resources by moving an on-screen pointer. The idea behind **Gopher** is to simplify the process of using network information. **Gopher** can point to text files, Telnet sites, **WAIS** databases, and a wide range of other data.
Gopherspace	A play on cyberspace. Gopherspace is a whimsical term for the worldwide system of **Gophers**.
header	A header appears as the first part of a data packet, and contains addressing information as well as providing provisions for error-checking. The word is also used to refer to the part of an e-mail message before the body of text.
hits	In network parlance, the term for results as applied to a database search. You might say, for example, that **Veronica** returned 65 hits when you searched under a particular keyword.
home directory	The directory on the service provider's computer that dial-up users are allocated for their accounts. This is the directory you are in when you log on.
host	A computer directly connected to the network.
hostname	The name of a computer on the Internet. Can be almost anything that the system administrator can dream up.
hypertext	Data that provides links between key elements, allowing you to move through information nonsequentially.
Internet	The worldwide matrix of connecting computers using the TCP/IP protocols. Does not include, but often moves traffic for, other networks like BITNET and UUCP. If you see the term internet (with a lowercase i), you are dealing with a TCP/IP network that is separate from the worldwide Internet.

Internet Architecture Board	Formerly the Internet Activities Board. Coordinates research and development of the TCP/IP protocols and oversees standards for the Internet Society.
Internet Engineering Task Force	A task force working as part of the IAB that develops standards for protocols and architecture on the Internet.
Internet Society	Promotes the growth of the Internet and works to assist those groups involved in its use and evolution.
InterNIC	Internet Network Information Center. Your first place to ask questions about the network itself. Maintains a wide variety of data, which it makes accessible to all users. Run by Network Solutions, Inc., AT&T, and General Atomics.
interoperability	The ability of diverse computer systems to work together by using common protocols. Without it, the Internet could not exist.
IP Address	A network address expressed in numbers.
ISO	The International Standards Organization. Creates standards for international use, not all of which take hold (see OSI).
Knowbot	A network tool that allows you to search several different databases consecutively to find network addresses and information.
LISTSERV	A program that manages mailing lists on BITNET by responding automatically to e-mail requests and distributing new messages.
LAN	A local area network, usually in a business office, connecting multiple computers to a server computer.
mail server	A computer that responds to electronic mail requests for information. You could ask a mail server, for example, to send you a particular file by giving a precise command, such as **send index**, etc.
mailing list	A group discussion carried on through electronic mail. BITNET is home to numerous mailing lists on a huge range of topics, but mailing lists are also found on the Internet itself.
MBONE	The Multicast Backbone is a testbed for moving audio and visual information over the Internet.
metanetwork	A network that is made up of numerous other networks. The Internet is the prime example.
MILNET	A network run by the Department of Defense, which serves the military. Split off from ARPANET in 1983.

MIME	Multipurpose Internet Mail Extensions; the system for providing graphics and other nontextual data through e-mail.
Mosaic	A graphical tool that allows you to access **World Wide Web** information in a point-and-shoot environment. Can be used only if you have direct network access; dial-up users would have to use a SLIP account to make **Mosaic** work.
multicast	As opposed to broadcasting, which would send data to everyone, multicasting means moving data from one point to multiple, specified network points. The term is used in connection with the operational procedures of the MBONE.
nameserver	A computer that manages Internet names and numeric addresses.
netfind	A network search tool that allows you to track down user information.
netiquette	The etiquette of using the network. Not a trivial issue, especially now that the rise in commercial Internet sites is raising questions about advertising and other business uses of the net.
network	Computers connected together to communicate information.
NIC	Network Information Center. An organization charged with maintaining a particular network.
nixpub	A list of public-access UNIX systems compiled and maintained by Phil Eschallier.
nn	A software program used to read USENET messages. See **trn**.
NNTP	Network News Transfer Protocol. The standard for the exchange of USENET messages across the Internet.
node	Any computer attached to a network can be called a node.
NSFNET	The National Science Foundation Network, an essential part of the research networking infrastructure.
OSI	Open Systems Interconnection is a standard for networking developed by the ISO (q.v.). It is used much more heavily in Europe than in the United States, where TCP/IP prevails.

packet	The basic unit of Internet data. A message sent across the net is broken into packets, each marked with the address and other pertinent information, such as error-checking data. The TCP/IP protocols see to it that the packets are rebuilt at their destination.
packet switching	The process of sending packets through the network, allowing for alternate routing if a particular network link fails.
PDIAL	A list of Internet dial-up providers maintained by Peter Kaminski.
pico	An easy-to-use text editor operating under UNIX.
pine	A program used to read and create electronic mail. Uses the **pico** text editor and provides on-line help as well as an intuitive interface and an address book.
postmaster	The person who takes care of the mail system at a given site. The postmaster responds to queries about users on the system and makes sure the mail gets through.
protocol	A protocol defines how computers communicate; it is an agreement between different systems on how they will work together. The set of TCP/IP protocols defines how computers on the Internet exchange information.
public data network	A network providing local numbers by which you can access computer services in different cities, using X.25 protocols to move data.
RARE	The Reseaux Associes pour la Recherche Europeenne, an association of network organizations in Europe. Serves a function similar to that of the IETF.
resolution	The process of translating an Internet name into its corresponding IP address.
RFCs	A series of documents that describe the protocols driving the Internet, along with diverse information about its operations.
RIPE	The Reseaux IP Europeens is an organization of European Internet providers. RIPE has now been incorporated into RARE.
router	A computer system that makes decisions about which path Internet traffic will take to reach its destination.
server	A computer that provides a resource on the network. Client programs access servers to obtain data.

service provider	A company that offers access to the Internet. Dial-up users obtain an account on the service provider's system and use its computers to log on to the net.
shell	A program that provides the interface users work with on UNIX systems. A variety of shells are available.
signature	A short note, usually containing your name, address, and other information (and including, often, a favorite quotation), which appears at the end of mail or newsgroup messages you send. A signature is set up by creating a special file in your home directory.
SLIP	Serial Line Internet Protocol. As opposed to regular dial-up accounts, a SLIP account allows your computer to receive an IP address. FTP sessions are thus handled directly between remote computers and your system, without going through your service provider's computers first. A SLIP account also allows you to run graphical front-end programs like **Mosaic**.
smiley	Also known as an emoticon. A group of ASCII characters that provide visual references to add commentary to text.
SMTP	Simple Mail Transfer Protocol is the Internet standard protocol for handling electronic mail messages between computers.
synchronous	The process of sending data communications at a fixed rate. Both sender and receiver must operate at the same rate to achieve synchronous communications.
T1	1.544 Megabits per second data transfer over a leased line.
T3	45 Mbps data transfer over a leased line.
tar	A method of file archiving.
TCP/IP	Transmission Control Protocol/Internet Protocol. This is the set of protocols that drives the Internet, regulating how data is transferred between computers.
Telnet	An Internet protocol that allows you to log on to a remote computer. Used, for example, in searching remote databases.
terminal emulation	The process of communicating with a remote computer as if your computer were actually a terminal connected to that computer. VT-100 is the most common form of terminal emulation.
tn3270	Works like Telnet, but designed to handle IBM systems, which require full-screen operations.

UUCP	UNIX to UNIX Copy Program is a method of transferring files between computers that includes electronic mail. Thousands of computers around the world use the UUCP network to exchange mail over dial-up telephone lines.
UNIX	An operating system used by most service providers. Dial-up users usually encounter UNIX when they log on to a service provider's system, and must use UNIX commands to handle routine chores like file management. Berkeley UNIX comes with the TCP/IP protocols already built in.
USENET	A worldwide network of newsgroups on thousands of subjects which can be accessed by newsreader programs like **trn**.
WAIS	Wide Area Information Servers is a system that allows you to search databases by keyword and refine your search through relevance feedback techniques.
WAN	A Wide Area Network can be any network whose components are geographically dispersed.
workstation	Workstations are generally more powerful than desktop IBM-compatible or Apple computers, and usually run UNIX as their operating system.
worm	A computer program that can make copies of itself. The Internet Worm was a program that caused network havoc in late 1988 when it duplicated itself at sites around the world.
Veronica	A program that allows you to search **Gopher** menus for particular keywords.
vi	A text editor with an inscrutable interface that is widely distributed over the Internet. **pico** is much easier to use.
VMS	An operating system used by Digital Equipment Corporation VAX computers.
WHOIS	A program that allows you to search a database for people or network addresses.
World Wide Web	A program that works through hypertext links to data, allowing you to explore network resources from multiple entry points.
X.25	A standard that defines how connection-based services operate. X.25 requires a connection to be made before data is transmitted.
X.500	A directory standard based on OSI (q.v.).

Index

Accessing. *See also* Reference guide;
    Resources; Search strategies; User guide;
  archie
    direct methods, 13
    with a client program, 30
    with e-mail, 13, 244–246
    with Telnet, 14–30
  audio, with Gopher, 72–75
  BITNET, with e-mail, 262
  finger, with e-mail, 258
  Gopher, 42
    direct access, 51
    with a client program, 42
    with GopherMail, 253–258
    with Telnet, 43
  HYTELNET
    with Gopher, 195
    with Telnet, 184
  Jughead, 97
  Knowbot
    with e-mail, 235
    with Telnet, 233
  library resources
    with CATALYST, 204
    with Gopher, 202
    with HYTELNET, 194
    with LIBS, 200
    with LIBTEL, 197
  LISTSERV, with e-mail, 262
  mail servers, 270–274

  netfind, with Telnet, 225
  software, with WAISmail, 252
  USENET, with WWW (World Wide Web),
    153
  Veronica
    with a Gopher client, 79
    with GopherMail, 256
    with Telnet, 80
  video, with Gopher, 72–75
  WAIS
    with a client program, 102
    with e-mail, 246
    with Gopher, 103, 118–121
    with waissearch, 121–123
  WHOIS
    with a client program, 223
    with e-mail, 259
    with Telnet, 216
  WWW (World Wide Web)
    with a client program, 137
    with a GUI, 137
    with lynx browser, 161
    with Telnet, 137, 161
Address (Internet). *See also* Accessing
  IP Address
    checking with e-mail, 260–262
    (glossary), 289
  obtaining
    for people, 207–242
    with archie, 9

ANSI (American National Standards
    Institute)
    (glossary), 285
archie, 9–36. *See also* Search strategies;
    User guide
    accessing
        direct methods, 13
        with a client program, 30
        with e-mail, 13, 244–246
        with Telnet, 14–30
    characteristics, 9–36, 11, 12
    development history, 11
    (glossary), 285
    name derivation, 78
    overview, 6
    problems and gotchas, 26
        search limitation issues, 18
        whatis command limitations, 27, 28
    reference guide
        changing search parameters, 21
        command options, 20–26
        command switches, 30–33
        e-mail access, 244
        mailing results, 25
        miscellaneous commands, 25
        output, choosing a format, 24
        output, controlling, 23
        specifying where to search, 22
    resources
        about archie, 11, 13
        worldwide server list, 14
    search strategies, 33
        constraining, 18, 19
        search screen characteristics, 15
        Software Description Database, 27
        specifying domain and directories, 22
        with e-mail, 245
    user guide, 13–20, 244–246
ARPA (Advanced Research Projects Agency)
    (glossary), 285
ARPANET (Advanced Research Projects
    Agency Network)
    (glossary), 285
ASCII (American Standard Code for Infor-
    mation Interchange)
    (glossary), 285
Asynchronous
    (glossary), 285
ATM (Asynchronous Transfer Mode)
    (glossary), 286
Audio
    accessing, with Gopher, 72–75

Backbone (Internet)
    (glossary), 286

Bandwidth
    (glossary), 286
BITNET (Because It's Time Network). *See
    also* Search strategies; User guide
    accessing, with e-mail, 262
    (glossary), 286
    search strategies, e-mail access, 262–270
Bookmarks, 53–59. *See also* Gopher
Browsing. *See also* Search engines; Search
    strategies
    Gopher, characteristics, 39
    hypertext characteristics, 133–134
    WWW (World Wide Web)
        compared with precise searching, 5
        with a local client, 140
        with lynx browser, 161
        with Mosaic GUI browser, 168–181
        with NJIT browser, 165
Bulletin board systems (BBSs)
    (glossary), 286

CATALYST. *See also* Search strategies;
    User guide
    accessing library resources with, 204
CCIRN (Coordinating Committee for Inter-
    continental Research Networks)
    (glossary), 286
ClariNet
    (glossary), 286
Client programs
    accessing
        WAIS with, 102
        WHOIS with, 223
        WWW (World Wide Web) with, 137, 140
    archie, 13, 30
    (glossary), 286
    Gopher, 42
CMC (Computer Mediated Communication)
    (glossary), 286
CNIDR (Clearinghouse for Networked Infor-
    mation Discovery and Retrieval), 275–
    285
    (glossary), 286
    overview, 8
Commercial use, possibilities and concerns,
    275-285
Compression
    (glossary), 286
Content navigation
    characteristics as WAIS search strategy, 108
CSO name servers. *See also* Search strategies;
    User guide
    (glossary), 286
    Gopher use with, 70, 236
    locating people with, 236

CWIS (Campus Wide Information Systems)
  (glossary), 286
  locating people with, 240
Cyberspace
  (glossary), 287

Dial-up
  user, (glossary), 287
Directory-based information retrieval. *See*
    archie; X-500 distributed directory
    standard
Domain. *See also* Address (Internet)
  (glossary), 287
  specifying in a archie search, 22
Domain Name System (DNS)
  (glossary), 287
Downloading
  (glossary), 287

E-mail, 243–274. *See also* Search strategies;
    Telnet; FTP (File Transfer Protocol);
    User guide
  accessing
    archie with, 13, 244–246
    finger with, 258
    Gopher with, 253–258
    Knowbot with, 235
    WAIS with, 246
    WHOIS with, 259
  (glossary), 287
  locating people with, 240–242
  noninteractive searching with, 243–274
  obtaining archie output via, 25
  search strategies, archie, 245
Emoticons
  (glossary), 287

FAQ (Frequently Asked Questions). *See also*
    Resources
  (glossary), 287
FARNET (Federation of American Research
    Networks)
  (glossary), 287
Files. *See also* FTP (File Transfer Protocol)
  locating with archie, 16
finger. *See also* People, locating; Search
    strategies; User guide
  accessing, with e-mail, 258
  characteristics, 231
  (glossary), 287
Flame
  (glossary), 287
fred (Front End to Directories). *See also*
    Interfaces
  reference guide, 210–212

Free-Net
  (glossary), 287
FSF (Free Software Foundation)
  (glossary), 287
FTP (File Transfer Protocol)
  anonymous, (glossary), 285
  characteristics, 10
  (glossary), 288
  Gopher, 66–70
  WWW (World Wide Web) use of, 146
full-text information retrieval. *See* FTP (File
    Transfer Protocol); WAIS (Wide Area In-
    formation Servers); WWW (World Wide
    Web)
FYI (For Your Information)
  (glossary), 288

Gateways
  (glossary), 288
Glossary, 288
Gopher, 37–75. *See also* Search strategies;
    User guide
  accessing, 42
    audio and video files, 72–75
    direct access, 51
    HYTELNET with, 195
    Veronica with, 79
    WAIS with, 103, 118–121
    with a client program, 42
    with GopherMail, 253–258
    with Telnet, 43
  accessing library resources with, 202
  browsing, characteristics, 39
  characteristics, 37–42
    Gopherspace, 38
    unregistered, 44
    what is available, 44
  CSO name server
    use by, 70
    use of, 236
  development history, 37
  FTP, 66–70
  (glossary), 288
  Gopherspace
    characteristics, 38
    (glossary), 288
  name derivation, 38, 78
  overview, 4
  problems and gotchas
    file content search limitations, 99
    locking up of, 70
    search difficulties, 60
  reference guide
    bookmark commands, 58
    commands, 61

data type definitions, 64, 85
files, management commands, 52
files, viewing commands, 51
search commands, 59–60
resources
    development, 75
    examining, 62
    Gopher Jewels, 46
    public access sites (table), 43
    sample list of subjects, 45
    software, 43
    Yanoff Special Internet Connections
        list, 44
search strategies
    bookmarks, 53–59
    foraging expedition, 57
    FTP sample search, 66
    Gopherspace characteristics, 38
    search command reference guide, 59–60
    Telnet sample search, 62–66
    with GopherMail, 254–258
Telnet, 62–66
user guide, 46–51
    bookmarks, 53–59
    Telnet, 62–70
    WAIS, 70
    CSO, 70–71
    audio and video files, 72–75
Veronica, data type use, 84
WAIS use by, 70
WWW (World Wide Web) use of, 155
X.500 search with, 214
GUI (graphical user interface). *See also*
        Interfaces
    accessing, WWW (World Wide Web) with,
        137
    Gopher, 42
    Mosaic
        (glossary), 290
        WWW (World Wide Web) use of,
            168–181

Header
    (glossary), 288
History
    archie, 11
    Gopher, 37
    HYTELNET, 183
    Veronica, 77
    WAIS, 100
    WWW (World Wide Web), 162–163
Hits
    (glossary), 288
Home directory
    (glossary), 288

Host
    (glossary), 288
Hostname
    (glossary), 288
How to Find it tips. *See also* Resources
    archie
        developer address, 13
        development information, 11
    FTP site lists, 10
    lynx browser command list, 164
HTML (Hypertext Markup Language)
    WWW (World Wide Web) use of, 144
http (HyperText Transport Protocol)
    WWW (World Wide Web) use of, 144
Hypertext
    characteristics, 133–134
    (glossary), 288
    HYTELNET, 6, 183–206
    WWW (World Wide Web), 5, 133–182
HYTELNET, 183–197. *See also* Library
        resources; Search strategies; User guide
    accessing, 184
        with Gopher, 195
        with Telnet, 186
    characteristics, 183
    development history, 183
    reference guide, 190
    resources, 196
        servers, 184
    search strategies, 190-193
    user guide, 184-207

IAB (Internet Architecture Board)
    (glossary), 289
IETF (Internet Engineering Task Force)
    (glossary), 289
Indexed database
    directory contents, archie database as, 6
Information retrieval, Internet. *See also*
        People, locating; Search strategies;
        Resources
    applications. *See* E-mail; FTP (File Trans-
        fer Protocol); Telnet
    tools
        list of. *See* User guide
        search strategies. *See* Search strategies
        limitations. *See* Problems and gotchas
    possibilities and concerns, 275-285
Interfaces
    GUI (graphical user interface)
        Gopher, 42
        Mosaic, 168–181
        Mosaic, (glossary), 290
        WWW (World Wide Web) access with, 137
    menu-based. *See* Gopher

Interfaces *(continued)*
  Problems and gotchas, swais interface,
    104, 106, 108
  X.500 standard
    fred (Front End to Directories),
      210–212
    PARADISE project, 212–214
Internet
  applications. *See* E-mail; FTP (File Trans-
    fer Protocol); Telnet
  future possibilities and concerns, 275–285
  (glossary), 289
  Internet Society (ISOC), (glossary), 289
InterNIC (Internet Network Information
    Center)
  (glossary), 289
Interoperability
  (glossary), 289
IP address. *See* Address (Internet), IP ad-
    dress
ISO (International Standards Organiza-
    tion), 208
  (glossary), 289

Jughead. *See also* Search strategies; User
    guide
  accessing, 97
  name derivation, 78, 96
  reference guide, 97
  user guide, 96

Knowbot. *See also* Search strategies; User
    guide
  accessing
    with e-mail, 235
    with Telnet, 233
  (glossary), 289
  locating people with, 233–236
  reference guide, 234

LAN (Local Area Network)
  (glossary), 289
Library resources, accessing
  with CATALYST, 204
  with Gopher, 202
  with HYTELNET, 194
  with LIBS, 6, 200
  with LIBTEL, 6, 197
LIBS (Library Internet Browsing Software).
    See also Search strategies; User guide
  accessing library resources with, 200
LIBTEL. *See also* Search strategies; User
    guide
  accessing library resources with, 197
  problems and gotchas, 199

LISTSERV (BITNET). *See also* BITNET
    (Because Its Time). *See also* Search
    strategies; User guide
  accessing, with e-mail, 262–270
  (glossary), 289
lynx browser. *See also* browsing; Search
    strategies
  accessing, WWW (World Wide Web) with,
    161
  reference guide, 164

Mail servers. *See also* BITNET (Because Its
    Time); Search strategies; User guide
  finding and using, 270–274
  mailing lists (glossary), 289
  (glossary), 289
  resources, 272
MBONE (Multicast Backbone)
  (glossary), 289
menu-based systems. *See* Gopher
Metanetwork. *See also* Internet
  (glossary), 289
MILNET
  (glossary), 289
MIME (Multi-purpose Internet Mail Exten-
    sions) standard. *See also* E-mail
  (glossary), 290
Mosaic GUI browser. *See also* Interfaces;
    WWW (World Wide Web)
  (glossary), 290
  WWW (World Wide Web) use of, 168–181
Multicasting
  (glossary), 290

Name derivation
  archie, 78
  Gopher, 38, 78
  Jughead, 78, 96
  Veronica, 78
Name servers. *See also* People, locating
  CSO name servers
    (glossary), 286
    Gopher use with, 70, 236
    locating people with, 236
  (glossary), 290
netfind program. *See also* People, locating;
    Search strategies; User guide
  accessing, with Telnet, 225
  characteristics, 227–229
  (glossary), 290
  locating people with, 225–231
  resources, servers, 225
  search strategies, 229–231
Netiquette
  (glossary), 290

Network
    (glossary), 290
NIC (Network Information Center)
    (glossary), 290
nixpub public access UNIX site list
    (glossary), 290
NJIT browser
    accessing, WWW (World Wide Web) with, 165
nn program
    (glossary), 290
NNTP (Network News Transfer Protocol)
    (glossary), 290
Node
    (glossary), 290
NSFNET (National Science Foundation Network)
    (glossary), 290

OSI (Open Systems Interconnection), 208
    (glossary), 290

Packet
    (glossary), 291
    switching, (glossary), 291
PARADISE project. *See also* People, locating
    X.500 interface, 212–214
PDIAL (Public Dialup Internet Access List)
    (glossary), 291
PDNs (Public Data Networks)
    (glossary), 291
People, locating. *See also* Resources; Search strategies
    CSO name servers, Gopher use with, 70
    problems and gotchas, 207
    tools for, 6, 207–242
    with CSO, 236
    with CWIS, 240
    with e-mail, 240–242
    with finger, by e-mail, 258
    with Knowbot, 233–236
    with netfind, 225–231
    with WHOIS, 216–225
        by e-mail, 259
pico text editor
    (glossary), 291
pine e-mail program
    (glossary), 291
Postmaster
    (glossary), 291
Problems and gotchas. *See also* Reference guide; Resources; User guide
    archie, 26
        search limitation issues, 18
        whatis command limitations, 27, 28

Gopher
    file content search limitations, 99
    locking up of, 70
    search difficulties, 60
Internet information quality, 275–285
LIBTEL, 199
locating people, 207, 225
netfind, 225
search limitations, overcoming with hypertext, 133
Veronica, 94
    file content search limitations, 99
    locking up, 82
WAIS
    Gopher limitations, 121
    keyword limitation, 110
    swais interface, 104, 106, 108
WWW (World Wide Web), 165
Protocols. *See also* TCP/IP (Transmission Control Protocol/Internet Protocol); X.500 distributed directory standard
    (glossary), 291

qarchie
    as simplified archie, 15

RARE (Reseaux Associes pour la Recherche Europeene)
    (glossary), 291
Reference guide. *See also* Accessing; Browsers; Problems and gotchas; Resources; Search strategies; User guide
archie
    changing search parameters, 21
    command options, 20–26
    command switches, 30–33
    e-mail access, 244
    mailing results, 25
    miscellaneous commands, 25
    output, choosing a format, 24
    output, controlling, 23
    specifying where to search, 22
fred (Front End to Directories), 210–212
Gopher
    bookmark commands, 58
    commands, 61
    data type definitions, 64, 85
    files, management commands, 52
    files, viewing commands, 51
    search commands, 59–60
HYTELNET, 190–193
Jughead, 97
Knowbot, 234
regular expressions, 28–30
Veronica, 91–93

Reference guide *(continued)*
  WAIS
    movement commands, 109
    search commands, 110
    swais commands, 110
    WAISmail, 250
  WWW (World Wide Web), 155–158
    lynx browser, 164
Regular expressions, 22
  archie use, 19
  reference guide, 28–30
Relevance feedback. *See also* WAIS (Wide
    Area Information Servers)
  characteristics as WAIS search strategy,
    111–115
  search strategy recommendations, 117
Resolution
  (glossary), 291
Resources. *See also* Search strategies
  archie
    about archie, 11
    worldwide server list, 14
  Gopher
    development, 75
    examining, 62
    Gopher Jewels, 46
    public access sites (table), 43
    sample list of subjects, 45
    software, 43
    Yanoff Special Internet Connections
      list, 44
  HYTELNET, 196
    servers, 184
  library. *See* Library resources,
    accessing
  mail server sites, 272
  netfind servers, 225
  WAIS, 102
    about WAIS development, 130
    interesting sites, 123–130
    mailing list, 131
    public access clients, 102
  WWW (World Wide Web)
    samples of the riches available, 150–155
    servers available by Telnet, 137
    subject holdings, 134–136
RFC (Request for Comments)
  (glossary), 291
RIPE
  (glossary), 291
Router
  (glossary), 291

Search engines. *See* archie; Veronica; WAIS
    (Wide Area Information Servers)

Search strategies. *See also* Accessing;
    Browsers; People, locating; Problems
    and gotchas; Reference guide; Re-
    sources; User guide
  archie, 33
    examples of use, 15
    regular expression and wildcard use, 19
    Telnet sample search, 17
    with e-mail, 245
  BITNET, e-mail access, 262–270
  full text, WAIS, 4
  Gopher
    bookmarks, 53–59
    foraging expedition, 57
    FTP sample search, 66
    Gopherspace characteristics, 38
    search command reference guide,
      59–60
    Telnet sample search, 62–66
    with GopherMail, 254–258
  hypertext advantages, 133
  HYTELNET, 190
  mail servers, 271
  methodology recommendations, 7
  netfind, 229–231
  searching compared with, WWW (World
    Wide Web), 5
  Veronica, 80, 83, 85–91, 93
  WAIS, 101
    content navigation, 108
    recommendations, 115–118
    relevance feedback, 111–115
    using Telnet, 103–108
    with WAISmail, 247–260
  WHOIS, with Telnet, 220–223
  WWW (World Wide Web), 144–155,
    165–168
    index searches, 158–160
Server
  (glossary), 291
Service provider
  (glossary), 292
Shell
  (glossary), 292
Signature
  (glossary), 292
SLIP (Serial Line Internet Protocol)
  (glossary), 292
  Gopher access, 42
  requirements, 2
  WAIS access, 104
Smiley
  (glossary), 292
SMTP (Simple Mail Transfer Protocol)
  (glossary), 292

Software
  accessing, with WAISmail, 252
  Software Description Database, 27
  whatis database, 12
Synchronous
  (glossary), 292

T1 service
  (glossary), 292
T3 service
  (glossary), 292
tar program
  (glossary), 292
TCP/IP (Transmission Control Protocol/
    Internet Protocol)
  (glossary), 292
  X.400 compared with, 209
Telnet. *See also* E-mail; FTP (File Transfer
    Protocol)
  3270 considerations, 66
  accessing
    archie with, 14–30
    Gopher with, 43, 62–66
    HYTELNET with, 184
    netfind with, 225
    Veronica with, 80
    WAIS with, 102
    WHOIS with, 216–223
    WWW (World Wide Web) with, 137, 161
  (glossary), 292
  WAIS search strategy using, 103
Terminal emulation
  (glossary), 292
tn3270 program
  (glossary), 292
Tools (Internet), list of. *See* User guide

UNIX
  (glossary), 293
URL (Uniform Resource Locator)
  WWW (World Wide Web) use of, 144
USENET
  accessing, with WWW (World Wide Web),
    153
  archives, searching, 238
  (glossary), 293
User guide. *See also* Accessing; Problems
    and gotchas; Reference guide; Resources;
    Search strategies
  archie, 13–20, 244–246
  BITNET, 262–270
  CATALYST, 204
  CSO name servers, 236
  e-mail, 243–274
  finger, 231, 258

Gopher, 46–51, 62–75, 253–258
  HYTELNET, 184–207
  Jughead, 96
  Knowbot, 233–236
  LIBS, 200
  LIBTEL, 197–199
  LISTSERV, 262–270
  mail servers, 270–274
  netfind, 225–231
  Veronica, 79–91, 93, 256
  WAIS, 103–109, 111–123, 247–260
  whatis, 26–28
  WHOIS, 216–225, 259
  WWW (World Wide Web), 138–155,
    158–182
UUCP (UNIX-to-UNIX Copy Program)
  (glossary), 293

Veronica (Very Easy Rodent-Oriented Net-
    wide Index to Computerized Archives),
    77–98. *See also* Search strategies; User
    guide
  accessing
    with Gopher, 79
    with GopherMail, 256
    with Telnet, 80
  characteristics, 77, 78
  development history, 77
  (glossary), 293
  Gopher, data type use, 84
  Jughead use with, 96
  name derivation, 78
  overview, 4
  problems and gotchas, 94
    file content search limitations, 99
    locking up, 82
  reference guide, 91–93
  relationship to Gopher, 5
  search strategies, 80, 83, 85–91, 93
  user guide, 79–91, 93, 256
Version issues
  Bunyip response to via templates, 6
vi text editor
  (glossary), 293
Video
  accessing, with Gopher, 72–75
VMS (Virtual Memory System)
  (glossary), 293

WAIS (Wide Area Information Servers),
    99–132. *See also* Search strategies;
    User guide
  accessing
    with a client program, 102
    with e-mail, 246

WAIS *(continued)*
    with Gopher, 103, 118–121
    with Telnet, 102
    with waissearch, 121–123
    with WWW (World Wide Web) index
        searches, 158–160
    characteristics, 100
    development history, 100
    (glossary), 293
    Gopher use with, 70
    overview, 4
    problems and gotchas
        Gopher limitations, 121
        keyword limitation, 110
        swais interface, 104, 106, 108
    reference guide
        movement commands, 109
        search commands, 110
        swais commands, 110
        WAISmail, 250
    resources, 102
        about WAIS development, 130
        interesting sites, 123–130
        mailing list, 131
        public access clients, 102
    search strategies, 101
        content navigation, 108
        recommendations, 115–118
        relevance feedback, 111–115
        using Telnet, 103–108
        with WAISmail, 247–260
    user guide, 103–109, 111–123, 247–260
waissearch program
    accessing, WAIS with, 121–123
WAN (Wide Area Network)
    (glossary), 293
Web. *See* WWW (World Wide Web)
whatis, 26–28. *See also* Search strategies;
    User guide
    as outgrowth of archie, 12
White pages. *See* X.500 distributed directory
    standard
WHOIS. *See also* Search strategies;
    User guide
    accessing
        with a client program, 223
        with e-mail, 259
        with Telnet, 216–223
    (glossary), 293
    locating people with, 216–225
    search strategies, with Telnet, 220–223

Wildcards
    archie use, 19
Workstation
    (glossary), 293
World Wide Web. *See* WWW (World Wide
    Web)
Worm
    (glossary), 293
www client
    accessing WWW (World Wide Web)
        with, 141
WWW (World Wide Web), 133–182. *See also*
    Search strategies; User guide
    accessing
        with lynx browser, 161
        with Telnet, 161
        with USENET, 153
    development history, 162–163
    (glossary), 293
    overview, 5
    problems and gotchas, 165
    reference guide, 155–158
        lynx browser, 164
    resources
        samples of the riches available,
            150–155
        servers available by Telnet, 137
        subject holdings, 134–136
    search strategies, 144–155, 165–168
        index searches, 158–160
        typical example, 147
    user guide, 138–143, 144–155, 158–182
        browsing, with a local client, 140
        browsing, with Mosaic GUI, 168–181
        FTP use by, 146
        Gopher use by, 155

X.25 protocol. *See also* E-mail
    (glossary), 293
X.400 standard. *See also* E-mail
    characteristics, 209
    TCP/IP compared with, 209
X.500 distributed directory standard. *See
    also* E-mail; Protocols
    as directory service, 210
    characteristics, 208
    (glossary), 293
    interfaces
        fred (Front End to Directories), 210–212
        PARADISE project, 212–214
    searching with Gopher, 214